Cornelius Rea Douglas College

Study Guide

to accompany

Discovering Psychology
Second Edition

Don H. Hockenbury
Sandra E. Hockenbury

WORTH PUBLISHERS

Study Guide
by Cornelius Rea
to accompany
Hockenbury & Hockenbury: **Discovering Psychology**, Second Edition

Copyright © 2001, 1998 by Worth Publishers

Printed in the United States of America

ISBN 1-57259-965-0

Printing: 5 4 3 2
Year: 04 03 02 01

Cover credit: *Circle Dance* by Phoebe Beasley

Worth Publishers
41 Madison Avenue
New York, NY 10010
www.worthpublishers.com

Contents

To the Student

This study guide is designed to help you to study effectively and to learn the important concepts in *Discovering Psychology*, Second Edition, by Don and Sandy Hockenbury. Use this study guide in an active manner and as a complement to the textbook, not as a substitute for it. By actively interacting with the text material and this study guide, you will be able to master the chapter concepts in a straightforward and enjoyable manner. Our goal is to create independent, motivated students who enjoy learning for its own sake, who can think critically, and who have a deep conceptual understanding of the information presented in the text.

Your first course in psychology is very exciting but it is also challenging. Besides the volume of new information you will be asked to learn, you are faced with learning new terminology, novel concepts, unfamiliar theories, and, most important, the scientific way of thinking. "How to Use This Guide," which outlines this Study Guide, explains how best to use the study guide to learn all the new material. "Study Tips" (p. ix) provides some practical suggestions for improving your ability to learn, understand, and remember.

HOW TO USE THIS GUIDE

Scanning

Scanning is a useful strategy that can facilitate learning. When you scan a chapter, you get a better idea of what lies ahead. So survey the text chapter first. Spend some time looking at the graphics, and examine the special features, boxed inserts, and concept reviews; note the parts that look interesting to you. Pay attention to the diagrams, graphs, photographs, cartoons, and tables. This preview will give you a clearer impression of what is going to be covered in the chapter. Don't worry about the details at this point; just try to get the big picture.

Next read the chapter overview (Chapter . . . At A Glance) in the study guide. This will give you a general, but more detailed, summary of what you are about to encounter in the chapter. This type of previewing activity will help you to develop a conceptual framework (or cognitive map) that will allow you to more readily understand the details of what you are about to read and will make learning the material easier. For example, imagine trying to put together a large jigsaw puzzle without knowing what the finished picture looked like. Do you think it would be easier if you could see the finished picture? Of course it would! Likewise, when you scan the chapter and read the preview, you will have some idea of the big picture and of how the various pieces of the chapter fit together.

Advance Organizers and Preview Questions

The text authors have provided advance organizers at the beginning of each major section of a chapter. These will help you to start thinking about the material and will give you an overview of what lies ahead. The preview questions at the beginning of each main section in the study guide are derived from these advance organizers. Read these preview questions before you read each section of the text chapter and before you start the exercises in the study guide. Both the advance organizers and the preview questions are directly linked to the concept checks, true/false tests, matching exercises, progress tests, and graphic organizers in the study guide. Successful completion of these activities will prepare you for tests, quizzes, exams, and other evaluation procedures.

Structured Note Taking   Good note taking is very important to learning. So we encourage you to take notes. The study guide structures your note taking by prompting you to write definitions, to paraphrase information, and to integrate concepts. Simply highlighting sentences in the textbook is not sufficient. Highlighting does not involve active cognitive processing of the information, whereas writing, especially using your own words, does.

Graphic Organizers   An important aid to better understanding text material is the use of visualization. Completing the graphs, charts, and flow diagrams will provide a visual synopsis that will help you understand and remember the material. So be sure to complete all these exercises, and practice making up your own graphic organizers.

Corrective Feedback: Concept Checks, Matching Exercises, True/False Tests, and Progress Tests   At the end of each major section in the study guide are learning checks in the form of conceptual questions, matching exercises, and true/false tests. These exercises provide you with feedback as you progress through the chapter. Be sure to complete each of these before going on to the next section. Three progress tests containing multiple-choice questions conclude each chapter. These are designed to help you assess your mastery of the material. If you don't know the answers to these questions, go back and study the parts of the text that you didn't understand.

If your instructor gives a quiz or test after each chapter, complete all three progress tests before the exam. Testing, and the corrective feedback it provides, will give you a more realistic idea of how well prepared you actually are and thus reduces the tendency for "overconfidence."

If your exam covers a number of chapters, it is a good idea to complete progress tests 1 and 2 after you have studied each chapter, then create a "comprehensive pretest" from progress test 3 in all the relevant chapters. Taking this larger test will give you a better idea of what the exam is going to be like. Also, be sure to ask your instructor if material other than that covered in the textbook (e.g., material from lectures, videos, lab demonstrations, and tutorials) will be on the exam.

One additional point: It is important not to confuse your recognition ability with your ability to recall and write about a topic. Multiple-choice questions tap your ability to recognize the correct answer, but do not assess your ability to express your ideas logically and coherently. You need to develop both types of skills.

Something to Think About   Each study guide chapter concludes with a special feature called Something to Think About, which contains thought-provoking questions about the material. We encourage you to think actively about what you have read in the chapter. Discuss these topics with friends and family members. This will help you remember the concepts and make learning more enjoyable.

You can also use the ideas from these sections as a guide for writing short essays or papers or for preparing for a presentation.

Answers   The answers to all the questions are included at the end of each chapter. Check your answers as you work your way through the material: Getting immediate corrective feedback facilitates the learning process.

STUDY TIPS   What are the five or ten most effective ways to improve your ability to learn, comprehend, and remember the material in this course? The truth is that there is probably no single list of techniques, no matter who develops it, that will work for all learners all the time. Everyone has a different way or style of learning; becoming familiar with your own unique learning style is the first step in becoming a successful student. However, we can all improve our ability to learn and to remember what we have learned. On that optimistic note, here are some general strategies that can be of value and can benefit almost anyone who makes the effort to use them. So, when faced with the challenge of mastering a large amount of new material try some, or all, of the following:

Use Distributed Practice   You know that you should not cram. Cramming, or what psychologists called massed practice, is not good for long-term retention of material. Spacing out your studying, or distributed practice, on the other hand, enhances your ability to remember. This is one of the most well-established principles in psychology—the spacing effect. Instead of studying for five straight hours at one time, you would be much better off studying one hour a day over five days. This technique also works at shorter intervals. For example, if you have to memorize a formula, you will probably repeat it over and over (say, ten times) until you feel confident you have it memorized. This, of course, is massed practice, and the sense of confidence that typically accompanies it is often misleading. A better way to maximize the benefits of those ten rehearsals is to space them over time, allowing a longer interval after each rehearsal than the one before.

Reduce Interference   One reason we tend to forget new information is that other information (either previously learned or learned later) can interfere with the material we are trying to master. So, if you are studying for a number of courses at the same time, try to study subjects that are different from each other. The more similar they are, the greater the interference. Another source of interference comes from social activities, such as watching TV or interacting with friends. When you engage in these activities after studying, you increase the risk of interference. In addition, playing loud music, having the TV on, or listening to other people's conversations while you are studying can cause distraction and interfere with learning. The best advice? Go to sleep after studying. A good sleep is the best way to cut down on interference and it helps consolidate memories. The worst thing to do? Stay up all night cramming for an exam that is being given the next day.

Try Overlearning   Overlearning is another very effective, and relatively simple, technique for preventing forgetting. When you feel you have mastered the material in a chapter, and you have just answered all the progress test questions correctly, you usually feel relieved and put away the books. It is at this point, however, that overlearning is useful. If you had spent, say, an hour and a half getting to this level, what you need to do now is spend another 10 to 15 minutes reviewing the material one more time. These few extra minutes of studying are the most beneficial minutes you can spend in terms of consolidating your memory and preventing the forgetting of material you have just learned. Hermann Ebbinghaus showed, over a hundred years ago, that most of the information is lost very soon after it is learned. He was the first to demonstrate the powerful effect of overlearning as a way of dealing with this problem.

Get Corrective Feedback

If you studied hard and felt you really knew the material, it is a bit of a shock to find that you did poorly on the test. What could have happened? One possibility is that you only thought you knew the material and you were suffering from "the overconfidence effect." A simple way of prevent this is to get corrective feedback on what you know before taking the exam. For example, using the True/False tests and the Matching Tests, completing the Graphic Organizers, and, of course, taking the Progress Tests will give you the feedback you need.

Be aware, however, that this is not necessarily a perfect gauge of how you will do on the real exam. When you are testing yourself, you tend to be in a much more relaxed state: You have just studied the material and you are in no particular rush. If you make a mistake, it is no big deal; you can simply look up the answers at the end of the chapter (this is not something that you can do in the exam!). These factors often lead students to the false conclusion that the questions on the real exam were much harder than the ones in the progress tests, sample exams, and so forth. Try to make your self-testing as real as possible (get a little anxious); that way you will benefit most from corrective feedback.

Use Mnemonics

Use of memory aids, called mnemonics, can help in memorizing new material and in preventing forgetting. Visual imagery, in particular, is very effective with some material. Try to vividly imagine what it is you are attempting to memorize. A picture is worth a thousand words and is much more memorable. For other material, try making up a story that links elements together. Create acronyms for lists of terms or complex concept names, for example (it is easier to remember SCUBA than self-contained underwater breathing apparatus). Look ahead in your textbook to Chapter 6 and read about how memory works, why we forget, and how we can make memories last; specifically, read the Application for more study tips.

Develop Good Study Habits

Most top students get good grades because of effective study habits (not sheer brilliance). Evaluate your current study habits. Manage your time effectively. Remember, we are usually poor judges about how long things take to do (late papers are a typical example that is the result of our poor judgment). So, after you have made your plans, allow yourself some extra time.

Make studying a priority and firmly commit to doing well in school. Don't let other people interfere with your goal of mastering the material and getting good grades. Study by yourself (too much socializing takes place in study groups). Reward yourself with social activities, if that's what is important to you, AFTER you have successfully completed your study and have achieved an A+ on the progress tests. If you like music, play soft instrumental music. Take a short break after an hour or so of studying—walk around for a few minutes. Do some exercise. Don't study when you are sleep deprived, very tired, or stressed out. If you are getting nowhere and can't concentrate on the material. do something else for a while (a breath of fresh air, a brief nap, a little walk, a chat with a friend, a little meditation or exercise, can all be helpful).

Try Exercise   Exercising before you study will help relieve stress and will induce a more relaxed state. This is because exercise causes the brain to release pain-killing chemicals called endorphins (you have your own little drug-producing factory). It is also a good idea to exercise before a major exam for the same reasons. If aerobic exercise is not your thing (if it makes you tired and unable to concentrate), try something less strenuous, like walking. Anxiety interferes with performance, so anything you can do to effectively control and reduce your anxiety will help. Have fun, good luck, and enjoy your introductory psychology course.

Study Guide

Introduction and Research Methods

PREVIEW	Reading the section below first will give you a general sense of the chapter's contents and an initial introduction to some of the major concepts and terms. This will prime you for what you are about to read and help you to develop a "cognitive map" that will guide your study of the material in this chapter. Likewise, reading the **preview questions** at the beginning of each major section will improve your ability to understand, learn, and retain the information.

CHAPTER 1. . . AT A GLANCE

Chapter 1 first defines psychology, then gives a brief history of the people and events that influenced its development. Beginning with the contributions of philosophy and physiology, the chapter discusses the two early schools, structuralism and functionalism; the emergence of the major perspectives in twentieth-century psychology; and the major specialty areas.

The four goals of psychology are used to introduce the scientific method. The descriptive and experimental research methods are outlined, and the advantages and disadvantages of each are discussed.

Important issues such as the need for representative sampling and random selection are raised. The section concludes with a discussion of the uses and limitations of correlational studies. The concepts of correlation, the correlation coefficient, and negative and positive correlations are described and explained.

The experimental method is explained in detail, using a specific study to illustrate important concepts such as dependent and independent variables, experimental and control groups, and random assignment. Also presented are variations in experimental design.

The chapter concludes with an important discussion of the ethical guidelines that regulate psychological research and the role played by the American Psychological Association.

Introduction: The Origins of Psychology

Preview Questions

Consider the following questions as you study this section of the chapter.

- How is psychology defined today?
- Which two disciplines influenced the emergence of psychology as a science?
- Who founded psychology?
- What were the first two schools of psychology called, who is associated with their founding, and how do they differ?
- Who founded psychoanalysis, and what was its main focus?
- What are the goals of behaviorism, and who were the three main proponents of this perspective?
- What is the emphasis of humanistic psychology, and what are the names of its two major advocates?

*Read the section "Introduction: The Origins of Psychology" and **write** your answers to the following:*

1. Psychology is defined as _____
_____

2. The two disciplines that influenced the emergence of psychology were _____
_____

3. The founder of psychology was
_____

4. The first two schools of psychology were
_____ ,
and the people associated with their beginnings were _____

5. Structuralism emphasized _____
_____
_____
Functionalism stressed the importance of
_____
_____

6. The person who founded psychoanalysis was
_____ , and its main focus

was on _____
_____

7. Behaviorism focused on _____
_____
and rejected _____
_____
_____

8. The main proponents of behaviorism were
_____

9. Humanistic psychology emphasizes _____
_____
Its two major advocates were
_____

After you have carefully studied the preceding section, complete the following exercises.

Concept Check 1

Read the following and write the correct term in the space provided.

1. A psychologist who stresses the importance of how behavior enables organisms to adapt to their environment would be classified as belonging to the _____ school of psychology.

2. Dr. Levine adheres to the theory that emphasizes the role of unconscious conflicts in determining behavior and personality. This viewpoint is most consistent with the _____ school of psychology.

3. Environmental influences and overt measurable behavior are to _____ as conscious experience, psychological growth, and self-determination are to
_____ .

4. While researching a paper on the history of psychology, John discovered that René Descartes, a seventeenth-century philosopher and mathematician, promoted the idea that the mind and body are separate entities that interact to produce sensations, emotions, and other conscious

experiences. Descartes's view is called

_____ .

5. Dr. Brunac's research focuses on the question of the degree to which heredity and environment influence the development of human abilities such as intelligence and personality characteristics. Dr. Brunac is interested in the

_____ issue.

6. Alvira believes that our most complex conscious experiences can be broken down into elemental structures or basic components of sensations and feelings through the research method of introspection. Alvira's view is most consistent with the school of thought in psychology called

_____ .

Review of Terms, Concepts, and Names 1

Use the terms in this list to complete the Matching Test, then to help you answer the True/False items correctly.

psychology	Mary Whiton Calkins
interactive dualism	Margaret Floy
nature-nurture issue	Washburn
(heredity versus	Sigmund Freud
environment)	psychoanalysis
physiology	behaviorism
Wilhelm Wundt	Ivan Pavlov
Edward B. Titchener	John B. Watson
structuralism	B. F. Skinner
introspection	humanistic psychology
William James	Carl Rogers
functionalism	Abraham Maslow
G. Stanley Hall	

Matching Exercise

Match the appropriate term/name with its definition or description.

1. _____ American psychologist who conducted research on memory, personality, and dreams and was the first woman president of the American Psychological Association.

2. _____ Looking inward in an attempt to reconstruct feelings and sensations experienced immediately after viewing a stimulus object.

3. _____ School of psychology and theoretical viewpoint that emphasizes each

person's unique potential for psychological growth and self-direction.

4. _____ American psychologist who founded behaviorism, emphasizing the study of observable behavior and rejecting the study of mental processes.

5. _____ Early school of psychology that emphasized studying the purpose, or function, of behavior and mental experiences.

6. _____ The scientific study of behavior and mental processes.

7. _____ The idea that the mind and body are separate entities that interact to produce sensations, emotions, and other conscious experiences.

8. _____ German physiologist who founded psychology as a formal science and opened the first psychology research laboratory in 1879.

9. _____ British-born American psychologist who founded structuralism, the first school of psychology.

10. _____ School of psychology and theoretical viewpoint that emphasizes the study of observable behaviors, especially as they pertain to the process of learning.

11. _____ American psychologist who founded the school of humanistic psychology.

True/False Test

Indicate whether each statement is true or false by placing T or F in the blank space next to each item.

1. ____ G. Stanley Hall was an American psychologist who established the first psychology research laboratory in the United States and founded the American Psychological Association.

2. ____ Structuralism stresses the importance of how behavior functions to allow people and animals to adapt to their environment.

3. ____ Physiology is a branch of biology that studies the functions and parts of living organisms, including human beings.

4. ____ William James was an American philosopher and psychologist who was instrumental in establishing psychology in the United States and whose ideas became the basis for the psychological school called functionalism.

5. ___ The issue of heredity versus environment is the same as the nature-nurture issue and refers to the debate over which is more important, the inborn characteristics of the individual or the impact of the environment.

6. ___ Margaret Floy Washburn was an American psychologist who published research on mental processes in animals and was the first woman in the United States to earn a doctorate in psychology.

7. ___ Ivan Pavlov was an Austrian physician whose work focused on the unconscious causes of behavior and personality formation and who founded psychoanalysis.

8. ___ B. F. Skinner was a famous American psychologist who championed behaviorism.

9. ___ Abraham Maslow was a humanistic psychologist who developed a theory of motivation that emphasized psychological growth.

10. ___ Psychoanalysis studies environmental influences on behavior and personality without reference to mental processes and is concerned with understanding how we learn to become who we are.

11. ___ Sigmund Freud was a Russian physiologist whose pioneering research on learning contributed to the development of behaviorism and who discovered the basic learning process that is now called classical conditioning.

Check your answers and review any areas of weakness before going on to the next section.

Contemporary Psychology

Preview Questions

Consider the following questions as you study this section of the chapter.

- What are the seven major perspectives in contemporary psychology, and how do they differ?
- What are the main specialty areas in contemporary psychology?
- How do clinical psychologists and psychiatrists differ?

Read the section "Contemporary Psychology" and **write** *your answers to the following:*

1. The seven major perspectives in psychology are

   _____

   _____

   _____

2. The main specialty areas in contemporary psychology are _____

   _____

   _____

   _____

   _____

3. The difference between a clinical psychologist and a psychiatrists is _____

   _____

   _____

   _____

   _____

   _____

After you have carefully studied the preceding section, complete the following exercises.

Concept Check 2

Which specialty area is represented by each of the following?

1. Dr. Matthews studies the relationship between behavior and the nervous system. She would most likely be classified as a(n) _____ psychologist.

2. Michele wants to study physical, social, and psychological changes that occur over the lifespan when she attends graduate school. Michele is planning to be a(n) _____ psychologist.

3. Dr. Bowman studies the causes, treatment, and prevention of different types of psychological disorders. Dr. Bowman is most likely a(n) _____ psychologist.

4. Dr. Ying explores how individuals are affected by people and situations and the factors that influence conformity and obedience. Dr. Ying is a(n) _____ psychologist.

5. Dr. Steinberg examines individual differences and the characteristics that make each person unique. He is most likely a(n) _____ psychologist.

6. Ingrid is interested in investigating mental processes such as reasoning, thinking, and problem solving. Ingrid is probably planning a career as a(n) _____ psychologist.

7. Dr. Whinney develops instructional methods and materials used to train people in both educational and work settings; she also studies how people of all ages learn. She is a(n) _____ psychologist. Her colleague, Dr. Marx, focuses on designing programs that promote the intellectual, social, and emotional development of children, including those with special needs. He is a(n) _____ psychologist.

8. Dr. Barton is concerned with stress and coping, the relationship between psychological factors and well-being, and ways of promoting health-enhancing behaviors. Dr. Barton is probably a(n) _____ psychologist.

9. Pitor, who just completed his Ph.D., applied for a job concerned with the relationship between people and work, including the study of job satisfaction, worker productivity, personnel selection, and the interaction between people and equipment. Pitor has applied for a job as a(n) _____ psychologist.

Graphic Organizer 1

The statements in the table below represent some of the major perspectives and specialty areas in contemporary psychology. Which perspective is reflected by each statement, and which specialty area is being described? Write your answers in the spaces provided.

Statement	Perspective	Specialty
1. I'm interested in how different parenting styles and techniques influence each child's individual potential for growth and self-determination.		
2. I study the relationship between people and work and, more specifically, how to increase productivity. I believe that by changing environmental factors, increasing the use of rewards and praise for correct behavior, and providing corrective feedback, workers' overt behavior can be changed.		
3. I study how people of all ages learn, and I develop instructional methods and materials to help the learning process. In particular, I stress the roles played by thinking, problem solving, memory, and mental imagery.		
4. I work mostly with people who suffer from mental disorders, and I believe that the main causes of mental illness are either genetic or due to some malfunction in the central nervous system or endocrine system. I often prescribe medications and order medical procedures such as electroshock treatment.		
5. I often travel to different countries to research people's attitudes and group relations. My research tends to show that many behavioral patterns—for instance, the amount of personal space people require to feel comfortable—vary from one country to another.		
6. I believe that unconscious conflicts, early childhood experiences, and repressed sexual and aggressive feelings make us who we are, and I use this point of view in my work on individual differences and in trying to determine which characteristics make each of us unique.		
7. I focus on the relationship between psychological factors and health, in particular on how people cope with stress in their lives. It is not what happens to us that is important; rather, how we perceive and think about potentially stressful events determines our well-being.		
8. My research keeps me in the lab most of the time, and I focus on the principles and conditions of learning and motivation. Recently, I have been investigating how quickly rats learn the layout of a maze as a function of either large or small amounts of reinforcement.		
9. Psychological processes that have helped individuals adapt to their environment have also helped them to survive, reproduce, and pass those abilities onto their offspring. I adopt this point of view in my investigations of interpersonal attraction, prejudice, and aggression.		

Graphic Organizer 2

Origins of Psychology, First Schools, and Key Figures

Flow diagram exercise: To help you develop the technique of creating your own graphic organizers, we encourage you to try making a flow diagram/ timeline, using boxes, lines, and arrows, that contains the following information. Using a separate sheet of paper, generate your own graphic organizer, then compare it to the sample in the answer section. To help you in this early stage of your study, we've filled in portions of the first two boxes.

Philosophy (list key figures)	Physiology (list key figure)

1. Two areas that influenced the beginnings of psychology and the key figures in each.
2. The founder of psychology and the year the first psychology research lab was established.
3. First school in psychology and key figure.
4. First American school in psychology and key figures.
5. Two new approaches (and key figures in each) that challenged the first two schools in psychology.
6. New school that emerged in the 1950s and key figures.

Review of Terms and Names 2

Use the terms in this list to complete the Matching Test, then to help you answer the True/False items correctly.

perspective
specialty area
biological perspective
psychodynamic
  perspective
behavioral perspective
humanistic perspective
cognitive perspective
cross-cultural
  perspective
culture
ethnocentrism
individualistic cultures
collectivistic cultures
evolutionary perspective
Charles Darwin

biological psychology
cognitive psychology
experimental psychology
developmental
  psychology
social psychology
personality psychology
health psychology
educational
  psychologists
school psychology
industrial/organizational
  psychology
clinical psychologist
counseling psychologist
psychiatrist

Matching Exercise

Match the appropriate term/name with its definition or description.

1. _____ Psychologist who has a doctorate in psychology and intensive training in diagnosing and treating people with psychological disorders.

2. _____ The study of physical, social, and psychological changes over the lifespan, from infancy to old age.

3. _____ Mental health professional who has a medical degree plus years of specialized training in the diagnosis and treatment of psychological disorders.

4. _____ Specialists who study how people of all ages learn.

5. _____ General term that describes research focused on such basic psychological topics as learning, emotion, and motivation.

6. _____ Point of view or general framework that reflects a psychologist's emphasis in investigating psychological topics.

7. _____ Specific area in psychology in which psychologists are trained and in which they work or practice.

8. _____ Broad term that refers to the attitudes, values, beliefs, and behaviors shared by a group of people and communicated from one generation to another.

9. _____ Specialty area that investigates mental processes, including reasoning, thinking, language, and memory.

10. _____ British naturalist and scientist whose theory of evolution through natural selection was first published in *On the Origin of Species by Means of Natural Selection* in 1859.

11. _____ Area of psychology that examines individual differences and may also study the origins and development of those differences.

12. _____ Perspective in psychology that studies how behavior is acquired or modified by environmental consequences and whose focus is on observable behavior and the fundamental laws of learning.

13. _____ The tendency to use your own culture as the standard for judging other cultures.

14. _____ Perspective in psychology that emphasizes studying the physical bases of human and animal behavior, including the nervous system, endocrine system, immune system, and genetics.

True/False Test

Indicate whether each statement is true or false by placing T or F in the blank space next to each item.

1. ___ Biological psychology studies the physical bases of human and animal behavior.

2. ___ The evolutionary perspective uses Darwin's theory of evolution by natural selection to explain psychological processes and phenomena.

3. ___ Counseling psychology is concerned with the relationship between people and work, and it includes the study of job satisfaction, worker productivity, personnel selection, and the interaction between people and equipment.

4. ___ The cross-cultural perspective stresses the importance of cultural and ethnic influences on behavior.

5. ___ School psychology focuses on designing programs that promote the intellectual and social development of children in school.

6. ___ Psychologists who explore how individuals are affected by people and situations and what factors influence conformity, obedience, persuasion, interpersonal attraction, and other related phenomena are called social psychologists.

7. ___ Individualistic cultures emphasize the needs and goals of the group over the needs and goals of the individual.

8. ___ Health psychology focuses on the role of psychological factors in health, illness, medical treatment, and health-related behaviors.

9. ___ Industrial/organizational psychology aims to improve everyday functioning by helping people to cope more effectively with everyday problems and challenges.

10. ___ Psychologists who take the humanistic perspective emphasize the importance of unconscious influences, early life experiences, and interpersonal relationships in explaining the underlying dynamics of behavior or treating people with psychological problems.

11. ___ Collectivistic cultures emphasize the needs and goals of the individual over the needs and goals of the group.

12. ___ The psychodynamic perspective focuses on the motivation of people to grow psychologically, the influence of interpersonal relationships on a person's self-concept, and the importance of choice and self-direction in striving to reach one's potential.

13. ___ The cognitive perspective stresses the important role of mental processes in how people process information, develop language, solve problems, and think.

Check your answers and review any areas of weakness before going on to the next section.

The Scientific Method

Preview Questions

Consider the following questions as you study this section of the chapter.

- What are the four goals of psychology?
- What is the scientific method?
- What assumptions and attitudes guide psychologists?
- What is meant by empirical evidence, and what are the four basic steps of the scientific method?
- What are theories, how do they differ from hypotheses, and what principle do they reflect?

*Read the section "The Scientific Method" and **write** your answers to the following:*

1. The four basic goals of psychology are to _____
   _____
   _____

2. The scientific method refers to _____
   _____
   _____

3. Psychologists are guided by the basic assumptions that _____
   _____
   _____
   _____

4. Psychologists share a set of attitudes, including

   _____

   _____

5. Empirical evidence refers to _____

   _____

   The four basic steps of the scientific method
   are   _____

   _____

   _____

   _____

6. A theory is _____

   _____

   It is different from a hypothesis _____

   _____

   _____

   _____

7. The role of statistics in psychological research
   is to _____

   _____

   _____

8. Theories can evolve and change because they
   reflect the _____

   _____

   _____

   ***After you have carefully studied the preceding
   section, complete the following exercises.***

   _____

Concept Check 3

*Read the following and write the correct term in the
space provided.*

1. Dr. Marlow is interested in drinking and driving
   behavior and wants to know the frequency with
   which people will drive after receiving feedback
   from a breathalyzer test. In one condition, she
   sets up her equipment in a bar and administers
   the test to patrons who are leaving and planning to drive and then observes whether or not
   feedback on their level of intoxication influences
   their decision to drive. Dr. Marlow is using
   _____ research.

2. In the above example, Dr. Marlow makes this
   prediction: the majority of people who are told
   that they are over the legal limit will still drive;

the higher the level on the breathalyzer test, the
more likely it is that they will drive. Dr. Marlow
has formulated a _____ .

3. After collecting data over many weeks, Dr.
   Marlow performs calculations and mathematical
   tests to see if her prediction was correct. Dr.
   Marlow is using _____
   to analyze her data.

(d) Dr. Marlow next writes a report describing the
    background of this research and details her
    research design, data collection methods,
    results, analyses, and conclusions. She submits
    her report to a respected psychology journal for
    peer review and publication. She is following
    step _____ of producing scientific evidence
    by _____ .

Review of Terms and Concepts 3

*Use the terms in this list to complete the Matching
Test, then to help you answer the True/False items
correctly.*

scientific method	experimental method
critical thinking	statistics
empirical evidence	statistical significance
hypothesis	meta-analysis
variable	replicate
operational definition	theory
descriptive method	

Matching Exercise

*Match the appropriate term/name with its definition
or description.*

1. _____ Statistical technique that
   involves combining and analyzing the results of
   many research studies on a specific topic in
   order to identify overall trends.

2. _____ To repeat or duplicate a scientific study in order to increase confidence in
   the validity of the original findings.

3. _____ A set of assumptions, attitudes, and procedures that guide researchers in
   creating questions to investigate, in generating
   evidence, and in drawing conclusions.

4. _____ Tentative statement about
   the relationship between two or more variables.

5. _____ Precise description of how the variables in a study will be manipulated or measured.

6. _____ Method of investigation used to demonstrate cause-and-effect relationships by purposely manipulating a factor thought to produce change in a second factor.

7. _____ Mathematical methods used to summarize data and draw conclusions based on the data.

True/False Test

Indicate whether each statement is true or false by placing T or F in the blank space next to each item.

1. ___ A statistically significant finding is one that is not likely to have occurred by chance.

2. ___ Empirical evidence is evidence that is the result of observation, measurement, and experimentation.

3. ___ A variable is a tentative explanation that tries to integrate and account for the relationship of various findings and observations.

4. ___ Descriptive methods are research strategies for observing and describing behavior and include naturalistic observation, survey, case studies, and correlational studies.

5. ___ A theory is a factor that can vary, or change, in ways that can be observed, measured, and verified.

6. ___ Critical thinking is the active process of trying to minimize the influence of preconceptions and biases while rationally evaluating evidence, determining what conclusions can be drawn from the evidence, and considering alternative explanations.

Check your answers and review any areas of weakness before going on to the next section.

Descriptive Methods

Preview Questions

Consider the following questions as you study this section of the chapter.
- What are descriptive methods?
- How is naturalistic observation typically conducted?
- What are case studies, and when are they normally used?
- What is the survey method, and how do researchers ensure that their sample closely parallels the larger group on relevant characteristics?
- What is random selection, and why is it important for obtaining accurate results?
- What does a correlational study involve, and what are its limitations?
- What is the correlation coefficient, and how does a negative correlation differ from a positive correlation?

*Read the section "Descriptive Methods" and **write** your answers to the following:*

1. Descriptive statistics are _____

2. Naturalistic observation involves the _____

3. A case study is _____

Case studies are typically used to _____

4. In the survey method, the researcher _____

5. Researchers ensure that their sample closely parallels the population of interest by

6. Random selection refers to _____

It is important because _____

_____

_____

7. Correlational studies show _____

_____

_____

They are limited because _____

_____

8. The correlation coefficient is _____

_____

_____

The correlation coefficient has two parts:

_____

_____

_____

9. A positive correlation is one in which _____

_____

A negative correlation is one in which _____

_____

_____

After you have carefully studied the preceding section, complete the following exercises.

Concept Check 4

Read the following and decide which term applies in each case.

1. If a researcher found a correlation coefficient of –0.85, between amount of exercise and weight,

this would indicate that the _____ people exercise, the _____ they weigh.

2. If an organization wants to find out about the spending habits of high-income people, they would be advised to conduct a _____ , using a representative _____ that would be _____ selected from this population.

3. Dr. Klatz is interested in whether there is a difference in the way males and females carry objects such as textbooks, bags, and other large items, so she sets up a hidden camera on the main concourse of a large university and videotapes people at various times throughout the day. Dr. Klatz is using

_____ .

4. A psychologist discovers that the more control people feel they have over what happens in their work environments, the more productive they are. The psychologist has discovered a _____ correlation between perceived control and productivity.

5. A psychologist who wants to find out about the lives and experiences of people who claim to have been abducted by aliens and to know how these people are viewed by their families, friends, and coworkers would be advised to use the _____ method of research.

Graphic Organizer 3
Positive and Negative Correlations

The following box shows both positive and negative correlations between variables. In cells A through D the arrows indicate a relationship between the amount students study (variable X) and their grade point average (GPA) (variable Y). Fill in the appropriate term in each space provided.

Amount of Study (X)

1. Cell A indicates a _____ correlation, and cell D indicates a _____ correlation.

2. Cell C indicates a _____ correlation, and cell B indicates a _____ correlation.

3. Cell A: _____ amounts of X are associated with _____ levels of Y.

   Cell D: _____ amounts of X are associated with _____ levels of Y.

4. Cell C: _____ amounts of X are associated with _____ levels of Y.

   Cell B: _____ amounts of X are associated with _____ levels of Y.

Review of Terms and Concepts 4

Use the terms in this list to complete the Matching Test, then to help you answer the True/False items correctly.

descriptive methods
naturalistic observation
case study
survey
sample
representative sample

random selection
correlational study
correlation coefficient
positive correlation
negative correlation

Matching Exercise

Match the appropriate term with its definition or description.

1. _____ A questionnaire or interview designed to investigate the opinions, behaviors, or characteristics of a particular group.

2. _____ General term for scientific procedures that involve systematically observing behavior in order to describe the relationships among behaviors and events.

3. _____ Selected segment of the population under study.

4. _____ Selected segment of a population that very closely parallels the larger group being studied on relevant characteristics.

5. _____ Research strategy that allows the precise calculation of how strongly related two factors are to each other.

6. _____ Process in which participants are selected randomly from the larger group such that every member has an equal chance of being included in the study.

True/False Test

Indicate whether each statement is true or false by placing T or F in the blank space next to each item.

1. ____ A case study is an intensive, in-depth investigation of an individual.

2. ____ A negative correlation between two variables means that the two factors are totally unrelated.

3. ____ Naturalistic observation is the systematic observation and recording of behaviors as they occur in their natural setting.

4. ____ A correlation coefficient is a numerical indication of the magnitude and direction of the relationship between two variables.

5. ____ A positive correlation is one in which the two variables move in opposite directions; as one factor increases, the other decreases.

Check your answers and review any areas of weakness before going on to the next section.

The Experimental Method

Preview Questions

Consider the following questions as you study this section of the chapter.

- What is the experimental method, and what is its main purpose?
- What are independent and dependent variables, and why do researchers use random assignment?
- What is the experimental group, the control group, and the placebo control group?
- What is a double-blind study, why do researchers use this technique, and what is meant by demand characteristics?
- How do natural experiments differ from laboratory experiments?
- What are the five key provisions of the APA guidelines for research using humans?

Read the section "The Experimental Method" and **write** *your answers to the following:*

1. The experimental method of investigation is used to _____
   _____
   _____

2. The independent variable is the _____
   _____
   The dependent variable is the _____
   _____

3. Random assignment means that _____
   _____
   _____
   It helps ensure that _____
   _____
   _____

4. The experimental group (or experimental condition) is _____
   _____
   The control group (or control condition) is _____
   _____
   _____
   The placebo control group is _____
   _____
   _____

5. A double-blind study is one in which
   _____
   _____
   It is used to _____
   _____
   _____

6. Five key provisions of the APA ethical guidelines regulating research with human participants are
   (a) _____
   (b) _____
   (c) _____
   (d) _____
   (e) _____

After you have carefully studied the preceding section, complete the following exercises.

Concept Check 5

Read the following and decide which term applies in each case.

Dr. Denton studies the effects of marijuana on memory. He designs an ethically approved experiment that consists of two groups: group A gets the active ingredient in cannabis, THC, and group B gets a harmless inert substance. Neither the researcher nor the participants know who is getting the drug and who is not. Subjects are assigned to each group by chance, and all subjects are given a long list of word pairs to learn and are later given a memory test.

1. The independent variable in this study is
   _____ .

2. The dependent variable is the
   _____ .

3. Group A is the _____
   group, and group B is the
   _____ group.

4. Dr. Denton has used a _____ technique in designing the experiment; along with the control procedure used, this should help guard against _____ .

5. Subjects ended up in group A or group B on the basis of _____ .

Review of Terms and Concepts 5

Use the terms in this list to complete the Matching Test, then to help you answer the True/False items correctly.

experimental method
independent variable
dependent variable
Mozart effect
spatial reasoning
  abilities
random assignment
experimental group (or
  experimental condition)
control group (or control
  condition)
no-treatment control
  group
sham-treatment control
  group

treatment effect
practice effect
placebo control group
placebo
expectancy effect
double-blind study
single-blind study
demand characteristics
natural experiment
pseudoscience
paranormal phenomena
rule of falsifiability
illusory correlation

Matching Exercise

Match the appropriate term with its definition or description.

1. _____ Experimental technique in which the researchers, but not the participants, are aware of the critical information about the experiment.

2. _____ Method of investigation used to demonstrate cause-and-effect relationships by purposely manipulating a factor thought to produce change in a second factor.

3. _____ The factor that is observed and measured for change in an experiment.

4. _____ Alleged abilities that fall outside the range of normal experience and established scientific explanations.

5. _____ Change in a subject's behavior produced by the subject's belief that change should happen.

6. _____ A group of participants that is not exposed to the independent variable or treatment of interest and against which the experimental group is compared.

7. _____ In order for a claim to be scientifically tested and proved true, there must be identifiable evidence that could prove the claim false.

8. _____ Subtle cues or signals that communicate what is expected of particular subjects in an experiment.

9. _____ An inert substance or a treatment that has no known effects.

10. _____ Any change in performance due to repeating a task.

11. _____ Abilities involved in tasks that require the actual or mental manipulation of objects in space, such as mentally rotating objects, reading maps, or putting together a jigsaw puzzle.

12. _____ An illusory correlation is the mistaken belief that two factors are related when they are not.

True/False Test

Indicate whether each item is true or false by placing T or F in the blank space next to each item.

1. ___ Random assignment means that all subjects have an equal chance of being assigned to any of the conditions or groups in the study.

2. ___ Participants in the placebo control group receive a fake treatment or substance with no known effects.

3. ___ Participants in the experimental group (or condition) are exposed to the independent variable or treatment of interest.

4. ___ The independent variable in an experiment is purposely manipulated in order to effect a change in another variable.

5. ___ The experimental technique in which neither the participants nor the researcher is aware of the experimental conditions to which each subject has been assigned is called the double-blind technique.

6. ___ A pseudoscience is a fake or a false science.

7. ___ In a natural experiment, researchers carefully observe and measure the impact of naturally occurring events on their study participants.

8. ___ The change in behavior or mental processes after being exposed to the independent variable is called the treatment effect.

9. ___ In an experiment, the sham-treatment control group goes through all the experimental phases but is not exposed to the treatment of interest.

10. ___ The Mozart effect refers to a temporary increase in spatial reasoning that supposedly occurs after listening to Mozart's *Sonata for Two Pianos in D Major.*

11. ___ The group exposed to all phases of the experiment, including exposure to a fake or sham treatment, is called the no-treatment control group.

Check your answers and review any areas of weakness before going on to the next section.

Something to Think About

1. When family and friends find out you are taking a psychology course, someone typically makes some comment about "headshrinking" and "psychoanalyzing," or notes that "psychology is just plain old common sense." To prepare yourself for these remarks, think about how you would explain what psychology really is and how you might "educate" your family and friends about the difference between psychiatry and clinical psychology.

2. If you are like most introductory psychology students, you were probably motivated to take this course, at least in part, because of a number of questions you have about human behavior and mental processes. For example, students often wonder if hypnosis can really help recover repressed memories and memories of past lives; if a lie detector really can detect lies; if "satanic messages" embedded in the lyrics of rock music can cause people to commit suicide; if ESP really exists; or whether subliminal tapes can really improve memory, clear up acne, or improve self-esteem. Now that you know more about the science of psychology, take one of your questions and think about how a psychologist would try to answer it.

Check your answers and review any areas of weakness before doing the following progress tests.

Progress Test 1

Review the complete chapter (including Concept Reviews and the boxed inserts), review all your study notes, and then test yourself on the following progress test. Check your answers. If you make a mistake, review your notes, the relevant section in the study guide, and, if necessary, go back and read the appropriate part of your textbook.

1. Two disciplines influenced the founding of psychology. The discipline that concerns itself with questions such as mind-body dualism and the nature-nurture issue is _____ ; the discipline that is a branch of biology and studies functions and structures of living organisms is _____ .
   (a) chemistry; physics
   (b) neurology; sociology
   (c) physics; neurology
   (d) philosophy; physiology

2. A Japanese psychologist investigating the relationship between worker satisfaction and productivity was surprised to find that North American workers were less productive when working as part of a group than when working alone. In some Asian countries, he had found the opposite to be true. This researcher probably has a _____ perspective, and his specialty area is _____ psychology.
   (a) cross-cultural; developmental
   (b) behavioral; health
   (c) behavioral; developmental
   (d) cross-cultural; industrial/organizational

3. Dr. Hammersly focuses on the role of unconscious factors in his patients' behaviors and spends time analyzing their dreams and delving into their early childhood experiences. Dr. Finkleman is more concerned with the way her patients think and reason, and her psychotherapy involves teaching her patients how to recognize irrational thinking and to find different ways of thinking about their situation. Dr. Hammersly's perspective is _____ , and Dr. Finkleman's perspective is _____ .
   (a) cognitive; behavioral
   (b) psychodynamic; cognitive
   (c) humanistic; biological
   (d) cognitive; psychodynamic

4. In a replication of the Mozart Effect study, researchers randomly assigned participants to three different conditions (Mozart music, Glass music, or silence). Pretests and posttests of spatial abilities were given to all participants. In this study
   (a) the sham-treatment group heard no music, only silence.
   (b) the no-treatment group was exposed to the Glass music.
   (c) the experimental group was exposed to the Mozart music.
   (d) all of the above are true.

5. A researcher who investigates how people differ on such characteristics as shyness, assertiveness, and self-esteem is most likely a _____ psychologist.
   (a) clinical   (c) developmental
   (b) biological   (d) personality

6. To ensure that differences among participants are evenly distributed across all experimental conditions and that there is no bias in how participants are assigned to their respective groups, a researcher studying the effects of violence on TV and its effect on children should
   (a) operationally define the role each participant is expected to play and assign participants on the basis of how closely they fit the definition.
   (b) make sure that the smartest people are assigned to the experimental condition.
   (c) make sure that there is an equal number of males and females, young and old, smart and stupid, short and tall, and so on, in each group.
   (d) randomly assign the participants to each condition in the experiment.

7. A researcher is interested in how sleep deprivation affects performance and cognitive abilities. She proposes that there is a relationship between the amount of sleep deprivation and the ability to solve complex mental tasks; the more sleep-deprived people are, the more mistakes they are likely to make. She has
   (a) developed a theory.
   (b) formulated a hypothesis.
   (c) produced empirical evidence.
   (d) merely stated the obvious.

8. In a study investigating the effects of sleep deprivation and cognitive performance, a researcher discovers a statistically significant difference between the cognitive scores of participants who were sleep-deprived for one hour each night and those who were sleep-deprived for four hours per night. This finding indicates that
   (a) the group members were not randomly assigned.
   (b) sleep deprivation improves mental health.
   (c) smarter people need less sleep than less intelligent people.
   (d) the differences between the groups are not likely to have occurred by chance.

9. An experimenter who decides to repeat the essence of an earlier study using different participants is
   (a) replicating the previous study.
   (b) wasting his time.
   (c) doing a meta-analysis.
   (d) conducting a correlational study.

10. In an experiment designed to test the effects of alcohol on motor coordination, group 1 participants are given a precise amount of alcohol in a mixed drink and group 2 participants are given a drink that smells and tastes exactly like the alcoholic drink but contains no alcohol. Which of the following is true?
    (a) Group 1 is the control group.
    (b) Group 2 is the experimental group.
    (c) Group 2 is the placebo control group.
    (d) Group 1 will have much more fun than group 2.

11. A researcher is interested in whether people talk when they are riding in elevators, so she and her research assistants spend many hours riding in elevators and unobtrusively noting when they hear a conversation. This researcher is using
    (a) naturalistic observation.
    (b) experimental research.
    (c) correlational research.
    (d) case study research.

12. In an attempt to understand how traumatic brain injuries affect behavior, Dr. Nicolai extensively and carefully observes and questions three accident victims who had suffered brain injuries. Which research method is Dr. Nicolai utilizing?

    (a) naturalistic observation
    (b) experimental research
    (c) correlational research
    (d) the case study method

13. In her research, Dr. Cranshaw focuses on the application of principles of natural selection to explain psychological processes and phenomena. Dr. Cranshaw is most likely a(n) _____ psychologist.

    (a) evolutionary   (c) behavioral
    (b) biological   (d) psychodynamic

14. According to Culture and Human Behavior 1.1, individualistic cultures emphasize the needs and goals of the _____ over the needs and goals of the _____ .

    (a) individual; group
    (b) country; company
    (c) group; individual
    (d) collective; group

15. According to Science Versus Pseudoscience 1.3, which of the following is true of pseudoscience?

    (a) It is a legitimate science that uses both established and unorthodox methods in the search for the truth.
    (b) It is a fake or false science.
    (c) It is not accepted by most of the scientific establishment because pseudoscientists have discovered truths that threaten all the fundamental laws and principles of science.
    (d) It does not use sophisticated jargon, impressive-looking statistical graphs, or elaborate theories, and virtually no pseudoscientist has impressive-sounding credentials.

Progress Test 2

After you have checked your understanding of the material in Progress Test 1 and have done a complete chapter review with special focus on any areas of weakness, you are ready to assess your knowledge on Progress Test 2. Check your answers. If you make a mistake, review your notes and the relevant section of the study guide and, if necessary, review the appropriate part of your textbook.

1. In an experiment, children were randomly assigned to a group that watched a violent video or to a group that watched a nonviolent video; later, the level of aggression in both groups was measured under controlled laboratory conditions. In this example, the measure of the children's aggression was the

    (a) dependent variable.
    (b) independent variable.
    (c) control variable.
    (d) naturalistic variable.

2. Dr. Ames researches changes in people's intellectual abilities as they grow older. Dr. Ames's specialty area is _____ psychology.

    (a) social   (c) developmental
    (b) educational   (d) clinical

3. Which of the major perspectives in psychology today would Wilhelm Wundt say most resembled his point of view?

    (a) behavioral   (c) cognitive
    (b) psychodynamic   (d) humanistic

4. Dr. Sandman investigates the relationship between sleep deprivation and cognitive abilities. He decides to test subjects in his sleep research lab under varying conditions. First, he allows all his subjects to get a number of uninterrupted nights' sleep and records how long each subject sleeps on average. Next, he decides that sleep deprivation would be either two, three, or four hours fewer than the average for each subject. Dr. Sandman

    (a) has operationally defined one of his variables.
    (b) is using cruel and unusual punishment.
    (c) has empirically demonstrated a cause-and-effect relationship.
    (d) has proposed a theory.

5. An educational psychologist is interested in whether having students evaluate instructors' performance is actually a good measure of teaching ability. A review of the literature showed some inconsistent findings across hundreds of different studies. To get a sense of the overall trends in this body of research, the investigator would be advised to use a technique called

    (a) the correlation coefficient.
    (b) meta-analysis.
    (c) the case study method.
    (d) replication.

6. Compared to clinical psychologists, psychiatrists are more likely to
   (a) prescribe drugs and other medical procedures for their clients.
   (b) assume that psychological disorders result from unconscious conflicts.
   (c) use a cognitively based therapy rather than a biologically based therapy.
   (d) favor a humanistic perspective rather than a psychoanalytic perspective.

7. In an experiment testing the effects of subliminal persuasion on memory and self-esteem, group A participants listened to a memory tape and were told that it would improve their memory, group B heard the same tape but were told it would improve their self-esteem, group C participants listened to a self-esteem tape and were told that it would improve their self-esteem, and group D heard the same tape but were told that it would enhance memory. All subjects were given a pretest and posttest measure of self-esteem and memory. The dependent variable in the experiment was
   (a) the random assignment to the four groups.
   (b) the scores on the pretest and the posttest.
   (c) listening to either the self-esteem tapes or the memory tapes.
   (d) the level of deception used.

8. In the above experiment, participants were randomly assigned to one of four conditions. The purpose of random assignment is to
   (a) increase the probability that the same number of participants end up in each condition.
   (b) increase the likelihood that the participants are representative of people in general.
   (c) decrease the probability of expectancy effects.
   (d) reduce the possibility of bias and ensure that differences among participants are spread out across all experimental conditions.

9. Both researchers and participants in a study examining the effects of marijuana on memory are unaware of which subjects actually received the active ingredient and which were given a placebo. This study involves the use of
   (a) replication.
   (b) the single-blind procedure.
   (c) the double-blind procedure.
   (d) correlational techniques.

10. Researchers using a form of descriptive research have found that the bigger a person's line of credit, the more money he or she is likely to owe. The researchers have found a _____ between the size of a credit line and the amount of debt.
    (a) positive correlation
    (b) negative correlation
    (c) cause-and-effect relationship
    (d) zero correlation

11. Mary is interviewed in depth, and her friends, family, and coworkers are contacted for further information. She also takes a number of psychological tests, and her behavior in various situations is observed. This is an example of
    (a) a survey.
    (b) correlational research.
    (c) the case study method.
    (d) experimental research.

12. In an attempt to predict the winner in the next election, The Kneed to Know Kompany contacts a randomly selected representative sample of the voting population and questions them about their voting plans. This is an example of
    (a) correlational research.
    (b) a survey.
    (c) the case study method.
    (d) experimental research.

13. Behaviorism and psychoanalysis dominated psychology for many decades early in the twentieth century, but in the 1950s a new school of thought emerged, _____, which emphasized conscious experience, each person's unique potential for psychological growth, self-determination, and free will.
    (a) structuralism
    (b) functionalism
    (c) humanistic psychology
    (d) cross-cultural psychology

14. According to Culture and Human Behavior 1.1, ethnocentrism is
    (a) the tendency to use one's own culture as the standard for judging other cultures.
    (b) introspective, self-centered analysis.
    (c) much more common in individualistic cultures than in collectivistic cultures.
    (d) much more common in collectivistic cultures than in individualistic cultures.

15. When evaluating claims made in the media about psychology-related topics, the Application makes the point that
    (a) skepticism is the rule, not the exception, in science.
    (b) there is no way to sort out true claims from false claims.
    (c) testimonials are the most reliable source of information.
    (d) correlational research is the most valid type of research because it can clearly establish cause-and-effect relationships between two variables.

Progress Test 3

After you have checked your understanding of the material in Progress Tests 1 and 2 and have done a complete chapter review with special focus on any areas of weakness, you are ready to assess your knowledge on Progress Test 3. Check your answers. If you make a mistake, review your notes and the relevant section of the study guide and, if necessary, review the appropriate part of your textbook.

1. An emphasis on the physical bases of behavior is to the _____ perspective as an emphasis on the influence of culture on behavior is to the _____ perspective.
   (a) biological; evolutionary
   (b) behavioral; humanistic
   (c) biological; cross-cultural
   (d) behavioral; cognitive

2. The evolutionary perspective focuses on _____ , whereas the cognitive perspective emphasizes _____ .
   (a) the physical bases of behavior; environmental influences on behavior
   (b) unconscious influences on behavior and personality; psychological growth and personal potential
   (c) mental processes, information processing, problem solving, and thinking; the influence of culture on behavior
   (d) the application of principles of natural selection to explain psychological processes and phenomena; information processing, problem solving, and thinking

3. Psychologists went to Slogaria after the fall of the dictatorship. There they discovered that many children in orphanages had suffered extreme physical and psychological deprivation. Children from these orphanages, who were later adopted, were matched with a control group of children of the same ages, gender, and so on, who had not experienced deprived conditions. The psychological, emotional, cognitive, and physical development of each group was then measured and monitored over a number of years. This example best illustrates which kind of research?
   (a) correlational research
   (b) naturalistic observation
   (c) a natural experiment
   (d) a double-blind study

4. In the above example, the measurements of psychological and physical health taken over the years constitute the
   (a) independent variable.
   (b) expectancy effects.
   (c) dependent variable.
   (d) demand characteristics.

5. In conducting research on the effects of a new memory-enhancing drug, Dr. Simpleton used the double-blind technique. The purpose of doing so was to guard against the possibility that the researcher will inadvertently display
   (a) expectancy effects.
   (b) demand characteristics.
   (c) placebo effects.
   (d) ethnocentrism.

6. In order to find out students' opinions about the recent cut-backs at her university, Gira sent a questionnaire to every twentieth person on the list of currently enrolled students. Gira used the technique of
   (a) replication.   (c) random sampling.
   (b) meta-analysis.   (d) interviewing.

7. Research showing that students with the highest GPAs study approximately twice as many hours per week as those with the lowest GPAs would indicate that
   (a) there is a positive correlation between study behavior and GPA.
   (b) there is a negative correlation between study behavior and GPA.
   (c) high GPA causes good study behavior.
   (d) that the correlation coefficient would probably exceed +1.50.

8. Ethical principles developed by the American Psychological Association require psychologists to
   (a) always tell the participants the exact nature of the experiment and inform them of the hypothesis that will be tested.
   (b) never, under any circumstances, use deception with potential participants.
   (c) withhold all information about the nature, results, and conclusions of the study because of the confidentiality principle.
   (d) obtain informed consent and voluntary participation of potential participants.

9. Dr. Joyce supports the view that the goal of psychology should be to discover the fundamental principles of learning and that psychologists should focus exclusively on overt behavior rather than on mental processes. Dr. Joyce would be classified as a _____ psychologist.
   (a) behavioral   (c) psychodynamic
   (b) cognitive   (d) humanistic

10. An experimenter found that variable A and variable B had a correlation coefficient of +.55, and variable C and variable D had a correlation coefficient of −.75. She can conclude that
    (a) variables A and B have a stronger correlation than variables C and D.
    (b) variable A causes variable B, but C and D are unrelated.
    (c) variables A and B have a weaker correlation than variables C and D.
    (d) variables A and B are strongly correlated, but C and D have no relationship.

11. If researchers wanted to discover the extent to which education level can be used to predict political preferences, they would most likely use
    (a) correlational research.
    (b) naturalistic observation.
    (c) experimental research.
    (d) a natural experiment.

12. "Psychology should study the purpose of behavior and mental processes and how they function to allow organisms to adapt to their environment." This is what a _____ might say.
    (a) functionalist
    (b) structuralist
    (c) behaviorist
    (d) humanistic psychologist

13. According to In Focus 1.4, animal research is condoned by the American Psychological Association as long as the research
    (a) has an acceptable scientific purpose.
    (b) will likely increase knowledge about behavior.
    (c) will likely increase understanding of the species under study.
    (d) produces results that benefit the health and welfare of humans or other animals.
    (e) will do all of the above.

14. Misha believes that in order for a claim to be proved true, you must be able to identify some type of evidence that would refute the claim or prove that it is false. According to Science Versus Pseudoscience 1.3, Misha is referring to a basic rule of science called
    (a) an operational definition.
    (b) the rule of replication.
    (c) the rule of falsifiability.
    (d) statistical significance.

15. According to Critical Thinking 1.2, critical thinking involves
    (a) minimizing the influence of preconceptions and biases while rationally evaluating evidence.
    (b) determining the conclusions that can be drawn from the evidence.
    (c) considering alternative explanations.
    (d) all of the above.

Answers

Introduction: The Origins of Psychology

1. *Psychology is defined as* the science of behavior and mental processes.

2. *The two discipline that influenced the emergence of psychology were* philosophy and physiology.

3. *The founder of psychology was* Wilhelm Wundt.

4. *The first two schools of psychology were* structuralism and functionalism, *and the people associated with their beginnings were* Edward B. Titchener and William James.

5. *Structuralism emphasized* studying the most basic components, or structures, of conscious experience using a procedure called introspection. *Functionalism stressed the importance* of how behavior functions to allow people and animals to adapt to their environments.

6. *The person who founded psychoanalysis was* Sigmund Freud, *and its main focus was on* the role of unconscious factors in personality and behavior.

7. *Behaviorism focused on* the scientific study of overt behavior that could be objectively measured and verified *and rejected* the emphasis on consciousness promoted by structuralism and functionalism, as well as Freudian notions of unconscious influences.

8. *The main proponents of behaviorism were* Ivan Pavlov, John. B. Watson, and B. F. Skinner.

9. *Humanistic psychology emphasizes* each person's unique potential for psychological growth and self-direction. *Its two major advocates were* Carl Rogers and Abraham Maslow.

Concept Check 1

1. functionalist
2. psychoanalytic
3. behaviorism; humanistic psychology
4. interactive dualism
5. nature-nurture
6. structuralism

Matching Exercise 1

1. Mary Whiton Calkins
2. introspection
3. humanistic psychology
4. John B. Watson
5. functionalism
6. psychology
7. interactive dualism
8. Wilhelm Wundt
9. Edward B. Titchener
10. behaviorism
11. Carl Rogers

True/False Test 1

1. T	7. F
2. F	8. T
3. T	9. T
4. T	10. F
5. T	11. F
6. T	

Contemporary Psychology

1. *The seven major perspectives in psychology* are biological, psychodynamic, behavioral, humanistic, cognitive, cross-cultural, and evolutionary.

2. *The main specialty areas in contemporary psychology are* biological, cognitive, experimental, developmental, social, personality, health, educational, school, industrial/organizational, clinical, and counseling psychology.

3. *The difference between a clinical psychologist and a psychiatrist is* that a clinical psychologist typically has a doctorate in psychology, which includes intensive training in treating people with psychological disorders, and a psychiatrist has a medical degree plus additional specialized training in the treatment of psychological disorders. A psychiatrist also can prescribe medications and other biomedical treatments.

Concept Check 2

1. biological
2. developmental
3. clinical
4. social
5. personality
6. cognitive
7. educational; school
8. health
9. industrial/organizational

Graphic Organizer 1

PERSPECTIVE	SPECIALTY
1. humanistic	developmental
2. behavioral	industrial/organizational
3. cognitive	educational
4. biological	psychiatrist
5. cross-cultural	social
6. psychodynamic	personality
7. cognitive	health
8. behavioral	experimental
9. evolutionary	social

Graphic Organizer 2

Origins of Psychology, First Schools, and Key Figures

1.

Philosophy Aristotle René Descartes	and	Physiology Hermann von Helmholtz

2.

Wilhelm Wundt; 1879

3.

Structuralism
Edward B. Titchener

4.

Functionalism
William James
G. Stanley Hall
Mary Whiton Calkins
Margaret Floy Washburn

5.

Behaviorism Ivan Pavlov John B. Watson B. F. Skinner	Psychoanalysis Sigmund Freud

6.

Humanistic Psychology
Carl Rogers
Abraham Maslow

Matching Exercise 2

1. clinical psychologist
2. developmental psychology
3. psychiatrist
4. educational psychologists
5. experimental psychology
6. perspective
7. specialty area
8. culture
9. cognitive psychology
10. Charles Darwin
11. personality psychology
12. behavioral perspective
13. ethnocentrism
14. biological perspective

True/False Test 2

1. T		8. T	
2. T		9. F	
3. F		10. F	
4. T		11. F	
5. T		12. F	
6. T		13. T	
7. F			

The Scientific Method

1. *The four basic goals of psychology are to* describe, explain, predict, and control or influence behavior and mental processes.

2. *The scientific method refers to* a set of assumptions, attitudes, and procedures that guide researchers in creating questions to investigate, in generating evidence, and in drawing conclusions.

3. *Psychologists are guided by the basic assumptions that* all events are lawful, that behavior and mental processes follow consistent patterns, that events are explainable, and that behavior and mental processes have a cause or causes.

4. *Psychologists share a set of attitudes, including* open-mindedness, scientific skepticism, caution in making claims, and a willingness to critically evaluate the evidence for new findings.

5. *Empirical evidence refers to* evidence that is the result of objective observation, measurement, and experimentation. *The four basic steps of the scientific method are* formulate a question that can be tested, design a study to collect relevant data, analyze the data to arrive at conclusions, and, finally, report the results.

6. *A theory is* a tentative explanation that tries to account for diverse findings. *It is different from a hypothesis*—a specific question or prediction to be tested—in that a theory integrates and summarizes a large number of findings and observations and often generates predictions and new hypotheses that can be tested by further research.

7. *The role of statistics in psychological research is to* enable researchers to summarize, analyze, and draw conclusions about the data they have collected.

8. *Theories can evolve and change because they reflect the* self-correcting nature of the scientific enterprise; when new research findings challenge established ways of thinking about a phenomenon, theories are expanded, modified, or even replaced.

Concept Check 3

1. experimental (in a natural setting)
2. hypothesis
3. statistics
4. 4; reporting her findings

Matching Exercise 3

1. meta-analysis
2. replicate
3. scientific method
4. hypothesis
5. operational definition
6. experimental method
7. statistics

True/False Test 3

1. T		4. T	
2. T		5. F	
3. F		6. T	

Descriptive Methods

1. *Descriptive methods are* scientific procedures that involve systematically observing behavior in order to describe the relationship among behaviors and events.

2. *Naturalistic observation involves the* systematic observation and recording of behaviors as they occur in their natural settings.

3. *A case study is* an intensive, in-depth investigation of a single individual or event. *Case studies are typically used to* develop a complete profile of a psychotherapy client and are also used to investigate rare, unusual, or extreme conditions.

4. *In the survey method, the researcher* designs a questionnaire or conducts an interview designed to investigate the opinion, behaviors, or characteristics of a particular group.

5. *Researchers ensure that their sample closely parallels the population of interest by* selecting a representative sample that matches the larger group on relevant characteristics, such as age, sex, race, marital status, and educational level.

6. *Random selection refers to* the process in which subjects are selected randomly from a group such that every member has an equal chance of being included in the study. *It is important because* it ensures that the sample is representative of the larger population being studied on relevant characteristics.

7. *Correlational studies show* how strongly two factors, or variables, are related to one another and are used for making predictions. *They are limited because* they cannot be used to demonstrate cause-and-effect relationships (experimental research is used to do that).

8. *The correlation coefficient is* a numerical indication of the magnitude and direction of the relationship between two variables; it always falls in the range from −1.00 to +1.00. *The correlation coefficient has two parts:* the number indicates the strength of the relationship (the bigger the number, the stronger the relationship) and the sign (+ or −) indicates the direction of the relationship between the two variables.

9. *A positive correlation is one in which* the two factors vary in the same direction, increasing together or decreasing together. *A negative correlation is one in which* the two variables move in opposite directions, one increasing and the other decreasing.

Concept Check 4

1. more; less
2. survey; sample; randomly
3. naturalistic observation
4. positive
5. case study

Graphic Organizer 3

1. positive; positive
2. negative; negative
3. high; high; low; low
4. high; low; low; high

Matching Exercise 4

1. survey
2. descriptive methods
3. sample
4. representative sample
5. correlational study
6. random selection

True/False Test 4

1. T	4. T
2. F	5. F
3. T	

The Experimental Method

1. *The experimental method of investigation is used to* demonstrate cause-and-effect relationships by purposely manipulating a variable and observing the effect on a second variable.

2. *The independent variable is the* purposely manipulated factor thought to produce change. *The dependent variable is the* factor that is observed and measured for change as a result of the manipulation of the independent variable in an experiment.

3. *Random assignment means that* all participants in the study have an equal chance of being assigned to any of the groups or conditions in an experiment. *It helps ensure that* potential differences among subjects are spread out across all experimental conditions.

4. *The experimental group (or experimental condition) is* the group of participants that is exposed to the independent variable or treatment of interest. *The control group (or control condition) is* the group of participants that is not exposed

to the independent variable or treatment of interest and against which the experimental group is compared. *The placebo control group is* a group of participants that are exposed to an inert substance or treatment with no known effects; this group serves as a check for expectancy effects.

5. *A double-blind study is one in which* neither the participants nor the researcher who interacts with the participants is aware of the treatment or condition to which the participants have been assigned. *It is used to* guard against the possibility that the researcher will display subtle cues or signals that communicate what is expected from the participants (demand characteristics).

6. *Five key provisions of the APA ethical guidelines regulating research with human participants are*
   (a) Informed consent and voluntary participation of subjects is required.
   (b) Students must be given the option of not participating in research involving credits without being penalized in any way.
   (c) Psychologists are restricted in their use of deception.
   (d) All records must be kept confidential.
   (e) Participants must be allowed the opportunity to obtain information about the study once it is completed and must be debriefed about the nature of their involvement in the study.

Concept Check 5

1. the drug and placebo conditions
2. participants' scores on the memory tests
3. experimental; placebo control
4. double-blind; expectancy effects and demand characteristics
5. random assignment

Matching Exercise 5

1. single-blind study
2. experimental method
3. dependent variable
4. paranormal phenomena
5. expectancy effect
6. control group
7. rule of falsifiability
8. demand characteristics

9. placebo
10. practice effect
11. spatial reasoning abilities

True/False Test 5

1. T	5. T	9. F
2. T	6. T	10. T
3. T	7. T	11. F
4. T	8. T	

Something to Think About

1. (a) Psychology tackles questions that people have grappled with for thousands of years. Instead of using anecdotal evidence, intuition, philosophical discussion, and speculation, psychology uses the scientific method to answer questions that are amenable to empirical testing. It uses four steps in generating empirical evidence. First, questions are formulated into testable hypotheses; next, the study is designed and the data are collected, then statistical analyses are prepared and conclusions are drawn, and finally, the results are reported. Psychologists operationally define all variables and precisely specify the method of measurement or manipulation. Following this process, they can be confident of the reliability and validity of their results.

   (b) The difference between clinical psychologists and psychiatrists is training. Clinical psychologists have a doctorate in psychology and extensive training in the assessment, diagnosis, and treatment of people with psychological disorders. Psychiatrists, on the other hand, have an M.D. plus years of training in dealing with people with psychological disorders; because of their medical qualifications, they can prescribe drugs and order medical procedures such as electroshock therapy.

2. Many of the questions of students coming into psychology can be tested empirically, and quite a few have, in fact, been answered. For example, how would you test the claim that subliminal messages can influence our behavior? It turns out that psychologists have done just that.

   The essence of their experimental design was the use of two subliminal tapes, one claiming to improve self-esteem and the other claiming to improve memory. They randomly assigned subjects to one of four groups and gave them all pretests on measures of self-esteem and memory. Members of group 1 were given the memory tape to listen to for a set period of time and told it would help improve their memory; those in group 2 were given the same memory tape but were told it would improve their self-esteem. (Remember, on subliminal tapes you can't, by definition, hear the messages, only the surface music.) Group 3 was given the self-esteem tape and told it would improve self-esteem, and group 4 was given the same self-esteem tape but were told that it would improve memory. All subjects listened to their respective tapes for exactly the same length of time, at the same times of the day, etc. Later they were given another test of self-esteem and memory. The pretest and posttest scores for all conditions were compared.

What do you think the results showed? If you believe the claims of those who promote the power of subliminal tapes, then groups 1 and 3 should have shown significant improvement in memory and self-esteem scores, respectively. And, one would assume, if the results were not due to some placebo effect, then groups 2 and 4 should have shown some change—memory improvement for group 2 and self-esteem improvement for group 4—because that is what they were actually exposed to.

The results were clear and unequivocal: there was no improvement in any of the groups between their pretest and posttest scores. In contrast to the claims of their promoters, subliminal tapes were shown to be of no value in improving memory or self-esteem.

This is a good example of how useful the scientific method is in answering questions of a psychological nature. Can you apply what you know about scientific psychology to answer other questions you may have?

Progress Test 1

1. d	6. d	11. a
2. d	7. b	12. d
3. b	8. d	13. a
4. c	9. a	14. a
5. d	10. c	15. b

Progress Test 2

1. a	6. a	11. c
2. c	7. b	12. b
3. c	8. d	13. c
4. a	9. c	14. a
5. b	10. a	15. a

Progress Test 3

1. c	6. c	11. a
2. d	7. a	12. a
3. c	8. d	13. e
4. c	9. a	14. c
5. b	10. c	15. d

2

The Biological Foundations of Behavior

<table>
<tr>
<td>**PREVIEW**</td>
<td>Reading the section below first will give you a general sense of the chapter's contents and an initial introduction to some of the major concepts and terms. This will prime you for what you are about to read and help you to develop a "cognitive map" that will guide your study of the material in this chapter. Likewise, reading the **preview questions** at the beginning of each major section will improve your ability to understand, learn, and retain the information.</td>
</tr>
</table>

CHAPTER 2. . . AT A GLANCE

Chapter 2 first outlines the scope and diversity of biological psychology, then reminds you that biological psychologists investigate the physical processes underlying psychological experiences and behavior.

The first section describes the structure and functions of the neuron. Neural activation, synaptic transmission, and the role of neurotransmitters are outlined. The functions and effects of several neurotransmitters (acetylcholine, dopamine, serotonin, norepinephrine, GABA, and endorphins) are discussed.

The next section discusses the structures and functions of the divisions of the nervous system: the central nervous system, which consists of the brain and spinal cord; and the peripheral nervous system, with its two main subdivisions, the somatic and autonomic nervous systems. The sympathetic and parasympathetic systems, which make up the autonomic nervous system, are described. This section ends by focusing on the endocrine system, its glands, and its chemical messengers, called hormones.

The core section, on the brain, begins with a description of how the brain's complex operations are studied—through case studies, EEG, MRI, CAT scans, PET scans, and fMRI. A guided tour of the brain takes you through the regions of the hindbrain, midbrain, and forebrain, including their structures and functions. The different roles of the four lobes of the brain (temporal, occipital, parietal, and frontal) are explained, and the functions of forebrain structures in the limbic system—the thalamus, hypothalamus, hippocampus, and amygdala—are described.

The chapter ends with a discussion of hemispheric specialization and the part played by split-brain patients in discovering the specialized functions of the brain's hemispheres.

Introduction: The Scope of Biological Psychology

Preview Questions

Consider the following questions as you study this section of the chapter.

- What is biological psychology?
- What systems and structures are of interest to biopsychologists?

Read the section "Introduction: The Scope of Biological Psychology" and **write** *your answers to the following.*

1. Biological psychology is _____

    _____

    _____

2. The systems and structures that are of interest to biopsychologists are _____

    _____

    _____

The Neuron: The Basic Unit of Communication

Preview Questions

Consider the following questions as you study this section of the chapter.

- How is information in the nervous system transmitted?
- What are glial cells, and what are the three main types of neurons?
- What are the basic components of the neuron, and what are their functions?
- How is information communicated within and between neurons?
- What are some common neurotransmitters, and what are their primary roles?
- How can drugs affect synaptic transmission?

Read the section "The Neuron: The Basic Unit of Communication" and **write** *your answers to the following:*

1. Information is transmitted in the nervous system by _____ , of which there are three basic types: _____

    _____

2. Glial cells are _____

    _____

3. The neuron's basic components and their functions are _____

    _____

    _____

    _____

    _____

    _____

4. Within the neuron, information is communicated (describe the complete process) _____

    _____

    _____

    _____

    _____

    _____

    _____

5. Communication between neurons may be electrical or chemical. Chemically, it involves

    _____

    _____

    _____

6. Some important neurotransmitters (and their primary roles) are _____

    _____

    _____

    _____

    _____

    _____

    _____

    _____

7. Drugs can affect synaptic transmission _____

    _____

    _____

    _____

    _____

After you have carefully studied the preceding sections, complete the following exercises.

Concept Check 1

Read the following and decide which neurotransmitter is most likely involved:

1. Mrs. Cartwright's memory functions have deteriorated, and she has been diagnosed as suffering from Alzheimer's disease.

   _____

2. When Gerald was bitten by a black widow spider, he suffered severe, uncontrollable muscle spasms and had great difficulty breathing.

   _____

3. When Melanie was suffering from severe depression, her doctor prescribed Prozac, which he said would help alleviate the symptoms of her mood disorder by increasing the availability of a particular neurotransmitter.

   _____

4. Patients afflicted with Parkinson's disease suffer from rigidity, muscle tremors, and poor balance and have trouble initiating movements. These symptoms are believed to result from diminished production of the neurotransmitter

   _____ .

5. George suffers from chronic anxiety. His doctor has prescribed the antianxiety drug Valium because it works by increasing

   _____ , which inhibits action potentials and slows brain activity.

6. Mr. Lee had his back pain treated by an ancient Chinese medical technique called acupuncture. Inserting needles in various parts of his body may have reduced his perception of pain because of the involvement of

   _____ .

Graphic Organizer 1

Identify the parts of the neuron in the figure in the righthand column:

a. _____   f. _____

b. _____   g. _____

c. _____   h. _____

d. _____   i. _____

e. _____

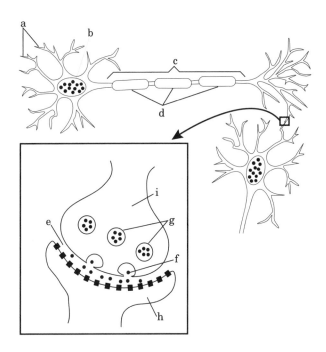

Review of Terms and Concepts 1

Use the terms in this list to complete the Matching Test, then to help you answer the True/False items correctly.

biological psychology	synapse
neuroscience	synaptic gap
neuron	axon terminals
glial cells	synaptic vesicles
sensory neuron	neurotransmitter
motor neuron	synaptic transmission
interneuron	reuptake
cell body	acetylcholine
dendrites	dopamine
axon	serotonin
myelin sheath	norepinephrine
action potential	GABA (gamma-
stimulus threshold	amniobutyric acid)
resting potential	endorphins
all-or-none law	

Matching Exercise

Match the appropriate term from the list with its definition or description.

1. _____ Highly specialized cell that communicates information in electrical and chemical form.

2. _____ Neurotransmitter that usually communicates an inhibitory message.

3. _____ Neurotransmitters that regulate pain perception.

4. _____ Type of neuron that signals muscles to contract or relax.

5. _____ Neurotransmitter that is involved in sleep, moods, and emotional states, including depression.

6. _____ The part of a neuron that contains the nucleus.

7. _____ A brief electrical impulse by which information is transmitted along the axon of a neuron.

8. _____ Chemical messenger manufactured in the synaptic vesicles of a neuron.

9. _____ The long, fluid-filled tube that carries a neuron's messages to other body areas.

10. _____ The point of communication between two neurons.

11. _____ Tiny pouches, or sacs, in the axon terminals that contain chemicals called neurotransmitters.

12. _____ The neurotransmitter that is involved in the regulation of bodily movements and pleasurable or rewarding sensations.

13. _____ Minimum level of stimulation required to activate a particular neuron.

14. _____ The scientific study of the nervous system.

True/False Test

Indicate whether each statement is true or false by placing T or F in the blank space next to each item.

1. ____ Norepinephrine is involved in activation of neurons throughout the brain, is critical in the body's response to danger, and is implicated in learning and memory retrieval.

2. ____ Biological psychology is the specialized branch of psychology concerned with the diagnosis and treatment of mental disorders.

3. ____ Reuptake is the process in which neurotransmitters are released by one neuron, cross the synaptic gap, and affect adjoining neurons.

4. ____ Glial cells assist neurons by providing structural support, nutrition, and removal of cell wastes; they also enhance the speed of communication between neurons by manufacturing myelin.

5. ____ Interneurons communicate information from one neuron to the next.

6. ____ Synaptic transmission is the process by which neurotransmitter molecules detach from a postsynaptic neuron and are reabsorbed by a presynaptic neuron so that they can be recycled and used again.

7. ____ Axon terminals are branches at the end of the axon that contain tiny pouches, or sacs, called synaptic vesicles.

8. ____ Sensory neurons communicate information to the muscles and glands of the body and signal muscles to contract or relax.

9. ____ Dendrites are the long, fluid-filled tubes that carry information *from* the neuron *to* other cells in the body, including other neurons, glands, and muscles.

10. ____ The myelin sheath is a white, fatty covering wrapped around the axons of some neurons that increases their speed of communication.

11. ____ The resting potential is a brief electrical impulse by which information is transmitted along the axon of a neuron.

12. ____ Acetylcholine is a neurotransmitter that produces muscle contractions and is involved in memory functions.

13. ____ The synaptic gap is a tiny space between the axon terminal of one neuron and the dendrite of an adjoining neuron.

14. ____ The all-or-none law states that either a neuron is sufficiently stimulated and an action potential occurs or a neuron is not sufficiently stimulated and an action potential does not occur.

Check your answers and review any areas of weakness before going on to the next section.

The Nervous System and the Endocrine System: Communication Throughout the Body

Preview Questions

Consider the following questions as you study this section of the chapter.

- What are the two main divisions of the nervous system, and what does each include?

- What are spinal reflexes?

- What are the key components of the peripheral nervous system, and what are their functions?

- What is the endocrine system, and how does it transmit information?

- How does the endocrine system interact with the nervous system?
- What are the specific functions of the pituitary gland and the adrenal glands?

*Read the section "The Nervous System and the Endocrine System: Communication Throughout the Body" and **write** your answers to the following:*

1. The two main divisions of the nervous system and their components are _____

   _____

   _____

   _____

2. Spinal reflexes are _____

   _____

3. The key components of the peripheral nervous system and their functions are_____

   _____

   _____

   _____

4. The two branches of the autonomic nervous system and their functions are _____

   _____

   _____

   _____

   _____

5. The endocrine system is made up of_____

   _____

   _____

6. The endocrine system interacts with the nervous system in a number of ways: _____

   _____

   _____

   _____

   _____

   _____

   _____

7. The hypothalamus serves as _____

   _____

   _____

8. The pituitary gland's hormones _____

   _____

   _____

   The adrenal glands (adrenal cortex and adrenal medulla) are involved in _____

   _____

   _____

After you have carefully studied the preceding section, complete the following exercises.

Concept Check 2

Read the following and complete the sentence with the correct term:

1. Allison accidentally touched a hot stove top and immediately withdrew her hand before becoming consciously aware of the sensation or movement. She was able to do this because of her

   _____ .

2. Always a daredevil, Miguel dove off the cliff into the river below. Unfortunately, he landed on his head and is now paralyzed from the shoulders down. Apart from his paralysis, all his mental functions are intact, and he is attempting to complete his college degree. His present inability to move the lower part of his body is a result of permanent damage to his

   _____ .

3. At home alone late one night, Jason had just finished watching the most frightening video he had ever seen when there was a sudden knock on the door. His heart rate suddenly increased, his breathing accelerated, and he began to sweat. These physiological changes were most likely triggered by his

   _____ .

4. When Jason answered the door, he discovered it was only the pizza delivery, and before long he calmed down and his blood pressure, heart rate, and breathing returned to their normal state. These physical reactions were most likely regulated by his _____ .

5. Jason's initial reaction to the knock on the door (his fight-or-flight response) resulted in his adrenal glands (in particular, the adrenal medulla) releasing the two hormones _____ and _____ .

Graphic Organizer 2

Mapping the Divisions and Functions of the Nervous System

In the following organizational chart of the nervous system, write the name of each division and choose the appropriate function of each from the list below (e.g., A is the appropriate choice for the nervous system).

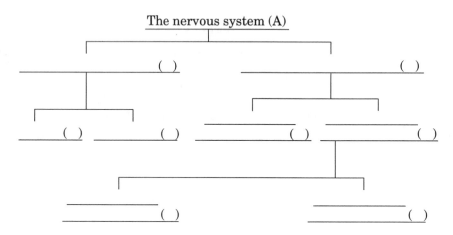

The nervous system (A)

A. Complex, organized communication system of nerves and neurons.
B. Maintains normal bodily functions and conserves physical resources.
C. Produces rapid physical changes to perceived threats and emergencies.
D. Includes all nerves lying outside the central nervous system.
E. Communicates sensory and motor information.
F. Consists of the brain and the spinal cord.
G. Regulates involuntary functions such as heartbeat and respiration.
H. Main organ of the nervous system; made up of billions of neurons.
I. System that handles both incoming and outgoing messages to and from the brain.

autonomic nervous system
sympathetic nervous system
parasympathetic nervous system
fight-or-flight response

endocrine system
hormones
hypothalamus
pituitary gland
adrenal glands
adrenal cortex
adrenal medulla

Review of Terms and Concepts 2

Use the terms in this list to complete the Matching Test, then to help you answer the True/False items correctly.

nervous system
central nervous system
nerve
spinal reflexes

peripheral nervous system
somatic nervous system

Matching Exercise

Match the appropriate term with its definition or description.

1. _____ Bundle of neuron axons that carries information in the peripheral nervous system.

2. _____ Communication system composed of glands located throughout the body that secrete hormones into the bloodstream.

3. _____ Simple, automatic behaviors that are processed in the spinal cord without any brain involvement.

4. _____ Set of endocrine glands that are involved in the human stress response.

5. _____ Branch of the autonomic nervous system that maintains normal bodily functions and conserves the body's physical resources.

6. _____ Brain structure that regulates the release of hormones by the pituitary gland.

7. _____ Outer portion of the adrenal glands.

8. _____ Division of the nervous system that includes all the nerves lying outside the central nervous system.

9. _____ Subdivision of the peripheral nervous system that regulates involuntary functions.

True/False Test

Indicate whether each statement is true or false by placing T or F in the blank space next to each item.

1. ___ The nervous system is the primary internal communication network of the body; it is divided into the central nervous system and the peripheral nervous system.

2. ___ The central nervous system is a major division of the nervous system and consists of the brain and the spinal cord.

3. ___ The pituitary gland is the inner portion of the adrenal medulla and secretes epinephrine and norepinephrine.

4. ___ The fight-or-flight response refers to physiological changes such as increased heart rate, accelerated breathing, dry mouth, and perspiration that occur in response to perceived threats or danger.

5. ___ The sympathetic nervous system maintains normal bodily functions and conserves physical resources.

6. ___ Hormones are chemical messengers that are secreted into the bloodstream by endocrine glands.

7. ___ The somatic nervous system regulates involuntary functions such as heartbeat, digestion, breathing, and blood pressure.

8. ___ The adrenal medulla is the outer portion of the adrenal glands.

Check your answers and review any areas of weakness before going on to the next section.

Studying the Brain: The Toughest Case to Crack

Preview Questions

Consider the following questions as you study this section of the chapter.

- Why have scientists used case studies of brain-damaged people to study the brain?

- How has the production of *lesions* and the use of electrical stimulation been useful in advancing knowledge of the brain?

- What are the five main imaging techniques used to study the brain, and how does each attempt to accomplish the task?

*Read the section "Studying the Brain: The Toughest Case to Crack" and **write** your answers to the following:*

1. Scientists used case studies to study the brain because _____

   _____

   _____

   _____

2. The production of lesions and electrically stimulating areas of the brain have been useful because _____

   _____

3. The five major imaging techniques used to study the brain are _____

   _____

   _____

A Guided Tour of the Brain

Preview Questions

Consider the following questions as you study this section of the chapter.

- How does the brain develop, and what are its three main divisions?

- What are the key structures of the hindbrain and midbrain, and what functions are associated with each structure?

- What are the two main structures of the forebrain, and what functions have been identified with each of the four lobes of the cerebral cortex?

- What are the key limbic system structures, and what role do they play in behavior?

Read the section "A Guided Tour of the Brain" and **write** *your answers to the following:*

1. The brain develops from _____
   _____
   _____
   _____
   _____

2. The three divisions of the developing brain are _____

3. The key structures of the hindbrain and their functions are _____
   _____
   _____
   _____
   _____
   _____

4. The midbrain contains _____
   _____
   _____

5. The forebrain includes _____
   _____
   _____

6. The four lobes and their functions are _____
   _____
   _____
   _____
   _____

7. The main structures of the limbic system and their functions are _____
   _____
   _____
   _____
   _____

After you have carefully studied the preceding sections, complete the following exercises.

Concept Check 3

Decide which area of the brain is most likely involved in each of the following.

1. Marcel had a stroke on the *right* side of his brain in an area that controls motor movement; as a result, he has trouble moving the *left* side of his body. This is because incoming sensory messages and outgoing motor messages cross over at the _____ level of the brain.

2. If this area of your brain was electrically stimulated while you were fast asleep, you would wake up instantly. _____

3. After being hit in the head by a baseball, Larry now has jerky, uncoordinated movements and can no longer type or play his guitar.
   _____

4. In the third round of a boxing match Bruno caught a right hook that snapped his head back; when he hit the canvas, his breathing stopped. _____

5. Ever since his automobile accident six months ago, Sam watches the same video day after day and each time responds to it as though he had never seen it before. All his other sensory functions appear to be intact, but it is clear that one brain area was damaged in the accident that prevents him from forming new memories.
   _____

6. Because of a tumor growing in her brain, Janna has lost her senses of taste, sight, hearing, and touch but not her sense of smell. The area of the brain involved in regulating behaviors related to survival is the _____ .

7. Following an industrial accident, Harinder has lost his ability to feel any sensation on the right side of his body. It is most likely that the accident damaged his _____ lobe.

Graphic Organizer 3

Chart Diagram Exercise: The Key Structures of the Limbic System

To help you develop the technique of creating your own graphic organizers, we encourage you to try to locate the structures listed below in the following outline of a brain. Then, on a separate piece of paper, write a description of each structure.

Locate and describe the following:
- (a) Hypothalamus
- (b) Thalamus
- (c) Amygdala
- (d) Hippocampus

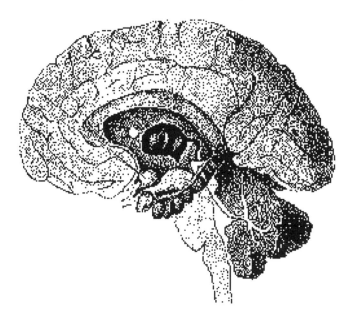

Review of Terms and Concepts 3

Use the terms in this list to complete the Matching Test, then to help you answer the True/False items correctly.

electroencephalograph (EEG)
computerized axial tomography (CAT or CT scan)
magnetic resonance imaging scanner (MRI)
positron emission tomography (PET scan)
functional magnetic resonance imaging (fMRI)

neurogenesis
brain stem
hindbrain
medulla
pons
cerebellum
reticular formation
midbrain
substantia nigra
forebrain
cerebral cortex
cerebral hemispheres
corpus callosum

temporal lobe
primary auditory cortex
occipital lobe
primary visual cortex
parietal lobe
somatosensory cortex
frontal lobe
primary motor cortex
association areas

prefrontal association cortex
limbic system
thalamus
hypothalamus
suprachiasmatic nucleus (SCN)
hippocampus
amygdala

Matching Exercise

Match the appropriate term with its definition or description.

1. _____ The nearly symmetrical left and right halves of the cerebral cortex.

2. _____ The area on each cerebral hemisphere located above the temporal lobe that processes somatic sensations.

3. _____ Midbrain area involved in motor control and containing a large concentration of dopamine-producing neurons.

4. _____ The part of the temporal lobe that enables hearing.

5. _____ Hindbrain structure that connects the medulla to the two sides of the cerebellum; helps coordinate and integrate movement on each side of the body.

6. _____ Forebrain structure that processes motor information and sensory information from all the senses except smell and relays it to higher brain centers.

7. _____ The part of the occipital lobe that receives information from the eyes.

8. _____ The curved forebrain structure that is part of the limbic system and is involved in learning and forming new memories.

9. _____ Region of the brain made up of the hindbrain and the midbrain.

10. _____ Band of tissue in the frontal lobe on which the movements of different parts of the body are represented.

11. _____ Large association area of the brain, situated in front of the primary motor cortex, that is involved in the planning of voluntary movements.

12. _____ Hindbrain structure that controls vital life functions such as breathing, circulation, heart rate, and digestion.

13. _____ Instrument that produces a graphic record of the brain's electrical activity by using large electrodes placed on the scalp.

14. _____ Network of nerve fibers located in the center of the medulla that helps regulate attention, arousal, and sleep.

15. _____ Imaging technique that provides three-dimensional, highly detailed images of the brain using electrical signals generated by the brain in response to magnetic fields.

16. _____ Area of the hypothalamus that plays a key role in regulating daily sleep-wake cycles and other rhythms of the body.

17. _____ The development of new neurons.

True/False Test

Indicate whether each statement is true or false by placing T or F in the blank space next to each item.

1. ____ The frontal lobe is the largest lobe of the cerebral cortex; processes voluntary muscle movement and is involved in thinking, planning, and emotional expression and control.

2. ____ The somatosensory cortex is a band of tissue on the parietal lobe that receives information from touch receptors in different parts of the body.

3. ____ The midbrain is a region at the base of the brain that controls several structures that regulate basic life functions.

4. ____ The cerebellum is an almond-shaped forebrain structure that is part of the limbic system and involved in emotion and memory.

5. ____ The forebrain, the largest and most complex brain region, contains centers for complex behaviors and mental processes.

6. ____ The cerebral cortex is the wrinkled outer portion of the forebrain that contains the most sophisticated brain centers.

7. ____ The amygdala is the large, two-sided hindbrain structure at the back of the brain that is responsible for muscle coordination and maintaining posture and equilibrium.

8. ____ The occipital lobe is a region at the back of each cerebral cortex hemisphere that is the primary receiving area for visual information.

9. ____ The association areas, which make up the bulk of the cerebral cortex and are the regions in which sensory and motor information is combined, produce complex, sophisticated human behaviors.

10. ____ The temporal lobe is an area on each hemisphere that is the primary receiving area for auditory information.

11. ____ The hindbrain is the middle and smallest brain region that is involved in processing auditory and visual sensory information.

12. ____ Computerized axial tomography (CAT scan or CT scan) is an imaging technique that provides color-coded images of brain activity by measuring the amount of a radioactive compound glucose, or oxygen, used in different brain regions.

13. ____ Three structures of the limbic system—the hypothalamus, amygdala, and hippocampus—are involved in emotions, motivation, learning, and memory.

14. ____ The hypothalamus is a peanut-sized forebrain structure that is part of the limbic system and is involved in diverse functions such as eating, drinking, sexual activity, and fear and aggression and exerts control over the secretion of endocrine hormones by directly influencing the pituitary gland.

15. ____ Positron emission tomography (PET scan) is an imaging technique that produces two-dimensional pictures of brain structures or other body parts using multiple X-rays that are reassembled by a computer; also called computed tomography.

16. ____ Functional magnetic resonance imaging (fMRI) is an imaging technique that uses magnetic fields to map brain activity by measuring changes in the brain's blood supply during different mental activities.

17. ____ A thick band of nerve fibers that connects the two cerebral hemispheres and acts as a communication link between them is called the corpus callosum.

Check your answers and review any areas of weakness before going on to the next section.

Specialization in the Cerebral Hemispheres

Preview Questions

Consider the following questions as you study this section of the chapter.

- What did Broca and Wernicke contribute to our knowledge of the brain?
- What is lateralization of function?
- What is aphasia, Broca's aphasia, and Wernicke's aphasia?
- What is the split brain-operation, and what did tests on split-brain patients reveal about differences in the abilities of the two hemispheres?
- What are the most important functions of each cerebral hemisphere?

Read the section "Specialization in the Cerebral Hemispheres" and **write** *your answers to the following:*

1. Broca and Wernicke provided the first evidence that _____
   _____

2. Lateralization of function (or lateralization) is
   _____
   _____

3. Aphasia refers to _____
   _____

   Broca's aphasia results in _____
   _____

   Wernicke's aphasia results in _____
   _____
   _____

4. The split-brain operation involves _____
   _____

5. In a specialized procedure, split-brain subjects are directed to focus on a point in the middle of a screen and then_____
   _____

   Split-brain subjects can _____
   _____
   _____
   _____

6. Tests on split-brain patients revealed that the left hemisphere is specialized for _____
   _____
   _____

   and the right hemisphere is specialized for
   _____
   _____
   _____

After you have carefully studied the preceding section, complete the following exercises.

Concept Check 4

Complete the following examples by placing the term right *or* left *in each blank:*

1. A blindfolded split-brain patient would be able to verbally identify an object placed in her _____ hand but not in her _____ hand.

2. When the picture of an apple was flashed to the _____ of the midpoint during an experiment with a split-brain patient, the patient was not able to say what he saw. However, he could draw a picture of the object with his _____ hand.

3. When a swear word was flashed to her _____ hemisphere, a split-brain patient could not say what she saw but showed some nonverbal signs of embarrassment.

4. The fact that a split-brain patient had trouble assembling colored blocks to match a design with his left hand but not his right hand suggests that the _____ hemisphere is superior to the _____ hemisphere at perceptual tasks that involve deciphering visual cues, reading maps, copying designs, and so on.

Review of Terms, Concepts, and Names 4

Use the terms in this list to complete the Matching Test, then to help you answer the True/False items correctly.

cortical localization
Pierre Paul Broca
Broca's area
Karl Wernicke
Wernicke's area
lateralization of function
aphasia

Broca's aphasia
Wernicke's aphasia
split-brain operation
Roger Sperry
functional plasticity
structural plasticity

Matching Exercise

Match the appropriate term/name with its definition or description.

1. _____ The American psychologist who received the Nobel Prize in Physiology or Medicine in 1981 for his pioneering research on brain specialization in split-brain patients.

2. _____ The partial or complete inability to articulate ideas or understand spoken or written language due to brain damage or injury.

3. _____ The language area on the left temporal lobe concerned with speech comprehension.

4. _____ The brain's ability to shift functions from damaged to undamaged areas.

5. _____ The notion that different functions are located, or localized, in different areas of the brain; also referred to as localization of function.

6. _____ The phenomenon in which brain structures physically change in response to environmental influences.

7. _____ The notion that specific psychological or cognitive functions are processed primarily on one side of the brain; also referred to as lateralization.

True/False Test

Indicate whether each statement is true or false by placing T or F in the blank space next to each item.

1. ___ Karl Wernicke was a German neurologist who discovered an area on the left temporal lobe that, when damaged, produces meaningless or nonsensical speech and difficulties in verbal or written comprehension.

2. ___ The split-brain operation was performed on patients specifically to enable psychologists to scientifically study hemispheric specialization in the cerebral cortex of humans.

3. ___ Broca's aphasia is a speech disorder that results from the surgical severing of the corpus callosum.

4. ___ Patients with Wernicke's aphasia can speak but may have problems finding the right words and typically have great difficulty understanding written or spoken communication.

5. ___ Broca's area is a language area on the lower left frontal lobe of the cerebral cortex.

6. ___ Pierre Paul Broca was a French surgeon and neuroanatomist who discovered an area on the lower left frontal lobe that, when damaged, produces speech disturbances but no loss of comprehension.

Check your answers and review any areas of weakness before going on to the next section.

Something to Think About

1. A biological psychologist who specializes in the assessment and diagnosis of people with brain-related problems is faced with the following cases. Based on what you now know about biological psychology, the brain, and the functions of the nervous system, give some thought to what the specialist's assessment might be.

   (a) Fraser slipped on ice and hit the back of his head on the sidewalk, and now his vision is seriously affected. Which brain area is most likely affected?

   (b) Following an operation to remove a brain tumor, Yoko is able to read and understand written and spoken language but has difficulty speaking and expressing herself clearly. It is likely that she has damage in which part of the brain?

   (c) Ever since a brain lesion destroyed part of her limbic system, Vanessa has had trouble controlling her appetite and has had a constant urge to eat and drink. Which structure was most likely damaged?

   (d) Mr. Ashley has a disorder that is characterized by rigidity, muscle tremors, poor balance, and difficulty in initiating movements.

2. Family members and friends who know you are taking a psychology course may ask you some interesting and curious questions. One often-asked question is, "I know that regular exercise helps keep me in shape physically, but is there anything I can do to prevent mental deterioration?" What advice would you give in response to that question?

Check your answers and review any areas of weakness before doing the following progress tests.

Progress Test 1

Review the complete chapter (including Concept Reviews and all boxed inserts), review all your study notes, and then test yourself on the following progress test. Check your answers. If you make a mistake, review your notes, the appropriate section in the study guide, and, if necessary, the relevant part of the chapter in your textbook.

1. A hunter in a South American jungle uses the poison curare on the tip of his arrow; when the arrow strikes an animal, the animal becomes almost instantly limp and quickly suffocates because its respiratory system has become paralyzed. The curare has _____ the neurotransmitter_____ .
   (a) blocked the release of; acetylcholine
   (b) blocked the receptors for; acetylcholine
   (c) increased the release of; acetylcholine
   (d) increased the reuptake of; acetylcholine

2. Miguel has been diagnosed with schizophrenia. His psychologist believes that Miguel's hallucinations and perceptual distortions may, in part, be caused by _____ amounts of the neurotransmitter _____ .
   (a) diminished; dopamine
   (b) excessive; dopamine
   (c) diminished; serotonin
   (d) excessive; serotonin

3. Jenny has just finished running a very tough marathon (26.22 miles) but seems to be very happy and elated. One cause of her "runner's high" may be due to abnormally high levels of chemical substances in her brain called
   (a) acetylcholines.   (c) endorphins.
   (b) serotonins.   (d) dopamines.

4. Mrs. Danvers has multiple sclerosis. She experiences muscle weakness, loss of coordination and speech, and visual disturbances that result from the slowdown or interruption of neural transmission. The cause of these symptoms probably involves the degeneration of the
   (a) dendrites.   (c) myelin sheath.
   (b) corpus callosum.   (d) synaptic vesicles.

5. When Dr. Maxwell electrically stimulated a specific area of a patient's right cerebral hemisphere, the patient's left hand twitched. The part of the cortex that was stimulated was
   (a) Broca's area.
   (b) the primary motor cortex.
   (c) Wernicke's area.
   (d) the somatosensory cortex.

6. While Rupert was reading a poem, researchers studied his brain activity by tracking changes in his brain's blood supply as a function of fluctuations in blood oxygen levels. They were most likely using an imaging technique called
   (a) functional magnetic resonance imaging (fMRI).
   (b) electroencephalography (EEG).
   (c) positron emission tomography (PET scan).
   (d) computerized axial tomography (CAT, or CT scan).

7. Neurotransmitters are to hormones as _____ is to _____ .
   (a) nervous system; endocrine system
   (b) nerves; neurons
   (c) hypothalamus; pituitary gland
   (d) brain; spinal cord

8. When Mike was faced with a final exam worth 80 percent of his grade in his graduate statistics class he was totally stressed out. The particular gland(s) in his endocrine system that is (are) likely to be stimulated is (are) the
   (a) thyroid gland.   (c) adrenal glands.
   (b) pituitary gland.   (d) nervous glands.

9. If researchers electrically stimulate the reticular formation in a sleeping cat, it is most likely that the cat will
   (a) aggressively attack the researchers.
   (b) stop breathing.
   (c) become paralyzed on both sides of the body.
   (d) instantly wake up, fully alert.

10. If researchers destroy or lesion the amygdala of a timid cat, it is likely that the cat will
    (a) become even more fearful.
    (b) lose its timidity and fearfulness.
    (c) become a vicious predator and start attacking large dogs.
    (d) stop breathing and die.

11. If a normal right-handed individual sustained severe damage to the right cerebral hemisphere, this would most likely reduce a number of abilities. Damage to the right hemisphere is *not* likely to affect his ability to
    (a) manipulate blocks to match a particular design.
    (b) recognize people's faces.
    (c) appreciate art and music.
    (d) decipher visual cues related to emotional expression.
    (e) produce and understand written and spoken language.

12. The occipital lobe is to _____ as the temporal lobe is to _____ .
    (a) anticipatory thinking; seeing
    (b) seeing; anticipatory thinking
    (c) seeing; hearing
    (d) hearing; seeing

13. If someone taps you on the back, you sense the touch because the _____ cortex in the _____ lobe receives this tactile information.
    (a) primary motor; frontal
    (b) primary visual; occipital
    (c) primary somatosensory; parietal
    (d) primary auditory; temporal

14. According to In Focus 2.2, most left-handed people
    (a) process language in the left hemisphere.
    (b) process language in the right hemisphere.
    (c) are intellectually challenged.
    (d) are female.

15. According to the Application, rats were exposed to either an enriched environment or an impoverished environment. Researchers found that enrichment
    (a) increases the number and length of dendrites, enlarges the size of neurons, and produces more synaptic connections.
    (b) results in a dramatic increase in the number of neurons in the brain.
    (c) has profound effects on the brains of young rats but no effect on those of mature rats.

    (d) dramatically affects the limbic system but has little or no effect on the cerebral cortex.

Progress Test 2

After you have checked your understanding of the material in Progress Test 1 and have done a complete chapter review with special focus on any areas of weakness, you are ready to further assess your knowledge on Progress Test 2. Check your answers. If you make a mistake, review your notes, the appropriate parts of the study guide, and, if necessary, the relevant sections of your textbook.

1. A patient is suffering from a number of symptoms, including depression, sleep disturbances, and mood fluctuations, and has problems in learning and memory retrieval. Her doctor prescribes Prozac and some other drugs, because the patient's problems are probably due to abnormal levels of the neurotransmitters
   (a) dopamine and acetylcholine.
   (b) serotonin and endorphins.
   (c) acetylcholine and norepinephrine.
   (d) serotonin and norepinephrine.

2. Signal reception is to _____ as signal transmission is to _____ .
   (a) myelin sheath; cell body
   (b) dendrite; axon
   (c) action potential; resting potential
   (d) axon; dendrite

3. As a result of a stroke, 75-year-old Mrs. Yee suffered brain damage. While she is no longer able to speak, she can understand what is being said to her. Mrs. Yee suffers from
   (a) damage to her occipital lobe.
   (b) Wernicke's aphasia.
   (c) damage to her left temporal lobe.
   (d) Broca's aphasia.

4. Your brain is involved in every perception, thought, and emotion, as are its neurons and their neurotransmitters. Neurotransmitters are chemical messengers that
   (a) carry information primarily in the endocrine system.
   (b) travel from the cell body along the axon and create an action potential.
   (c) assist neurons by providing physical support, nutrition, and waste removal.
   (d) travel across the synaptic gap and affect adjoining neurons.

5. If a patient suffers damage to the hippocampus, she is likely to have problems
   (a) learning and forming new memories.
   (b) remembering events and things that happened before her brain injury.
   (c) comprehending spoken and written language.
   (d) controlling emotions such as aggression, fear, anger, and disgust.

6. After Eduardo's serious skiing accident, doctors detected damage to his cerebellum. Eduardo is most likely to have trouble
   (a) swallowing, coughing, and breathing.
   (b) sleeping.
   (c) staying awake.
   (d) playing tennis, typing, and walking with a smooth gait.

7. In a typical test situation with a split-brain patient, a picture of an apple is briefly presented to the right of the center point. If the patient is asked to name the object, she will
   (a) be unable to say what she saw.
   (b) be able to draw a picture of the object with her left hand.
   (c) report that she saw nothing.
   (d) say she saw an apple.

8. If a researcher anesthetizes the entire right hemisphere of a right-handed patient who is asked to recite the alphabet aloud while reclining on the operating table with both arms extended upward, it is most probable that the patient's
   (a) left arm will fall limp but she will continue saying the alphabet.
   (b) right arm will fall limp but she will continue saying the alphabet.
   (c) left arm will fall limp and she will become speechless.
   (d) right arm will fall limp and she will become speechless.

9. A champion athlete loses his medal after officials discover that he has taken anabolic steroids, a synthetic version of the male sex hormone testosterone. Anabolic steroids, like other hormones, circulate through the _____ and act as _____ chemical messengers.
   (a) cerebrospinal fluid; central nervous system
   (b) bloodstream; endocrine system
   (c) cerebrospinal fluid; peripheral nervous system
   (d) bloodstream; limbic system

10. In response to an exam question, Leilani carefully draws a picture of a neuron and indicates the sequence of events that are typically involved when a neuron communicates. She is likely to note that information is carried from
    (a) the axon terminals to the cell body and then down the dendrites to the synapse.
    (b) from the cell body to the dendrites and then down the axon to the axon terminals and the synapse.
    (c) from the dendrites to the axon and then down the axon to the cell body and the synapse.
    (d) the dendrites to the cell body and then along the axon to the axon terminals and the synapse.

11. Dr. Jones systematically observes and records the behavior of people whose brains have been damaged by illness or injury. He is using an investigative technique called
    (a) fMRI.   (c) PET scan.
    (b) CAT scan.   (d) the case study.

12. The parietal lobe is to _____ as the frontal lobe is to _____ .
    (a) anticipatory thinking; hearing
    (b) sensing touch; anticipatory thinking
    (c) seeing; hearing
    (d) tasting; smelling

13. The chapter prologue tells the story of Asha, who suffered a stroke. This story illustrates that the brain has a remarkable ability to gradually shift functions from damaged to undamaged areas, a phenomenon called
    (a) lateralization of function.
    (b) structural plasticity.
    (c) synaptic transmission.
    (d) functional plasticity.

14. Structural plasticity refers to the capacity of some brain structures to
    (a) change in response to environmental stimulation.
    (b) remain rigid or "hard-wired" for life.
    (c) deteriorate with age and cause forgetfulness.
    (d) wear out if they are used too much.

15. Despite the fact that phrenology was eventually dismissed as a pseudoscience, it was pointed out in Science Versus Pseudoscience 2.1 that phrenology played a significant role in advancing the scientific study of the brain by triggering interest in
    (a) split-brain operations for epilepsy.
    (b) the role neurotransmitters play in regulating behavior.
    (c) cortical localization, or localization of function.
    (d) how drugs affect synaptic transmission.

Progress Test 3

After you have checked your understanding of the material in Progress Tests 1 and 2 and have done a complete chapter review with special focus on any areas of weakness, you are ready to further assess your knowledge on Progress Test 3. Check your answers. If you make a mistake, review your notes, the appropriate parts of the study guide, and, if necessary, the relevant sections of your textbook.

1. When doctors removed a tumor from Andrew's occipital lobe, they also had to remove healthy brain tissue from the same area. When he recovers, Andrew is most likely to suffer some loss of
   (a) language comprehension.
   (b) muscular coordination.
   (c) visual perception.
   (d) taste perception.

2. Nancy suffers from severe epilepsy that so far has not responded to any treatment. As a final resort, her doctor operates on her brain and surgically cuts the
   (b) amygdala.
   (b) hippocampus.
   (c) corpus callosum.
   (d) adrenal cortex.

3. After a police car with flashing lights and blaring siren passes him and pulls over another driver for speeding, Jerry's heartbeat soon slows down, his blood pressure decreases, and he stops sweating so much. These calming physical reactions are most directly regulated by his
   (a) sympathetic nervous system.
   (b) parasympathetic nervous system.
   (c) somatic nervous system.
   (d) central nervous system.

4. While cooking dinner for a large family gathering, Mindy was so distracted by the conversations around her that she forgot to use an oven mitt when she grabbed a very hot roaster pan. She instantly withdrew her hand before becoming consciously aware of the sensation or her own hand movement. Mindy was able to do this because of her
   (a) spinal reflexes.
   (b) parasympathetic nervous system.
   (c) high levels of endorphins.
   (d) limbic system.

5. As a result of a stroke, Mr. Nelson can no longer understand what he reads or what is being said to him, and he often has trouble finding the right words when he tries to speak. Mr. Nelson suffers from
   (a) Wernicke's aphasia.
   (b) Broca's aphasia.
   (c) Parkinson's disease.
   (d) Alzheimer's disease.

6. If a picture of a hammer is flashed to the left of the midpoint during an experiment with a split-brain patient and she is asked to indicate what she saw, the patient will
   (a) verbally report what she saw.
   (b) be able to draw a picture of the hammer with her right hand.
   (c) be unable to verbally report what she saw.
   (d) most likely draw a picture of a nail with her right hand.

7. In order to determine which area of Drucilla's brain was most active when she read a passage from a book, neuroscientists radioactively tagged glucose and used a technique involving a(n)
   (a) PET scan.
   (b) CAT scan.
   (c) fMRI.
   (d) EEG.

8. Sonny suffered brain damage when he was knocked down in a boxing match; he can no longer hear in one ear. It is most probable that one of his _____ lobes was injured.
   (a) ear
   (b) occipital
   (c) temporal
   (d) frontal
   (e) parietal

9. In an effort to relax after a stress-filled week, Joanne had a couple of glasses of wine, and her coworker Jim took a Valium. Both alcohol and Valium work by increasing the activity of the neurotransmitter _____ , which inhibits action potentials and slows brain activity.
   (a) GABA
   (b) dopamine
   (c) norepinephrine
   (d) serotonin

10. If Dr. Doonan's research showed that the left hemisphere is dominant for speech and language in virtually all right-handed people and the majority of left-handers, this would argue strongly for the notion of
    (a) lateralization of function.
    (b) the all-or-none law.
    (c) structural plasticity.
    (d) functional plasticity.

11. In his medical practice, Dr. Setiadi uses acupuncture, an ancient Chinese procedure, which involves inserting needles at various points in the body. This pain-killing technique is assumed to involve the production of _____ by the brain.
    (a) endorphins
    (b) dopamine
    (c) GABA
    (d) acetylcholine

12. During a lecture on the brain, Professor Chiga notes that an action potential will not occur unless a neuron is sufficiently stimulated. The principle that she is referring to is the
    (a) all-or-none law.
    (b) law of phrenology.
    (c) principle of lateralization.
    (d) principle of fight-or-flight.

13. A researcher plans to survey 1,000 randomly selected individuals about hand preference. According to In Focus 2.2, the results are likely to indicate that about
    (a) 50 percent will be left-handed.
    (b) 25 percent will be left-handed.
    (c) 8 percent will be left-handed.
    (d) one-third will be left-handed, one-third right-handed, and one-third ambidextrous.

14. During the early 1800s, Franz Gall developed a theory that the shape of the skull reflects abilities and personality characteristics. According to Box 2.1, this idea was called
    (a) philosophy.
    (b) bumpology.
    (c) phrenology.
    (d) physiology.

15. According to the Application, research has shown that compared with high school dropouts, university graduates had 40 percent more
    (a) synaptic connections.
    (b) brain mass.
    (c) neurons in their brains.
    (d) axons in the corpus callosum.

Answers

Introduction: The Scope of Biological Psychology

1. *Biological psychology is* the specialized branch of psychology that studies the relationship between behavior and bodily processes and systems.

2. *The systems and structures that are of interest to biopsychologists are* the nervous system, particularly its neurons and the structures of the brain, and the endocrine system.

The Neuron: The Basic Unit of Communication

1. *Information is transmitted in the nervous system by* neurons, *of which there are three basic types:* sensory neurons, motor neurons, and interneurons.

2. *Glial cells are* cells that assist neurons by providing structural support, nutrition, and removal of cell wastes; they also enhance the speed of communication between neurons by manufacturing myelin.

3. *The neuron's basic components and their functions are* the cell body, which contains the nucleus and provides energy for the neuron to carry out its functions; the dendrites, which extend out from the cell body and receive messages from other neurons or specialized cells; and the axon (often surrounded by a myelin sheath), which carries information from the neuron to other cells in the body, including other neurons, glands, and muscles.

4. *Within the neuron, information is communicated* in the form of brief electrical impulses,

called action potentials, which are produced by the movement of electrically charged particles, called ions, across the membrane of the axon. The resting potential is the state in which a neuron is prepared to activate and communicate its message if it receives sufficient stimulation. For a action potential to occur, stimulation must be above the stimulus threshold, the minimum level of stimulation required to activate a particular neuron. In addition, neurons either respond or they don't, the all-or-none law.

5. *Communication between neurons may be electrical or chemical. Chemically, it involves* neurostransmitters from one neuron crossing over the synapse, the junction between two neurons, and affecting adjoining neurons.

6. *Some important neurotransmitters (and their primary roles) are* acetylcholine, which is involved in memory, learning, general intellectual functioning, and muscle contraction; dopamine, which is involved in movement, attention, learning, and pleasurable or rewarding sensations; serotonin, which is involved in sleep, moods, and emotional states; norepinephrine, which is involved in the activation of neurons, memory, learning, and physical arousal; GABA, which inhibits brain activity; and endorphins, which affect pain perceptions and positive emotions.

7. *Drugs can affect synaptic transmission* by increasing or decreasing the amount of neurotransmitter released by the neuron, by blocking the reuptake of the neurotransmitter by the sending neuron, by mimicking specific neurotransmitters and producing the same effects, or by mimicking a neurotransmitter and blocking its effect by occupying its receptor sites and preventing it from acting.

Concept Check 1

1. acetylcholine
2. acetylcholine
3. serotonin
4. dopamine
5. GABA
6. endorphins

Graphic Organizer 1

a. dendrites
b. cell body
c. axon

d. myelin sheath
e. synaptic gap
f. neurotransmitter
g. synaptic vesicles
h. postsynaptic neuron
i. presynaptic neuron

Matching Exercise 1

1. neuron
2. GABA (gamma-amniobutyric acid)
3. endorphins
4. motor neuron
5. serotonin
6. cell body
7. action potential
8. neurotransmitter
9. axon
10. synapse
11. synaptic vesicles
12. dopamine
13. stimulus threshold
14. neuroscience

True/False Test 1

1. T	6. F	11. F
2. F	7. T	12. T
3. F	8. F	13. T
4. T	9. F	14. T
5. T	10. T	

The Nervous System and the Endocrine System: Communication Throughout the Body

1. *The two main divisions of the nervous system and their components are* the central nervous system, which includes the brain and spinal cord, and the peripheral nervous system, which includes all the nerves lying outside the central nervous system.

2. *Spinal reflexes are* simple, automatic behaviors that are processed in the spinal cord.

3. *The key components of the peripheral nervous system and their functions are* the somatic nervous system, which communicates sensory information to the central nervous system and carries motor messages from the central nervous system to the muscles, and the autonomic

nervous system, which regulates involuntary functions, such as heartbeat, blood pressure, breathing, and digestion.

4. *The two branches of the autonomic nervous system and their functions are* the sympathetic nervous system, which produces rapid physical arousal in response to perceived threats or emergencies, and the parasympathetic nervous system, which maintains normal bodily functions and conserves the body's physical resources.

5. *The endocrine system is made up of* glands that transmit information via chemical messengers called hormones.

6. *The endocrine system interacts with the nervous system in a number of ways:* by interacting with the nervous system and affecting internal organs and bodily tissue, hormones regulate such things as metabolism, growth rate, digestion, blood pressure, sexual development, and reproduction; endocrine hormones can promote or inhibit the generation of nerve impulses (the release of hormones, in turn, can be stimulated or inhibited by certain parts of the nervous system); and finally, because some hormones and neurotransmitters are chemically identical, the same molecules can act as either a hormone or a neurotransmitter.

7. *The hypothalamus serves as* the main link between the endocrine system and the nervous system and controls the pituitary gland.

8. *The pituitary gland's hormones* affect the function of other glands as well as regulate the production of other hormones. *The adrenal glands (adrenal cortex and adrenal medulla) are involved in* the human stress response.

Concept Check 2

1. spinal reflexes
2. spinal cord
3. sympathetic nervous system
4. parasympathetic nervous system
5. norepinephrine; epinephrine

Graphic Organizer 2

Mapping the Divisions and Functions of the Nervous System

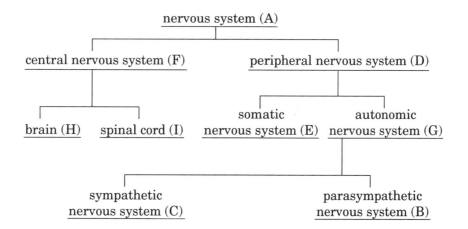

Matching Exercise 2

1. nerve
2. endocrine system
3. spinal reflexes
4. adrenal glands
5. parasympathetic nervous system
6. hypothalamus
7. adrenal cortex
8. peripheral nervous system
9. autonomic nervous system

True/False Test 2

1. T   5. F
2. T   6. T
3. F   7. F
4. T   8. F

Studying the Brain: The Toughest Case to Crack

1. *Scientists used case studies to study the brain because* the brain is encased entirely by bone, and it was not possible to directly observe a normal, living brain in action; observing and recording the behavior of people whose brains have been damaged by illness or injury has provided valuable insights into behavior in such areas as memory, speech, emotion, movement, and personality.

2. *The production of lesions and electrically stimulating areas of the brain have been useful because* by surgically altering, removing, or destroying specific portions of the brain (in humans, usually for medical reasons) researchers can observe subsequent changes in behavior; electrical stimulation produces the opposite behavioral effect of a lesion in the same area.

3. *The five major imaging techniques used to study the brain are* electroencephalography, computerized axial tomography (CAT scan or CT scan), magnetic resonance imaging (MRI), positron emission tomography (PET scan), and functional magnetic resonance imaging (fMRI).

A Guided Tour of the Brain

1. *The brain develops from* a fluid-filled neural tube, which forms about two weeks after conception, into separate fluid-filled cavities called ventricles; as the human fetus develops, brain cells multiply, differentiate, and migrate to their final locations; between conception and birth, the number of neurons increases at a dramatic rate and compete to form synaptic connections.

2. *The three divisions of the developing brain are* the hindbrain, midbrain, and forebrain.

3. *The key structures of the hindbrain and their functions are* the medulla, which controls breathing, heartbeat, digestion, and other vital life functions; the pons, which connects the medulla to the two sides of the cerebellum and helps coordinate and integrate movements from each side of the body; and the cerebellum, which is responsible for muscle coordination and maintaining posture and equilibrium. The reticular formation, which is a network of neurons at the core of the pons and the medulla, plays a role in regulating attention and sleep.

4. *The midbrain contains* centers important to the processing of auditory and visual sensory information, and an area involved in motor control, called the substantia nigra, which contains a large concentration of dopamine-producing neurons.

5. *The forebrain includes* the cerebral cortex (the wrinkled outer portion of the forebrain) and the limbic system structures, which are involved in emotion, motivation, learning, and memory.

6. *The four lobes and their functions are* the temporal lobe, the primary receiving area for auditory information; the occipital lobe, the primary receiving area for visual information; the parietal lobe, which processes somatic sensations; and the frontal lobe, which processes voluntary muscle movements and is involved in thinking, planning, and emotional control.

7. *The main structures of the limbic system and their functions are* the thalamus, which processes sensory information for all senses, except smell, and relays it to the cerebral cortex; the hypothalamus, which regulates behaviors related to survival, such as eating, drinking, and sexual behavior; the hippocampus, which is involved in learning and forming new memories; and the amygdala, which is involved in emotions such as fear, anger, and disgust, and in learning and memory.

Concept Check 3

1. hindbrain (more specifically, the medulla is the point at which neural messages cross over)

2. reticular formation

3. cerebellum

4. medulla

5. hippocampus

6. hypothalamus

7. left parietal

Graphic Organizer 3
Chart Diagram Exercise: The Key Structures of the Limbic System

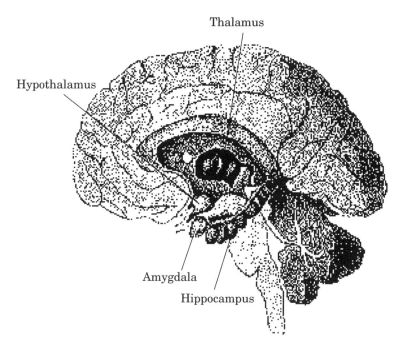

Thalamus

Hypothalamus

Amygdala

Hippocampus

(a) Hypothalamus: a peanut-sized forebrain structure that regulates both divisions of the autonomic nervous system as well as behaviors related to survival, such as eating, drinking, and sexual activity

(b) Thalamus: a forebrain structure that processes motor information and sensory information for all the senses except smell and relays it to the cerebral cortex

(c) Amygdala: an almond-shaped forebrain structure that is involved in emotion and in learning and forming memories

(d) Hippocampus: a curved forebrain structure that is involved in learning and forming new memories

Matching Exercise 3

1. cerebral hemispheres
2. parietal lobe
3. substantia nigra
4. primary auditory cortex
5. pons
6. thalamus
7. primary visual cortex
8. hippocampus

9. brain stem
10. primary motor cortex
11. prefrontal association area
12. medulla
13. electroencephalograph (EEG)
14. reticular formation
15. magnetic resonance imaging (MRI)
16. suprachiasmatic nucleus (SCN)
17. neurogenesis

True/False Test 3

1. T		7. F		13. T
2. T		8. T		14. T
3. F		9. T		15. F
4. F		10. T		16. T
5. T		11. F		17. T
6. T		12. F		

Specialization in the Cerebral Hemispheres

1. *Broca and Wernicke provided the first evidence that* the left and right hemispheres were specialized for different functions (cortical localization or localization of function), and in particu-

lar that language is processed primarily in the left hemisphere.

2. *Lateralization of function (or lateralization) is* the notion that specific psychological or cognitive functions are processed primarily on one side of the brain.

3. *Aphasia refers to* the partial or complete inability to articulate ideas or understand spoken or written language because of brain injury or damage. *Broca's aphasia results in* the inability to produce speech, but comprehension is relatively unaffected. *Wernicke's aphasia results in* problems in finding the correct word and comprehension of written or spoken communication, but speech is relatively unaffected unless the damage is severe.

4. *The split-brain operation involves* surgically cutting the corpus callosum, the thick band of axons that connects the two hemispheres.

5. *In a specialized procedure, split-brain subjects are directed to focus on a point in the middle of a screen and then* visual information is differentially projected either to the left or right hemisphere. *Split-brain subjects can* verbally identify the object when it is projected to the left hemisphere but not the right, however, the left hand (which is controlled by the right hemisphere) can correctly pick out the object projected to the right hemisphere.

6. *Tests on split-brain patients revealed that the left hemisphere is specialized for* language abilities, speech, reading and writing, and *the right hemisphere is specialized for* nonverbal emotional expression, visual-spatial tasks, facial recognition, reading maps, copying designs, drawing, and musical appreciation or responsiveness (but not necessarily musical ability, which involves the left hemisphere as well).

Concept Check 4

1. right; left
2. left; left
3. right
4. right; left

Matching Exercise 4

1. Roger Sperry
2. aphasia
3. Wernicke's area
4. functional plasticity

5. cortical localization
6. structural plasticity
7. lateralization of function

True/False Test 4

1. T   3. F   5. T
2. F   4. T   6. T

Something to Think About

1. (a) The occipital lobe is most likely affected because it includes the primary visual cortex where visual information is received, so damage to this area could affect vision.

   (b) Yoko probably has damage to the left frontal lobe, Broca's area. Damage here would not affect comprehension but would influence speech production.

   (c) Vanessa's hypothalamus was most likely damaged. The hypothalamus is part of the limbic system and regulates appetite, among its many functions.

   (d) Mr. Ashley suffers from Parkinson's disease, which is caused by the degeneration of neurons that produce dopamine in one brain area. Symptoms can be alleviated by the drug L-dopa, which converts to dopamine in the brian.

2. In answer to this question, the news is good. Because of the brain's structural plasticity, some brain structures can change in response to environmental stimulation. Research with rats has demonstrated that, in addition to other changes, an enriched environment increases the number and length of dendrites, enlarges the size of neurons, and increases the number of neural connections. More important, there is an impressive amount of correlational research showing that the human brain also seems to benefit from enriched environments. Getting a good education, as long as the process is challenging, is one way to "exercise" the brain. Another piece of advice is to remain mentally active throughout the lifespan and to get involved in complex and stimulating activities.

   It is important to point out that intellectual decline is not the inevitable result of aging. To increase the number of synaptic connections and dendritic growth, the best advice is to get involved in novel, challenging, and unfamiliar pursuits. Keep pumping those neurons and remember, "If you don't use it, you lose it!"

Progress Test 1

1. b	6. a	11. e
2. c	7. a	12. c
3. c	8. c	13. c
4. c	9. d	14. a
5. b	10. b	15. a

Progress Test 2

1. d	6. d	11. d
2. b	7. d	12. b
3. d	8. a	13. d
4. d	9. b	14. a
5. a	10. d	15. c

Progress Test 3

1. c	6. c	11. a
2. c	7. a	12. a
3. b	8. c	13. c
4. a	9. a	14. c
5. a	10. a	15. a

Sensation and Perception

CHAPTER 3. . . AT A GLANCE   Chapter 3 describes both sensation and perception. Beginning with the basic principles of sensation—sensory threshold, Weber's law, and sensory adaptation—the chapter then explains the senses of vision, hearing, smell, taste, and touch. This is followed by a discussion of pain, pain perception, and the gate-control theory of pain. The section concludes with the kinesthetic and vestibular senses.

The discussion of perception first distinguishes between bottom-up and top-down processing. How we perceive shape and depth are explained, including a description of monocular and binocular cues. The perception of motion is explained, followed by the phenomenon of perceptual constancy. How we misperceive objects and events in our world is illustrated through various illusions. That perception is a psychological process is made clear through a discussion of how perceptual sets—expectations, learning experiences, and cultural factors—influence our interpretations.

The Application at the end of the chapter is devoted to how we can use various perceptual strategies and techniques in the control of pain.

Introduction: What Are Sensation and Perception?

Preview Questions

Consider the following questions as you study this section of the chapter.

- What are the definitions of sensation and perception?
- How do sensation and perception differ?

*Read the section "Introduction: What Are Sensation and Perception?" and **write** your answers to the following:*

1. The primary function of the nervous system is

   _____

2. Sensation refers to _____

   _____

   and perception occurs _____

   _____

3. The difference between sensation and perception is _____

   _____

Some Basic Principles of Sensation

Preview Questions

Consider the following questions as you study this section of the chapter.

- What are sensory receptors; how do they help us hear, taste, smell, feel, and see; and what is transduction?
- What are the two types of sensory thresholds?
- How does Weber's law relate to the just noticeable difference (jnd)?
- Why does sensory adaptation occur, and why is it important?

*Read the section "Some Basic Principles of Sensation" and **write** the answers to the following:*

1. Sensory receptors help us hear, taste, smell, feel, and see by_____

   _____

2. Transduction is _____

   _____

   _____

3. The two types of sensory threshold are _____

   _____

   _____

   _____

4. Another name for the difference threshold is

   _____

5. Weber's law states _____

   _____

6. Sensory adaptation occurs because _____

   _____

   _____

   _____

After you have carefully studied the preceding sections, complete the following exercises.

Concept Check 1

Read the following and write the correct term in the space provided.

1. When Anton went to have his hearing tested, he was presented with many different tones; in fact, some were at such a low level of intensity he could not detect them. These sounds were below Anton's _____ threshold.

2. Detecting a sequence of sounds as a series of different tones involves the process of _____ ; recognizing the sequence of sounds as a melody is _____ .

3. Jan was exposed to a 100-watt light. When its brightness was increased by 5 watts, she was not aware of the increase. However, when a 20-watt light was increased by 5 watts, she detected the increase immediately. Jan's experience illustrates a principle of sensation called

   _____ .

4. The school bell rings at lunch time. The process by which our ears convert the sound waves from the bell into a coded neural signal that can be processed by the nervous system is called _____ .

5. Not realizing how cold it is after you have been on the ski slope for a while is an example of

   _____ .

6. Not being able to detect a sound because its level is too low is to the _____ threshold as being able to just barely notice that two sounds are not the same is to the _____ threshold.

Review of Terms and Concepts 1

Use the terms in this list to complete the Matching Test, then to help you answer the True/False items correctly.

sensation
perception
sensory receptors
transduction
threshold
absolute threshold

difference threshold
(just noticeable
difference or jnd)
Weber's law
sensory adaptation
subliminal perception

Matching Exercise

Match the appropriate term with its definition or description.

1. _____ The level at which a stimulus is strong enough to be detected by activating sensory receptors.

2. _____ The process by which a form of physical energy is converted into a coded neural signal that can be processed by the nervous system.

3. _____ The smallest possible strength of a stimulus that can be detected half the time.

4. _____ Specialized cells unique to each sense organ that respond to a particular form of sensory stimulation.

5. _____ The smallest possible difference between two stimuli that can be detected half the time; also called the just noticeable difference.

True/False Test

Indicate whether each statement is true or false by placing T or F in the blank space next to each item.

1. ___ Perception refers to the process of detecting a physical stimulus, such as sound, light, heat, or pressure.

2. ___ Sensory adaptation refers to the decline in sensitivity to a constant stimulus.

3. ___ Weber's law is a principle of sensation that holds that the size of the just noticeable difference will vary depending on its relation to the strength of the original stimulus.

4. ___ The process of integrating, organizing, and interpreting sensations is called sensation.

5. ___ The perception of stimuli that are below the threshold of conscious awareness is called subliminal perception.

Check your answers and review any areas of weakness before going on to the next section.

Vision: From Light to Sight

Preview Questions

Consider the following questions as you study this section of the chapter.

- How do we see, and what is the electromagnetic energy spectrum?

- What are the key structures of the eye?

- What are the functions of the rods and cones, and how do the bipolar and ganglion cells process visual information for transmission to the brain?

- What properties of light determine our experience of color, and how do the two theories of color vision explain the process?

Read the section "Vision: From Light to Sight" and ***write*** *your answers to the following.*

1. The process of seeing begins with _____ _____ _____

2. The electromagnetic spectrum is _____ _____ _____

3. The key structures of the eye are _____ _____ _____

4. The function of rods is to _____ _____ _____ ;

the function of cones is to _____

_____

5. Bipolar cells process visual information by

_____

_____

6. The optic disk is _____

_____

7. Our experience of color involves _____

_____

_____

_____

8. According to the trichromatic theory,

_____

_____

_____

This theory explains_____

_____

9. According to the opponent-process theory,

_____

_____

_____

This theory explains_____

_____

*After you have carefully studied the preceding
section, complete the following exercises.*

Concept Check 2

*Read the following and write the correct term in the
space provided.*

1. According to the trichromatic theory, if Mr.
    Colorado's red- , green- , and blue-sensitive
    cones are stimulated simultaneously, he should
    see _____ .

2. If a person with normal vision stares at a red
    circle for a couple of minutes, then shifts his or
    her eyes to a white surface, the afterimage of
    the circle will be _____ .

3. Following an accident the fovea in Harbinder's
    right eye was destroyed. Although he can still
    see with this eye, it is likely that he will have
    trouble seeing _____ and
    _____ when his left eye is closed.

4. Frederico's dog Fido lacks receptor cells for long
    wavelengths of about 700 nanometers. Most
    likely, Fido cannot see the color

    _____ .

5. According to the opponent-process theory, if cer-
    tain cells in Dale's retina are stimulated by
    exposure to green light, they are likely to be
    inhibited by exposure to _____
    light.

Graphic Organizer 1

*Identify each part of the eye by writing the name on
the appropriate line; then match its function by placing the corresponding number next to the name. (For
example, "1. retina" is the first answer.)*

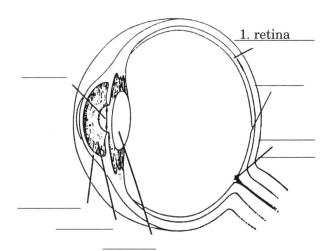

1. retina _____

1. A light-sensitive membrane located at the back
    of the eye that contains sensory receptors for
    vision.

2. The black opening in the middle of the eye that
    changes size to let in different amounts of light.

3. A clear membrane covering the visible part of
    the eye that helps gather and direct incoming
    light.

4. The colored part of the eye that is the muscle
    that controls the size of the pupil.

5. A transparent structure located behind the
    pupil that actively focuses, or bends, light as it
    enters the eye.

6. A small area in the center of the retina that
    contains cones but not rods.

7. The area of the retina without rods or cones,
    where the optic nerve leaves the eye.

Review of Terms and Concepts 2

Use the terms in this list to complete the Matching Test, then to help you answer the True/False items correctly.

wavelength
cornea
pupil
iris
lens
accommodation
retina
rods
cones
fovea
optic disk
blind spot
bipolar cells

ganglion cells
visual acuity
optic nerve
optic chiasm
color
hue
saturation
brightness
trichromatic theory
color blindness
afterimage
opponent-process theory

Matching Exercise

Match the appropriate term with its definition or description:

1. _____ The visual ability to see fine details.

2. _____ Visual experience that occurs after the original source of stimulation is no longer present.

3. _____ Distance from one wave peak to another.

4. _____ Process by which the lens changes shape to focus incoming light so that it falls on the retina.

5. _____ Perceived intensity of color that corresponds to the amplitude of the light wave.

6. _____ Thick nerve that exits from the back of the eye and carries visual information to the visual cortex in the brain.

7. _____ Theory that the sensation of color is due to cones in the retina that are especially sensitive to red, green, or blue light.

8. _____ Short, thick, pointed sensory receptors of the eye that detect color and are responsible for color vision and visual acuity.

9. _____ Property of wavelengths of light, what we know as color, in which different wavelengths correspond to our subjective experience of different colors.

10. _____ Long, thin, blunt sensory receptors that are highly sensitive to light but not color and are primarily responsible for peripheral vision and night vision.

11. _____ Specialized neurons in the retina that collect sensory information from the rods and cones and then funnel it to other specialized neurons before it is transmitted to the brain.

12. _____ Perceptual experience of different wavelengths of light, involving hue, saturation (purity), and brightness (intensity).

13. _____ Area of the retina without rods or cones, where the optic nerve exits the back of the eye.

True/False Test

Indicate whether each statement is true or false by placing T or F in the blank space next to each item.

1. ____ The cornea is the transparent structure located behind the pupil that actively focuses, or bends, light as it enters the eye.

2. ____ The opponent-process theory states that color vision is the product of opposing pairs of color receptors, red-green, black-white, and blue-yellow; when one member of a color pair is stimulated, the other is inhibited.

3. ____ The lens is the clear membrane covering the visible part of the eye that helps gather and direct incoming light.

4. ____ A single ganglion cell might receive information from only one or two cones or it might receive information from a hundred or more rods.

5. ____ The retina is a small area in the center of the back of the eye that is composed entirely of cones, where visual information is most sharply focused.

6. ____ The colored part of the eye, which is actually a ring of muscles that controls the size of the pupil, is called the iris.

7. ____ The pupil is the opening in the middle of the iris that changes size to let in different amounts of light.

8. ____ The fovea is a thin, light-sensitive membrane located at the back of the eye that contains two kinds of sensory receptors for light and vision.

9. ___ The optic chiasm is the point in the brain where the optic fibers from each eye meet and partly cross over to the opposite side of the brain.

10. ___ Saturation is the property of color that corresponds to the purity of the light wave.

11. ___ Color blindness occurs because there are no receptor cells in the area where the optic nerve exits the eye.

12. ___ The blind spot is the point where the optic nerve leaves the eye, producing a small gap in the field of vision.

Check your answers and review any areas of weakness before going on to the next section.

Hearing: From Vibration to Sound

Preview Questions

Consider the following questions as you study this section of the chapter.

- What is audition, and how do we hear?
- What properties of a sound wave correspond to our perception of sound?
- What are the key structures of the ear, and what are their functions?
- How do place theory and frequency theory explain pitch?

*Read the section "Hearing: From Vibration to Sound" and **write** your answers to the following:*

1. Audition is _____

_____

_____

2. Our perception of sound is directly related to the physical properties of _____

_____

_____

3. The key structures of the ear are _____

_____

_____

4. The process of hearing begins when _____

_____

It then involves _____

_____

_____

5. According to frequency theory, _____

_____

_____

_____

This theory explains_____

_____

_____

6. According to place theory, _____

_____

_____

_____

_____

This theory explains_____

_____

_____

After you have carefully studied the preceding section, complete the following exercises.

Concept Check 3

Read the following and write the correct term in the space provided.

1. The retina in the eye performs a function that parallels the function of the _____ in the ear.

2. Rita, who has suffered damage to the bones in her middle ear, has been told by the experts that a hearing aid that artificially amplifies sounds will help restore her hearing. Rita probably has _____ deafness.

3. After a small area of his basilar membrane was damaged, Hamish could no longer hear high-pitched sounds. This loss of hearing can best be explained by the _____ theory.

4. Mrs. Newbold is 75 years old and has had some hearing loss due to stiffness of the tiny bones in her middle ear. It is possible that her deafness can be helped by a _____ .

5. Dr. Emison's research, which found that high-frequency sounds trigger activity near the stirrup end of the basilar membrane, supports the _____ theory of pitch.

Graphic Organizer 2

Identify each part of the ear by writing the name on the appropriate line and then match its function by placing the corresponding number next to the name. (For example, "1. pinna" is the first answer.)

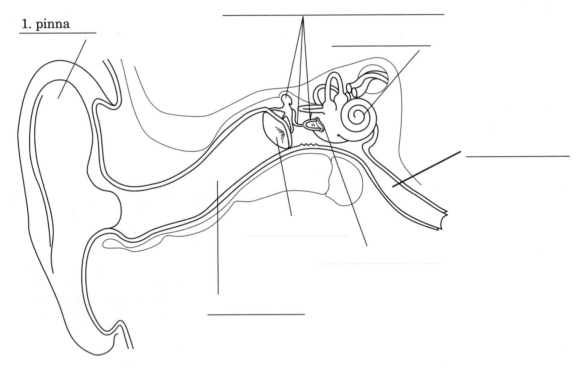

1. pinna

1. The oddly shaped flap of skin and cartilage that is attached to each side of the head.

2. A tightly stretched membrane at the end of the ear canal that vibrates when sound waves hit it.

3. A fluid-filled coiled structure that contains the sensory receptors for sound.

4. The tunnel through which sound waves travel to reach the eardrum.

5. The tightly stretched membrane that separates the middle ear from the inner ear.

6. The small structures of the middle ear whose joint action almost doubles the amplification of the sound.

7. The nerve that carries the neural information to the thalamus and the auditory cortex in the brain.

Review of Terms and Concepts 3

Use the terms in this list to complete the Matching Test, then to help you answer the True/False items correctly.

audition
sound waves
amplitude
decibels
pitch
frequency
hertz
timbre
outer ear
pinna
ear canal
eardrum

oval window
middle ear
hammer, anvil,
    and stirrup
conduction deafness
inner ear
cochlea
basilar membrane
hair cells
nerve deafness
frequency theory
place theory

Matching Exercise

Match the appropriate term with its definition or description.

1. _____ Type of deafness due to damage to the hair cells or auditory nerve.

2. _____ Technical term for the sense of hearing.

3. _____ Rate of vibration, or number of waves per second.

4. _____ Hairlike sensory receptors for sound embedded in the basilar membrane.

5. _____ Physical stimuli that produce our sensory experience of sound.

6. _____ The distinctive quality of a sound, determined by the complexity of the sound waves.

7. _____ Part of the ear that collects sound waves and consists of the pinna, the ear canal, and the eardrum.

8. _____ Relative highness or lowness of a sound, determined by the frequency of the sound wave.

9. _____ The view that different frequencies cause larger vibrations at different locations along the basilar membrane.

10. _____ Unit of measurement for loudness.

11. _____ Intensity or amount of energy of a wave, reflected in the height of the wave; determines a sound's loudness.

12. _____ The part of the ear that amplifies sound waves; consists of three small bones—the hammer, the anvil, and the stirrup.

True/False Test

Indicate whether each statement is true or false by placing T or F in the blank space next to each item.

1. ____ According to frequency theory, the basilar membrane vibrates at the same frequency as the sound wave, thereby enabling low-frequency sound to be transmitted to the brain.

2. ____ The oval window is a tightly stretched membrane that separates the middle ear from the inner ear.

3. ____ Conduction deafness results from mechanical problems that prevent parts of the ear from conducting vibrations to the hair cells in the inner ear.

4. ____ The hammer, anvil, and stirrup are important transduction structures in the inner ear.

5. ____ The cochlea is a coiled, fluid-filled structure that contains the sensory receptors for sound.

6. ____ Hertz refers to the number of wave peaks per second.

7. ____ The ear canal is the fluid-filled section of the ear that contains the cochlea.

8. ____ The structure within the cochlea that contains the hair cells is called the basilar membrane.

9. ____ The eardrum is a tightly stretched membrane at the end of the ear canal that vibrates when sound waves hit it.

10. ____ The pinna is the oddly shaped flap of skin and cartilage that is attached to each side of your head.

11. ____ The inner ear is the part of the ear where sound is transduced into neural impulses; it consists of the cochlea and semicircular canals.

Check your answers and review any areas of weakness before going on to the next section.

The Chemical and Body Senses (Part 1)

Preview Questions

Consider the following questions as you study this section of the chapter.

- How are olfaction and gustation defined, and what is meant by the chemical senses?
- How do airborne molecules result in the sensation of odor?
- What are the primary tastes, and how do we perceive different tastes?

*Read the section "The Chemical and Body Senses" (through taste) and **write** your answers to the following:*

1. Olfaction is the technical term for

   _____

   and gustation is the technical term for

   _____

2. They are called chemical senses because

   _____

   _____

3. Our sense of smell begins when _____

   _____

   and then involves _____

   _____

   _____

4. Our sense of taste begins when _____

   _____

   and then involves _____

   _____

   _____

5. The four primary taste qualities are

   _____

The Chemical and Body Senses (Part 2)

Preview Questions

Consider the following questions as you study this section of the chapter.

- What are the skin and body senses, and what sensory receptors are involved in touch and temperature?
- How is the sensation of pain produced, and what causes pain?

- What is the gate-control theory of pain?
- What are the kinesthetic and vestibular senses, and where are their receptors located?

*Read the section "The Chemical and Body Senses" ("Movement, Position, and Balance") and **write** your answers to the following:*

1. The skin and body senses include _____

   _____

2. The skin responds to _____

   _____

3. One receptor for touch is _____

   and it works by _____

   _____

4. Pain is the sensation of _____

   _____

5. According to gate-control theory, _____

   _____

   _____

   _____

   _____

6. The experience of pain is also influenced by

   _____

   _____

7. Our kinesthetic sense involves _____

   _____

   _____

8. Our vestibular sense provides us with

   _____

9. The two sources of vestibular sensory information are _____

   _____

After you have carefully studied the preceding sections, complete the following exercises.

Concept Check 4

Read the following and write the correct term in the space provided.

1. After eating his salad with vinegar dressing, Mario thinks that his very expensive vintage wine tastes strange. This change in perceived

taste is probably due to the vinegar causing some disruption to his

_____ .

2. As a result of damage to her olfactory bulb, Danielle has lost the ability to detect the _____ of whatever she eats or drinks.

3. If a person experiences damage to the thalamus, his or her sense of _____ will be least affected.

4. If Klara's gustatory sense is relatively normal, she can experience the four primary qualities of _____ , _____ , _____ , and _____ .

5. On the day of her final statistics exam, Nadia has a sore ankle. According to the gate-control theory, it is likely that Nadia's anxiety about the exam will _____ her perception of the pain in her ankle.

6. While fishing in a small boat, Mortimer becomes nauseated from the motion of the waves. Mortimer's _____ and _____ are most likely responsible for making him feel ill.

7. If Dr. Farnaz investigates certain aspects of gate-control theory, his research is concerned with the sensation of _____ .

8. If you are blindfolded and asked to touch your chin, nose, and forehead with your index finger, you probably will have no trouble doing so. This ability is due to your _____ sense.

9. Arleigh accidentally scrapes the skin off his knuckles while working on his car. The pain he feels following the injury is caused in part by the release of the neurotransmitter _____ .

Review of Terms and Concepts 4

Use the terms in this list to complete the Matching Test, then to help you answer the True/False items correctly.

olfaction	body senses
gustation	Pacinian corpuscle
chemical senses	pain
airborne molecules	gate-control theory
olfactory receptor cells	free nerve endings
olfactory nerves	substance P
olfactory bulb	endorphins
olfactory cortex	kinesthetic sense
olfactory tract	proprioceptors
pheromones	vestibular sense
taste buds	semicircular canals
skin senses	vestibular sacs

Matching Exercise

Match the appropriate term with its definition or description.

1. _____ Technical term for our sense of taste.

2. _____ Fluid-filled sacs that are lined with hairlike receptor cells that shift in response to motion, changes in body position, and gravity.

3. _____ Touch receptor located beneath the skin; when stimulated by pressure, it converts the stimulation into neural messages that are relayed to the brain.

4. _____ The name sometimes given to our senses of taste and smell because they both involve sensory receptors for chemical substances.

5. _____ Small-diameter sensory fibers in the skin, muscles, or internal organs that, when activated by an intense stimulus, begin the process of pain perception.

6. _____ Cells located high in the nasal cavity that are stimulated by inhaled molecules in the air.

7. _____ Enlarged ending of the olfactory cortex at the front of the brain where the sensation of smell is registered.

8. _____ Specialized sensory receptors for taste that are located on the tongue and inside the mouth and throat.

9. _____ Tract formed by bundles of axons from the olfactory bulb that projects to different brain area, including the temporal lobe and structures in the limbic system.

10. _____ The sense of balance or equilibrium.

11. _____ The body's natural painkillers that are produced in many parts of the brain and the body.

12. _____ The sense of location and position of body parts in relation to one another.

True/False Test

Indicate whether each item is true or false by placing T or F in the space next to each item.

1. ____ Pain is the unpleasant sensation of physical discomfort or suffering that can occur in varying degrees of intensity.

2. ____ Gate-control theory suggests that pain is the product of both physiological and psychological factors that cause spinal "gates" to open and relay patterns of intense stimulation to the brain, which perceives them as pain.

3. ____ Airborne chemical molecules are emitted by the substances we are smelling; we inhale them through the nose and through the opening in the palate at the back of the throat.

4. ____ The olfactory nerves connect directly to the olfactory bulb, where smells are perceived by the brain.

5. ____ Proprioceptors are sensory neurons in the spinal cord that regulate the release of endorphins.

6. ____ Olfaction is the technical term for our sense of smell.

7. ____ The semicircular canals are fluid-filled structures lined with hairlike receptors that shift in response to motion, changes in bodily position, and gravity and are a source of information for our vestibular sense.

8. ____ The olfactory cortex is at the front of the brain and is directly linked to the outside world via neural pathways.

9. ____ The body senses provide essential information about our physical status and our physical interaction with objects in our environment.

10. ____ Substance P is one of the body's natural painkillers and is produced in many parts of the brain and body in response to intense stimulation.

11. ____ The skin senses keep us informed as to our position and orientation in space.

12. ____ Chemical signals used by animals to communicate boundaries and sexual receptiveness are called pheromones.

Check your answers and review any areas of weakness before going on to the next section.

Perception (Part 1)

Preview Questions

Consider the following questions as you study this section of the chapter.

- What is perception?
- How does bottom-up processing differ from top-down processing?
- What three questions does perception answer about the stimuli we sense?
- Who founded Gestalt psychology, and what is the main focus of this perspective?

Read the section "Perception" (the introduction only) and **write** *your answers to the following:*

1. Perception is the process of _____

    _____

2. Bottom-up processing refers to _____

    _____

    _____

3. Top-down processing refers to _____

    _____

    _____

4. The three basic questions of perception are

    _____

    _____

    _____

5. Gestalt psychology was founded by _____

    _____

    and is concerned with _____

    _____

Perception: The Perception of Shape (Part 2)

Preview Questions

Consider the following questions as you study this section of the chapter.

- What is the figure-ground relationship, and how significant is it to perception?
- What perceptual principles do we follow in determining figure-ground relationships?
- What perceptual principles do we follow when we group visual elements?
- What is the law of Prägnanz, and what does it explain?

*Read the section "Perception: The Perception of Shape" (up to depth perception) and **write** your answers to the following:*

1. The figure-ground relationship describes

   _____

   _____

   _____

   It is important because it demonstrates that

   _____

   _____

2. The perceptual principles involved in grouping

   visual elements are _____

   _____

   _____

3. The law of Prägnanz states _____

   _____

   _____

   _____

   It is important because it encompasses _____

   _____

   and suggests that_____

   _____

   _____

Perception: Depth Perception (Part 3)

Preview Questions

Consider the following questions as you study this section of the chapter.

- Why is depth perception important, and how is it defined?
- What are monocular cues, and how do they contribute to depth perception?
- What are binocular cues, and how do they differ from monocular cues?
- How is binocular disparity involved in our ability to see three-dimensional images in stereograms?

*Read the section "Perception: Depth Perception" (up to motion perception) and **write** your answers to the following:*

1. Depth perception refers to _____

   _____

   It is important because _____

   _____

2. Monocular cues are defined as _____

   _____

   _____

   and include _____

   _____

   _____

3. Binocular cues are defined as _____

   _____

   _____

   and include _____

   _____

4. A stereogram is _____

   _____

Perception: The Perception of Motion (Part 4)

Preview Questions

Consider the following questions as you study this section of the chapter.

- Which sources of information contribute to our perception of motion?
- Who first studied induced motion, and how did he go about demonstrating this phenomenon?
- How does stroboscopic motion work, and how does it relate to the perception of motion?

*Read the section "Perception: The Perception of Motion" (up to perceptual constancies) and **write** your answers to the following:*

1. The perception of motion involves _____

   _____

   _____

   _____

2. Induced motion refers to _____

   _____

   and was first studied by _____

3. Stroboscopic motion creates _____

   _____

   It is caused by   _____

   _____

   _____

   _____

   _____

After you have carefully studied the preceding sections, complete the following exercises.

Concept Check 5

Read the following and write the correct term in the space provided.

1. Dr. Schwartz, whose research focus is perceptual organization, believes that we perceive whole objects or figures rather than isolated bits and pieces of sensory information. Dr. Schwartz is most likely a _____ psychologist.

2. At a noisy party, Ben focuses on his girlfriend's conversation, while tuning out the other conversations. Using a Gestalt perceptual principle to analyze this example, the noisy environment is the _____ and his girlfriend's voice is the _____ .

3. While viewing a stereogram, Nina experiences the perceptual illusion of three-dimensional depth from the two-dimensional scene. The binocular cue responsible for this phenomenon is _____ .

4. Chan knows that the red bicycle in the parking lot is closer to him than the green bicycle because the red one casts a larger retinal image. This illustrates the distance cue known as _____ .

5. Emily paints a long garden pathway bordered with flowers. She shows the flowers as decreasing in size as they approach the horizon, where they seem to meet; Emily is using _____ to convey depth on the canvas.

6. Ricardo uses sequentially flashing Christmas lights in front of his house to make it look as though Santa and his sleigh are moving from the garden to the roof. Ricardo is using the perceptual illusion of _____ .

7. To make the task of completing the jigsaw puzzle more challenging, Zahra attempted to assemble it without the finished picture in front of her. Zahra is most likely to use _____ , or data-driven processing, to accomplish the task.

Review of Terms, Concepts, and Names 5

Use the terms in this list to complete the Matching Test, then to help you answer the True/False items correctly.

perception	depth perception
bottom-up processing (data-driven processing)	monocular cues relative size overlap
top-down processing (conceptually driven processing)	aerial perspective texture gradient linear perspective
extrasensory perception (ESP)	motion parallax pictorial cues
parapsychology	accommodation
Gestalt psychology	binocular cues
Max Wertheimer	convergence
figure-ground relationship	binocular disparity stereogram
figure-ground reversal	induced motion
law of Prägnanz (law of simplicity)	Karl Dunker stroboscopic motion

Matching Exercise

Match the appropriate term with its definition or description.

1. _____ School of psychology founded in Germany in the early 1900s that maintained that our sensations are actively processed according to consistent perceptual rules that result in meaningful whole perceptions.

2. _____ Law that states that when several perceptual organizations are possible, the perceptual interpretation that will occur will be the one that produces the best, simplest, and most stable shape.

3. _____ Monocular cue that suggests that faraway objects often appear hazy or slightly blurred by the atmosphere.

4. _____ Binocular cue that relies on the fact that our eyes are set a couple of inches apart and thus cast slightly different images on the retina of each eye.

5. _____ Gestalt principle of perceptual organization that states that we automatically separate the elements of a perception into the feature that clearly stands out from its less distinct background.

6. _____ Monocular cue in which an object partially blocked or obscured by another object is perceived as being farther away.

7. _____ Distance or depth cues that require the use of both eyes.

8. _____ Monocular cue that utilizes information about changes in the shape of the lens of the eye to help us gauge depth and distance.

9. _____ German Gestalt psychologist who is best known for his studies on the perception of motion.

10. _____ An illusion of movement that results when two separate, carefully timed flashing lights are perceived as one light moving back and forth.

11. _____ The use of visual cues (either monocular or binocular) to perceive the distance or three-dimensional characteristics of objects.

12. _____ The perception of an image in which the ground can be perceived as the figure and the figure as the ground; underscores that our perception of figure and ground is a psychological phenomenon.

13. _____ German psychologist who founded Gestalt psychology in the early 1900s.

14. _____ The scientific investigation of claims of various paranormal phenomena.

True/False Test

Indicate whether each item is true or false by placing T or F in the space next to each item.

1. ____ Perception is defined as the process of integrating, organizing, and interpreting sensory information in a meaningful way.

2. ____ Induced motion occurs because we have a strong tendency to assume that the background is stationary and that it is the object or figure that moves.

3. ____ Relative size is the monocular cue in which an object partially blocked or obscured by another object appears farther away.

4. ____ Monocular cues for distance or depth require information from both eyes.

5. ____ The depth cue that occurs when parallel lines seem to meet in the distance (and the closer together the lines appear to be, the greater the perception of depth) is called linear perspective.

6. ____ Convergence is a binocular cue that relies on the degree to which muscles rotate the eyes to focus on an object; the less convergence, the farther away the object appears to be.

7. ____ When we are in motion, we can use the speed of passing objects to estimate their distance; nearby objects will appear to move much faster relative to distant objects. This monocular cue is called motion parallax.

8. ____ Texture gradient is a binocular cue for distance in which parallel lines seem to meet in the distance and their surface or texture become less clearly defined the farther away they are.

9. ____ Monocular cues used by artists to create the perception of distance or depth in paintings are called pictorial cues.

10. ____ Top-down processing is information processing that emphasizes the importance of sensory receptors in detecting the basic features of

a stimulus in the process of recognizing a whole pattern; it involves analysis from the parts to the whole.

11. ___ A stereogram is a picture that uses the principle of binocular disparity to create the perception of a three-dimensional image.

12. ___ Bottom-up processing is information processing that emphasizes the importance of the observer's knowledge, expectations, and other cognitive processes in arriving at meaningful perceptions and involves analysis from the whole to the parts.

13. ___ Extrasensory perception (ESP) is based on the idea that sensory information can be detected by some means other than through the normal processes of sensation.

Check your answers and review any areas of weakness before going on to the next section.

Perception: Perceptual Constancies (Part 5)

Preview Questions

Consider the following questions as you study this section of the chapter.

- What is perceptual constancy?
- What principles guide our perception of size constancy?
- What are shape constancy and brightness constancy?

*Read the section "Perception: Perceptual Constancies" and **write** your answers to the following:*

1. Perceptual constancy refers to _____

   _____

   _____

2. Size constancy is _____

   _____

   An important aspect of size constancy is _____

   _____

   _____

3. Shape constancy is _____

   _____

   _____

   _____

4. Brightness constancy is _____

   _____

   _____

Perceptual Illusions and the Effects of Experience on Perceptual Interpretations

Preview Questions

Consider the following questions as you study this section of the chapter.

- What are perceptual illusions, and why are psychologists interested in them?
- How are the Müller-Lyer and moon illusions explained?
- How do perceptual sets influence the perceptual conclusions we reach?

*Read the sections "Perceptual Illusions" and "The Effects of Experience on Perceptual Interpretations" and **write** your answers to the following:*

1. Perceptual illusions involve _____

   _____

   _____

2. The Müller-Lyer illusion is _____

   _____

   _____

3. The moon illusion is _____

   _____

   _____

   and may be the result of _____

   _____

   _____

4. Perceptions can be influenced by _____

   _____

   _____

5. A perceptual set is _____

_____

_____

After you have carefully studied the preceding sections, complete the following exercises.

Concept Check 6

Read the following and write the correct term in the space provided.

1. Stereotypes are mental conceptions that we have about individuals belonging to specific racial or ethnic groups and can influence how we interpret their behaviors. Stereotypes are most similar to the perceptual phenomenon of

   _____ .

2. William noticed that the full moon seemed to be much larger on the horizon than when it was overhead. His friend Jane, a psychology major, explained that the illusion results from distance cues that make the horizon moon seem _____ (farther away/closer) than an overhead moon.

3. Your unopened introductory psychology textbook produces a trapezoidal retinal image, but you typically perceive the book as a rectangular object. This is due to _____ constancy.

4. When asked to judge the length of two equal lines, people consistently report the one with outward-pointing arrows as being longer than the one with inward-pointing arrows. These people are experiencing the _____ illusion.

Review of Terms and Concepts 6

Use the terms in this list to complete the Matching Test, then to help you answer the True/False items correctly.

perceptual constancy   perceptual illusion
size constancy   Müller-Lyer illusion
shape constancy   moon illusion
brightness constancy   perceptual set

Matching Exercise

Match the appropriate term with its definition or description.

1. _____ The influence of prior assumptions and expectations on perceptual interpretations.

2. _____ The tendency to perceive objects, especially familiar objects, as constant and unchanging despite changes in sensory input.

3. _____ Famous visual illusion involving the misperception of the identical length of two lines, one with arrows pointed inward and one with arrows pointed outward.

4. _____ The perception of an object as maintaining the same size despite changing images on the retina.

True/False Test

Indicate whether each item is true or false by placing T or F in the space next to each item.

1. ___ A perceptual illusion is the tendency to perceive objects as constant and unchanging despite changes in sensory input.

2. ___ The moon illusion involves the misperception that the moon is larger when it is on the horizon than when it is directly overhead.

3. ___ The perception of a familiar object as maintaining the same shape regardless of the image produced on the retina is called shape constancy.

4. ___ Brightness constancy is the perception that the brightness of an object remains the same even though the lighting conditions change.

Check your answers and review any areas of weakness before going on to the next section.

Something to Think About

1. Many people have reported strange experiences that they interpret as extrasensory perception, or ESP. Suppose that a friend or family member told you about such an experience. This person might be convinced that something extraordinary has occurred. Based on what you have learned in this chapter, how would you go about explaining to them what has most likely taken place?

2. Imagine that you have decided to become an artist. You want to paint a picture that includes a variety of elements such as buildings, fields, a river, a mountain, and some people and animals. Using what you know about sensation and perception, think of all the monocular cues that you could use to give your masterpiece a sense of depth. In addition, can you think of any perceptual components that might add interest to your canvas?

Check your answers and review any areas of weakness before doing the progress tests.

Progress Test 1

Review the complete chapter (including Concept Reviews and all boxed inserts), review all your study notes, and then test yourself on the following progress test. Check your answers. If you make a mistake, review your notes, the appropriate section in the study guide, and if necessary, the relevant part of the chapter in your textbook.

1. Dr. Kandola's research showed that the vibrations of hair cells in the basilar membrane were at the same frequency as the low-frequency sound waves that stimulated them. This research supports the _____ theory of pitch.
   - (a) place
   - (b) frequency
   - (c) timbre
   - (d) amplitude

2. Dr. Frankenstein's younger brother built a monster but omitted a very important part of his anatomy. As a result, the monster cannot transform sounds into neural messages. The missing part is the
   - (a) eardrum.
   - (b) middle ear with its tiny bones.
   - (c) vestibular sacs.
   - (d) basilar membrane.

3. A red pen is displayed in Roger's peripheral vision while he stares straight ahead. He correctly identifies the object but is unable to name the color. The reason for this is that
   - (a) there are many rods but very few cones in the periphery of the retina.
   - (b) there are many cones but very few rods in the periphery of the retina.
   - (c) there are no receptor cells for vision in the periphery of the retina.
   - (d) the stimulus was below Roger's difference threshold.

4. After staring at a blue light for a few minutes, Yoko shifts her gaze to a white wall and experiences an afterimage in the color _____; Yoko's experience provides support for the _____ theory of color vision.
   - (a) red; opponent-process
   - (b) yellow; opponent-process
   - (c) red; trichromatic
   - (d) yellow; trichromatic

5. Neville is color-blind and cannot see red or green, yet he can see blue with no problem. Which theory of color vision can most easily explain this?
   - (a) trichromatic theory
   - (b) place theory
   - (c) opponent-process theory
   - (d) frequency theory

6. Ever since her operation, Madame Burgundi can no longer experience the flavors of the gourmet foods and wines she serves in her restaurant. It is most likely that she has suffered damage to her
   - (a) kinesthetic sense.
   - (b) sense of smell.
   - (c) sense of humor.
   - (d) vestibular sense.

7. The dizziness and disorientation Shelly felt after she rolled down the hill are a function of her
   - (a) basilar membrane.
   - (b) Pacinian corpuscles.
   - (c) semicircular canals and vestibular sacs.
   - (d) proprioceptors.

8. As Pancho gazed down the railway tracks it seemed to him that the two parallel rails actually met in the distance. Pancho is experiencing the monocular depth cue
   - (a) linear perspective.
   - (b) aerial perspective.
   - (c) motion parallax.
   - (d) texture gradient.

9. Many people have mistaken a floating log for Ogopogo, the alleged Okanagan Lake monster. The most likely reason for this misperception is
   - (a) a perceptual set.
   - (b) monocular vision.
   - (c) rye whisky.
   - (d) extrasensory perception.

10. If Fred holds a letter very close to his nose as he reads it and Charlie holds it at arm's length when he reads it, Fred will experience _____ Charlie.
    (a) more convergence than
    (b) the identical level of convergence as
    (c) less convergence than
    (d) more motion parallax than

11. In an experiment, you are seated in a darkened room and shown a large lighted frame with a single dot of light inside it. The frame slowly moves to the left, and the dot remains stationary. It is very probable that you will perceive
    (a) induced motion.
    (b) the dot moving to the right.
    (c) the frame as remaining stationary.
    (d) all of the above.

12. As Demi moves away from the camera, her image on the screen grows smaller and smaller, yet viewers do not perceive Demi as the incredible shrinking woman. This illustrates
    (a) convergence.   (c) size constancy.
    (b) binocular disparity. (d) motion parallax.

13. Dr. DeSilva scientifically investigates claims of telepathy, clairvoyance, and precognition. Dr. DeSilva researches
    (a) gate-control theory.
    (b) parapsychology.
    (c) opponent-process theory.
    (d) Gestalt psychology.

14. Whether perceptual principles are universal and inborn (nativist position) or vary from culture to culture and are influenced by experience and learning (empiricist position) has been the subject of a longstanding debate. According to Culture and Human Behavior 3.4, research using the Müller-Lyer illusion tends to support
    (a) the nativist position.
    (b) the empiricist position.
    (c) neither the nativist nor the empiricist position.
    (d) the nativist position slightly more than the empiricist position.

15. If advertisers were to expose moviegoers to the subliminally flashing words EAT POPCORN and DRINK COKE during a movie
    (a) sales of popcorn and Coke would increase dramatically.
    (b) the moviegoers would feel hungry and thirsty for days after seeing the movie.
    (c) the subliminal messages are not likely to have any discernible effect on the sale of popcorn and Coke.
    (d) the moviegoers will have recurring nightmares involving popcorn and Coke.

Progress Test 2

After you have checked your understanding of the material in Progress Test 1 and have done a complete chapter review with special focus on any areas of weakness, you are ready to further assess your knowledge on Progress Test 2. Check your answers. If you make a mistake, review your notes, the relevant sections of the study guide, and if necessary, review the appropriate parts of your textbook.

1. Detection of stimulus energy is to the interpretation of the information as _____ is to _____ .
    (a) transduction; accommodation
    (b) hue; saturation
    (c) hearing; vision
    (d) sensation; perception

2. When Julius returns from getting a drink of water, he resumes weightlifting a 150-pound free weight and doesn't notice that someone has added a five-pound ring to each end. For Julius the additional ten pounds
    (a) is not a just noticeable difference (jnd).
    (b) is below his absolute threshold.
    (c) is not sensed because of sensory adaptation.
    (d) is easy to lift because water releases endorphins.

3. When Vincent arrived home, the first thing he noticed was the smell of freshly baked bread. The process by which the odor of baking bread was converted into neural signals that Vincent's brain could interpret is called
    (a) sensory adaptation.
    (b) transduction.
    (c) accommodation.
    (d) conduction.

4. In an experimental situation, Malgorzata is able to detect a very small difference in the loudness of two tones. It is very likely that the researchers are investigating
   (a) the difference threshold.
   (b) sensory adaptation.
   (c) the absolute threshold.
   (d) subliminal perception.

5. When Tony was painting a landscape, he used many different colors. The technical term for each of the different wavelengths of light that produce the subjective sensation of different colors in Tony's painting is
   (a) saturation.   (c) brightness.
   (b) hue.   (d) timbre.

6. As Rodney was setting up the equipment for the concert, he adjusted the amplitude of the speaker system. This is most likely to affect the _____ of the music.
   (a) pitch   (c) timbre
   (b) frequency   (d) loudness

7. Eight-year-old Sean can hear sounds close to 20,000 hertz. This sensory capacity is best explained by
   (a) extrasensory perception (ESP) theory.
   (b) opponent-process theory.
   (c) frequency theory.
   (d) place theory.

8. When Derrick removed all visual distance cues, he noticed that the moon on the horizon looked to be the same size as it was when directly overhead. Derrick concluded correctly that the distance cues make the horizon moon seem _____ the overhead moon.
   (a) farther away than   (c) smaller than
   (b) closer than   (d) the same size as

9. In terms of the transduction of physical energy into coded neural messages, the _____ is to the eye as the _____ is to the ear.
   (a) lens; oval window
   (b) fovea; auditory nerve
   (c) retina; cochlea
   (d) iris; eardrum

10. On the day of an important job interview, Madeline wakes up with a slight toothache. As the time for the stressful interview approaches, her anxiety increases and so does her perception of the pain from her tooth. When the interview is over, Madeline is elated because she feels it has gone well and, to her surprise, she feels hardly any pain from her tooth. Madeline's experience is best explained by the _____ theory and the contribution of her psychological and emotional state.
    (a) opponent-process   (c) place
    (b) gate-control   (d) frequency

11. Astrid holds a pencil quite close to her nose and opens and closes her left and right eyes a couple of times in succession. She notices that the images are quite different. When she views the same pencil in a similar manner from across the room, she sees almost identical images. Astrid has demonstrated the _____ cue of _____ .
    (a) binocular; binocular disparity
    (b) monocular; motion parallax
    (c) binocular; overlap
    (d) monocular; convergence

12. With his eyes closed, Shahin can accurately touch his nose, lips, and ears with his right index finger. Shahin's ability to do this is due to specialized sensory neurons called _____ that are involved in his _____ sense.
    (a) Pacinian corpuscles; vestibular
    (b) ganglion cells; visual
    (c) proprioceptors; kinesthetic
    (d) pheromones; olfactory

13. As dusk descends, Carmen thinks that the yellow tulips are just as yellow as they had been earlier when there was more daylight. Despite the changing lighting conditions, Carmen's perception of the color of the flowers did not change. This is best explained by _____ constancy and the fact that objects always reflect the same _____ of available light.
    (a) brightness; amount
    (b) brightness; proportion
    (c) size; degree
    (d) shape; amount

14. According to the Application, the process of learning voluntary control over largely autonomic body functions such as heartbeat, blood pressure, and muscle tension by using specialized sensitive equipment is called
    (a) proprioception.   (c) acupuncture.
    (b) psychokinesis.   (d) biofeedback.

15. Willard believes he can influence the mechanical systems within slot machines with the power of his mind alone. Willard is claiming to possess the power of
    (a) telepathy.   (c) psychokinesis.
    (b) clairvoyance.   (d) precognition.

Progress Test 3

After you have checked your understanding of the material in Progress Tests 1 and 2 and have done a complete chapter review with special focus on any areas of weakness, you are ready to further assess your knowledge on Progress Test 3. Check your answers. If you make a mistake, review your notes, the appropriate parts of the study guide, and if necessary, the relevant sections of your textbook.

1. During a psychology lab demonstration, the instructor set up two flashing lights about three feet apart in a darkened room. About one-tenth of a second after the first light flashed, the second light flashed, and then the first light flashed again, and so on. Most of the students experienced the illusion of apparent motion, perceiving just one light traveling back and forth. The instructor is most likely to explain this phenomenon in terms of
   (a) the principles of stroboscopic motion.
   (b) the kinesthetic sense.
   (c) motion parallax.
   (d) binocular disparity.

2. You have just arrived at the beach and the texture of the sand toward the water appears smooth, even, and perfectly flat, yet the sand beneath your feet is rough and uneven and you can see individual small stones, seashells, and other debris. You are experiencing the monocular distance cue of
   (a) motion parallax.
   (b) aerial perspective.
   (c) linear perspective.
   (d) texture gradient.

3. José notices that near the horizon the moon appears larger than when it is overhead in the sky. The effect is mainly the result of
   (a) distance cues that make the horizon moon seem farther away.
   (b) the retinal image of the horizon moon being larger than the retinal image of the overhead moon.
   (c) distance cues that make the horizon moon seem nearer.
   (d) having to tilt your head upward when looking at the overhead moon.

4. While carrying out a sensory demonstration in which a small object is positioned so that its retinal image would be cast on the exact spot where her optic nerve exits the eye, Deidre should expect the image of the object to
   (a) change to its opposite color.
   (b) look twice as large as it had before.
   (c) produce an afterimage if she shifts her gaze to a white surface.
   (d) disappear from sight.

5. Analysis that moves from the parts to the whole is to _____ as analysis that moves from the whole to the parts is to _____ .
   (a) figure-ground relationship; figure-ground reversal
   (b) bottom-up processing; top-down processing
   (c) size constancy; shape constancy
   (d) the moon illusion; the Müller-Lyer illusion

6. While strolling through the garden, Jamal suddenly noticed the beautiful odor of roses. Jamal is using her _____ sense, and the process by which the odor is converted into neural signals that her brain can understand is called _____ .
   (a) gustatory; saturation
   (b) olfactory: transduction
   (c) gustatory; adaptation
   (d) olfactory; accommodation

7. Whenever Robyn looks at her boyfriend, her pupils dilate. The eye structure responsible for this response is called the
   (a) retina.   (c) iris.
   (b) fovea.   (d) optic disk.

8. When looking carefully at a picture of a country scene we are able to detect fine visual details, especially those that are focused on the fovea. One reason for this visual acuity is that
   (a) the fovea contains rods, which have many individual neural connections to the cortex.
   (b) the fovea contains cones, which have many individual neural connections to the cortex.
   (c) the fovea is the spot where the optic nerve leaves the eye.
   (d) there are only bipolar cells in the fovea, and these are specialized for feature detection.

9. After Jackson has been in the hot tub for a few minutes, he no longer notices how hot the water is. This is because of
   (a) sensory adaptation.
   (b) the just noticeable difference.
   (c) Jackson's thick skin.
   (d) sensory saturation.

10. After playing in a heavy metal rock band for most of his young adult life, Edwin has suffered a significant hearing loss. Unfortunately for Edwin, his hearing problem cannot be helped by a hearing aid. It is most likely that he is suffering from
    (a) damage to the auditory cortex in his left temporal lobe.
    (b) nerve deafness.
    (c) damage to his proprioceptors.
    (d) conduction deafness.

11. Ari is asked to list the parts of the eye that are involved in vision. Which of the following is *not* likely to be on Ari's list?
    (a) the retina   (c) the lens
    (b) ganglion cells   (d) proprioceptors

12. Mehnroosh believes that the size of the just noticeable difference varies depending on its relation to the strength of the original stimulus. Her views are most consistent with
    (a) Weber's law.
    (b) place theory.
    (c) the opponent-process theory.
    (d) gate-control theory.

13. To reduce the experience of pain, Dexter looks away and focuses on a picture on the wall as a nurse sticks a hypodermic needle into his arm. Dexter is using the pain control technique of
    (a) counter-irritation.   (c) biofeedback.
    (b) relaxation.   (d) distraction.

14. Dr. Frederick believes that people living in urban, industrialized environments have a great deal of perceptual experience in judging lines, corners, edges, and other rectangular, manufactured objects, and thus should be more susceptible to the Müller-Lyer illusion than people in cultures whose experience has been primarily with more natural objects. This idea is called
    (a) Weber's law.
    (b) gate-control theory.
    (c) the carpentered-world hypothesis.
    (d) the opponent-process theory.

15. Maxwell is a male pig and, like most male pigs, he releases a chemical substance in the sweat glands to communicate territorial boundaries and sexual receptiveness. Female pigs use their _____ sense to detect these airborne chemical scents called _____ .
    (a) gustatory; vestibulars
    (b) olfactory; pheromones
    (c) gustatory; pheromones
    (d) olfactory; vestibulars

Answers

Introduction: What Are Sensation and Perception?

1. *The primary function of the nervous system is* communication—the transmission of information from one part of the body to another.

2. *Sensation refers to* the detection and basic sensory experience of environmental stimuli, *and perception occurs when* we integrate, organize, and interpret sensory information in a way that is meaningful.

3. *The difference between sensation and perception is* that sensation involves responding to stimulation and transmitting it to the brain, whereas perception involves the organization and interpretation of sensation. However, there is no clear definitive boundary between the two.

Some Basic Principles of Sensation

1. *Sensory receptors help us hear, taste, smell, feel, and see by* using specialized cells called sensory receptors that respond to stimulation by some form of energy.

2. *Transduction is* the process by which a form of physical energy is converted into a coded neural signal that can be processed by the nervous system.

3. *The two types of sensory threshold are* the absolute threshold, which is the smallest possible strength of a stimulus that can be detected half the time, and the difference threshold, which is the smallest possible difference between two stimuli that can be detected half the time.

4. *Another name for difference threshold is* the just noticeable difference (jnd).

5. *Weber's law states* that for each sense, the size of the jnd is a constant proportion of the size of the initial stimulus.

6. *Sensory adaptation occurs because* sensory receptor cells become less responsive to a constant stimulus; it is relative to the duration of exposure.

Concept Check 1

1. absolute

2. sensation; perception

3. Weber's law

4. transduction

5. sensory adaptation

6. absolute; difference

Matching Exercise 1

1. threshold

2. transduction

3. absolute threshold

4. sensory receptors

5. difference threshold

True/False Test 1

1. F	3. T	5. T
2. T	4. F	

Vision: From Light to Sight

1. *The process of seeing begins with* stimulation of visual receptors cells in the eye, which are sensitive to the physical energy of light.

2. *The electromagnetic spectrum is* made up of many different forms of electromagnetic energy, which vary in wavelength; humans are capable of visually detecting only a tiny portion of the spectrum (visual light).

3. *The key structures of the eye are* the cornea, pupil, iris, lens, retina (rods and cones).

4. *The function of rods is to* detect light (but not color); *the function of cones is to* detect color and fine details (most cones are concentrated in the fovea, the point of central focus in the retina).

5. *Bipolar cells process visual information by* collecting information from the rods and cones and funneling it to the ganglion cells, whose bundled axons form the optic nerve; from the optic chiasm (the point of partial crossover of the optic nerves from each eye) information is sent to the thalamus and then on to the visual cortex.

6. *The optic disk is* the point at which the fibers that make up the optic nerve exit the back of the eye and create a blind spot in our field of vision.

7. *Our experience of color involves* three properties of light waves: hue (color), saturation (purity), and brightness (intensity). Different wavelengths correspond to our subjective experience of different colors.

8. *According to the trichromatic theory,* there are three types of cones, each of which is especially sensitive to certain wavelengths: red light (long wavelengths), green light (medium wavelengths), or blue light (short wavelengths); other colors are a result of stimulation of a combination of cones. *This theory explains* the most common form of color blindness, red-green color blindness.

9. *According to the opponent-process theory,* there are four basic colors, which are divided into two pairs of color-sensitive neurons, red-green and blue-yellow (black and white also act as an opposing pair), and when one member of a pair is stimulated, the other member is inhibited. *This theory explains* afterimages.

Concept Check 2

1. white

2. green

3. color; fine detail

4. red

5. red

Graphic Organizer 1

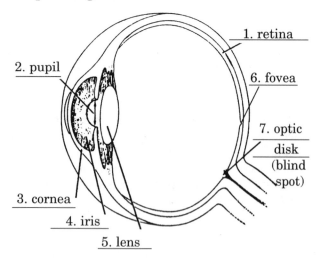

1. retina

2. pupil

6. fovea

7. optic disk (blind spot)

3. cornea

4. iris

5. lens

Matching Exercise 2

1. visual acuity
2. afterimage
3. wavelength
4. accommodation
5. brightness
6. optic nerve
7. trichromatic theory
8. cones
9. hue
10. rods
11. bipolar cells
12. color
13. optic disk

True/False Test 2

1. F	5. F	9. T
2. T	6. T	10. T
3. F	7. T	11. F
4. T	8. F	12. T

Hearing: From Vibration to Sound

1. *Audition is* the technical term for the sense of hearing.

2. *Our perception of sound is directly related to the physical properties of* sound waves and involves intensity (amplitude, measured in decibels), pitch (the relative highness or lowness determined by frequency), and timbre (distinctive quality of a sound).

3. *The key structures of the ear are* the outer ear (pinna, ear canal, and eardrum), the middle ear (the hammer, anvil, and stirrup), and the inner ear (cochlea and semicircular canals).

4. *The process of hearing begins when* sound waves are caught by the outer ear and funneled down the ear canal. *It then involves* the sound waves being amplified in the middle ear and transformed into neural messages by hair cells in the basilar membrane, which runs the length of the cochlea in the inner ear.

5. *According to the frequency theory,* the basilar membrane vibrates at the same frequency as the sound waves. *This theory explains* how low-frequency sounds (up to about 1000 hertz) are transmitted to the brain but cannot explain the transmission of higher-frequency sounds.

6. *According to place theory,* different frequencies cause larger vibrations at different locations along the basilar membrane. *This theory explains* our discrimination of higher pitched sounds, and for intermediate frequencies both place and frequency theories are involved.

Concept Check 3

1. cochlea
2. conduction
3. place
4. hearing aid
5. place

Graphic Organizer 2

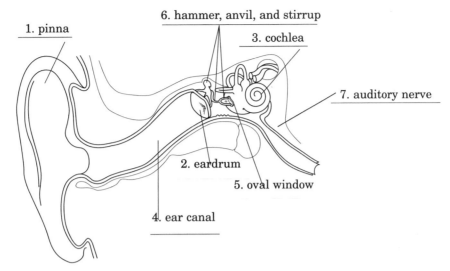

1. pinna
6. hammer, anvil, and stirrup
3. cochlea
7. auditory nerve
2. eardrum
5. oval window
4. ear canal

Matching Exercise 3

1. nerve deafness
2. audition
3. frequency
4. hair cells
5. sound waves
6. timbre
7. outer ear
8. pitch
9. place theory
10. decibels
11. amplitude
12. middle ear

True/False Test 3

1. T	5. T	9. T
2. T	6. T	10. T
3. T	7. F	11. T
4. F	8. T	

The Chemical and Body Senses (Part 1)

1. *Olfaction is the technical term for* the sense of smell, *and gustation is the technical term for* the sense of taste.

2. *They are called chemical senses because* the sensory receptors for taste and smell are specialized to respond to different types of chemical substances.

3. *Our sense of smell begins when* airborne molecules emitted by substances we smell stimulate olfactory receptor cells high in the nasal cavity, *and then involves* the resulting neural mes-sages being passed along the olfactory nerves, which are directly connected to the olfactory bulb (the enlarged ending of the olfactory cortex). From there, the messages pass along the olfactory tract to various brain areas, including the temporal lobe and the limbic system.

4. *Our sense of taste begins when* specialized receptors in the taste buds located on the tongue and inside the mouth and throat are stimulated *and then involves* neural messages being sent along neural pathways to the thalamus, which, in turn, directs the information to several other regions in the brain.

5. *The four primary taste qualities are* sweet, sour, salty, and bitter.

The Chemical and Body Senses (Part 2)

1. *The skin and body senses include* touch, pain, position, and balance.

2. *The skin responds to* stimulation such as pressure, warmth, and cold.

3. *One receptor for touch is* the Pacinian corpuscle, *and it works by* converting pressure stimulation into a neural message that is relayed to the brain. If pressure is constant, sensory adaptation takes place.

4. *Pain is the sensation of* physical discomfort or suffering that can occur in varying degrees of intensity.

5. *According to the gate-control theory,* the sensation of pain is controlled by a series of gates that open (pain is experienced) and close (pain is not experienced) in the spinal cord. It results from both physiological and psychological factors.

6. *The experience of pain is also influenced by* both negative and positive emotions, and by social and cultural learning experiences about the meaning of pain and how people should react to pain.

7. *Our kinesthetic sense involves* stimulation of proprioceptors, which constantly communicate information to the brain about changes in body position and muscle tension, and provide information about the location and position of body parts in relation to one another.

8. *Our vestibular sense provides us with* a sense of balance, or equilibrium, by responding to changes in gravity, motion, and body position.

9. *The two sources of vestibular sensory information are* the semicircular canals and the vestibular sacs, both of which are located in the ear.

Concept Check 4

1. taste buds
2. smell (olfaction)
3. smell (olfaction)
4. sweet; salty; sour; bitter
5. intensify
6. semicircular canals; vestibular sacs
7. pain
8. kinesthetic
9. substance P

Matching Exercise 4

1. gustation
2. vestibular sacs
3. Pacinian corpuscle
4. chemical senses
5. free nerve endings
6. olfactory receptor cells
7. olfactory bulb
8. taste buds
9. olfactory tract
10. vestibular sense
11. endorphins
12. kinesthetic sense

True/False Test 4

1. T	5. F	9. F
2. T	6. T	10. F
3. T	7. T	11. F
4. T	8. T	12. T

Perception (Part 1)

1. *Perception is the process of* integrating, organizing, and interpreting sensory information in a meaningful way.

2. *Bottom-up processing refers to* the flow of information from the sensory receptors to the brain; this type of analysis moves from the parts to the whole (data-driven processing).

3. *Top-down processing refers to* analysis that moves from the whole to the parts; it occurs when we use our knowledge, experience, expectations, and other cognitive processes to arrive at meaningful perceptions (conceptually driven processing).

4. *The three basic questions of perception are* What is it?, How far away is it?, and Where is it going? (Bottom-up and top-down processing are both necessary for arriving at perceptual conclusions.)

5. *Gestalt psychology was founded by* Max Wertheimer *and is concerned with* the fact that we tend to perceive whole objects or figures (gestalts) rather than isolated bits and pieces of sensory information.

Perception: The Perception of Shape (Part 2)

1. *The figure-ground relationship describes* how we automatically separate the elements of perception into the feature that clearly stands out (the figure) and its less distinct background (the ground). *It is important because it demonstrates that* the separation of a scene into figure and ground is not a property of the actual elements in the scene but instead is a psychological accomplishment.

2. *The perceptual principles involved in grouping visual elements are* similarity, closure, good continuation, and proximity.

3. *The law of Prägnanz states* that when several perceptual organizations of an assortment of visual elements are possible, the perceptual interpretation that occurs will be one that produces the best, simplest, and most stable shape (also called the law of simplicity). *It is important because it encompasses* all other Gestalt principles, including the figure-ground relationship *and suggests that* we actively and automatically construct a perception that reveals the essence of something.

Perception: Depth Perception (Part 3)

1. *Depth perception refers to* the ability to perceive the distance of an object as well as its three-dimensional characteristics. *It is important*

because being able to perceive the distance of an object has obvious survival value, especially regarding potential threats or danger.

2. *Monocular cues are defined as* distance or depth cues that can be processed by either eye alone *and include* relative size, overlap, aerial perspective, texture gradient, linear perspective, motion parallax, and accommodation. (Monocular cues used by artists are called pictorial cues.)

3. *Binocular cues are defined as* distance or depth cues that require the use of both eyes *and include* convergence and binocular disparity.

4. *A stereogram is* a picture that uses the principles of binocular disparity to create the perception of a three-dimensional image.

Perception: The Perception of Motion (Part 4)

1. *The perception of motion involves* the integration of information from several sources, including microfine eye muscle movements, the changing retinal image, and the contrast of the moving object with its stationary background.

2. *Induced motion refers to* our strong tendency to assume that the background is stationary and that it is the object or figure that moves. *It was first studied by* Karl Dunker.

3. *Stroboscopic motion creates* an illusion of movement with two carefully timed flashing lights going on and off in succession. *It is caused by* the brain's visual system combining the rapid sequence of visual information (the two lights going on and off and being detected at two different points on the surface of the retina) and arriving at the conclusion of movement, even though no movement has occurred (the perception of smooth motion in movies is due to the same phenomenon).

Concept Check 5

1. Gestalt
2. ground; figure
3. retinal disparity
4. relative size
5. linear perspective
6. stroboscopic motion
7. bottom-up processing

Matching Exercise 5

1. Gestalt psychology
2. law of Prägnanz

3. aerial perspective
4. binocular disparity
5. figure-ground relationship
6. overlap
7. binocular cues
8. accommodation
9. Karl Dunker
10. stroboscopic motion
11. depth perception
12. figure-ground reversal
13. Max Wertheimer
14. parapsychology

True/False Test 5

1. T	6. T	11. T
2. T	7. T	12. F
3. F	8. F	13. T
4. F	9. T	
5. T	10. F	

Perception: Perceptual Constancies (Part 5)

1. *Perceptual constancy refers to* the tendency to perceive objects as unchanging despite changes in sensory input.

2. *Size constancy is* the perception that an object remains the same size despite its changing image on the retina. *An important aspect of size constancy is* that if the retinal image of an object does not change, but the perception of its distance increases, the object is perceived as larger.

3. *Shape constancy is* the tendency to perceive familiar objects as having a fixed shape regardless of the image they cast on the retina.

4. *Brightness constancy is* the perception that the brightness of an object remains the same even though the lighting conditions change.

Perceptual Illusions and the Effects of Experience on Perceptual Interpretations

1. *Perceptual illusions involve* the misperception of a stimulus; they are used to study perceptual principles.

2. *The Müller-Lyer illusion is* a famous illusion involving the misperception of the length of two identical lines, one with arrows pointing outward and one with arrows pointed inward.

3. *The moon illusion is* a visual illusion involving the misperception that the moon is larger when

it is on the horizon than when it is overhead *and may be the result of* the misapplication of the principle of size constancy—distance cues make the horizon moon seem farther away, and thus we perceive the moon as being larger, even though the retinal image of the moon remains constant.

4. *Perceptions can be influenced by* a variety of learning experiences, including educational, cultural, and social factors.

5. *A perceptual set is* the tendency for prior assumptions and expectations to influence our perceptual interpretations.

Concept Check 6

1. perceptual sets
2. farther away
3. shape
4. Müller-Lyer

Matching Exercise 6

1. perceptual set
2. perceptual constancy
3. Müller-Lyer illusion
4. size constancy

True/False Test 6

1. F		3. T
2. T		4. T

Something to Think About

1. First, you would note that these strange experiences happen to many people, that there is nothing particularly unique about them. The problem arises in the way people interpret these experiences. These experiences, of course, do not constitute proof of ESP, no matter how strongly someone believes they do. Two less extraordinary concepts can explain these occurrences: coincidence and the fallacy of positive instances. Coincidence, which refers to an event occurring simply by chance, can account for many of the experiences reported by people. Combine coincidence with our tendency to remember coincidental events that seem to confirm our belief about unusual phenomena—the fallacy of positive instances—and the feeling that something unusual has happened can be very strong, even though there are no rational grounds for it. Finally, there is no strong scientific evidence for the existence of ESP, despite years of intensive study by psychologists interested in this topic. To date, no parapsychology experiment that has claimed to show evidence of ESP has been successfully replicated. This, of course, does not prove conclusively that ESP does not exist; however, although one should keep an open mind, there is not a shred of evidence or any rational reason to believe in its existence.

2. Some of the most common monocular or pictorial cues that are useful in conveying a sense of depth on the canvas are overlap, in which "nearer" objects are depicted as blocking or obscuring more "distant" objects; linear perspective, in which parallel lines are depicted as converging toward the top of the painting, for instance; and texture gradient, in which surfaces that are supposed to be close to the observer have distinct, clearly defined textures and those that are gradually less and less clearly defined depict distance. Relative size and aerial perspective are also useful devices to convey depth.

   To make your picture more interesting you might want to attempt to incorporate some of the elements from impossible figures (such as the Escher drawings) or perceptual illusions.

Progress Test 1

1. b	6. b	11. d
2. d	7. c	12. c
3. a	8. a	13. b
4. b	9. a	14. b
5. a	10. a	15. c

Progress Test 2

1. d	6. d	11. a
2. a	7. d	12. c
3. b	8. a	13. b
4. a	9. c	14. d
5. b	10. b	15. c

Progress Test 3

1. a	6. b	11. d
2. d	7. c	12. a
3. a	8. b	13. d
4. d	9. a	14. c
5. b	10. b	15. b

Consciousness and Its Variations

4

PREVIEW   Reading the section below first will give you a general sense of the chapter's contents and an initial introduction to some of the major concepts and terms. This will prime you for what you are about to read and help you to develop a "cognitive map" that will guide your study of the material in this chapter. Likewise, reading the **preview questions** at the beginning of each major section will improve your ability to understand, learn, and retain the information.

CHAPTER 4 . . . AT A GLANCE   Chapter 4 examines the different forms of human consciousness, beginning with how biological and environmental "clocks" regulate our circadian rhythms and sleep-wake cycles. The discovery of REM sleep and how the EEG is used to measure brain-wave activity are discussed. This is followed by an examination of the different stages of sleep and their associated brain-wave activity and behavioral patterns, including the various sleep disorders. The section concludes with an exploration of dreams and mental activity during sleep. Two major theories of the meaning of dreams and their relevance to psychological and physiological functioning are presented.

Altered states of consciousness are introduced next, and both hypnosis and meditation are discussed in this context. Under hypnosis, profound sensory and perceptual changes may be experienced. This section focuses on phenomena such as posthypnotic suggestion, posthypnotic amnesia, and hypermnesia. Hilgard's notions of dissociation and the hidden observer are examined, and the controversy surrounding how to explain hypnosis is discussed. Finally, meditation is defined, and techniques for inducing a meditative state are presented along with research findings on transcendental meditation, or TM.

The final section of the chapter is concerned with using drugs to alter consciousness. The psychoactive drugs are classified and listed along with their various effects on brain activity and physiological and psychological functioning. Drug dependence, drug tolerance, withdrawal symptoms, and drug abuse are discussed.

Introduction: Consciousness: Experiencing the "Private I"

Preview Questions

Consider the following questions as you study this section of the chapter.

- How is consciousness defined, and what did William James mean by "stream of consciousness"?
- Why was research on consciousness abandoned for a time, and why did it regain legitimacy?

*Read the section "Introduction: Consciousness: Experiencing the 'Private I'" and **write** your answers to the following:*

1. Consciousness is defined as the _____ _____

2. William James's idea of "stream of consciousness" refers to the fact that _____ _____ _____

3. Research on consciousness was abandoned because _____ _____

   Psychologists turned instead to _____ _____

4. Psychologists returned to studying consciousness in the late 1950s for two reasons: _____ _____ _____

The Biological and Environmental "Clocks" Regulating Consciousness

Preview Questions

Consider the following questions as you study this section of the chapter.

- What are circadian rhythms?
- What roles do the suprachiasmatic nucleus (SCN), sunlight, and melatonin play in regulating circadian rhythms?
- How do "free-running" conditions affect circadian rhythms?
- Why do people suffer jet-lag symptoms, and what role does melatonin play in producing these symptoms?

*Read the section "The Biological and Environmental 'Clocks' Regulating Consciousness" and **write** the answers to the following:*

1. Circadian rhythms are _____ _____

2. The suprachiasmatic nucleus (SCN) is _____ _____ _____

   Its role in sleep-wake cycles and other circadian rhythms is to _____ _____ _____

3. Melatonin is a _____ _____

4. Free-running conditions are created by _____ _____

   They have two distinct effects: First, _____ _____

   Second, _____ _____

5. People suffer from jet-lag symptoms because _____ _____

6. Melatonin plays a key role in jet-lag symptoms by _____ _____

After you have carefully studied the preceding sections, complete the following exercises.

Concept Check 1

Read the following and write the correct term in the space provided.

1. Sheena works night shifts and has found that she can sleep quite well during the day now that she has hung heavy curtains in her bedroom that effectively block out any daylight. She is able to get restful sleep in the daytime because her _____ are staying in sync with her night work schedule, and she has prevented sunlight from resetting her _____ .

2. Although Marvin was very tired after pulling an "all-nighter" to finish a paper, he began to feel much less drowsy as the morning proceeded. His reaction is probably due to decreased levels of the hormone

_____ .

3. David typically experiences a slump in his mental alertness around midafternoon but feels very energetic in the early evening. These daily highs and lows are examples of

_____ .

4. During a history lecture, Alfie is listening and taking notes but at times he is also thinking about his girlfriend and the argument they had last night. He wonders what he will say to her when he phones her that afternoon, which gets him thinking about how often his parents fight and whether arguing is genetic, which reminds him about his biology exam next week. This description reflects Alfie's _____ .

5. Dr. Parizeau arranges for volunteers to spend several weeks in underground bunkers without exposure to sunlight, clocks, or other environmental time cues, and during this time he monitors their sleep-wake cycles and other biological changes. Dr. Parizeau is attempting to create _____ in his research on circadian rhythms.

Review of Terms, Concepts, and Names 1

Use the terms in this list to complete the Matching Test, then to help you answer the True/False items correctly.

consciousness
William James
introspection
circadian rhythm
biological clock
suprachiasmatic nucleus
  (SCN)

melatonin
pineal gland
free-running condition
jet lag
biorhythms

Matching Exercise

Match the appropriate term/name with its definition or description:

1. _____Personal awareness of mental activities, internal sensations, and the external environment.

2. _____Subjective verbal reports that try to capture the structure of conscious experience through examining one's present mental state.

3. _____Cluster of neurons in the brain's hypothalamus that governs the timing of circadian rhythms.

4. _____Symptoms such as physical and mental fatigue, depression, irritability, disrupted sleep, and fuzziness in concentration, thinking, and memory that result from circadian rhythms being out of sync with daylight/darkness cues.

5. _____ Hormone manufactured by the pineal gland that produces sleepiness.

6. _____ A pseudoscience based on the unproven notion that from birth onward, three rigidly fixed natural rhythms reflect high, low, and critical periods of a person's physical, emotional, and intellectual functioning.

True/False Test

Indicate whether each statement is true or false by placing T or F in the blank space next to each item.

1. ___ The "biological clock" is another name for the tiny cluster of neurons in the hypothalamus, called the suprachiasmatic nucleus, or SCN.

2. ___ William James was the American psychologist who proposed that psychology should not study consciousness because it could not be objectively investigated; instead, psychology should emphasize the scientific study of overt, observable behavior.

3. ___ The pineal gland is an endocrine gland located in the brain that regulates the production of the hormone melatonin.

4. ___ Researchers have had volunteers live in underground bunkers, depriving them of all environmental time cues for various periods of time, in order to create free-running conditions.

5. ___ Circadian rhythm refers to a cycle or rhythm that is roughly 24 hours long and involves cyclical daily fluctuations in biological and psychological processes.

Check your answers and review any areas of weakness before going on to the next section.

Sleep

Preview Questions

Consider the following questions as you study this section of the chapter.

- How did the invention of the electroencephalograph and the discovery of REM sleep contribute to modern sleep research?
- What are the characteristics of the sleep stages?
- How do sleep patterns change over the lifespan?

*Read the section "Sleep" (up to "Why Do We Sleep?") and **write** your answers to the following:*

1. An electroencephalograph is _____
   _____
   _____

2. By studying EEGs, sleep researchers have established that _____
   _____

3. Use of the EEG led to the discovery of _____
   _____

4. Beta brain waves are associated with _____
   _____

   Alpha brain waves are associated with_____
   _____

5. Hypnagogic hallucinations are _____
   _____

6. The four NREM sleep stages are characterized by different brain and body activity:
   Stage 1 NREM: _____
   _____

   Stage 2 NREM: _____
   _____

   Stage 3 and 4 NREM: _____
   _____

7. REM sleep is characterized by _____
   _____
   _____

8. Over the course of the lifespan, the quantity and quality of our sleep _____
   _____
   _____

Why Do We Sleep?

Preview Questions

Consider the following questions as you study this section of the chapter.

- Why do we need to sleep?
- How do the restorative and adaptive theories of sleep explain the function of sleep?

*Read the section "Why Do We Sleep?" and **write** your answers to the following:*

1. Sleep deprivation studies demonstrate that
   _____
   _____

2. The phenomena of REM and NREM rebound seem to indicate that _____
   _____

3. The restorative theory of sleep suggests that
   _____
   _____

4. The adaptive theory of sleep suggests that
   _____
   _____
   _____

Sleep Disorders: Troubled Sleep

Preview Questions

Consider the following questions as you study this section of the chapter.

- What are sleep disorders, who suffers from them, and how common are they?
- How is insomnia defined?
- What are the characteristics of sleep apnea, sleepwalking, night terrors, REM sleep behavior disorder, and narcolepsy?

*Read the section "Sleep Disorders: Troubled Sleep" and **write** your answers to the following:*

1. Sleep disorders are _____
   _____
   _____
   _____

2. Insomnia is _____
   _____

3. With sleep apnea, _____
   _____

4. Sleepwalking is characterized by _____
   _____

5. A night terror is characterized by _____
   _____
   _____

6. In REM sleep behavior disorder, _____
   _____

7. Narcolepsy is characterized by _____
   _____
   _____

After you have carefully studied the preceding sections, complete the following exercises.

Concept Check 2

Read the following and write the correct term in the space provided.

1. James went to bed a short while ago; although his eyes are closed and he is very relaxed, he has not yet fallen asleep. If James's brain is relatively normal, it is probably generating _____ brain waves.

2. Shortly after falling asleep, James experiences a muscle spasm that jolts him awake. James has most likely experienced the most common hypnagogic hallucination of _____ accompanied by a _____ .

3. Bjorn, who has been under a lot of stress ever since he started college, is having trouble sleep-ing. He repeatedly complains about the quality and duration of his sleep, and worry about not sleeping well often keeps him awake at night. Bjorn is most likely to be diagnosed as suffering from _____ .

4. In an attempt to deal with his sleep disturbance, Bjorn decides to try an over-the-counter sleep medication combined with alcohol. Bjorn's approach is most likely to make his problem _____ (better/worse) in the long run.

5. After being asleep for about 2 hours, eight-year-old Soo Mee suddenly sits up in bed screaming incoherently. Her mother has trouble waking her and calming her down. Soo Mee is experiencing a(n) _____ and is probably in stage _____ or _____ of NREM sleep.

6. Salim is enjoying a night out with a bunch of his college friends at Yuk Yuks comedy club. While laughing heartily at a very funny act, he suddenly goes limp and falls asleep for a few minutes. It is likely that Salim is suffering an attack of _____ and has instantly entered REM sleep and experienced _____ .

7. Mrs. Eastman has just turned 65 and is worried because she is waking up more easily nowadays, sleeps less than 7 hours most nights, and feels less rested and less satisfied after sleeping. A sleep specialist is most likely to say that she _____
   _____ .

8. Azra has been asleep for about ten minutes and is now in stage 2 sleep. Her brain-wave activity is likely to be predominantly _____ waves and to be marked by _____ .

Graphic Organizer 1

The diagram below shows the brain waves typical of each stage in a 90-minute (approximately) sleep cycle. Match the term or description with the correct brain-wave pattern.

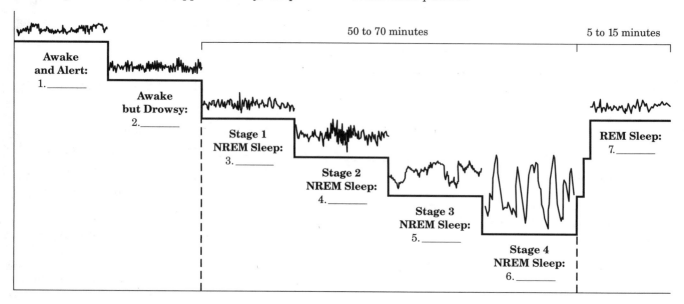

A. Brain waves associated with dreaming

B. Sleep spindles

C. Beta brain waves

D. Mixture of theta and delta brain waves

E. Alpha brain waves

F. Delta brain waves

G. Mixture of alpha and theta brain waves

Review of Terms and Concepts 2

Use the terms in this list to complete the Matching Test, then to help you answer the True/False items correctly.

electroencephalograph
electroencephalogram
  (EEG)
REM sleep (active or
  paradoxical sleep)
NREM sleep (quiet
  sleep)
beta brain waves
alpha brain waves
hypnagogic
  hallucinations
myoclonic jerk
  (sleep starts)
theta brain waves
sleep spindles
slow-wave sleep
delta brain waves
microsleeps
REM rebound

NREM rebound
restorative theory of
  sleep
adaptive (evolutionary)
  theory of sleep
sleep disorders
insomnia
sleepwalking
  (somnambulism)
nocturnal enuresis
night terrors
  (sleep terrors)
sleep bruxism
parasomnias
REM sleep behavior
  disorder
sleep apnea
narcolepsy
sleep paralysis

Matching Exercise

Match the appropriate term with its definition or description.

1. _____ Condition in which a person regularly is unable to fall asleep, stay asleep, or feel adequately rested by sleep.

2. _____ Type of sleep during which rapid eye movements and dreaming occur, and voluntary muscle activity is suppressed; also called active sleep or paradoxical sleep.

3. _____ The view that sleep and dreaming are essential to normal physical and mental functioning.

4. _____ Brain-wave pattern associated with relaxed wakefulness and drowsiness.

5. _____ Sleep disorder in which the person repeatedly stops breathing during sleep.

6. _____ Graphic record of brain activity produced by an electroencephalograph.

7. _____ Short bursts of brain activity that characterize stage 2 NREM sleep.

8. _____ Vivid sensory phenomena that can occur during the onset of sleep.

9. _____ Term applied to the combination of stage 3 and stage 4 sleep.

10. _____ Involuntary muscle spasm of the whole body that jolts the person completely awake and often accompanies the hypnagogic hallucination of falling.

11. _____ Bodily state of narcoleptics when, during a sleep attack, their muscles go limp and they collapse.

12. _____ Sleep disorder in which the sleeper acts out his or her dreams.

13. _____ Phenomenon in which a person who is deprived of REM sleep greatly increases the amount of time spent in REM sleep at the first opportunity for uninterrupted sleep.

14. _____ Instrument that uses electrodes placed on the scalp to measure and record the brain's electrical activity.

True/False Test

Indicate whether each statement is true or false by placing T or F in the blank space next to each item.

1. ___ NREM rebound is a phenomenon in which a person who is deprived of stage 3 and 4 NREM sleep spends less time in these stages when permitted to sleep undisturbed.

2. ___ The adaptive (evolutionary) theory of sleep suggests that unique sleep patterns of different animals evolved over time to help promote survival and environmental adaptation.

3. ___ Sleep disorders are serious disturbances in the normal sleep pattern that interfere with daytime functioning and cause subjective distress.

4. ___ Narcolepsy is a sleep disorder in which the person repeatedly stops breathing during sleep and awakens momentarily.

5. ___ Sleep bruxism is a sleep disorder in which people grind their teeth loudly during sleep.

6. ___ Sleepwalking (somnambulism) is a sleep disturbance characterized by an episode of walking or performing other actions during stage 3 or stage 4 NREM sleep.

7. ___ Parasomnias are sleep disorders characterized by arousal or activation during sleep or sleep transitions; they include sleepwalking, night terrors, sleep bruxism, and REM sleep behavior disorder.

8. ___ Beta brain waves are patterns of electrical activity that begin in stage 1 NREM sleep and predominate in stage 2 NREM sleep.

9. ___ Episodes of sleep lasting only a few seconds that occur during wakefulness are called microsleeps; they can occur after as little as one day's sleep deprivation.

10. ___ Night terrors typically occur during stage 3 or stage 4 NREM sleep and are characterized by increased physiological arousal, intense fear and panic, frightening hallucinations, and with no recall of the episode the next morning.

11. ___ NREM sleep is quiet sleep, which is divided into four stages and does not involve dreaming.

12. ___ Theta brain waves are small, fast waves of electrical activity in the brain that reflect an awake and reasonably alert state of consciousness.

13. ___ *Nocturnal enuresis* is another name for night terrors or sleep terrors.

14. ___ Delta brain waves are the long, slow waves associated with stage 3 and stage 4 of NREM sleep.

Check your answers and review any areas of weakness before going on to the next section.

Dreams and Mental Activity During Sleep

Preview Questions

Consider the following questions as you study this section of the chapter.

- What is the difference between sleep thinking and dreaming?

- What are the main characteristics of dreams, and what are the most common themes in dreams?

- Why do we remember some dreams and forget others?

- How does Freud's theory of the meaning of dreams differ from the activation-synthesis model?

- What conclusions can we draw about the meaning of dreams?

*Read the section "Dreams and Mental Activity During Sleep" and **write** your answers to the following:*

1. Sleep thinking refers to_____

_____

whereas a dream is _____

_____

2. The main characteristics of dreams are

_____

_____

_____

3. Most dreams are _____

_____

_____

with the most common themes being _____

_____

_____

4. We are most likely to remember a dream if

_____

_____

5. We are more likely to forget dreams because

_____

_____

_____

6. Freud's explanation for dreams suggests that

_____

_____

7. The manifest content refers to _____

_____

The latent content is the _____

_____

8. The activation-synthesis model of dreaming

maintains that _____

_____

9. Current research concludes that dreams reflect

_____

_____

_____

_____

***After you have carefully studied the preceding
section, complete the following exercises.***

_____

Concept Check 3

*Read the following and write the correct term in the
space provided.*

1. Meredith recalls having a dream about dancing
in a ballet with a very big, strong, muscled
male dancer when suddenly the music switches
to loud rock music and the man disappears.
According to Freud, Meredith's account represents the _____ of the
dream.

2. Dr. Dormo believes that Meredith's dream could
be the result of a burst of neural activity that
spread upward from the brain stem and activated more sophisticated brain areas. This
interpretation is most consistent with the
_____ model of dreaming.

3. After falling asleep, Ricardo finds that his mind
keeps returning to the material he has been
studying all day in preparation for his exam the
next morning. Ricardo is experiencing the most
common form of mental activity during sleep,
called _____ .

4. Dr. Roach is a cross-cultural psychologist interested in investigating sleep and dreams. His
cross-cultural data are likely to show that the
dreams of people in various parts of the world
have _____ (common/no common)
themes.

5. Maxwell claims that he has no recollection of
any dream when he wakes up in the morning,
and he is convinced that he never dreams. One
way to demonstrate to Maxwell that he does
dream is to wake him up after he has been
asleep for about _____ minutes,
when he is clearly in _____ sleep.

6. After a visit to the natural history museum,
young Jamila had a very scary dream about
dinosaurs, which caused her to wake up in a
very frightened state. Jamila has experienced
an unpleasant anxiety dream called a(n)

_____ .

Review of Terms, Concepts, and Names 3

Use the terms in this list to complete the Matching Test, then to help you answer the True/False items correctly.

sleep thinking
dream
nightmare
Sigmund Freud
manifest content
latent content

J. Allan Hobson
Robert McCarley
activation-synthesis
    model
lucid dream

Matching Exercise

Match the appropriate term/name with its definition or description:

1. _____ Contemporary American psychiatrist and neurobiologist who extensively researched sleep and dreaming; proposed the activation-synthesis model of dreaming with coresearcher Robert McCarley.

2. _____ The founder of psychoanalysis, who proposed that dream images are disguised and symbolic expressions of unconscious wishes and urges.

3. _____ Repetitive, bland, and uncreative ruminations about real-life events during sleep.

4. _____ Contemporary American psychiatrist and neuroscientist who extensively researched sleep and dreaming; proposed the activation-synthesis model of dreaming with coresearcher J. Allan Hobson.

5. _____ Dream in which the sleeper is aware that he or she is dreaming.

True/False Test

Indicate whether each item is true or false by placing T or F in the space next to each item

1. ___ A nightmare is a frightening or unpleasant anxiety dream that occurs during REM sleep.

2. ___ In Freud's psychoanalytic theory, the latent content of a dream refers to the elements that are consciously experienced and remembered by the dreamer.

3. ___ A dream is a storylike episode of unfolding mental imagery during sleep.

4. ___ The activation-synthesis model of dreaming states that brain activity during sleep produces dream images (*activation*), which are combined by the brain into a dream story (*synthesis*).

5. ___ In Freud's psychoanalytic theory, the manifest content of a dream refers to the unconscious wishes, thoughts, and urges that are concealed in the latent content of a dream.

Check your answers and review any areas of weakness before going on to the next section.

Hypnosis

Preview Questions

Consider the following questions as you study this section of the chapter.

- What is hypnosis, and what are the characteristics of the hypnotic state?

- What are the main characteristics of people who are susceptible to hypnosis?

- What are the effects of hypnosis, and what are its limits?

- How has hypnosis been explained?

*Read the section "Hypnosis" and **write** your answers to the following:*

1. Hypnosis is a _____
_____

2. Hypnosis is characterized by _____
_____
_____
_____
_____

3. The best candidates for hypnosis are _____
_____
_____
_____

4. The effects of hypnosis include _____
_____
_____
_____
_____

5. The limits of hypnosis are that_____
_____
_____
_____

6. Hilgard's neodissociation theory of hypnosis suggests that _____

_____

_____

_____

Meditation

Preview Questions

Consider the following questions as you study this section of the chapter.

- What is meditation, and what is it intended to accomplish?
- What are the two general categories of meditation?
- What are the effects of meditation?

*Read the section "Meditation" and **write** your answers to the following:*

1. Meditation refers to _____

_____

_____

2. The two general types of meditation differ in that _____

_____

_____

_____

_____

3. The effects of meditation include _____

_____

_____

_____

After you have carefully studied the preceding sections, complete the following exercises.

Concept Check 4

Read the following and write the correct term in the space provided.

1. Janna quickly becomes deeply absorbed while reading novels or watching movies. It is very likely that Janna is among the 15 percent of adults who are _____ to hypnosis.

2. While under hypnosis, Karl describes a very frightening experience of being lost at the fairground when he was 6 years old. When his therapist makes the suggestion that Karl will soon forget this traumatic event, he is attempting to induce _____ .

3. During every final exam period, Declan gets very uptight and anxious. At the suggestion of a friend, he has tried using a meditation technique in which he focuses his awareness and attention by repeating a simple phrase over and over to himself. Declan is using a _____ technique of meditation.

4. A researcher suggests to a hypnotized subject that the letter D does not exist. After being brought out of the trance, the subject is asked to recite the alphabet; when she does, she skips the letter D. This example illustrates the use of

_____ .

5. An eyewitness to a robbery (who couldn't remember much of the incident) was hypnotized. When the hypnotherapist suggested that there had been three white men and one black woman involved in the robbery, the subject agreed and described them in some detail. All the other five witnesses reported that only one white male robber was involved. The hypnotherapist has created a

_____ .

6. Lynda has an irrational fear and dislike of cats but has no conscious memory of when or how her phobia developed. In an attempt to enhance her memory, Lynda's therapist hypnotizes her. If the hypnotic suggestions actually work, this would demonstrate _____ .

Review of Terms, Concepts, and Names 4

Use the terms in this list to complete the Matching Test, then to help you answer the True/False items correctly.

hypnosis
posthypnotic suggestion
posthypnotic amnesia
hypermnesia
pseudomemory
Ernest R. Hilgard
dissociation

neodissociation theory of hypnosis
hidden observer
meditation
concentration technique
opening-up techniques
transcendental meditation (TM)

Matching Exercise

Match the appropriate term/name with its definition or description.

1. _____ Ernest Hilgard's theory that attributes hypnotic effects to the splitting of consciousness into two simultaneous streams of mental activity, only one of which is unavailable to the consciousness of the hypnotized subject.

2. _____ Meditative technique that has been widely used in research in which practitioners sit quietly with eyes closed, mentally repeat the mantra they have been given, and practice a strategy for getting rid of distracting thoughts.

3. _____ A cooperative social interaction in which the hypnotized person responds to the hypnotist's suggestions with changes in perception, memory, and behavior.

4. _____ The splitting of consciousness into two or more simultaneous streams of mental activity.

5. _____ Suggestion made during hypnosis that the person carry out a specific instruction following the hypnotic session.

6. _____ Hypnotic suggestion that supposedly enhances the person's memory for past events.

7. _____ Hilgard's term for the hidden, or dissociated, stream of mental activity during hypnosis.

True/False Test

Indicate whether each item is true or false by placing T or F in the space next to each item.

1. ___ Ernest Hilgard was an Austrian physician who discovered "animal magnetism" and whose pioneering work is associated with the origins of hypnotism.

2. ___ A concentration meditative technique involves a present-centered awareness of the passing moment without mental judgment and does not involve concentrating on a mantra or object or activity.

3. ___ In posthypnotic amnesia, the result of a posthypnotic suggestion, the subject is unable to recall specific information or events that occurred before or during hypnosis.

4. ___ Pseudomemories are false memories (even though the person may be very confident that the memories are real) that result when suggestions are made during hypnosis that create distortions and inaccuracies in recall.

5. ___ The opening-up meditative techniques involve focusing awareness on a visual image or your breathing, or mentally repeating a sound called a mantra.

6. ___ Meditation is any of a number of sustained concentration techniques that focus attention and heighten awareness.

Check your answers and review any areas of weakness before going on to the next section.

Psychoactive Drugs

Preview Questions

Consider the following questions as you study this section of the chapter.

- What are psychoactive drugs, and what properties do they have in common?
- How do depressants work, and what effects do alcohol, barbiturates, and tranquilizers have?
- What are opiates, and what effects do they have?
- How do stimulants affect the brain and psychological functioning?
- How do the most common psychedelic drugs influence perception, mood, and thinking?

*Read the section "Psychoactive Drugs" and **write** your answers to the following:*

1. Psychoactive drugs are _____
   _____

2. Addiction is a broad term that refers to _____
   _____

   More specific terms for addiction-related conditions are _____
   _____

3. The effects of a drug may be influenced by
   _____
   _____
   _____

4. Depressants have several effects; they
   _____
   _____

   Examples include _____
   _____

5. Alcohol depresses _____
   _____

   and impairs _____
   _____
   _____
   _____

6. Barbiturates are depressant drugs that _____
   _____
   _____

7. Tranquilizers are depressants that _____
   _____
   _____

8. The opiates are a group of addictive drugs that
   _____
   _____

   Examples include _____
   _____

9. Stimulant drugs _____
   _____

   Examples include _____
   _____

10. The psychedelic drugs create _____
    _____
    _____

    Examples include _____
    _____

11. Marijuana and its active ingredient, THC,
    produce _____
    _____
    _____

    THC has been shown to be useful in _____
    _____
    _____

After you have carefully studied the preceding section, complete the following exercises.

Concept Check 5

Read the following and write the correct term in the space provided.

1. Sian regularly drinks five or six cups of strong coffee a day. If she is like most people, she would probably be surprised to find out that caffeine is a _____ drug and is _____ addictive.

2. Zachary has been using a mood-altering, euphoria-enhancing psychoactive drug; with continued use, he needs to take larger and larger doses in order to experience its original effects. Zachary is developing _____ for the drug.

3. At a party where he has had too much to drink, the normally shy Darryl keeps people entertained for quite a while with his silly antics. Darryl's unusual behavior is probably caused by the fact that alcohol lessens inhibitions by depressing the brain centers responsible for _____ and _____ .

4. If he continues drinking at the party, Darryl will probably lose his coordination and balance; the next day, he might _____ (remember/not remember) very clearly the events of the evening before.

5. While undergoing chemotherapy for cancer, Brendan is given marijuana to help prevent nausea and vomiting. It is very likely that Brendan _____ (will/will not) develop tolerance and physical dependence.

6. Dora has been suffering from severe anxiety, so her doctor prescribes a depressant drug called Valium, which is a commonly prescribed

_____ .

7. Shortly after "snorting" an illegal psychoactive drug, Samuel experiences intense euphoria, mental alertness, and self-confidence that lasts for several minutes. It is most likely that Samuel has inhaled the stimulant drug

_____ .

Graphic Organizer 2

Read the following examples, identify the drug involved, and indicate the type of drug it is.

Example	Drug Name	Drug Class
1. During a party Jordy becomes less and less inhibited as the night wears on, and by the time the party is nearly over, he is very uncoordinated and unbalanced and has trouble walking.		
2. After taking her prescription drug for a number of weeks, Janet no longer feels the intense anxiety she used to suffer.		
3. Mrs. Smothers, who suffers from glaucoma, and Mr. Hartley, who has asthma, have both been given an ordinarily illegal drug at the university hospital.		
4. Harold has used a powerful synthetic drug for a number of years to create sensory and perceptual distortions and to alter his mood, but now he is experiencing flashbacks, depression, and occasional psychotic reactions.		
5. Henrietta was a very heavy coffee drinker until she quit cold turkey. She is now experiencing headaches, irritability, drowsiness, and fatigue.		
6. Following surgery, Gregory was given a common prescription drug under medical supervision in order to alleviate his pain.		
7. Just before his exam, Juan smokes a couple of cigarettes and finds he is less tired, more mentally alert, and yet fairly relaxed.		

Review of Terms and Concepts 5

Use the terms in this list to complete the Matching Test, then to help you answer the True/False items correctly.

psychoactive drug
physical dependence
tolerance
withdrawal symptoms
drug-rebound effect
drug abuse
depressants
binge-drinking
delirium tremens (DTs)
barbiturates
tranquilizers
opiates (narcotics)
opium
morphine
stimulants

caffeine
nicotine
amphetamines
cocaine
stimulant-induced
   psychosis
psychedelic drugs
mescaline
LSD
psilocybin
marijuana
THC
hashish
sleep inertia
   (morning brain fog)

Matching Exercise

Match the appropriate term with its definition or description.

1. _____ The active ingredient of marijuana and other preparations derived from the hemp plant.

2. _____ Category of psychoactive drugs that depress or inhibit brain activity.

3. _____ Stimulant drug found in tobacco products.

4. _____ Recurrent drug use that results in disruptions in academic, social, or occupational functioning or in legal or psychological problems.

5. _____ Drug that alters normal consciousness, perception, mood, and behavior.

6. _____ Schizophrenia-like symptoms that can occur as the result of prolonged amphetamine or cocaine use.

7. _____ Psychedelic drug derived from the peyote cactus.

8. _____ Condition in which increasing amounts of a physically addictive drug are needed to produce the original, desired effect.

9. _____ Potent form of marijuana made from the resin of the hemp plant.

10. _____ Unpleasant physical reactions, combined with intense drug cravings, that occur when a person abstains from a drug on which he or she is physically dependent.

11. _____ Stimulant drug derived from the coca tree.

12. _____ Class of stimulant drugs that arouse the central nervous system and suppress appetite.

13. _____ The collective term for withdrawal symptoms associated with high levels of alcohol dependence; may involve confusion, hallucinations, severe tremors, or seizures.

14. _____ Feelings of grogginess upon waking from sleep that interfere with the ability to perform mental or physical tasks.

True/False Test

Indicate whether each item is true or false by placing T or F in the space next to each item.

1. ___ Marijuana is a psychoactive drug derived from the hemp plant.

2. ___ Barbiturates are a category of depressant drugs that reduce anxiety and produce sleepiness.

3. ___ When withdrawal symptoms occur that are the opposite of a physically addictive drug's action, this is referred to as the drug-rebound effect.

4. ___ Caffeine is the stimulant drug found in tobacco products.

5. ___ Opium is a natural opiate derived from the opium poppy.

6. ___ Binge-drinking is defined as five or more drinks in a row for men, or four or more drinks in a row for women.

7. ___ Psilocybin is a psychedelic drug derived from the psilocybe mushroom, which is sometimes called "magic mushroom."

8. ___ LSD is the active ingredient of marijuana and other preparations derived from the hemp plant.

9. ___ Morphine is the active ingredient of the natural opiate called opium.

10. ___ Tranquilizers such as Valium and Librium are depressants that are prescribed to relieve anxiety.

11. ___ Psychedelic drugs are a category of psychoactive drugs that increase brain activity, as reflected in aroused behavior and increased mental alertness.

12. ___ Physical dependence is a condition in which a person has physically adapted to a drug so that the person must take the drug regularly in order to avoid withdrawal symptoms.

13. ___ Opiates are a category of psychoactive drugs that are chemically similar to morphine and have strong pain-relieving properties.

14. ___ Stimulants are a category of psychoactive drugs that create sensory and perceptual distortions, alter mood, and affect judgment by altering brain chemistry or activity.

Check your answers and review any areas of weakness before going on to the next section.

Something to Think About

1. We've all heard the complaint, "there's so much to do, and so little time!" When people are busy and feel pressured, they often end up sleep-deprived, making them less efficient or productive than well-rested people. More important, they are more likely to make potentially dangerous mistakes. Those most at risk are shift workers or people who suffer jet-lag symptoms for other reasons.

   Imagine you are a consultant and have been asked to prepare a report for an organization concerned with these problems among its employees. Based on what you have learned about the sleep-wake cycle, circadian rhythms, biological and environmental clocks, and so on, what would you recommend in your report?

2. Almost everybody has some fascination with dreams and what they mean. Some people believe that dreams can foretell the future or are important in other mysterious ways. Suppose a friend tells you that she has dreamed that she could not understand a single question on a very important math exam. She just stared at the exam until the professor announced the exam was over and removed the paper from in front of her. At this point, she awoke in a very anxious state. Now she is worried that when she takes the real exam next week, her dream will come true. What would you say to her about dreams and their meaning, lucid dreaming, theories of dreams, and such?

Check your answers and review any areas of weakness before doing the progress tests.

Progress Test 1

Review the complete chapter (including Concept Reviews and the boxed inserts), review all your study notes, and then test yourself on the following progress test. Check your answers. If you make a mistake, review your notes, the relevant section of the study guide, and, if necessary, go back and read the appropriate part of your textbook.

1. Nightmares are to _____ as night terrors are to _____ .
   (a) sleep spindles; beta waves
   (b) alpha waves; beta waves
   (c) REM sleep; slow-wave NREM sleep
   (d) slow-wave NREM sleep; REM sleep

2. Bernita witnessed a robbery, but her recall of the event was vague. Police investigators therefore used hypnosis in an attempt to enhance her memory. The hypnotic effect that the investigators hope for is called _____ , which research shows is _____ to be successful.
   (a) hypermnesia; very likely
   (b) posthypnotic suggestion; not very likely
   (c) hypermnesia; not very likely
   (d) posthypnotic suggestion; very likely

3. After ingesting a small dose of a psychoactive drug, Graham experiences vivid visual hallucinations and other perceptual distortions; he feels as if he is floating above his body. Graham is most likely experiencing the effects of
   (a) cocaine.   (d) LSD.
   (b) barbiturates.   (e) cappuccino.
   (c) tranquilizers.

4. "Consciousness is like a stream or river; it is continuous and cannot be divided or broken down into component parts." The person most likely to have made that statement is
   (a) Sigmund Freud.   (c) Ernest Hilgard.
   (b) William James.   (d) J. Allan Hobson.

5. After flying from San Diego to New York, Jasmine experiences a restless, sleepless night; the next day, she is irritable and cannot concentrate on her work. Jasmine's problems are likely due to
   (a) disruption in her circadian rhythms.
   (b) high blood levels of melatonin.
   (c) jet lag.
   (d) all of the above.

6. Justine believes that dreaming is simply our subjective awareness of the brain's internally generated signals during sleep, which start with automatic activation of brain stem circuits that then arouse more sophisticated brain areas. Justine's views are most consistent with which theory of dreams?
   (a) adaptive theory
   (b) restorative theory
   (c) activation-synthesis theory
   (d) wish-fulfillment theory

7. In order to find out what goes on in people's brains during a typical night's sleep, researchers are most likely to
   (a) ask people to try to remember as much as possible when they awake in the morning
   (b) closely watch the actions of subjects sleeping in the sleep research lab.
   (c) wake people up every fifteen minutes and ask them what is going on in their mind.
   (d) use an electroencephalograph to measure their brain-wave activity throughout the night.

8. Just as you are about to fall asleep, you have the sudden feeling of falling and your body gives an involuntary spasm. You have experienced
   (a) a sleep spindle.
   (b) a myoclonic jerk.
   (c) sleep apnea.
   (d) a microsleep.

9. Harry has been asleep for about an hour or so, and his heart begins to beat faster, his breathing becomes irregular, his voluntary-muscle activity is suppressed, and his closed eyes move rapidly back and forth. It is most probable that Harry is in _____ and is therefore experiencing _____ .
   (a) REM sleep; a myoclonic jerk
   (b) NREM: sleep spindles
   (c) REM; paradoxical sleep
   (d) NREM; quiet sleep

10. Eight-year-old Billy gets out of bed at 1 A.M. and starts to sleepwalk. He is most likely
   (a) in slow-wave stage 3 or 4 NREM sleep.
   (b) suffering from narcolepsy.
   (c) in REM sleep.
   (d) suffering from sleep apnea.

11. After Zufina has been asleep for a period of time in the sleep lab, the EEG monitor indicates the presence of theta waves and sleep spindles. Zufina is in _____ sleep.
   (a) stage 3 NREM   (c) stage 2 NREM
   (b) REM   (d) stage 4 NREM

12. Mr. Jensen repeatedly complains about the quality and duration of his sleep; he claims that he can't fall asleep and stay asleep and usually wakes up before it is time to get up. Mr. Jensen apparently suffers from
   (a) sleep apnea.   (c) nocturnal enuresis.
   (b) narcolepsy.   (d) insomnia.

13. People have no problem staying up a little later each night on the weekend. The most likely explanation for this is that
   (a) the SCN naturally tends toward a 25-hour day.
   (b) the SCN naturally tends toward a 23-hour day.
   (c) there are no obvious environmental time cues during the weekend.
   (d) there are much better late-night movies on TV during the weekend.

14. According to the Application, Improving Sleep and Mental Alertness, sleep inertia refers to
   (a) feelings of grogginess upon awakening from sleep that interfere with the ability to perform mental or physical tasks.
   (b) a sleep disorder in which the person stops breathing during sleep and awakens momentarily, only to return immediately to sleep.
   (c) the paralysis that accompanies stage 3 and 4 deep sleep.
   (d) the sudden involuntary spasm of the whole body during stage 1 sleep.

15. According to Critical Thinking 4.4, _____ theory suggests that hypnotic subjects are responding to social demands by acting the way they think good hypnotic subjects should act and by conforming to expectations and situational cues.
   (a) neodissociation   (c) activation-synthesis
   (b) social-cognitive   (d) adaptive

Progress Test 2

After you have checked your understanding of the material in Progress Test 1 and have done a complete chapter review with special focus on any areas of weakness, you are now ready to assess your knowledge in Progress Test 2. Check your answers. If you make a mistake, review your notes, the relevant section of the study guide, and, if necessary, the appropriate part of your textbook.

1. Dr. Benjamin hypnotizes a client and suggests that she will no longer feel a craving for chocolates. Dr. Benjamin is making use of
   (a) posthypnotic suggestion.
   (b) hypermnesia.
   (c) posthypnotic amnesia.
   (d) meditation.

2. Amber sits in a relaxed position, closes her eyes, and begins to recite her mantra. Amber is practicing
   (a) hypnosis.   (d) dissociation.
   (b) meditation.   (e) laziness.
   (c) sleep inertia.

3. Researchers who have found evidence that subjects appear to have a "hidden observer" are likely to suggest that hypnosis involves
   (a) dissociation.
   (b) social factors.
   (c) stages 3 and 4 NREM sleep.
   (d) experimenter bias.

4. John drinks five or six cups of coffee every day; if he doesn't, he feels irritable, drowsy, and fatigued. John is _____ a(n) _____ drug.
   (a) addicted to; psychedelic
   (b) physically dependent on; opiate
   (c) addicted to; depressant
   (d) physically dependent on; stimulant

5. Richard has just finished his fourth night shift and is driving home from work in the bright morning light. The most likely effect of this exposure is that
   (a) the bright light will reset his body clock to a day schedule.
   (b) he will become very drowsy and sleepy.
   (c) he will experience an increase in the production of melatonin.
   (d) all of the above will occur.

6. Nancy's parents took her to the doctor because she grinds her teeth loudly in her sleep. The doctor is likely to diagnose her with _____ called _____ .
   (a) a parasomnia; nocturnal enuresis
   (b) a hypermnesia; somnambulism
   (c) a parasomnia; sleep bruxism
   (d) a hypermnesia; sleep inertia

7. Phelan has just had a very painful operation. His doctors are most likely to prescribe _____ for pain relief.
   (a) a tranquilizer   (c) morphine
   (b) marijuana   (d) alcohol

8. Mr. Godfrey has cancer and was given marijuana to counter the nausea and vomiting following chemotherapy. The active ingredient that makes this a useful drug in such cases is
   (a) psilocybin.   (c) LSD.
   (b) cannabis.   (d) THC.

9. Sleep researchers deprive subjects of REM sleep for a number of nights but allow them an otherwise normal sleep; the subjects are likely to experience _____ when next allowed to sleep uninterrupted.
   (a) narcolepsy   (c) sleep inertia
   (b) REM rebound   (d) NREM rebound

10. Harold dreams that he is on a train traveling through mountains in what he thinks is Switzerland. He can see the train very clearly going in and out of tunnels over and over again. Harold's therapist suggests that the dream is not about travel in a foreign country but about Harold's concern with his sexual performance. The therapist adheres to the _____ theory of dreams and is attempting to reveal the _____ of Harold's dream.
    (a) evolutionary; adaptive aspects
    (b) Freud's wish fulfillment; manifest content
    (c) Freud's wish fulfillment; latent content
    (d) activation-synthesis; restorative aspects

11. During a very intense game of pool, Gary attempts a very difficult shot that will win him the game when he suddenly collapses and falls fast asleep on the pool table. Gary probably suffers from _____ and is experiencing _____ .
    (a) sleep apnea; sleep paralysis
    (b) narcolepsy; a sleep attack
    (c) insomnia; sleep inertia
    (d) REM sleep behavior disorder; sleep paralysis

12. Nicotine is to alcohol as a _____ drug is to a _____
    (a) stimulant; depressant
    (b) psychedelic; stimulant
    (c) depressant; stimulant
    (d) depressant; psychedelic

13. Dr. Tirian's research is concerned with the effects of psychedelic drugs on brain functioning. Which of the following is she most likely to test in her experiments?
    (a) LSD, psilocybin, and mescaline
    (b) amphetamines and cocaine
    (c) alcohol, nicotine, and caffeine
    (d) barbiturates and tranquilizers

14. According to In Focus 4.2, which of the following is true?
    (a) Research suggests that very low levels of a naturally occurring compound in the body called adenosine cause sleepiness.
    (b) It is extremely dangerous to awaken a sleepwalker.
    (c) If you dream you are falling and you hit the ground, you will wake up dead.
    (d) In a relatively common phenomenon called sleep paralysis, the paralysis of REM sleep carries over to the waking state for up to 10 minutes.

15. According to In Focus 4.3, What You Really Want to Know About Dreams, which of the following is true?
    (a) People who have been blind all their lives don't dream.
    (b) Up until the widespread use of color TV, most people dreamed in black and white.
    (c) Virtually all mammals experience sleep cycles in which REM sleep alternates with slow-wave NREM sleep, and it is reasonable to conclude that they all experience dreams.
    (d) People who frequently experience lucid dreams have more nightmares than normal because they have little or no control over their dreams.

Progress Test 3

After you have checked your understanding of the material in Progress Tests 1 and 2, and have done a complete chapter review with special focus on any areas of weakness, you are ready to further assess your knowledge on Progress Test 3. Check your answers. If you make a mistake, review your notes, the appropriate parts of the study guide, and if necessary, the relevant sections of your textbook.

1. Mrs. Cadogan complains that her overweight 65-year-old husband snores and snorts throughout the night and appears to be gasping for breath. She notes that this happens most often when he is sleeping on his back. Mr. Cadogan suffers from
    (a) sleep apnea.   (c) sleep inertia.
    (b) sleep terrors.   (d) sleep bruxism.

2. Dr. Gerhardt believes that sleep promotes physiological processes that repair and rejuvenate the body and mind. Dr. Gerhardt's view is consistent with the _____ theory of sleep.
    (a) evolutionary
    (b) activation-synthesis
    (c) wish-fulfillment
    (d) restorative

3. Brianna, who has a very warm, loving relationship with her husband, dreamed that she had an intense, emotional argument with him in which she shouted and screamed and called him horrible names. Her psychoanalyst suggested that Brianna must have some deeply repressed anger and frustration toward her father that is expressed symbolically in the dream about her husband. Brianna's account of the dream represents the _____ , and her therapist's account represents the _____ .
    (a) latent content; manifest content
    (b) activation phase; synthesis phase
    (c) manifest content; latent content
    (d) synthesis phase; activation phase

4. Stage 2 sleep is to _____ as stage 4 is to _____ .
    (a) beta waves; alpha waves
    (b) alpha waves; beta waves
    (c) sleep spindles; delta waves
    (d) dreams; nightmares

5. Dr. Hayward uses hypnosis on a patient during a root canal procedure. When he asks her to raise her hand if some part of her can feel pain, she raises her hand. This illustrates

   (a) the hidden observer.
   (b) paradoxical sleep.
   (c) posthypnotic amnesia.
   (d) tolerance.

6. In a class discussion of sleep and dreams, Anouk suggests that different sleep patterns exhibited by various animals, including humans, evolved as a way of preventing a particular species from interacting with the environment when it is most dangerous and hazardous to do so. Anouk is promoting the

   (a) restorative theory.
   (b) the activation-synthesis model.
   (c) the adaptive theory.
   (d) the neodissociation theory.

7. Due to prolonged and heavy use of cocaine, Andrew suffered schizophrenia-like symptoms, including auditory hallucinations of "voices," bizarre paranoid ideas, and the "cocaine bugs" hallucination in which he felt like insects were crawling under his skin. Andrew's symptoms suggest that he has

   (a) stimulant-induced psychosis (cocaine psychosis).
   (b) delirium tremens (DTs).
   (c) hypermnesia.
   (d) a parasomnia.

8. Research indicates that the percentage of total sleep spent in REM sleep is higher in _____ than in _____ .

   (a) infants; adults   (c) old people; children
   (b) females; males   (d) cats; dogs

9. After he abruptly stops taking a depressant psychoactive drug, Ernie suffers from sleep problems, excitability, and restlessness. Ernie is suffering from

   (a) drug-rebound effect. (c) inertia.
   (b) parasomnia.   (d) apnea.

10. Maya uses the zazen, or the "just sitting" technique of Zen Buddhism, in which she engages in quiet awareness of the "here and now" without any distracting thoughts. Maya is using a type of _____ meditation.

    (a) opening-up
    (b) inertia
    (c) concentration
    (d) parasomnia

11. According to his wife, 70-year-old Hugo sometimes jumps out of bed during the night and appears to be acting out his dreams. It is very likely that Hugo suffers from a sleep disorder called

    (a) narcolepsy.
    (b) REM sleep behavior disorder.
    (c) sleep apnea.
    (d) nocturnal enuresis.

12. Jason frequently experiences morning brain fog. One way to deal with his sleep inertia, according to the Application, is to

    (a) stay in bed, in a deep sleep, until the last possible minute after the alarm has gone off.
    (b) get up very gradually and spend the first 30 minutes or so in very low-level light conditions.
    (c) set his alarm clock 15 minutes earlier than usual, get up as soon as it goes off, sip some coffee, and expose himself to bright light.
    (d) Stay up about 15 minutes later than usual each night for a week, but get up at the same time each morning.

13. In an attempt to determine the effect of circadian rhythms on traffic problems, Dr. Nappertandy analyzed thousands of fatigue-related motor vehicle accidents. It is very likely that his research will reveal that the number of accidents peaks at

    (a) 3 A.M. and 3 P.M.
    (b) 8 A.M. and 5 P.M.
    (c) 12 A.M. and 12 P.M.
    (d) 6 A.M. and 6 P.M.

14. Biorhythms are discussed in Science Versus Pseudoscience 4.1. Which of the following point(s) is (are) made?

    (a) Biorhythms is a popular pseudoscience.
    (b) The notion that there are three "natural biorhythms" rigidly fixed from birth on is unproved.
    (c) Although "biorhythms" and "biological rhythms" sound very similar, they have virtually nothing in common.
    (d) The legitimate scientific study of biological rhythms examines the consistent but potentially varying cycles of living organisms over time.
    (e) All of the above points were made.

15. In Focus 4.2 presents information about sleep. Which of the following is (are) true according to this section?
    (a) Deaf people who use sign language sometimes "sleep sign" during sleep.
    (b) Yawning is caused by too little oxygen or too much carbon dioxide and is highly contagious.
    (c) It is possible to learn foreign languages, chemistry, etc., by listening to tape recordings while fast asleep.
    (d) All of the above are true.

Answers

Introduction: Consciousness: Experiencing the "Private I"

1. *Consciousness is defined as the* personal awareness of mental activities, internal sensations, and the external environment.

2. *William James's idea of "stream of consciousness" refers to the fact that* although consciousness is always changing, it is perceived as unified and unbroken, in much the same way that a river or stream is seen as one thing, yet is constantly changing.

3. *Research on consciousness was abandoned because* introspective self-reports were not objectively verifiable. *Psychologists turned instead to* overt behavior that could be directly observed and measured.

4. *Psychologists returned to studying consciousness in the late 1950s for two reasons:* first, because it became clear that a complete understanding of behavior would not be possible without considering the role of conscious mental processes in behavior, and, second, because psychologists devised more objective ways to study the phenomenon (technological advances in studying brain activity and more objective means of inferring conscious experience from behavior).

The Biological and Environmental "Clocks" Regulating Consciousness

1. *Circadian rhythms are* biological processes that systematically vary over a 24-hour period

2. *The suprachiasmatic nucleus (SCN) is* a cluster of neurons in the hypothalamus that governs the timing of circadian rhythms, including the sleep-wake cycle and the mental alertness cycle (the master biological clock). *Its role in sleep-wake cycles and other circadian rhythms is to* detect, through its connections with the visual system, decreases in sunlight and, in turn, to trigger an increase in the production of melatonin, which makes you sleep. Exposure to sunlight suppresses melatonin levels.

3. *Melatonin is a* hormone manufactured by the pineal gland (an endocrine gland in the brain), which produces sleepiness.

4. *Free-running conditions are created by* the absence of environmental time cues like sunlight and clocks. *They have two distinct effects: First,* in the absence of normal light, darkness, and other time cues, people tend to drift to the natural rhythm of the SCN, which is approximately a 25-hour day, and consequently people go to sleep about an hour later each night. *Second,* circadian rhythms lose their normal synchronization with one another.

5. *People suffer from jet-lag symptoms because* time cues are out of sync with their internal biological clocks, and these symptoms can be produced by travel across multiple time zones, working night shifts, or working rotating shifts.

6. *Melatonin plays a key role in jet-lag symptoms by* causing sleepiness, grogginess, etc., at a time when the external environmental cues suggest that you should be alert and awake (your internal body clock says it is 3:00 A.M. so melatonin levels are high, but the external time is 10:00 A.M. and you need to be awake).

Concept Check 1

1. biological clock/circadian rhythms; SCN (body clock)
2. melatonin
3. circadian rhythms
4. consciousness
5. free-running conditions

Matching Exercise 1

1. consciousness
2. introspection
3. suprachiasmatic nucleus (SCN)
4. jet lag
5. melatonin
6. biorhythms

True/False Test 1

1. T	3. T	5. T
2. F	4. T	

Sleep

1. *An electroencephalograph is* an instrument that uses electrodes placed on the scalp to measure and record the brain's electrical activity and produces an electroencephalogram (EEG).

2. *By studying EEGs, sleep researchers have established that* brain-wave activity systematically changes throughout sleep.

3. *Use of the EEG led to the discovery of* rapid eye movement sleep, or REM sleep, and this marked the beginning of modern sleep research.

4. *Beta brain waves are associated with* being alert and awake. *Alpha brain waves are associated with* drowsiness and relaxation.

5. *Hypnagogic hallucinations are* vivid sensory phenomena that occur during the onset of sleep.

6. *The four NREM sleep stages are characterized by different brain and body activity:*

   Stage 1 NREM: a mixture of alpha and theta waves, lasts only a few minutes, and is a transitional stage from wakefulness to being asleep.

   Stage 2 NREM: the appearance of sleep spindles (bursts of brain activity that last a second or two), and the brain waves are mainly theta waves with perhaps a few delta waves.

   Stages 3 and 4 NREM: delta brain-wave activity (20 percent in stage 3, and 50 percent in stage 4); in combination, they are referred to as slow-wave sleep.

7. *REM sleep is characterized by* increased brain activity (smaller, faster brain waves), dreaming, suppression of voluntary muscle activity, and considerable physiological arousal.

8. *Over the course of the lifespan, the quantity and quality of our sleep* changes considerably; from birth onward, the average amount of time spent sleeping gradually decreases, and the amount of time devoted to REM and slow-wave NREM also gradually decreases.

Why Do We Sleep?

1. *Sleep deprivation studies demonstrate that* we have a biological need to sleep; when deprived of sleep (either REM or stage 3 and 4 NREM), people will experience rebound effects when allowed to sleep undisturbed.

2. *The phenomena of REM and NREM rebound seem to indicate that* the brain needs to make up for missing components of sleep.

3. *The restorative theory of sleep suggests that* sleep promotes physiological processes that restore and rejuvenate the body and the mind.

4. *The adaptive theory of sleep suggests that* the sleep patterns exhibited by different animals, including humans, are the result of evolutionary adaptation and that different sleep patterns evolved as a way of preventing a particular species from interacting with the environment when it may be dangerous to do so.

Sleep Disorders: Troubled Sleep

1. *Sleep disorders are* serious disturbances in the normal sleep pattern that interfere with daytime functioning and cause subjective distress. Virtually everyone is seriously troubled by the quality or quantity of their sleep at some point.

2. *Insomnia is* a condition in which a person regularly experiences an inability to fall asleep, to stay asleep, or to feel adequately rested by sleep; it is the most common sleep complaint among adults.

3. *With sleep apnea,* the person repeatedly stops breathing during sleep; it is the second most common sleep disorder.

4. *Sleepwalking is characterized by* an episode of walking or performing other actions during stage 3 or stage 4 NREM sleep; it is also called somnambulism.

5. *A night terror is characterized by* an episode of increased physiological arousal, intense fear and panic, and frightening hallucinations, with no recall of the episode in the morning; it usually occurs during stage 3 or stage 4 NREM sleep.

6. *In REM sleep behavior disorder,* the sleeper acts out his or her dreams.

7. *Narcolepsy is characterized by* excessive daytime sleepiness and brief lapses into sleep throughout the day.

Concept Check 2

1. alpha

2. falling; myoclonic jerk

3. insomnia

4. worse

5. night terror; 3; 4

6. narcolepsy; sleep paralysis

7. is experiencing sleep disturbances that are normal for her age

8. theta; sleep spindles

Graphic Organizer 1

1. C   4. B   6. F
2. E   5. D   7. A
3. G

Matching Exercise 2

1. insomnia
2. REM sleep
3. restorative theory of sleep
4. alpha brain waves
5. sleep apnea
6. electroencephalogram (EEG)
7. sleep spindles
8. hypnagogic hallucinations
9. slow-wave sleep
10. myoclonic jerk (sleep start)
11. sleep paralysis
12. REM sleep behavior disorder
13. REM rebound
14. electroencephalograph

True/False Test 2

1. F   6. T   11. T
2. T   7. T   12. F
3. T   8. F   13. F
4. F   9. T   14. T
5. T   10. T

Dreams and Mental Activity During Sleep

1. *Sleep thinking refers to* repetitive, bland, and uncreative ruminations about real-life events during sleep, *whereas a dream is* an unfolding episode of mental images that is storylike, involving characters and events.

2. *The main characteristics of dreams are* intense emotions, usually illogical content and organization, sometimes bizarre and uncritically accepted sensations, and difficult-to-remember dream images.

3. *Most dreams are* a reflection of everyday life including people we know and familiar locations, *with the most common themes being* falling, being chased, or being attacked, which are common across cultures.

4. *We are most likely to remember a dream if* we wake up during the dream; if it is vivid, bizarre, or emotionally intense; or if we minimize distractions upon awakening.

5. *We are most likely to forget dreams because* a fundamental change in brain chemistry during sleep makes the processing and storage of information in memory very difficult (neurotransmitters needed to acquire new memories, including serotonin, norepinephrine, and dopamine, are greatly reduced), and the brain is largely programmed to forget not only the vast majority of dreams but also any experiences that happen during sleep.

6. *Freud's explanation for dreams suggests that* because the sexual and aggressive instincts that motivate human behavior are so unacceptable to the conscious mind, they are pushed into the unconscious mind, or repressed.

7. *The manifest content refers to* the elements of a dream that are consciously experienced and remembered by the dreamer; *the latent content is the* disguised psychological meanings of the dream that are concealed in the manifest content.

8. *The activation-synthesis model of dreaming maintains that* dreaming is our subjective awareness of the brain's internally generated signals during sleep; brain activity produces dream images (activation), which are combined by the brain into a dream story (synthesis).

9. *Current research concludes that dreams reflect* the waking concerns and preoccupations of the dreamer and the active process of trying to make sense of stimuli produced by the brain during sleep; dream interpretation occurs when we are awake, and it may reveal more about the psychological characteristics of the interpreter than about the dream itself.

Concept Check 3

1. manifest content
2. activation-synthesis
3. sleep thinking
4. common

5. 70; REM

6. nightmare

Matching Exercise 3

1. J. Allan Hobson

2. Sigmund Freud

3. sleep thinking

4. Robert McCarley

5. lucid dream

True/False Test 3

1. T	3. T	5. F
2. F	4. T	

Hypnosis

1. *Hypnosis is a* cooperative social interaction in which the hypnotized person responds to the hypnotist's suggestions with changes in perception, memory, and behavior.

2. *Hypnosis is characterized by* highly focused attention, increased responsiveness to suggestions, vivid images and fantasies, and a willingness to accept distortions of logic or reality; during hypnosis, the subject temporarily suspends a sense of initiative and voluntarily accepts and follows the hypnotist's instructions.

3. *The best candidates for hypnosis are* individuals who approach the experience with positive, receptive attitudes and expect it to work and people who are fantasy prone and easily become absorbed in reading fiction, watching movies, or listening to music.

4. *The effects of hypnosis include* sensory and perceptual changes (blindness, deafness, or loss of sensation in some body part), hallucinations, carrying out posthypnotic suggestions, posthypnotic amnesia, and hypermnesia.

5. *The limits of hypnosis are that* you cannot be hypnotized against your will, you cannot become physically stronger than you are, you cannot exhibit talents that you don't already possess, and you cannot be made to perform behaviors that are contrary to your morals and values.

6. *Hilgard's neodissociation theory of hypnosis suggests that* hypnotic effects are due to the splitting of consciousness into two simultaneous streams of memory activity, only one of which the hypnotic participant is consciously aware of

during hypnosis (the dissociated stream is called the hidden observer).

Meditation

1. *Meditation refers to* techniques used to control or retrain attention so as to induce an altered state of focused attention and awareness.

2. *The two general types of meditation differ in that* concentration techniques involve focusing awareness on a visual image, your breathing, a word, or a phrase, and opening-up techniques involve a present-centered awareness of the passing moment, without mental judgment.

3. *The effects of meditation include* a state of lowered physiological arousal, lowered blood pressure, changes in brain waves, and enhanced physical and psychological functioning (beyond that provided by relaxation alone).

Concept Check 4

1. highly susceptible

2. posthypnotic amnesia

3. concentration

4. posthypnotic suggestion

5. pseudomemory

6. hypermnesia

Matching Exercise 4

1. neodissociation theory of hypnosis

2. transcendental meditation (TM)

3. hypnosis

4. dissociation

5. posthypnotic suggestion

6. hypermnesia

7. hidden observer

True/False Test 4

1. F	4. T
2. F	5. F
3. T	6. T

Psychoactive Drugs

1. *Psychoactive drugs are* drugs that alter consciousness, perception, mood, and behavior; they include depressants, opiates, stimulants, and psychedelic drugs.

2. *Addiction is a broad term that refers to* a condition in which a person feels psychologically and physically compelled to take a specific drug. *More specific terms for addiction-related conditions are* physical dependence, tolerance, withdrawal symptoms, and the drug-rebound effect.

3. *The effects of a drug may be influenced by* psychological and environmental factors, including personality characteristics, mood, expectations, experience with the drug, and the setting in which the drug is taken.

4. *Depressants have several effects; they* inhibit central nervous system activity; produce drowsiness, sedation, or sleep; relieve anxiety; and lower inhibitions. *Examples include* alcohol, barbiturates, and tranquilizers.

5. *Alcohol depresses* the activity of neurons throughout the brain *and impairs* cognitive abilities, such as concentration, memory, and speech, and physical abilities, such as muscle coordination and balance.

6. *Barbiturates are depressant drugs that* reduce anxiety and promote sleep by depressing activity in the brain centers that control arousal, wakefulness, and alertness.

7. *Tranquilizers are depressants that* relieve anxiety and, while chemically different from barbiturates, produce similar effects.

8. *The opiates are a group of addictive drugs that* relieve pain and produce euphoria by mimicking the brain's own natural painkillers called endorphins. *Examples include* opium, morphine, heroin, methadone, and the prescription painkillers Percodan and Demerol.

9. *Stimulant drugs* increase brain activity, arouse behavior, increase mental alertness. *Examples include* caffeine, nicotine, amphetamines, and cocaine.

10. *The psychedelic drugs create* sensory and perceptual distortions, alter mood, and affect judgment by mimicking the neurotransmitter serotonin (which is involved in regulating moods and sensations) and stimulating serotonin receptor sites. *Examples include* mescaline, psilocybin, and LSD.

11. *Marijuana and its active ingredient, THC, produce* a sense of well-being, mild euphoria, a dreamy state of relaxation. *THC has been shown to be useful in* the treatment of pain, epilepsy, hypertension, nausea, vomiting, glaucoma, and asthma.

Concept Check 5

1. psychoactive; physically
2. tolerance
3. judgment; self-control
4. not remember
5. will not
6. tranquilizer
7. cocaine

Graphic Organizer 2

1. alcohol; depressant
2. tranquilizer; depressant
3. marijuana; psychedelic
4. LSD; psychedelic
5. caffeine; stimulant
6. morphine; opiate
7. nicotine; stimulant

Matching Exercise 5

1. THC
2. depressants
3. nicotine
4. drug abuse
5. psychoactive drug
6. stimulant-induced psychosis
7. mescaline
8. tolerance
9. hashish
10. withdrawal symptoms
11. cocaine
12. amphetamines
13. delirium tremens (DTs)
14. sleep inertia

True/False Test 5

1. T	6. T	11. F
2. T	7. T	12. T
3. T	8. F	13. T
4. F	9. T	14. F
5. T	10. T	

Something to Think About

1. Generally speaking, humans are very adaptable; in fact, most people can easily adapt to shift work. If shifts are scheduled to take into account our natural tendencies and use knowledge about sleep-wake cycles, circadian rhythms, and the role of the SCN, they need not produce the usual jet-lag symptoms.

   Begin your report with a discussion of how to rotate a person's shifts. Because we tend to drift to longer days (the 25-hour day rather than the 24-hour day), as we often do on weekends, it would seem best to rotate shifts forward: first shift, 8 A.M. to 4 P.M., second shift 4 P.M. to 12 midnight, and then midnight to 8 A.M. for the third shift.

   The length of the shift rotation is the next issue to address. Every shift change is going to take some time to get used to and will be accompanied by some jet-lag symptoms, so the less someone has to change the better. It would probably be best to have people do the same shift for at least a month before changing to the next shift forward.

   Shift workers should be given as much information as possible about circadian rhythms, sleep-wake cycles, and the role of the SCN in the production of melatonin. People finishing a night shift, for example, could be told the value of black-out curtains to avoid having their biological clock reset by bright light; those suffering from sleep inertia could be given the information presented in the Application section (Improving Sleep and Mental Alertness). For instance, for the midnight to 8 A.M. shift, having bright lights, especially in the early part of the shift, can help people adjust to the night shift.

   Finally, present the organization with a somewhat radical idea. Introduce the idea of the siesta or nap and explain how the low points in our circadian rhythms produce fatigue, especially in sleep-deprived people. Taking a nap is a normal, even beneficial, aspect of our daily sleep-wake cycle. In fact, research has shown that naps reduce fatigue and sleepiness, improve mood and mental alertness, and can improve overall productivity.

2. This dream sounds like a real nightmare. The first thing to tell your friend is that dreams cannot predict the future. She is not likely to fail the exam because of her dream. Her dream reflects the fact that she is concerned and worried about the course. The best way to do well on the exam, and to deal with exam anxiety, is to study the material completely. The text presents two theories of dreams. Freud's view is that the manifest content is relatively unimportant; he would suggest looking for disguised symbolic meaning that reflects the latent content. The activation-synthesis theory suggests that if someone is worried and anxious, these concerns are likely to show up in a dream if these well-worn neural pathways are activated. In other words, the brain produces dream images that are synthesized into a meaningful story using memories about daily events, past experiences, concerns, and worries.

   The person's interpretation of the dream may tell us more about the dreamer than anything else. If that is the case, it would be fairly safe to assume that this dreamer is experiencing some perceived difficulty with the course (or some aspect of it) and/or the course material itself.

   Finally, you could suggest that she try lucid dreaming. If she is not already a lucid dreamer, you could present the suggestions outlined in the text for increasing this ability. It is quite possible that she could go to sleep and have the same dream again, but this time, with her lucid dreaming ability, have a completely different and much more positive outcome.

Progress Test 1

1. c	6. c	11. c
2. c	7. d	12. d
3. d	8. b	13. a
4. b	9. c	14. a
5. d	10. a	15. b

Progress Test 2

1. a	6. c	11. b
2. b	7. c	12. a
3. a	8. d	13. a
4. d	9. b	14. d
5. a	10. c	15. c

Progress Test 3

1. a	6. c	11. b
2. d	7. a	12. c
3. c	8. a	13. a
4. c	9. a	14. e
5. a	10. a	15. a

CHAPTER

5

Learning

PREVIEW

Reading the section below first will give you a general sense of the chapter's contents and an initial introduction to some of the major concepts and terms. This will prime you for what you are about to read and help you to develop a "cognitive map" that will guide your study of the material in this chapter. Likewise, reading the **preview questions** at the beginning of each major section will improve your ability to understand, learn, and retain the information.

CHAPTER 5. . . AT A GLANCE

Chapter 5 answers the question "What is learning?" in its discussions of classical conditioning, operant conditioning, and observational learning. Conditioning focuses on how we form associations between environmental events and behavioral responses. Classical conditioning (discovered by Ivan Pavlov) involves repeatedly pairing a neutral stimulus with a stimulus that naturally elicits a response until the neutral stimulus elicits the same response. Behaviorism was founded by John B. Watson and was concerned with the scientific study of observable behaviors, especially as they pertain to learning. Classical conditioning is used to explain conditioned emotional reactions and conditioned physiological responses. Contemporary psychology has modified the basics of classical conditioning to account for cognitive functioning and biological predispositions.

Operant conditioning (developed by B. F. Skinner) demonstrates how voluntary, active behaviors are acquired through shaping, reinforcement (positive and negative), and punishment (by application and by removal). Once acquired, behaviors are maintained through different schedules of reinforcement. Behaviors that are partially reinforced are more resistant to extinction than are behaviors that are continuously reinforced. Behavior modification is the application of principles of operant conditioning to help people develop more adaptive behaviors. Operant conditioning theory has also been modified by contemporary cognitive and biological views.

Observational learning (studied by Albert Bandura) shows how new behaviors can be acquired through watching the actions of others; it involves the processes of attention, memory, motor skills, and motivation. This type of learning is not limited to humans but has been demonstrated in many nonhuman animals as well. Applications involve education, work performance, psychotherapy, and counseling.

Introduction: What Is Learning?

Preview Questions

Consider the following questions as you study this section of the chapter.

- How is learning defined?
- What is conditioning?
- What are three basic types of learning?

*Read the section "Introduction: What Is Learning?" and **write** your answers to the following:*

1. Learning refers to _____

   _____

2. Conditioning is the _____

   _____

3. The three basic types of learning are

   _____

   _____

Classical Conditioning: Associating Stimuli

Preview Questions

Consider the following questions as you study this section of the chapter.

- Who discovered classical conditioning, and how did he investigate it?
- What is the basic process of classical conditioning?
- What factors can affect the strength of a classically conditioned response?
- What phenomena did Pavlov discover when he varied the stimuli during conditioning?

*Read the section "Classical Conditioning: Associating Stimuli" and **write** your answers to the following:*

1. The person who discovered classical conditioning was _____

   He investigated the phenomenon by_____

   _____

   _____

2. Classical conditioning is the process of (describe the elements involved in the process)

   _____

   _____

   _____

   _____

3. The two factors that can affect the strength of a classically conditioned response are _____

   _____

   _____

4. Pavlov also discovered four other phenomena when additional stimuli were presented:

   _____

   _____

   _____

   _____

From Pavlov to Watson: The Founding of Behaviorism

Preview Questions

Consider the following questions as you study this section of the chapter.

- Who founded behaviorism, and what were its basic assumptions?
- How can classical conditioning be used to explain emotional responses, and how does it affect physiological reactions?

*Read the section "From Pavlov to Watson: The Founding of Behaviorism" and **write** your answers to the following:*

1. Behaviorism was founded by _____

   and was defined as _____

   _____

   _____

2. The fundamental assumptions of behaviorism are _____

   _____

   _____

   _____

   _____

3. Watson identified three innate emotions

_____

each of which could be _____

_____

With regard to these emotions, Watson showed
that classical conditioning could be used to

_____

_____

4. The classical conditioning components in the
Little Albert study were as follows:

CS: _____

UCS: _____

UCR: _____

CR: _____

5. Physiological responses, such as immune system functioning, can be classically conditioned

by_____

_____

_____

Contemporary Views of Classical Conditioning

Preview Questions

*Consider the following questions as you study this
section of the chapter.*

- How does the cognitive explanation of learning
  differ from the behavioral explanation?

- What kinds of cognitive processes are involved
  in classical conditioning, and how have they
  been demonstrated experimentally?

- How does the evolutionary perspective account
  for the conditioning process?

- How do taste aversions challenge the principles
  of classical conditioning, and how can they be
  explained?

- What is biological preparedness?

*Read the section "Contemporary Views of Classical
Conditioning" and **write** your answers to the following:*

1. According to the cognitive perspective, learning

   _____

   _____

whereas the traditional behavioral perspective
holds that_____

_____

2. In his research with rats, Robert Rescorla
   demonstrated that _____

   _____

   _____

3. According to the evolutionary perspective,

   _____

   This is because_____

   _____

   _____

4. Taste aversion is a _____

   _____

   Taste aversions violate two basic principles of
   classical conditioning: _____

   _____

   _____

   _____

5. John Garcia demonstrated that taste aversions
   could be produced under controlled laboratory
   conditions by _____

   _____

   He found that _____

   _____

   _____

6. Biological preparedness refers to _____

   _____

   _____

_____

*After you have carefully studied the preceding
sections, complete the following exercises.*

Concept Check 1

*Read the following and write the correct term in the
space provided.*

1. Dr. Munchausen believes that the general principles of learning apply to virtually all species
   and all learning situations, whereas his colleague Dr. Milstein believes that an animal's
   natural behavioral patterns and unique charac-

teristics can influence what it is capable of learning. Dr. Munchausen supports the _____ perspective, and Dr. Milstein's views are consistent with an _____ perspective.

2. Dr. Wells decided to classically condition some rats. He used a tone (CS) followed by a shock (UCS) for group 1; for group 2, he used a taste (CS) followed by a shock. It is very _____ (likely/unlikely) that the rats in group 1 will be classically conditioned; it is very _____ (likely/unlikely) that the rats in group 2 will be classically conditioned.

3. It appears that Dr. Wells in the above example is investigating how _____ affects learning through classical conditioning.

4. Dr. Manly believes that classical conditioning depends on the information the CS provides about the UCS and that for learning to occur, the CS must be a reliable signal that predicts the presentation of the UCS. Dr. Manly's views are most consistent with the _____ perceptive.

5. About five hours after extinguishing the classically conditioned response (CR) in an experimental animal, Dr. Taylor presented the conditioned stimulus (CS) and obtained a CR. Dr. Taylor has demonstrated _____ .

6. Fido drools whenever he hears the sound of the electric can opener but does not drool when he hears the sound of the blender, which makes a similar noise. It appears that Fido has learned to _____ between the two sounds.

7. Ahmood, who is a regular coffee drinker, notices that he now feels alert at just the sight and smell of the coffee. In classical conditioning terms, Ahmood's physiological response to these cues is called a _____ .

8. Ahmood also observed that he has a similar physiological response to the smell of other beverages such as herbal tea and hot chocolate. In this situation, he is experiencing a phenomenon called _____ .

9. Research with cancer patients who had undergone a series of chemotherapy treatments indicates that the human immune system can be classically conditioned. Initially, only the chemotherapy treatments affected the patients' immune systems, but after many treatments, cues related to the hospital environment produced reduced immune functioning. Using this example, identify the components that constitute the CS, UCS, UCR, and CR.

(a) The UCS in this research was the _____ , and the _____ was the UCR.

(b) After repeated treatments, the _____ related to the hospital environment (called the CS) became associated with the chemotherapy treatments.

(c) Now, the CS produced a response of _____ , which is the CR.

Graphic Organizer 1

In his classic experiment Pavlov repeatedly presented a neutral stimulus, such as a tone, just before putting food in the dog's mouth, which automatically elicited salivation. After several repetitions the tone alone triggered the salivation. Label the following graph using the correct terms (UCS, UCR, CS, CR):

Before Conditioning

Food in the mouth is the ____ and the salivation is the ____ .	The neutral stimulus is the ___. It elicits no salivation before conditioning.

During Conditioning

The neutral stimulus is the ___ .	+	Food in the mouth is the ____ .	→	The salivation is the ____ .

After Conditioning

The tone alone is the ___ .	→	The salivation is now the ___ .

Review of Terms, Concepts, and Names 1

Use the terms in this list to complete the Matching Test, then to help you answer the True/False items correctly.

learning
conditioning
Ivan Pavlov
classical conditioning
elicit
unconditioned stimulus
unconditioned response
conditioned stimulus
conditioned response
extinction
spontaneous recovery
stimulus generalization
stimulus discrimination
John B. Watson
behaviorism
cognitive perspective
Robert A. Rescorla
taste aversion
John Garcia
biological preparedness
phobia

Matching Exercise

Match the appropriate term/name with its definition or description.

1. _____ The gradual weakening and disappearance of conditioned behavior; in classical conditioning, it occurs when the conditioned stimulus is repeatedly presented without the unconditioned stimulus.

2. _____ The process of learning associations between environmental events and behavioral responses.

3. _____ A relatively enduring change in behavior or knowledge as a result of past experience.

4. _____ Classically conditioned dislike for and avoidance of a particular food that develops when an organism becomes ill after eating the food.

5. _____ American psychologist who founded behaviorism in the early 1900s.

6. _____ School of psychology and theoretical viewpoint that emphasizes the scientific study of observable behaviors, especially as they pertain to the process of learning.

7. _____ Natural stimulus that reflexively elicits a response without the necessity of prior learning.

8. _____ Russian physiologist who first described the basic learning process of associating stimuli that is now called classical conditioning.

9. _____ Extreme, irrational fear of a specific object, animal, or situation.

10. _____ Unlearned, reflexive response that is elicited by an unconditioned stimulus.

11. _____ In learning theory, the idea that an organism is innately predisposed to form associations between certain stimuli and not others.

True/False Test

Indicate whether each statement is true or false by placing T or F in the blank space next to each item.

1. ____ Classical conditioning is the basic learning process that involves repeatedly pairing a neutral stimulus with a response-producing stimulus until the neutral stimulus elicits the same response.

2. ____ "Elicit" means to draw out or bring forth and causes an existing behavior to occur.

3. ____ The American psychologist who experimentally demonstrated the involvement of cognitive processes in classical conditioning is John Garcia.

4. ____ The occurrence of a learned response not only to the original stimulus but to other similar stimuli as well, is called stimulus discrimination.

5. ____ The conditioned stimulus is a formerly neutral stimulus that acquires the capacity to elicit a reflexive response.

6. ____ The reappearance of a previously extinguished conditioned response after a period of time without exposure to the conditioned stimulus is called spontaneous recovery.

7. ____ Stimulus generalization occurs when a learned response is made to a specific stimulus but not to other similar stimuli.

8. ____ Robert A. Rescorla is the American psychologist who experimentally demonstrated the learning of taste aversions in animals.

9. ____ The conditioned response is the learned, reflexive response to a conditioned stimulus.

10. ____ The cognitive perspective holds that mental processes as well as external events are an important component in the learning of new behaviors.

Check your answers and review any areas of weakness before going on to the next section.

Operant Conditioning: Associating Behaviors and Consequences (Part 1)

Preview Questions

Consider the following questions as you study the first three parts of this section of the chapter (up to and including Punishment).

- What was Thorndike's contribution to learning theory?

- What were B. F. Skinner's key assumptions, and what is the fundamental premise of operant conditioning?

- How are positive and negative reinforcement similar, and how are they different?

- What is punishment, and what factors influence its effectiveness?

- What negative effects are associated with the use of punishment?

*Read the section "Operant Conditioning: Associating Behaviors and Consequences" (up to Discriminative Stimuli) and **write** your answers to the following:*

1. Edward L. Thorndike was the first person to

   _____

   _____

   He concluded that   _____

   _____

   _____

   _____

   _____

2. B. F. Skinner believed that   _____

   _____

   _____

   _____

   _____

3. Operant conditioning is   _____

   _____

   It explains _____

   _____

4. The basic premise of operant conditioning is

   _____

5. Reinforcement refers to   _____

   _____

   _____

6. Positive reinforcement involves _____

_____

_____

Negative reinforcement involves _____

_____

_____

Negative and positive reinforcement are similar in that _____

_____

They differ in that _____

_____

7. A primary reinforcer is_____

_____

and a conditioned reinforcer (secondary reinforcer) is_____

_____

8. Punishment is a _____

_____

_____

9. The factors that influence the effectiveness of punishment are _____

_____

_____

The drawbacks of punishment are that

_____

_____

_____

After you have carefully studied the preceding section, complete the following exercises.

Concept Check 2

Read the following and write the correct term in the space provided.

1. Ashley holds the view that responses followed by a satisfying state of affairs are strengthened and are more likely to occur again in the same situation and that responses followed by an unpleasant or annoying state of affairs are less likely to recur. This view is most consistent with a fundamental principle of learning called the _____ .

2. April burned her fingers when she picked up a hot saucepan with her bare hands. She now always dons her oven mitts before touching any hot pan or pot. The aversive stimulus of getting burned reduced her tendency to pick up pots with her bare hands and is therefore an example of _____ ; her increased tendency to use oven mitts because doing so reduces the possibility of getting burned is an example of _____ .

3. Whenever young Simon wants something, such as a new toy or candy, he cries and screams until his parents give in and give him what he wants. Simon's whining behavior is _____ reinforced by his parents giving in, and the parents behavior is _____ reinforced because it stops the annoying crying and screaming.

4. While researching a term paper for his history of psychology class, Rupert discovered the name of the first psychologist to investigate how voluntary behaviors are influenced by their consequences. That psychologist was _____ .

5. The following are examples of negative reinforcement. Decide which illustrate *escape* and which illustrate *avoidance*.

   (a) You go to the dentist on a regular basis; as a result, you don't experience problems such as toothaches. This an example of

   _____ .

   (b) Your partner is complaining about your messy habits, so you put on your running gear and go for a five-mile jog. This is an example of _____ .

   (c) You study hard all semester because you don't want to end up with a low grade-point average. This is an example of

   _____ .

(d) You turn the air conditioner on when the temperature in your room gets too hot and uncomfortable. This is an example of

_____ .

6. For each of the following, decide whether the example illustrates negative reinforcement (N) or punishment (P).

(a) _____ Marco always wears his seatbelt whenever he drives his car because he doesn't want to be thrown against the windshield if his car is hit from behind.

(b) _____ Darryl has tried some new aftershave lotion. "It smells like diesel oil!" complains his girlfriend. Darryl never uses that aftershave lotion again.

(c) _____ Maria does not misbehave at the dinner table because she knows that misbehavior will result in her forfeiting dessert.

(d) _____ Greta's cigarette lighter ignites the hair spray she has just put on her hair and burns her bangs and eyebrows. Greta no longer smokes when she is doing her hair.

(e) _____ Jim no longer picks up hitchhikers after the last one robbed him at gun point.

(f) _____ Before pouring milk on her cereal, Carmelita smells the carton to make sure the milk has not gone sour.

(g) _____ Astrid brushes her teeth after every meal because she wants to cut down on the number of visits she needs to make to the dentist.

Graphic Organizer 2

The following is a very useful way to organize the procedures used in operant conditioning. The arrow

(↑ or ↓) indicates whether the behavior increases or decreases. Fill in the blanks in cells 1, 2, 3, and 4.

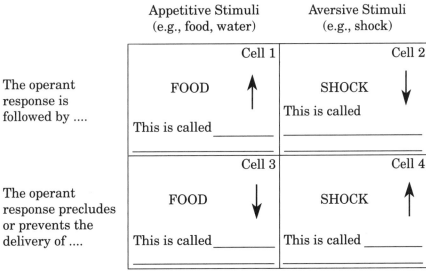

Review of Terms, Concepts, and Names 2

Use the terms in this list to complete the Matching Test, then to help you answer the True/False items correctly.

Edward L. Thorndike
law of effect
B. F. Skinner
operant
operant conditioning
reinforcement
positive reinforcement

negative reinforcement
primary reinforcer
conditioned reinforcer
punishment
punishment by
  application
punishment by removal

Matching Exercise

Match the appropriate term/name with its definition or description.

1. _____ American psychologist who developed the operant conditioning model of learning.

2. _____ Situation in which a response results in the removal of, avoidance of, or escape from a punishing stimulus, increasing the likelihood of the response being repeated in similar situations.

3. _____ American psychologist who was the first to study animal behavior experimentally and document how active behaviors are influenced by their consequences.

4. _____ Presentation of a stimulus or event following a behavior that acts to decrease the likelihood of the behavior being repeated.

5. _____ Stimulus or event that has acquired reinforcing value by being associated with a primary reinforcer; also called a secondary reinforcer.

6. _____ Occurrence of a stimulus or event following a response that increases the likelihood of the response being repeated.

7. _____ Skinner's term for an actively emitted behavior that operates on the environment to produce consequences.

True/False Test

Indicate whether each statement is true or false by placing T or F in the blank space next to each item.

1. ___ A primary reinforcer is a stimulus or event that is naturally or inherently reinforcing for a given species, such as food, water, or other biological necessities.

2. ___ Punishment by application involves the loss or withdrawal of a reinforcing stimulus following a response.

3. ___ Positive reinforcement refers to a situation in which a response is followed by the addition of a reinforcing stimulus, increasing the likelihood of the response being repeated in a similar situation.

4. ___ Punishment by removal involves the presentation of an unpleasant or aversive event or stimulus following a response.

5. ___ The law of effect states that responses followed by a satisfying effect become strengthened and are more likely to recur in a particular situation, whereas responses followed by a dissatisfying effect are weakened and less likely to recur in a particular situation.

6. ___ Operant conditioning is the basic learning process that involves changing the probability of a response being repeated by manipulating the consequences of that response.

Check your answers and review any areas of weakness before going on to the next section.

Operant Conditioning: Associating Behaviors and Consequences (Part 2)

Preview Questions

Consider the following questions as you study the last parts of this section of the chapter (up to and including Applications of Operant Conditioning).

• What are discriminative stimuli, and what important role do they play in operant conditioning?

• What is shaping, and how does it work?

• How does partial reinforcement affect behavior?

• What are the four basic schedules of reinforcement?

• What are some practical applications of operant conditioning principles?

• How has behavior modification been used to change human behavior?

*Read the section "Operant Conditioning: Associating Behaviors and Consequences" and **write** your answers to the following:*

1. Discriminative stimuli are _____

_____

_____

_____

According to Skinner, they are important

because _____

_____

_____

_____

2. Shaping involves _____

_____

_____

_____

_____

3. Partial reinforcement is more effective than continuous reinforcement because it _____

_____

_____

4. The four basic schedules of reinforcement are

_____

_____

_____

_____

5. Behavior modification is _____

_____

_____

_____

_____

_____

After you have carefully studied the preceding section, complete the following exercises.

Concept Check 3

Read the following and write the correct term in the space provided.

1. Your instructor, Dr. Jones, decides to give surprise quizzes throughout the semester. Your studying will be reinforced on a

_____ schedule.

2. A ringing telephone is a

_____ for picking up the receiver.

3. Your instructor, Dr. Wong, schedules a quiz every two weeks throughout the semester. Your studying will be reinforced on a

_____ schedule.

4. A rat gets a food pellet for every 20 responses. It is reinforced on a

_____ schedule.

5. If parents use praise and encouragement to gradually teach a child how to dress herself, they are using a _____ procedure.

6. Maria sells magazine subscriptions over the phone. She makes many calls but only gets paid for making a sale. She is reinforced on a

_____ schedule.

7. Juanita and her colleagues assemble TV sets in a factory. They get paid a bonus for every ten TVs they produce. They are being rewarded on a _____ schedule.

Graphic Organizer 3

Fill in each cell with the name of the appropriate partial reinforcement schedule.

	Based on the number of responses made	Based on the elapsed time
Fixed	Cell 1 _____	Cell 2 _____
Variable	Cell 3 _____	Cell 4 _____

Review of Terms, Concepts, and Names 3

Use the terms in this list to complete the Matching Test, then to help you answer the True/False items correctly.

discriminative stimulus
Skinner box
shaping
continuous reinforcement
partial reinforcement
extinction
partial reinforcement effect

schedule of reinforcement
fixed ratio
variable ratio
fixed interval
variable interval
behavior modification

Matching Exercise

Match the appropriate term/name with its definition or description:

1. _____ The application of learning principles to help people develop more effective or adaptive behaviors.

2. _____ Schedule of reinforcement in which every occurrence of a particular response is reinforced.

3. _____ The popular name for an operant chamber, the experimental apparatus invented by B. F. Skinner to study the relationship between environmental events and active behaviors.

4. _____ Reinforcement schedule in which a reinforcer is delivered after a fixed number of responses has occurred.

5. _____ Operant conditioning procedure in which successively closer approximations of a goal behavior are selectively reinforced until the goal behavior is displayed.

6. _____ Reinforcement schedule in which a reinforcer is delivered for the first response that occurs after a fixed time interval has elapsed.

7. _____ The delivery of a reinforcer according to a preset pattern based on the number of responses or the time interval between responses.

True/False Test

Indicate whether each statement is true or false by placing T or F in the blank space next to each item.

1. ____ Partial reinforcement refers to a situation in which the occurrence of a particular response is only sometimes followed by a reinforcer.

2. ____ A variable-ratio schedule is one in which a reinforcer is delivered for the first response that occurs after an average time interval has elapsed, but the time varies unpredictably from trial to trial.

3. ____ A discriminative stimulus is a specific stimulus in the presence of which a particular response is more likely to be reinforced.

4. ____ A variable-interval schedule is one in which a reinforcer is delivered after an average number of responses, but the number varies unpredictably from trial to trial.

5. ____ The partial reinforcement effect refers to the fact that continuously reinforced behaviors are more resistant to extinction than behaviors that are only sometimes reinforced.

6. ____ The gradual weakening and disappearance of conditioned behavior in operant conditioning is called extinction; it occurs when an emitted behavior is no longer followed by a reinforcer.

Check your answers and review any areas of weakness before going on to the next section.

Contemporary Views of Operant Conditioning

Preview Questions

Consider the following questions as you study this section of the chapter.

- What factors do contemporary learning researchers suggest are involved in operant conditioning?
- How did Tolman's research demonstrate the involvement of cognitive processes in learning?
- What are cognitive maps and latent learning?
- How is operant conditioning influenced by an animal's natural behavior pattern?
- How does the phenomenon of instinctive drift challenge the traditional behavioral view of operant conditioning?

*Read the section "Contemporary Views of Operant Conditioning" and **write** your answers to the following:*

1. Contemporary learning researchers confirm the basic principles of operant conditioning but also acknowledge _____

   _____

2. Unlike Skinner and Thorndike, Tolman believed that _____

   _____

3. A cognitive map is _____

   Latent learning refers to _____

   _____

   _____

4. Operant conditioning may also be influenced by

   _____

   _____

   _____

5. The phenomenon of instinctive drift challenged the traditional behavioral view by _____

   _____

   _____

   _____

Observational Learning: Imitating the Actions of Others

Preview Questions

Consider the following questions as you study this section of the chapter.

- What type of learning is indirect?
- What four mental processes are involved in observational learning?
- How has observational learning been applied?

*Read the section "Observational Learning: Imitating the Actions of Others" and **write** your answers to the following:*

1. Observational learning is _____

   _____

   The person most strongly identified with work in this area is _____

2. The four cognitive processes that interact to determine if imitation will occur are _____

   _____

   _____

   _____

   _____

3. Observational learning has been applied in a variety of settings, including _____

   _____

   _____

   _____

After you have carefully studied the preceding sections, complete the following exercises.

Concept Check 4

Read the following and write the correct term in the space provided.

1. Maria watches the cooking show Cucina Amore on public TV on Saturday afternoon and often cooks one of the dishes she sees the chef prepare. Maria's culinary ability is the result of _____ learning.

2. Dr. Bristow believes that reinforcement is not necessary for learning to occur but that the *expectation* of reinforcement can affect the performance of what has been learned. Dr. Bristow is emphasizing the importance of _____ factors in learning.

3. If a rat has been allowed to explore a maze for a number of trials without ever getting a reinforcer, it is very _____ (likely/unlikely) that when food is made available in the goal box, the rat will find it very quickly with few errors.

4. An animal trainer has a hard time operantly conditioning a pig to pick up a large wooden penny and put it in a big "piggy bank" because the pig seems to prefer to push the coin with its snout even though it is not reinforced for this behavior. The Brelands called this phenomenon _____ .

5. Mr. and Mrs. Delbrook both stopped smoking when they started a family because they wanted to model healthy behavior patterns for their children. They are apparently aware of the importance of _____ learning in children's development.

Review of Terms, Concepts, and Names 4

Use the terms in this list to complete the Matching Test, then to help you answer the True/False items correctly.

Edward C. Tolman   instinctive drift
cognitive map   Albert Bandura
latent learning   observational learning
learned helplessness

Matching Exercise

Match the appropriate term/name with its definition or description:

1. _____ Learning that occurs through observing the actions of others.

2. _____ Tolman's term for learning that occurs in the absence of reinforcement but is not behaviorally demonstrated until a reinforcer becomes available.

3. _____ American psychologist who used the terms *cognitive map* and *latent learning* to describe experimental findings that strongly suggested that cognitive factors play a role in animal learning.

4. _____ Tolman's term for the mental representation of the layout of a familiar environment.

5. _____ American psychologist who experimentally investigated observational learning, emphasizing the role of cognitive factors.

6. _____ The tendency of an animal to revert to instinctive behaviors, which can interfere with the performance of an operantly conditioned response.

7. _____ A phenomenon in which exposure to inescapable and uncontrollable aversive events produces passive behavior.

Check your answers and review any areas of weakness before going on to the next section.

Something to Think About

1. Imagine that you are a behavioral therapist whose client has a real fear of going to the dentist. Despite the need for some important dental work, he can't bring himself to make an appointment. Using what you know about classical conditioning, explain how his phobia might have come about, and describe how to extinguish the fear.

2. Mrs. Denton can't understand why scolding her ten-year-old son for misbehaving only seems to make the problem worse. Using what you know about operant conditioning techniques, what advice would you give Mrs. Denton about how she might (a) reduce the disruptive behavior and (b) encourage more appropriate behavior.

3. Imagine that your family has decided to adopt a puppy. Using what you know about operant conditioning techniques, what advice would you give them about how they should train the dog to be obedient and do some neat pet tricks?

Check your answers and review any areas of weakness before doing the progress tests.

Progress Test 1

Review the complete chapter (including Concept Reviews and all the boxed inserts), review all your study notes, and then test yourself on the following progress test. Check your answers. If you make a mistake, review your notes, review the relevant section of the study guide, and, if necessary, go back and read the appropriate part of your textbook.

1. Dr. Ramos is a behavioral psychologist who conducts basic research using animals in carefully controlled laboratory studies. The goal of his research is most probably to
   (a) train animals to do tricks.
   (b) collect and sell saliva from dogs and other animals.
   (c) identify the general learning principles of learning that apply across a wide range of species, including humans.
   (d) observe changes in animal behavior that result from biological maturation.

2. Dr. Frolov classically conditioned a dog to flex his hind leg at the sound of a bell by pairing the ringing of a bell with a mild electric shock to the leg. In this example, the ringing bell is the
   (a) unconditioned stimulus (UCS).
   (b) conditioned response (CR).
   (c) unconditioned response (UCR).
   (d) conditioned stimulus (CS).

3. Some forms of chemotherapy make patients sick. A patient who has eaten vegetarian pizza just before the therapy (and is then sick) later feels ill when she sees or smells pizza. In this example of taste aversion learning, the conditioned response is the
   (a) vegetarian pizza.
   (b) chemotherapy.
   (c) illness induced by the therapy.
   (d) nausea felt at the sight or smell of pizza.

4. Zoran has a classically conditioned fear of rivers and lakes after he was attacked by an alligator while swimming in a river near his home. A behavioral psychologist is likely to suggest that his conditioned response (CR) can be weakened and may eventually disappear through a process called
   (a) spontaneous recovery.
   (b) extinction.
   (c) instinctive drift.
   (d) stimulus generalization.

5. Dr. Redner believes that classical conditioning depends on the information the conditioned stimulus provides about the unconditioned stimulus and that for learning to occur, the conditioned stimulus must be a reliable signal that predicts the presentation of the unconditioned stimulus. Dr. Redner's views are most consistent with those of the learning theorist
   (a) Robert A. Rescorla.
   (b) Edward L. Thorndike.
   (c) Ivan Pavlov.
   (d) B. F. Skinner.

6. Ricardo always gets nervous and apprehensive whenever his professor uses the word "exam" but he seldom feels the same anxiety when the word "quiz" is mentioned. Assuming that classical conditioning is involved in these two different reactions at the mention of tests, it appears that Ricardo is exhibiting
   (a) stimulus discrimination.
   (b) spontaneous recovery.
   (c) latent learning.
   (d) stimulus generalization.

7. About five hours after she had successfully extinguished a dog's classically conditioned response of salivating to the sound of a bell, Dr. Sheckenov discovered that the dog once again salivated in the presence of the bell. This example illustrates the phenomenon of
   (a) stimulus generalization.
   (b) spontaneous recovery.
   (c) latent learning.
   (d) instinctive drift.

8. Dr. Radersched conducts research on the phenomenon of biological preparedness. She is most likely to discover that
   (a) organisms are innately predisposed to form associations between some stimuli and responses and not others.
   (b) that the general principles of learning apply to virtually all animal species and all learning situations.
   (c) classical conditioning occurs because two stimuli are associated closely in time and that frequency and contiguity are the only variables that affect learning.
   (d) mental processes, but not innate predispositions, are the crucial variables involved in classical conditioning.

9. After studying very hard last semester Sasha got very good grades in all her courses. This semester, Sasha is once again studying very hard. It appears that good grades are _____ for Sasha's studying behavior.
   (a) conditioned stimuli
   (b) discriminative stimuli
   (c) positively reinforcing
   (d) negatively reinforcing

10. Rachel studies very hard to avoid getting bad grades because for her a bad grade is a devastating experience. Rachel's studying behavior is maintained by
    (a) negative reinforcement.
    (b) primary reinforcement.
    (c) positive reinforcement.
    (d) punishment by removal.

11. Helmut is employed by his university as a telephone solicitor for a fund-raising drive. He is paid a set amount of money for every ten calls he makes regardless of whether he is successful in raising funds. Helmut's telephoning is reinforced on a _____ schedule of reinforcement.
    (a) fixed-interval (FI)
    (b) variable-interval (VI)
    (c) fixed-ratio (FR)
    (d) variable-ratio (VR)

12. Ever since Thelma got her new fax machine and hooked up her computer to the Internet, her phone line is often busy. It is difficult for her parents to know when to call her so they try at random times. It appears that phoning Thelma is reinforced on a _____ schedule.
    (a) fixed-interval (FI)
    (b) variable-interval (VI)
    (c) fixed-ratio (FR)
    (d) variable-ratio (VR)

13. After they had been watching Superman cartoons all morning, five-year-old Jim and six-year-old John, each using a beach towel as a cape, climbed on top of the garage roof and got ready to fly. Their startled mother stopped them in time and realized the powerful influence of _____ on behavior.
    (a) observational learning
    (b) classical conditioning
    (c) operant conditioning
    (d) stimulus generalization

14. According to the Critical Thinking 5.4, B. F. Skinner maintained that
    (a) human freedom is an illusion.
    (b) all behavior arises from causes that are within the individual, and environmental factors have little or no influence.
    (c) cognitive factors are the crucial elements in all learning.
    (d) the evolutionary perspective best explains animal behavior but can't be applied to human beings.

15. According to In Focus 5.5, the phenomenon of learned helplessness demonstrates that
    (a) cognitive factors, such as expectations, are involved in learning.
    (b) fixed-ratio schedules produce greater responding than fixed-interval schedules do.
    (c) biological predispositions are involved in classical conditioning.
    (d) continuously reinforced behaviors are more resistant to extinction than are partially reinforced behaviors.

Progress Test 2

After you have checked your understanding of the material in Progress Test 1 and have done a complete chapter review with special focus on any areas of weakness, you are now ready to assess your knowledge on Progress Test 2. Check your answers. If you make a mistake, review your notes, the relevant section of the study guide, and, if necessary, the appropriate part of your textbook.

1. Which of the following best illustrates classical conditioning?
   (a) Henry feels ill at the sight or smell of peanut butter because it once made him sick.
   (b) Annalee studies hard because she wants to get good grades.
   (c) Virginia goes shopping for new clothes fairly frequently because it makes her feel good.
   (d) Lyndle drives at the posted speed limit after getting a number of speeding tickets.

2. Erv developed a fear of attics after he was accidentally locked in his own attic by his wife. Erv's present fear and apprehension of the attic is a(n)
   (a) example of instinctive drift.
   (b) conditioned emotional response.

(c) form of observational learning.

(d) conditioned physiological response.

3. Little Richard receives attention from his teacher in the form of a scolding every time he misbehaves. As a result, Richard misbehaves quite frequently. In this instance, it would appear that the teacher's scolding is a

(a) form of punishment by application.

(b) positively reinforcing stimulus.

(c) form of punishment by removal.

(d) negatively reinforcing stimulus.

4. A group of four-year-old children watch a video showing an adult hitting, kicking, and punching a large Bobo doll. These children are later asked to imitate the model and are promised a reward for every behavior they can imitate. It is very probable that the children will

(a) not imitate the adult model.

(b) verbally describe what they saw but will refuse to imitate the adult model.

(c) quite readily imitate the adult's aggressive behavior.

(d) become very upset as a result of watching the aggressive behavior.

5. Lauren spent the first week of the semester exploring the campus. Later, she had no trouble locating the library, although she had never been there before. According to Tolman, Lauren

(a) has developed biological preparedness.

(b) has formed a cognitive map.

(c) is suffering from instinctive drift.

(d) has developed a sense of direction.

6. Gerry puts up her umbrella soon after it starts to rain in order prevent her clothes from getting any wetter. This example illustrates _____ behavior and _____ reinforcement.

(a) avoidance; positive

(b) escape; negative

(c) avoidance; negative

(d) escape; positive

7. When Juanita gets paid, she uses her money to buy food to feed her family. For Juanita, money is a _____ reinforcer and food is a _____ reinforcer.

(a) conditioned; primary

(b) primary; negative

(c) conditioned; secondary

(d) primary; positive

8. At dinner one night, Amanda created quite a disturbance using her spoon as a drumstick. Her mother told her that she would get no dessert if she persisted with her unruly behavior. Amanda soon stopped the banging. This example most clearly illustrates

(a) negative reinforcement.

(b) punishment by removal.

(c) positive reinforcement.

(d) punishment by application.

9. Dr. Penrose uses a fixed-interval schedule of tests throughout the term. It is likely that her students' studying behavior will

(a) be slow, steady, and moderate.

(b) demonstrate a burst-pause-burst pattern.

(c) follow a scallop-shaped pattern.

(d) be extinguished because of lack of consistent reinforcement.

10. Zeno tried to train his potbellied pig to pick up the newspaper on the doorstep and bring it into the house. However, the pig pushed the paper with his snout into the garden, even though this behavior would not be rewarded. It appears that Zeno's attempt to operantly condition his pig has been subject to

(a) instinctive drift.

(b) stimulus discrimination.

(c) spontaneous recovery.

(d) extinction.

11. Greta loves playing the slot machines even though she wins money only once in a while. Greta's gambling behavior is likely to be very resistant to extinction because of

(a) the partial reinforcement effect.

(b) spontaneous recovery.

(c) the law of effect.

(d) instinctive drift.

12. Dalbir believes that reinforcement is not necessary for learning to occur but it does affect the performance of what has been learned. Dalbir's view is most consistent with the phenomenon of

(a) instinctive drift.

(b) biological preparedness.

(c) shaping.

(d) latent learning.

13. Sebastian has often had stir-fried yak with his girlfriend at their favorite Mongolian restaurant. On one occasion, he got very sick a few hours later. In the future, he will most likely avoid which of the following?
    (a) his girlfriend
    (b) Mongolians
    (c) stir-fried yak
    (d) all restaurants

14. According to the Application, we often choose a short-term reinforcer over a more valuable long-term goal. Your text suggests that we do this because
    (a) the relative value of a reinforcer can shift over time.
    (b) as the availability of a reinforcer gets closer, the subjective value of the reinforcer increases.
    (c) when we make our decision, we'll choose whichever reinforcer has the greatest subjective value.
    (d) of all of the above reasons.

15. According to Seligman (In Focus 5.2), people are more likely to develop phobias of spiders, snakes, or heights—as compared to doorknobs, knives, washing machines, and ladders—because
    (a) of instinctive drift.
    (b) we are biologically prepared to do so.
    (c) doorknobs, knives, and ladders are inherently safer than spiders, snakes, and heights.
    (d) of latent learning.

Progress Test 3

After you have checked your understanding of the material in Progress Tests 1 and 2, and have done a complete chapter review with special focus on any areas of weakness, you are ready to further assess your knowledge on Progress Test 3. Check your answers. If you make a mistake, review your notes, the appropriate parts of the study guide, and, if necessary, the relevant sections of your textbook.

1. Arturo, a psychology major, was asked by his roommate to explain conditioning. He is most likely to point out
    (a) that conditioning is the process of learning associations between environmental events and behavioral responses.
    (b) that there are two basic types of conditioning, operant conditioning and classical conditioning.

    (c) that contemporary learning theorists also consider the process of observational learning.
    (d) all of the above.

2. When Harjit jumped into the swimming pool, she was surprised by the coldness of the water and reflexively started shivering. Her automatic shivering response to the cold temperature is a(n)
    (a) conditioned response (CR).
    (b) unconditioned stimulus (UCS).
    (c) unconditioned response (UCR).
    (d) conditioned stimulus (CS).

3. Justine got sick after eating a chicken burger. Now she not only has an intense dislike of chicken burgers but feels nauseated at the sight of beef burgers, fish burgers, soybean burgers, or anything that even resembles a burger. It would appear that Justine has experienced the phenomenon Pavlov called
    (a) stimulus discrimination.
    (b) spontaneous recovery.
    (c) extinction.
    (d) stimulus generalization.

4. By presenting the CS over and over again without the UCS, Dr. Laslove discovered that the subject's conditioned response (CR) gradually weakened and disappeared. Dr. Laslove has carried out a procedure called
    (a) latent learning.
    (b) spontaneous recovery.
    (c) extinction.
    (d) stimulus discrimination.

5. Rolando got very sick after eating a big dish of oysters. Ever since that experience Rolando feels ill whenever he sees or smells oysters. It appears that Rolando
    (a) has developed a taste aversion.
    (b) has experienced latent learning.
    (c) is suffering from instinctive drift.
    (d) is experiencing spontaneous recovery.

6. Dr. Alonzo takes a cognitive perspective in his research on learning. He is most likely to suggest that classical conditioning
    (a) involves learning the relations between events and that the CS must be a reliable predictor of the UCS.
    (b) results from simply pairing the CS with the UCS for a number of trials.

(c) is constrained by biological predispositions.

(d) follows general principles of learning that apply to virtually all animals species and all learning situations.

7. Positive reinforcement is to _____ as negative reinforcement is to _____ .

   (a) increased responding; decreased responding
   (b) decreased responding decreased responding
   (c) increased responding; decreased responding
   (d) increased responding; increased responding

8. When Bella used his knife to release a piece of toast that was jammed in the toaster he got a severe electric shock. Bella has never used his knife to get toast out of the toaster again. It appears that Bella's behavior has been changed by

   (a) punishment by application.
   (b) negative reinforcement.
   (c) punishment by removal.
   (d) extinction.

9. Whenever the doorbell rings, Rex runs to the door and barks and growls. For Rex the ringing doorbell is a(n) _____ for his growling and barking behavior.

   (a) discriminative stimulus
   (b) unconditioned stimulus
   (c) reinforcing stimulus
   (d) primary reinforcer

10. Tammy wants to train her dog to "shake hands" with people, so she reinforces closer and closer approximations to the desired behavior. First she rewards him for sitting on command, then for slightly raising his front paw, then for fully raising his paw, then for moving his paw up and down until it is grasped, and so on. Tammy has used a process called

    (a) latent learning.
    (b) extinction.
    (c) partial reinforcement.
    (d) shaping.

11. Arnie always drives at the posted speed limit and obeys all the rules of the road because he can't afford to pay fines for driving offenses. Arnie's good driving habits are maintained by

    (a) positive reinforcement.
    (b) partial reinforcement.
    (c) secondary reinforcement.
    (d) negative reinforcement.

12. Harry works on an assembly line as part of a team of eight workers. They get paid a bonus for every one hundred products they assemble. Harry and his coworkers are being rewarded on a _____ schedule of reinforcement.

    (a) fixed-interval (FI)
    (b) variable-interval (VI)
    (c) fixed-ratio (FR)
    (d) variable-ratio (VR)

13. Wilma's psychology instructor schedules tests every two weeks throughout the semester, but her sociology instructor has surprise quizzes throughout the semester. The psychology instructor is using a _____ schedule and the sociology instructor is using a _____ schedule.

    (a) fixed-interval (FI); variable-interval (VI)
    (b) variable-interval (VI); variable-ratio (VR)
    (c) fixed-ratio (FR); variable-ratio (VR)
    (d) variable-ratio (VR); fixed-interval (FI)

14. According to In Focus 5.1, John B. Watson

    (a) believed that punishment was the best and most desirable way to change behavior.
    (b) vehemently opposed Skinner's idea that freedom is just an illusion.
    (c) was a pioneer in the application of classical conditioning principles to advertising.
    (d) discovered the phenomenon of latent learning.

15. According to In Focus 5.3, which of the following is true?

    (a) Punishment is the most effective way to change undesirable behavior.
    (b) Punishment works better than any other behavioral strategy in changing undesirable behavior.
    (c) There are no effective strategies for reducing undesirable behaviors.
    (d) A number of strategies other than punishment can be used to change undesirable behavior.

Answers

Introduction: What Is Learning?

1. *Learning refers to* a relatively enduring change in behavior or knowledge as a result of past experience.

2. *Conditioning is the* process of learning associations between environmental events and behavioral responses.

3. *The three basic types of learning are* classical conditioning, operant conditioning, and observational learning.

Classical Conditioning: Associating Stimuli

1. *The person who discovered classical conditioning was* Ivan Pavlov. *He investigated the phenomenon by* studying how dogs learned to salivate to the presence of a stimulus (that would not normally elicit saliva) after it had been associated with food in the mouth, which reflexively elicits saliva.

2. *Classical conditioning is the process of (describe the elements involved in the process)* learning an association between two stimuli: the neutral stimulus (later to be the conditioned stimulus, or CS) that does not normally produce the response of interest and the natural stimulus (the unconditioned stimulus, or UCS), which automatically elicits the response (the unconditioned response, or UCR). Following this association, the CS will elicit a new learned response (the conditioned response, or CR).

3. *The two factors that can affect the strength of a classically conditioned response are* the frequency of the presentations of the two stimuli (the more frequently the CS and UCS are paired, the stronger the conditioning) and the timing of the stimulus presentations (the CS needs to be presented about a half-second before the UCS).

4. *Pavlov also discovered four other phenomena when additional stimuli were presented:* generalization, the ability to respond to new stimuli that were similar to the CS; discrimination, the ability to distinguish between two stimuli, responding only to the one that had been followed by food; extinction, the gradual weakening and disappearance of the CR after repeated exposure to the CS alone (without the UCS); and spontaneous recovery, the reappearance of a previously extinguished conditioned response following a rest period when the CS is once again presented.

From Pavlov to Watson: The Founding of Behaviorism

1. *Behaviorism was founded by* John B. Watson *and was defined as* the scientific study of observable behaviors, especially as they pertain to learning.

2. *The fundamental assumptions of behaviorism are* that psychology is an objective science, the goals of which are the prediction and control of behavior; introspection and the study of consciousness are not part of scientific psychology; overt, observable, measurable behavior is the subject matter; and virtually all human behavior can be explained in terms of conditioning and learning.

3. *Watson identified three innate emotions:* fear, rage, and love, *each of which could be* reflexively triggered by a small number of specific stimuli. *With regard to these emotions, Watson showed that classical conditioning could be used to* deliberately establish a conditioned emotional response (i.e., a new learned response).

4. *The classical conditioning components in the Little Albert study were as follows: CS:* the sight of the white rat (initially neutral); *UCS:* the loud noise caused by hitting the steel bar with a hammer; *UCR:* the fear experienced to the loud noise; *CR:* the fear experienced to the white rat after conditioning had taken place.

5. *Physiological responses, such as immune system functioning, can be classically conditioned by* frequently pairing the UCS (chemotherapy), which produces a drop in the patient's immune system responses (the UCR), with hospital cues (CS); eventually these cues elicit the CR (a drop in immune responses).

Contemporary Views of Classical Conditioning

1. *According to the cognitive perspective, learning* involves mental processes as well as external events, *whereas the traditional behavioral perspective holds that* conditioning results from a simple association of the CS and the UCS.

2. *In his research with rats, Robert Rescorla demonstrated that* classical conditioning involves cognitive processes such as learning the relationship between events and assessing the reliability of signals and that organisms actively process information about the predictive value of stimuli they encounter in their environments.

3. *According to the evolutionary perspective,* biological predispositions, shaped by evolution, affect the conditioning process. *This is because* animals have developed unique forms of behavior to adapt to their natural environment, and so some responses and behavioral patterns are more readily conditioned than others.

4. *Taste aversion is a* classically conditioned dislike for and avoidance of a particular food that develops when an organism becomes ill after eating the food. *Taste aversions violate two basic principles of classical conditioning:* first, conditioning requires only a single pairing of the CS and UCS, not multiple pairings; second, the time span between the CS and UCS can be several hours, not necessarily a matter of seconds, as Pavlov claimed.

5. *John Garcia demonstrated that taste aversions could be produced under controlled laboratory conditions by* pairing saccharin-flavored water (the CS) with poison (the UCS), which produced illness (the UCR). *He found that* even though the interval between the presentation of the two stimuli was several hours, the rats developed a taste aversion (CR) to the CS and refused to drink the saccharin-flavored water.

6. *Biological preparedness refers to* the idea that organisms are innately predisposed to form associations between certain stimuli and not others.

Concept Check 1

1. behavioral; evolutionary
2. likely; unlikely
3. biological preparedness
4. cognitive
5. spontaneous recovery
6. discriminate
7. conditioned response (CR)
8. generalization
9. (a) chemotherapy treatment; drop in immune response
   (b) cues
   (c) reduced immune functioning

Graphic Organizer 1

Before Conditioning

Food in the mouth is the <u>UCS</u> and the salivation is the <u>UCR</u>.	The neutral stimulus is the <u>CS</u>. It elicits no salivation before conditioning.

During Conditioning

The neutral stimulus is the <u>CS</u>.	+	Food in the mouth is the <u>UCS</u>.	→	The salivation is the <u>UCR</u>.

After Conditioning

The tone alone is the <u>CS</u>.	→	The salivation is now the <u>CR</u>.

Matching Exercise 1

1. extinction
2. conditioning
3. learning
4. taste aversion
5. John B. Watson
6. behaviorism
7. unconditioned stimulus (UCS)
8. Ivan Pavlov
9. phobia
10. unconditioned response (UCR)
11. biological preparedness

True/False Test 1

1. T	5. T	9. T
2. T	6. T	10. T
3. F	7. F	
4. F	8. F	

Operant Conditioning: Associating Behaviors and Consequences (Part 1)

1. *Edward L. Thorndike was the first person to* experimentally study how voluntary behaviors are influenced by their consequences. *He concluded that* (according to his law of effect) animals use the process of trial-and-error, rather than reasoning, to acquire new behaviors and that behaviors followed by satisfying outcomes were "strengthened" (more likely to occur again), and those behaviors followed by unpleasant consequences were "weakened" (less likely to occur).

2. *B. F. Skinner believed that* psychology should restrict itself to studying only overt observable behavior that could be objectively measured and verified, that subjective factors such as internal thoughts, expectations, and perceptions should not be included in psychology, and that the most important form of learning was demonstrated by new behaviors that were actively emitted by the organism (operants).

3. *Operant conditioning is* the learning of active, nonreflexive behavior. *It explains* how we acquire everyday voluntary behaviors.

4. *The basic premise of operant conditioning is* that behavior is shaped and maintained by its consequences.

5. *Reinforcement refers to* the occurrence of a stimulus or event following a response that increases the likelihood of that response being repeated.

6. *Positive reinforcement involves* following an operant with a reinforcing stimulus, thus increasing the likelihood that the response will be repeated. *Negative reinforcement involves* the removal of an aversive or unpleasant stimulus from a situation, thereby increasing the future probability of the behavior that brought about the removal of the stimulus (can involve escape from, or avoidance of, the stimulus). *Negative and positive reinforcement are similar in that* they both increase the probability of the behavior occurring again. *They differ in that* positive reinforcement involves the addition of a reinforcing stimulus, and negative reinforcement involves the removal of a punishing stimulus.

7. *A primary reinforcer is* one that is naturally reinforcing for a given species, *and a conditioned reinforcer (secondary reinforcer) is* one that has acquired reinforcing value by being associated with a primary reinforcer.

8. *Punishment is a* process that decreases the occurrence of behavior and may involve punishment by application (of a punishing stimulus), or punishment by removal (of a reinforcing stimulus).

9. *The factors that influence the effectiveness of punishment are* the consistency and immediacy of the delivery of the punishment following the response. *The drawbacks of punishment are that* it doesn't teach the correct response, it may produce undesirable results, and its effects are likely to be temporary.

Concept Check 2

1. law of effect

2. punishment by application; negative reinforcement

3. positively; negatively

4. Edward L. Thorndike

5. (a) avoidance
   (b) escape
   (c) avoidance
   (d) escape

6. (a) N   (e) P
   (b) P   (f) N
   (c) P   (g) N
   (d) P

Graphic Organizer 2

	Appetitive Stimuli (e.g., food, water)	Aversive Stimuli (e.g., shock)
The operant response is followed by	**Cell 1** FOOD ↑ This is called <u>positive</u> <u>reinforcement</u>	**Cell 2** SHOCK ↓ This is called <u>punishment by</u> <u>application</u>
The operant response precludes or prevents the delivery of	**Cell 3** FOOD ↓ This is called <u>punishment by removal</u>	**Cell 4** SHOCK ↑ This is called <u>negative</u> <u>reinforcement</u>

Matching Exercise 2

1. B. F. Skinner
2. negative reinforcement
3. Edward L. Thorndike
4. punishment
5. conditioned reinforcer
6. reinforcement
7. operant

True/False Test 2

1. T	3. T	5. T
2. F	4. F	6. T

Operant Conditioning: Associating Behaviors and Consequences (Part 2)

1. *Discriminative stimuli are* environmental cues in the presence of which a particular response is likely to be reinforced, and in the absence of which a particular response is not reinforced. *According to Skinner, they are important because* behavior is determined and controlled by the stimuli that are present in a given situation (discriminative stimuli) and not by personal choice or conscious decisions.

2. *Shaping involves* reinforcing successively closer approximations of a behavior until the correct behavior is displayed; it works by allowing the animal to gradually learn the correct response by making reinforcement dependent on getting closer and closer to the target behavior with each attempt.

3. *Partial reinforcement is more effective than continuous reinforcement because it* makes the target behavior more resistant to extinction than behavior that has been continuously reinforced (called the partial reinforcement effect).

4. *The four basic schedules of reinforcement are* fixed-ratio (FR), in which a fixed number of responses are required for reinforcement; variable-ratio (VR), in which an average number of responses, which varies from trial to trial, are needed for reinforcement; fixed-interval (FI), in which a reinforcer is delivered for the first response after a fixed amount of time; and variable-interval (VI), in which a reinforcer is delivered for the first response after an average, and unpredictable, amount of time.

5. *Behavior modification is* the application of learning principles to help people develop more effective or adaptive behaviors, and it has been used in such diverse situations as improving worker performance, increasing social skills, and in the specialized training of animals to help the physically challenged.

Concept Check 3

1. variable-interval (VI)
2. discriminative stimulus
3. fixed-interval (FI)
4. fixed-ratio (FR)
5. shaping
6. variable-ratio (VR)
7. fixed-ratio (FR)

Graphic Organizer 3

	Based on the number of responses made	Based on the elapsed time
Fixed	Cell 1 Fixed ratio	Cell 2 Fixed interval
Variable	Cell 3 Variable ratio	Cell 4 Variable interval

Matching Exercise 3

1. behavior modification
2. continuous reinforcement
3. Skinner box
4. fixed ratio (FR)
5. shaping
6. fixed interval (FI)
7. schedule of reinforcement

True/False Test 3

1. T	3. T	5. F
2. F	4. F	6. T

Contemporary Views of Operant Conditioning

1. *Contemporary learning researchers confirm the basic principles of operant conditioning but also acknowledge* the importance of both cognitive and evolutionary factors in operant conditioning.

2. *Unlike Skinner and Thorndike, Tolman believed that* cognitive processes played an important role in the learning of complex behavior, and he demonstrated their importance with his research on cognitive maps and latent learning.

3. *A cognitive map is* Tolman's term for the mental representation of the layout of a familiar environment. *Latent learning refers to* learning that occurs in the absence of reinforcement but is not demonstrated in overt behavior until a reinforcer becomes available.

4. *Operant conditioning may also be influenced by* biological predispositions to perform natural, or instinctive, behaviors that can interfere with the performance of an operantly conditioned response, a tendency called instinctive drift.

5. *The phenomenon of instinctive drift challenged the traditional behavioral view by* demonstrat-

ing that reinforcement is not the sole determinant of behavior and that instinctive behavior patterns can interfere with the operant conditioning of arbitrary responses.

Observational Learning: Imitating the Actions of Others

1. *Observational learning is* learning that occurs through observing the action of others. *The person most strongly identified with work in this area is* Albert Bandura.

2. *The four cognitive processes that interact to determine if imitation will occur are* attention (you must pay attention to the model), memory (you must remember the model's behavior), motor skills (you must be able to transform the mental representation into actions that you are capable of reproducing), and motivation (you must have some expectation of the outcome of your imitation of the behavior).

3. *Observational learning has been applied in a variety of settings, including* education, vocational and job training, psychotherapy, and counseling.

Concept Check 4

1. observational
2. cognitive
3. likely
4. instinctive drift
5. observational

Matching Exercise 4

1. observational learning
2. latent learning
3. Edward C. Tolman
4. cognitive map
5. Albert Bandura
6. instinctive drift
7. learned helplessness

Something to Think About

1. The first assumption that someone who adheres to the behavioral perspective would make is that the irrational fear, or phobia, was the result of a classical conditioning process. In the past, the client had a very unpleasant experience at a dentist's office. One could speculate that as a child he was taken to the dentist and

experienced pain and fear when a hypodermic needle was inserted into his gum or a drill struck a nerve. If this were the case, the dentist (CS) has become associated with the needle or drill (UCS), which elicited pain and fear (UCR). The dentist (CS) now evokes a fear response (CR), which may have generalized to all dentists.

One way to get rid of the irrational fear would be to use an extinction procedure in which the CS (the dentist) is presented over and over without the UCS until the fear subsides. This might mean that the client will have to find a very understanding dentist who will allow him to make many visits to the office without having any work done. The behavioral perspective predicts that this would eventually result in a reduction of the irrational fear and therefore allow the client to get some much-needed dental work done. It would also be important to point out that following a prolonged absence from the dentist, spontaneous recovery may occur.

2. It is possible that Mrs. Denton's "scolding" may in fact be reinforcing the undesirable behavior. Attention, in almost any form, from an adult can be a powerful positive reinforcer for a child. If this is the case, then withholding reinforcement (scolding) will tend to extinguish the target behavior, but only if it is consistent. Inconsistent or intermittent reinforcement will make the behavior very resistant to extinction.

In addition, she should encourage desirable behavior. She should pay attention to any instance of good behavior, or any close approximation of the goal behavior, by praising her son or providing some other positive reinforcer. In other words, she should use a shaping procedure initially, then use partial reinforcement to ensure that the desirable behavior becomes resistant to extinction. It is also important that she model the appropriate behavior and avoid punishing the child, especially using punishment by application.

3. Operant conditioning techniques can be used to train animals. Decide on the target behavior(s) and start by using a shaping procedure and continuous positive reinforcement. Pick one of the behaviors you want to train—for example, having the dog sit at the command "sit"—and use a reinforcer such as "good dog!" while patting the dog on the head or chest. The command "sit" should be followed with gentle pressure on the dog's rear end to make him sit; he should be reinforced immediately. After just a few trials, the dog will sit on command without the application of pressure to his back; he should always be immediately reinforced. It is important to let the dog know who is in command at all times without using punishment. After the dog is obeying the commands regularly, then switch to a partial reinforcement schedule, only occasionally reinforcing the dog for obeying. This will ensure greater resistance to extinction. Dogs can be trained to do many tricks in this manner, but remember to work with the animal's natural repertoire of behaviors (biological predispositions). Dogs can learn some behaviors more easily than others.

Progress Test 1

1. c	6. a	11. c
2. d	7. b	12. b
3. d	8. a	13. a
4. b	9. c	14. a
5. a	10. a	15. a

Progress Test 2

1. a	6. b	11. a
2. b	7. a	12. d
3. b	8. b	13. c
4. c	9. c	14. d
5. b	10. a	15. b

Progress Test 3

1. d	6. a	11. d
2. c	7. d	12. c
3. d	8. a	13. a
4. c	9. a	14. c
5. a	10. d	15. d

Memory

PREVIEW

Reading the section below first will give you a general sense of the chapter's contents and an initial introduction to some of the major concepts and terms. This will prime you for what you are about to read and help you to develop a "cognitive map" that will guide your study of the material in this chapter. Likewise, reading the **preview questions** at the beginning of each major section will improve your ability to understand, learn, and retain the information.

CHAPTER 6 . . . AT A GLANCE

Chapter 6 examines memory and the mechanisms involved in remembering and forgetting. The first section begins with the fundamental processes of encoding, storage, and retrieval, followed by a discussion of the capacity, duration, and function of each of the three stages of memory: sensory memory, short-term memory, and long-term memory. Elaborative rehearsal is discussed next, along with the types of information stored in long-term memory and the ways in which that information is organized.

How retrieval works and the problems associated with retrieval failure, as in the tip-of-the-tongue phenomenon, are examined. How the serial position effect, encoding specificity principle, and flashbulb memories contribute to our ability to remember—or not remember—information is explored. An explanation of the fact that memories are constructed and reconstructed lays the groundwork for a discussion of the sources of potential memory problems resulting from schema distortion, source confusion, and the misinformation effect. The influence of such problems on eyewitness testimony and false memories are also considered in this section.

Forgetting, theories of forgetting, and relevant research findings are explored next. Finally, the biological basis of memory is explained and the contributions of empirical research and case studies of people with amnesia are presented. The chapter ends with an examination of the role played by brain structures such as the hippocampus and the amygdala.

Introduction: What Is Memory?

Preview Questions

Consider the following questions as you study this section of the chapter.

- How is memory defined?
- What are encoding, storage, and retrieval?
- What is the three-stage model of memory, and what are the characteristics of each stage?
- How do the stages differ, and how do they interact?

*Read the section "Introduction: What Is Memory?" and **write** your answers to the following:*

1. Memory refers to _____

   _____

   _____

2. Encoding is the process of _____

   _____

   Storage is the process of _____

   _____

   Retrieval is the process of _____

   _____

3. The stage model of memory describes memory

   as _____

   _____

   _____

   _____

4. The three stages differ in three ways: _____

   _____

   _____

   _____

   They interact by_____

   _____

   _____

Sensory Memory: Fleeting Impressions of Reality

Preview Questions

Consider the following questions as you study this section of the chapter.

- How long is information from the environment held in sensory memory?

- How did Sperling's experiment establish the duration of visual sensory memory?
- What are the functions of sensory memory?

*Read the section"Sensory Memory: Fleeting Impressions of Reality" and **write** your answers to the following:*

1. Information is held in sensory memory for

   _____

2. Sperling's classic experiment demonstrated

   _____

   _____

   _____

3. An important function of sensory memory (iconic and echoic) is _____

   _____

   _____

Short-Term, Working Memory: The Workshop of Consciousness

Preview Questions

Consider the following questions as you study this section of the chapter.

- What is the main function of short-term, or working, memory?
- What is the duration and capacity of short-term memory?
- How do we overcome the limitations of short-term memory?

*Read the section "Short-term, Working Memory: The Workshop of Consciousness" and **write** your answers to the following:*

1. Short-term, working memory is the stage of

   memory in which _____

   _____

2. The duration of short-term memory is _____

   _____

3. The capacity of short-term memory is _____

   _____

   It can be increased by _____

   _____

Long-Term Memory

Preview Questions

Consider the following questions as you study this section of the chapter.

- How much information can be stored in long-term memory?
- What factors increase the efficiency of encoding?
- What three major categories of information are stored in long-term memory?
- What is the difference between explicit memory and implicit memory?
- How is information organized in long-term memory, and what is one of the best-known models of organization?

*Read the section "Long-Term Memory" and **write** your answers to the following:*

1. The amount of information that can be held in long-term memory is _____

2. Three ways to increase the efficiency of encoding are _____
   _____

3. The major categories of information stored in long-term memory are _____
   _____

4. Explicit memory is _____
   _____

   Implicit memory is _____
   _____

5. Information is organized in long-term memory by_____

6. The best-known model of how information is organized in memory is _____
   _____

   which describes long-term memory as _____
   _____
   _____

After you have carefully studied the preceding sections, complete the following exercises.

Concept Check 1

Read the following and write the correct term in the space provided.

1. During a math exam, Trevor is desperately trying to think of the correct formula for the area of a triangle. Although he knew the formula when he was studying last week, it just won't come to mind, despite all his efforts. Trevor is experiencing trouble with one of the three fundamental processes of memory, called

   _____ .

2. To help learn the number of days in each month, eight-year-old Gloria has been reciting a short rhyme over and over: "Thirty days hath September, April, June, and November; all the rest have thirty-one except February, which has twenty-eight." She is using the fundamental process of _____ to transform the information into a form that can be entered and retained by the memory system.

3. In the above example, Gloria is using a type of rehearsal that is giving some meaning to an otherwise hard-to-remember string of numbers; this is called _____ rehearsal.

4. After looking up a phone number, Alysha is able to remember it only long enough to press all the correct numbers on the keypad. The phone number is in her _____ memory and is briefly stored there by the use of _____ rehearsal.

5. Vito is an excellent chess player and can easily recall the exact positions of most of the chess pieces after a brief glance at the board. He explains his ability by pointing out that he does not try to memorize the locations of all the individual pieces but instead focuses on their relatively few attack patterns. Vito is using _____ to improve the capacity of his short-term memory.

6. Fifty-five-year-old Mr. Adams put on roller skates for the first time in over forty years; much to his surprise, he had no trouble remembering how to skate. In this instance, Mr. Adams is using one of the three categories of information stored in long-term memory, called _____ information.

7. When Stephan was consciously reviewing the information he had researched for a term paper, he was using a dimension of long-term memory called _____ (or declarative memory); later, when he was typing his paper without conscious awareness of the exact layout of the letters on the keyboard, he was using _____ (or nondeclarative memory).

Review of Terms, Concepts, and Names 1

Use the terms in this list to complete the Matching Test, then to help you answer the True/False items correctly.

memory
encoding
storage
retrieval
stage model of memory
sensory memory
short-term memory
  (working memory)
long-term memory
George Sperling
visual sensory memory
  (iconic memory)
auditory sensory
  memory
  (echoic memory)

maintenance rehearsal
chunking
elaborative rehearsal
self-reference effect
visual imagery
procedural information
episodic information
semantic information
explicit memory
implicit memory
clustering
association
semantic network model

Matching Exercise

Match the appropriate term/name with its definition or description.

1. _____ Rehearsal that involves focusing on the meaning of information to help encode and transfer it to long-term memory.

2. _____ Model that describes units of information in long-term memory as being organized in a complex network of associations.

3. _____ The process of recovering information stored in memory so that we are consciously aware of it.

4. _____ Organizing items into related groups during recall from long-term memory.

5. _____ Mental representations, or pictures, especially vivid ones, used to enhance encoding.

6. _____ Active stage of memory in which information is stored for about thirty seconds.

7. _____ Long-term memory of personally experienced events.

8. _____ The process of transforming information into a form that can be entered and retained by the memory system.

9. _____ Model that describes memory as consisting of three distinct stages: sensory memory, short-term memory, and long-term memory.

10. _____ The mental processes that enable us to retain and use information over time.

11. _____ Long-term memory of how to perform different skills, operations, and actions.

12. _____ American psychologist who identified the duration of visual sensory memory in a series of classic experiments in 1960.

True/False Test

Indicate whether each statement is true or false by placing T or F in the blank space next to each item.

1. ____ Information or knowledge that can be consciously recollected is called implicit, or nondeclarative, memory.

2. ____ Visual sensory memory is sometimes referred to as iconic memory because it is a brief memory of an image, or icon.

3. ____ Applying information to yourself to help you remember that information is called the self-reference effect.

4. ____ Semantic information is the general knowledge of facts, names, concepts, and ideas stored in long-term memory.

5. ___ When people are presented with the stimulus word *salt*, they frequently respond with the word *pepper*, and this suggests that there is some logical association between bits of information in long-term memory.

6. ___ Storage is the process of transforming information into a form that can be entered and retained by the memory system.

7. ___ Sensory memory is the stage of memory that registers information from the environment and holds it for a very brief period of time.

8. ___ Maintenance rehearsal involves focusing on the meaning of information to help people encode and transfer it to long-term memory.

9. ___ Increasing the amount of information that can be held in short-term memory by grouping related items together as a single unit is called chunking.

10. ___ Auditory sensory memory is sometimes referred to as echoic memory, meaning a brief memory that is like an echo.

11. ___ Information or knowledge that affects behavior or task performance but cannot be consciously recollected is called explicit, or declarative, memory.

12. ___ Long-term memory is the stage of memory that represents the storage of information over extended periods of time.

Check your answers and review any areas of weakness before going on to the next section.

Retrieval: Getting Information from Long-Term Memory

Preview Questions

Consider the following questions as you study this section of the chapter.

- How is retrieval defined, and what is a retrieval cue?
- What does the TOT experience tell us about the nature of memory?
- How is retrieval tested, and what is the serial position effect?
- What is the encoding specificity principle, and how is it reflected in context effects and mood congruence?

- What role does distinctiveness play in retrieval, and how accurate are flashbulb memories?

*Read the section "Retrieval: Getting Information from Long-Term Memory" and **write** your answers to the following:*

1. Retrieval refers to _____
   _____

   A retrieval cue is _____
   _____

   Retrieval cue failure refers to _____
   _____

2. The tip-of-the-tongue (TOT) experience is
   _____
   _____

   It illustrates the fact that_____
   _____
   _____
   _____

3. Retrieval is tested by _____
   _____
   _____
   _____

4. The serial position effect is _____
   _____
   _____

5. The encoding specificity principle states that
   _____
   _____

6. The context effect (one example of encoding specificity) refers to _____
   _____
   _____

   Mood congruence (another example of encoding specificity) refers to _____

7. Distinctiveness plays a role in retrieval because
   _____
   _____

8. A flashbulb memory is _____
   _____
   _____
   _____

Reconstructing Memories: Sources of Potential Errors

Preview Questions

Consider the following questions as you study this section of the chapter.

- Why do errors and distortions in memory occur during the process of retrieval?
- What are schemas, and what has research shown about how they contribute to memory distortion?
- What is source confusion, and how can it produce false memories?
- What factors can reduce the accuracy of eyewitness testimony?

*Read the section "Reconstructing Memories: Sources of Potential Errors" and **write** your answers to the following:*

1. Errors and distortions occur during the process of retrieval because _____
   _____
   _____

2. A schema is _____
   _____

   Research has demonstrated that our schemas
   _____
   _____
   _____

3. Source confusion is _____
   _____

   It can produce false memories because _____
   _____
   _____
   _____

4. The misinformation effect (one phenomenon that can reduce the accuracy of eyewitness testimony) refers to _____
   _____
   _____

   _____

   After you have carefully studied the preceding sections, complete the following exercises.

Concept Check 2

Read the following and write the correct term in the space provided.

1. When Cathy feels depressed, she remembers certain sad childhood events that she never thinks about otherwise. Cathy is experiencing the effects of _____ .

2. Hendrik has a vivid memory of exactly what he was doing when he heard that President Clinton was impeached. This example illustrates a _____ memory.

3. Although elderly Mrs. Haggerty always answers her family's questions completely, she appears to be filling in blanks with logical, though often incorrect, information. This example illustrates the _____ nature of memory.

4. Jessie cannot remember the newer name of the small Central American country that was formerly called British Honduras until she is told it starts with the letter B. The letter B acts as a _____ for the name *Belize*.

5. The progress tests in this study guide use which measure of memory? _____

6. When Mr. Melvin questioned a witness, he deliberately kept referring to the murder weapon as large scissors instead of garden shears. When the witness was later asked to identify the garden shears as the murder weapon, he appeared slightly confused and said he believed the weapon was a large pair of scissors. Mr. Melvin has successfully used the

   _____ .

7. Research subjects memorized long lists of words while in a room full of fresh flowers. Later, half the subjects were tested in the same room, and half were tested in a room with no flowers. Those tested in the same room recalled significantly more than those in the different room. This is one form of the _____ principle, called the _____ .

Graphic Organizer 1

Read the definitions and fill in the correct term next to the appropriate number in the puzzle below (items 1–6). When you have finished, the letters in the boxes will spell a significant memory term. Write out the definition of this term (item 7).

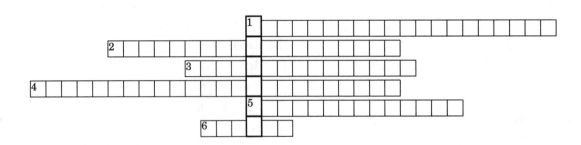

1. The tendency to remember items at the beginning and end of a list better than the items in the middle.

2. The inability to recall long-term memories because of inadequate or missing retrieval cues.

3. The recall of very specific images or details surrounding a vivid, rare, or significant personal event.

4. A memory phenomenon that involves the sensation of knowing that specific information is stored in long-term memory but being temporarily unable to retrieve it.

5. An encoding specificity phenomenon in which a given mood tends to evoke memories that are consistent with that mood.

6. A test of long-term memory that involves retrieving information without the aid of retrieval cues.

7. Write the definition of the memory term:

_____

_____

_____

Review of Terms, Concepts, and Names 2

Use the terms in this list to complete the Matching Test, then to help you answer the True/False items correctly.

retrieval
retrieval cue
retrieval cue failure
tip-of-the-tongue (TOT) experience
recall
cued recall
recognition
serial position effect
serial recall
primacy effect
recency effect

encoding specificity principle
context effect
mood congruence
distinctiveness
flashbulb memory
schema
false memory
source confusion
eyewitness testimony
Elizabeth Loftus
misinformation effect
cryptomnesia

Matching Exercise

Match the appropriate term with its definition or description.

1. _____ Tendency to recover information more easily when the retrieval occurs in the same setting as the original learning of the information.

2. _____ The process of accessing stored information.

3. _____ Organized cluster of information about a particular topic.

4. _____ The tendency to remember items at the beginning and end of a list better than items in the middle.

5. _____ A memory distortion that occurs when the true source of the memory is forgotten.

6. _____ American psychologist who has conducted extensive research on the memory distortions that can occur in eyewitness testimony.

7. _____ Test of long-term memory that involves remembering an item of information in response to a retrieval cue.

8. _____ Memory distortion in which people's existing memories can be altered by exposing them to misleading information.

9. _____ Clue, prompt, or hint that helps trigger recall of a given piece of information stored in long-term memory.

10. _____ Encoding specificity phenomenon in which a given mood tends to evoke memories that are consistent with that mood.

11. _____ Principle that when the conditions of information retrieval are similar to the conditions of information encoding, retrieval is more likely to be successful.

12. _____ Memory distortion in which "hidden," or unremembered, memory becomes the basis for a seemingly "new" memory.

True/False Test

Indicate whether each statement is true or false by placing T or F in the blank space next to each item.

1. ____ The primacy effect refers to the tendency to recall the final items in a list during serial recall.

2. ____ Eyewitness testimony is the most reliable and accurate source of information about events that people have observed and almost always results in the conviction of only the guilty people.

3. ____ A test of long-term memory that involves retrieving information without the aid of retrieval cues is called recall, or free recall.

4. ____ The tip-of-the-tongue (TOT) experience involves the sensation of knowing that specific information is stored in long-term memory but being temporarily unable to retrieve it.

5. ____ Serial recall refers to remembering a list of items in their original order.

6. ____ When the encoded information represents a unique, different, or unusual memory, it is said to be characterized by a high degree of distinctiveness.

7. ____ A distorted or inaccurate memory that feels completely real and is often accompanied by all the emotional impact of a real memory is called a false memory.

8. ____ The inability to recall long-term memories because of inadequate or missing retrieval cues is called retrieval cue failure.

9. ____ The recency effect refers to the tendency to recall the first items in a list during serial recall.

10. ____ Recognition refers to a test of long-term memory that involves identifying correct information from several possible choices.

11. ____ Flashbulb memory refers to recall of very specific images or details surrounding a vivid, rare, or significant personal event.

Check your answers and review any areas of weakness before going on to the next section.

Forgetting: You *Forgot* the Tickets?!

Preview Questions

Consider the following questions as you study this section of the chapter.

- How is forgetting defined?
- What did Ebbinghaus contribute to the study of forgetting?
- What are the four potential causes of forgetting?

Read the section "Forgetting: You Forgot the Plane Tickets?!" and **write** *your answers to the following:*

1. Forgetting is the _____

   _____

2. The Ebbinghaus forgetting curve reveals two distinctive patterns about forgetting:

   (a) _____

   _____

   (b) _____

   _____

3. Encoding failure refers to _____

   _____

4. Interference theory is the theory that _____

   _____

   The two basic types of interference affect memory in the following ways:_____

   _____

   _____

5. Motivated forgetting refers to the idea that

_____

_____

There are two forms of motivated forgetting:

_____

_____

6. According to decay theory_____

_____

_____

The Search for the Biological Basis of Memory

Preview Questions

Consider the following questions as you study this section of the chapter.

- How did research by Lashley and Thompson contribute to our understanding of the physical basis of memory?
- How do neurons change when a memory is formed?
- How have case studies of people with retrograde and anterograde amnesia provided important insights into the brain structures involved in memory?
- What brain structures are involved in normal memory, and what roles do they play?

*Read the section "The Search for the Biological Basis of Memory" and **write** your answers to the following:*

1. Lashley and Thompson contributed to our understanding of the physical basis of memory by_____

_____

2. When a new memory is formed, neurons change in two ways: _____

_____

_____

3. Amnesia refers to _____
   Retrograde amnesia is _____

_____

   Anterograde amnesia is _____

_____

4. The brain structures (and their functions) involved in normal memory are _____

_____

_____

_____

After you have carefully studied the preceding sections, complete the following exercises.

Concept Check 3

Read the following and write the correct term in the space provided.

1. When he first moved to his new apartment, Adam could not remember his new phone number; instead, he would give people his old phone number. Adam's inability to remember his new number is due to _____ interference.

2. At a recent orientation meeting, Juan was introduced to five of the directors; much to his embarrassment, after a short while he could not remember their names. Juan's memory lapse is probably due to _____ .

3. Later that night, while thinking about his embarrassment at the meeting, Juan decided that because it was normal to forget names under such circumstances, he was just not going to think about it any more. Juan is using a form of motivated forgetting called

_____ .

4. Bruno, who was knocked out in his last boxing match, cannot remember anything about the fight or events that happened before the bout. Bruno is most likely suffering from a form of amnesia called _____ amnesia.

5. Mrs. O'Meara, whose hippocampus was removed during a recent brain operation, is most likely to have trouble forming _____ memories.

6. Jackson has just finished a course in Spanish and is experiencing problems in remembering the Italian he learned last semester. Jackson's memory problem is a result of

_____ .

Graphic Organizer 2

Use the following to review forgetting due to interference in the test phase. Write in the type of *interference that is responsible for forgetting in the test phase.*

Memorizing Phase	Test Phase	Type of Interference
1. Learn A first; later learn B	Test A	
2. Learn A first; later learn B	Test B	

Review of Terms, Concepts, and Names 3

Use the terms in this list to complete the Matching Test, then to help you answer the True / False items correctly.

forgetting
Hermann Ebbinghaus
nonsense syllable
forgetting curve
encoding failure
interference theory
retroactive interference
proactive interference
motivated forgetting
suppression
repression
decay theory

memory trace
engram
Karl Lashley
Richard F. Thompson
amnesia
retrograde amnesia
memory consolidation
anterograde amnesia
hippocampus
infantile amnesia
amygdala
senile dementia

Matching Exercise

Match the appropriate term / name with its definition or description.

1. _____ Motivated forgetting that occurs consciously.

2. _____ Loss of memory caused by the inability to store new memories; forward-acting amnesia.

3. _____ The brain changes associated with a particular stored memory.

4. _____ Severe memory loss.

5. _____ American psychologist and neuroscientist who conducted extensive research on the neurobiological foundations of learning and memory.

6. _____ The inability to recall previously available information.

7. _____ Theory that forgetting is due to normal metabolic processes that occur in the brain over time.

8. _____ Motivated forgetting that occurs unconsciously.

9. _____ The theory that forgetting is caused by one memory competing with or replacing another.

10. _____ German psychologist who originated the scientific study of forgetting; plotted the first "forgetting curve," which describes the basic pattern by which learned information is forgotten over time.

11. _____ Inability to recall specific information because of insufficient encoding for storage in long-term memory.

12. _____ The inability to remember infant experiences during adulthood.

True/False Test

Indicate whether each item is true or false by placing T or F in the space next to each item.

1. ____ Karl Lashley was the American physiological psychologist who attempted to find the specific brain location of particular memories.

2. ____ With retroactive interference, an old memory interferes with remembering a new memory; forward-acting memory interference.

3. ____ The idea that forgetting occurs because an undesired memory is held back from awareness is called motivated forgetting.

4. ____ Memory consolidation is the gradual, physical process of converting new long-term memories to stable, enduring long-term memory codes.

5. ___ Retrograde amnesia is the loss of memory caused by the inability to store new memories; forward-acting amnesia.

6. ___ Damage or destruction of the hippocampus can affect the ability to transfer short-term memories into long-term memories.

7. ___ Hermann Ebbinghaus used nonsense syllables to study memory and the forgetting of completely new material rather than information that had preexisting associations in memory.

8. ___ The engram is the name given to the memory trace in the brain associated with the formation of long-term memories.

9. ___ Proactive interference is forgetting in which a new memory interferes with remembering an old memory; backward-acting memory interference.

10. ___ Damage or destruction of the amygdala will make monkeys lose their normal fear of snakes and other natural predators.

11. ___ The forgetting curve reveals two distinct patterns in the relationship between forgetting and the passage of time; much of what is learned is forgotten relatively quickly, and the amount of forgetting eventually levels off.

12. ___ Senile dementia is a condition characterized by impairment of memory and intellectual functions, and its most common cause is Alzheimer's disease.

Check your answers and review any areas of weakness before going on to the next section.

Something to Think About

1. You may have met that rare person who seems to have a perfect memory and rarely forgets anything. Most of us, however, have to struggle to learn and retain at least some of the vast amount of material we are constantly exposed to in the "information age." If someone were to ask you what you have learned about memory and forgetting that could help them, what would you say?

2. Suppose a friend of yours is falsely identified as being the culprit in a grocery store hold-up and comes to you for help. Based on what you know about eyewitness testimony and related phenomena, what advice would you give him?

Check your answers and review any areas of weakness before doing the progress tests.

Progress Test 1

Review the complete chapter (including Concept Reviews and the boxed inserts), review all your study notes, and then test yourself on the following progress test. Check your answers. If you make a mistake, review your notes and the relevant section of the study guide, and, if necessary, go back and read the appropriate part of your textbook.

1. In preparation for his biology exam, Lionel repeats the list of terms and their definitions over and over. Lionel's rehearsal strategy involves the fundamental memory process of
   (a) encoding.   (c) retrieval.
   (b) storage.   (d) wasting his time.

2. Michael, whose aggressive, arrogant behavior and indifferent attitude have resulted in the break-up of many relationships, is contemplating getting married for the third time. Michael is confident that this time it will work and that his previous relationship problems were never his fault. Michael is either actively _____ or unconsciously _____ memory of his own behavior.
   (a) consolidating; schematizing
   (b) schematizing; consolidating
   (c) suppressing; repressing
   (d) repressing; suppressing

3. Five-year-old Betty can recite the alphabet perfectly every time she is asked to do so. Betty's ability to do this involves the fundamental memory process of
   (a) repression.   (c) retrograde amnesia.
   (b) retrieval.   (d) encoding.

4. Acquisition is to retention as _____ is to _____ .

   (a) retrograde; retroactive
   (b) procedural; episodic
   (c) encoding; storage
   (d) storage; retrieval

5. Dirk can remember in vivid detail where he was and what he was doing when he heard about the tragic shooting of students in Littleton, Colorado. Dirk's flashbulb memory is stored in his

   (a) iconic memory.   (c) long-term memory.
   (b) short-term memory. (d) echoic memory.

6. Whenever Killian is introduced to someone, he usually remembers the name by repeating it over and over to himself. Killian is using a memory strategy called

   (a) rehearsal.
   (b) retroactive interference.
   (c) clustering.
   (d) chunking.

7. One conclusion that can be drawn from Ebbinghaus's work on forgetting is that

   (a) we can remember only about seven nonsense syllables at one time.
   (b) when we memorize new information, most forgetting occurs relatively soon after we learn it.
   (c) the duration of visual sensory memory is less than half a second.
   (d) the capacity of long-term memory is large but fleeting.

8. Mrs. Carson was very busy when she phoned her husband and quickly listed the twelve items she wanted him to pick up at the store. After she hung up, Mr. Carson attempted to write down the items. It is likely that he will

   (a) forget the items in the middle.
   (b) remember only the middle and the last items.
   (c) remember only the first and middle items.
   (d) forget the first and last items and remember the items in the middle.

9. At her high school reunion, Chychi met a girl who used to sit next to her in tenth grade, but she could not recall the girl's name. In an attempt to jog her memory, Chychi began reciting the alphabet. When she came to the letter M, she immediately remembered that her schoolfriend's name was Maureen. In this example, the letter of the alphabet

   (a) eliminated source confusion.
   (b) served as a retrieval cue.
   (c) provoked a flashbulb memory.
   (d) reversed encoding failure.

10. Charlie finds it easier to remember a list of words that includes *automobile, cigarettes, encyclopedia, lampshade, geranium,* and *seashell,* compared to a list of the same length that includes *philosophy, processes, justice, abstraction, fundamental,* and *inherent,* because with the first list it is easier to use

    (a) echoic processing.
    (b) maintenance rehearsal.
    (c) procedural memory.
    (d) visual imagery.

11. Karen can remember very clearly when and where she met Jim and how she felt when he first spoke to her. This information, which is stored in Karen's long-term memory, is called

    (a) procedural information.
    (b) episodic information.
    (c) semantic information.
    (d) retroactive information.

12. After his hippocampus was destroyed by a tumor, Mr. Locke is likely to experience problems

    (a) forming procedural memories.
    (b) recognizing common objects.
    (c) correctly repeating items over and over.
    (d) transferring short-term memories into long-term memory.

13. Mr. Locke (in the above example) is likely to be classified as suffering from

    (a) retrograde amnesia.
    (b) anterograde amnesia.
    (c) retrieval cue failure.
    (d) cryptomnesia.

14. According to the Application, one way to make memories last is to learn material over several sessions rather than cramming learning into one long session. This method of study is called
    (a) distributed practice.
    (b) massed practice.
    (c) maintenance rehearsal.
    (d) serial position learning.

15. According to Critical Thinking 6.2, which of the following regarding childhood sexual abuse is true?
    (a) Physical and sexual abuse in childhood can contribute to psychological problems in adulthood.
    (b) It is possible that memories of abuse can become repressed in childhood and surface later in life.
    (c) Repressed memories recovered in therapy need to be regarded with caution.
    (d) A person's confidence in a memory is no guarantee that the memory is accurate.
    (e) All of the above are true.

Progress Test 2

After you have checked your understanding of the material in Progress Test 1 and have done a complete chapter review with special focus on any areas of weakness, you are ready to assess your knowledge in Progress Test 2. Check your answers. If you make a mistake, review your notes, the relevant section of the study guide, and, if necessary, the appropriate part of your textbook.

1. When Gary was preparing for an exam, he tried to make the material more meaningful by using strategies such as visual imagery, creating short stories involving the terms, self-referencing, and so on. Gary is using _____ to help him remember the information.
   (a) elaborative rehearsal
   (b) maintenance rehearsal
   (c) retroactive interference
   (d) proactive interference

2. Shortly after he finished reading an exciting novel, Sean fell down the stairs and suffered a concussion; now, he has no recall of ever having read the novel. Sean's memory problem is probably the result of
   (a) retrieval cue failure.
   (b) source confusion.
   (c) disruption of memory consolidation.
   (d) mood incongruence.

3. Sean (in the above example) is most likely to be classified as suffering from
   (a) anterograde amnesia.
   (b) proactive forgetting.
   (c) retrograde amnesia.
   (d) retroactive forgetting.

4. Richard F. Thompson classically conditioned rabbits to eye-blink to a tone; he later found that there was change in brain activity in the rabbit's cerebellum. This result suggests that some long-term memories
   (a) are stored in a localized region of the brain.
   (b) are distributed and stored across multiple brain locations.
   (c) have no biological or physical basis in the brain.
   (d) are very vulnerable if they are not given enough time to consolidate.

5. Dr. Dement believes that forgetting is due to memory traces being eroded by normal metabolic processes in the brain. Dr. Dement supports the
   (a) interference theory.
   (b) motivated forgetting theory.
   (c) semantic network theory.
   (d) decay theory.

6. When Manfred, who used to be a compulsive gambler, is asked how he did, he recalls losing much less money than was actually the case. Manfred's memory failure best illustrates
   (a) motivated forgetting.
   (b) retrieval cue failure.
   (c) retroactive interference.
   (d) proactive interference.

7. Natasha has memorized the new personal identity code she was given by security; now, she can't remember her old personal identity code. Natasha is experiencing the effects of
   (a) mood congruence.
   (b) source confusion.
   (c) proactive interference.
   (d) retroactive interference.

8. Jeffery, who was an eyewitness to a robbery, initially thought the robber looked like a female. During questioning, a police detective suggested to him many times that the robber was probably a man with long hair. Later, when he was giving testimony on the witness stand, Jeffery was quite sure that it was a man who robbed the store. This example illustrates
   (a) the serial position effect.
   (b) mood congruence.
   (c) a flashbulb memory.
   (d) the misinformation effect.

9. Arvind believes that studying and learning course material in the same room in which the exam is going to be held can help improve his test score. Arvind believes in an encoding specificity principle called
   (a) the context effect.
   (b) the serial position effect.
   (c) the flashbulb memory effect.
   (d) the cued recall effect.

10. The smell of cherry blossoms awakened in Mrs. Yamomoto vivid memories of her childhood in Osaka. The aroma of the blossoms apparently acted as an effective
    (a) schema.   (c) flashbulb cue.
    (b) echoic cue.   (d) retrieval cue.

11. During a discussion about old movies, Grace could not bring to mind the name of the actor who played Sidney Greenstreet's sidekick in *The Maltese Falcon*, despite the fact that she felt she knew the name and had, in fact, talked about his role in the movie on other occasions. Grace is experiencing
    (a) the serial position effect.
    (b) encoding failure.
    (c) the tip-of-the-tongue (TOT) phenomenon.
    (d) anterograde amnesia.

12. Multiple-choice exam questions measure _____ ; short essay questions measure _____ .
    (a) recall; recognition
    (b) recognition; recall
    (c) short-term memory; long-term memory
    (d) long-term memory; short-term memory

13. Harold, who was in the kitchen, asked Jane, who was reading a book in the living room, whether she wanted a diet or a regular soft drink. Jane replied, "What did you say?" but before Harold could respond, Jane said, "Make it a regular Coke, please." This example illustrates
    (a) iconic memory.
    (b) repression.
    (c) echoic memory.
    (d) a flashbulb memory.

14. The Application lists a number of strategies that can be used to improve memory for important information. Which of the following is *not* one of those strategies?
    (a) Use visual imagery.
    (b) Organize the information.
    (c) Counteract the serial position effect.
    (d) Use contextual cues to jog memories during a test.
    (e) Always use massed practice, especially during all-night cramming sessions before a test.

15. According to Science Versus Pseudoscience 6.1, which of the following is true?
    (a) There is ample scientific evidence that people can remember actual past lives.
    (b) There is good reason to believe that many memories of past lives are examples of cryptomnesia.
    (c) Most reincarnation memories can only be recovered by a skilled hypnotherapist.
    (d) Most people cannot recall memories of past lives because of repression.

Progress Test 3

After you have checked your understanding of the material in Progress Tests 1 and 2 and have done a complete chapter review with special focus on any areas of weakness, you are ready to further assess your knowledge on Progress Test 3. Check your answers. If you make a mistake, review your notes, the appropriate parts of the study guide, and, if necessary, the relevant sections of your textbook.

1. Memory with awareness is to _____ as memory without awareness is to _____ .
   (a) explicit memory; implicit memory
   (b) retroactive interference; proactive interference
   (c) implicit memory; explicit memory
   (d) proactive interference; retroactive interference

2. Dr. Rhodes believes that when the conditions of information retrieval are similar to the conditions of information encoding, retrieval is more likely to be successful. This view is most consistent with
   (a) the stage model of memory.
   (b) the semantic network model.
   (c) the encoding specificity principle.
   (d) interference theory.

3. Elizabeth Loftus's story, presented in the Prologue, demonstrates how it is possible to form an extremely vivid, but inaccurate, memory. A common cause of such false memories is
   (a) retrograde amnesia.
   (b) source confusion.
   (c) anterograde amnesia.
   (d) retrieval cue failure.

4. The _____ is to encoding emotional aspects of memory as the _____ is to the encoding and transfer of new information from short-term to long-term memory.
   (a) amygdala; hippocampus
   (b) prefrontal cortex; amygdala
   (c) hippocampus; amygdala
   (d) cerebellum; hippocampus

5. When Danny "the Dynamo" was thrown out of the ring during a wrestling match, he hit his head on the floor and was knocked unconscious. When he finally came to, he had no recollection of the wrestling match or the events leading up to it. It is most probable that Danny is suffering from
   (a) anterograde amnesia.
   (b) cryptomnesia.
   (c) retrograde amnesia.
   (d) senile dementia.

6. Neddy cannot accurately remember the order of the numbers on the small calculator he has owned for ten years and uses quite frequently. Neddy's problem in recall is most likely a function of
   (a) retrieval cue failure.
   (b) proactive interference.
   (c) encoding failure.
   (d) retroactive interference.

7. Most subjects in an experiment responded with *sky* and *grass* to the stimulus words *blue* and *green*. Results such as these support
   (a) the semantic network model.
   (b) decay theory.
   (c) the tip-of-the-tongue (TOT) experience.
   (d) interference theory.

8. Emelia can quite easily list all fifty U.S. states and Canada's ten provinces and two territories. This type of information in long-term memory is called _____ information.
   (a) procedural   (c) semantic
   (b) episodic   (d) implicit

9. Marcus, like most adults, cannot recall events and experiences from the first few years of his life. His infantile amnesia most likely reflects
   (a) the fact that early childhood events were never effectively encoded and stored in the first place.
   (b) motivated repressed memories.
   (c) the fact that childhood memories are forgotten after they have been encoded and stored.
   (d) the fact that the brain does not contain brain structures, such as the hippocampus and amygdala, until after the age of three.

10. Lisa took a strong mood-altering prescription medication while studying for her exam; the following week, she took the same pills before the exam because she wanted to be in the same positive emotional state on both occasions. Lisa appears to believe in the effects of
    (a) maintenance rehearsal.
    (b) elaborative rehearsal.
    (c) mood congruence.
    (d) source confusion.

11. When Kirk was given a long list of items to memorize, he found it easier to remember them when he regrouped all the items according to whether they were vegetables, furniture, animals, and so on. Kirk is using a memory aid called
    (a) the serial position effect.
    (b) the self-referencing technique.
    (c) the context effect.
    (d) chunking.

12. When she first transferred from a college to a university, Kelly had trouble remembering her new student number; she would always recall her old college student number instead. Kelly's memory problem is an example of
    (a) retrograde amnesia.
    (b) proactive interference.
    (c) anterograde amnesia.
    (d) retroactive interference.

13. Mrs. Kahn experienced no trouble skiing despite the fact that she had not been on the slopes for almost fifteen years. Mrs. Kahn's current skiing ability is probably due to _____ information stored in her long-term memory.
    (a) procedural
    (b) episodic
    (c) semantic
    (d) repressed

14. According to Culture and Human Behavior 6.3, declines in memory ability
    (a) are due entirely to a natural, biological aging process.
    (b) may be influenced by cultural expectations about aging and memory abilities.
    (c) are predominantly the function of diseases such as Alzheimer's.
    (d) are most evident in members of the deaf culture who communicate with American Sign Language.

15. According to Science Versus Pseudoscience 6.1, cryptomnesia refers to
    (a) memories of being buried in a mausoleum or crypt.
    (b) a memory distortion in which a seemingly "new" or "original" memory is actually based on an unrecalled previous memory.
    (c) loss of memory caused by the inability to store new memories.
    (d) severe memory loss following a near-death experience.

Answers

Introduction: What Is Memory?

1. *Memory refers to* the group of related mental processes that enable us to acquire, retain, and use information over time.

2. *Encoding is the process of* transforming information into a form that can be entered into and retained by the memory system. *Storage is the process of* retaining information in memory so that it can be used at a later time. *Retrieval is the process of* recovering information stored in memory so that we are consciously aware of it.

3. *The stage model of memory describes memory as* consisting of three distinct stages, sensory memory (the stage that registers information from the environment for a brief period of time), short-term, working memory (the active stage in which information is stored for about 30 seconds), and long-term memory (the stage that represents the long-term storage of information).

4. *The three stages differ in three ways:* capacity (how much information can be stored), duration (how long the information can be stored), and function (what is done with the stored information). *They interact by* transferring information from one to another. Transfer between short-term and long-term memory goes two ways.

Sensory Memory: Fleeting Impressions of Reality

1. *Information is held in sensory memory for* a few seconds or less.

2. *Sperling's classic experiment demonstrated* that our visual sensory memory holds a great deal of information very briefly (for about half a second); this information is available just long enough for us to pay attention to specific elements that are significant to us at that moment.

3. *An important function of sensory memory (iconic and echoic) is* to store sensory impressions very briefly so that they overlap slightly with one another; consequently, we perceive the world around us as continuous, rather than as a series of disconnected images or disjointed sounds.

Short-Term, Working Memory: The Workshop of Consciousness

1. *Short-term, working memory is the stage of memory in which* information transferred from sensory and long-term memory is temporarily stored.

2. *The duration of short-term memory is* approximately 30 seconds, unless the information is rehearsed (maintenance rehearsal).

3. *The capacity of short-term memory is* limited to about seven items, or bits of information (plus or minus two); *it can be increased by* chunking (grouping related items together into a single unit or chunk) and by maintenance rehearsal.

Long-Term Memory

1. *The amount of information that can be held in long-term memory is* essentially unlimited.

2. *Three ways to increase the efficiency of encoding are* to engage in elaborative rehearsal (focus on the meaning of information), use self-referencing (apply information to yourself), and use visual imagery.

3. *The major categories of information stored in long-term memory are* procedural information (how to perform different skills, operations, and actions), episodic information (personally experienced events or episodes), and semantic information (general knowledge that includes facts, names, definitions, concepts, and ideas).

4. *Explicit memory is* information or knowledge that can be consciously recollected (also called declarative memory). *Implicit memory is* information or knowledge that affects behavior or task performance, but cannot be consciously recollected (also called nondeclarative memory).

5. *Information is organized in long-term memory by* clustering and association.

6. *The best-known model of how information is organized in memory is* the semantic network model, *which describes long-term memory as* units of information organized in a complex network of associations.

Concept Check 1

1. retrieval
2. encoding
3. elaborative
4. short-term; maintenance
5. chunking
6. procedural
7. explicit memory; implicit memory

Matching Exercise 1

1. elaborative rehearsal
2. semantic network model
3. retrieval
4. clustering
5. visual imagery
6. short-term memory
7. episodic information
8. encoding
9. stage model of memory

10. memory
11. procedural information
12. George Sperling

True/False Test 1

1. F	6. F	11. F
2. T	7. T	12. T
3. T	8. F	
4. T	9. T	
5. T	10. T	

Retrieval: Getting Information from Long-Term Memory

1. *Retrieval refers to* the process of accessing stored information. *A retrieval cue is* a clue, prompt, or hint that helps trigger recall of a given piece of information stored in long-term memory. *Retrieval cue failure refers to* the inability to recall long-term memories because of inadequate or missing retrieval cues.

2. *The tip-of-the-tongue (TOT) experience is* a memory phenomenon that involves the sensation of knowing that specific information is stored in long-term memory but being temporarily unable to retrieve it. *It illustrates the fact that* retrieving information is not an all-or-nothing process; in many instances, information is stored in memory but is not accessible without the right retrieval cues. It also shows that information stored in memory is organized and connected in relatively logical ways.

3. *Retrieval is tested by* recall (retrieving information without the aid of retrieval cues), cued recall (remembering an item of information in response to a retrieval cue), and recognition (identifying correct information out of several possible choices).

4. *The serial position effect is* the tendency to remember items at the beginning of a list (primacy effect) and at the end of a list (recency effect) better than items in the middle of the list.

5. *The encoding specificity principle states that* when the conditions of information retrieval are similar to the conditions of information encoding, retrieval is more likely to be successful.

6. *The context effect (one example of encoding specificity) refers to* the tendency to recover information more easily when retrieval occurs in the same setting as the original learning of the information. *Mood congruence (another*

example of encoding specificity) refers to the idea that a given mood tends to evoke memories that are consistent with that mood.

7. *Distinctiveness plays a role in retrieval because* highly unusual, surprising, or even bizarre experiences are easier to retrieve from memory than are routine events.

8. *A flashbulb memory is* the recall of very specific images or details surrounding a vivid, rare, or significant event; although confidence about the recollection is usually high, accuracy is not (confidence in a memory is no guarantee of accuracy).

Reconstructing Memories: Sources of Potential Errors

1. *Errors and distortions occur during the process of retrieval because* retrieval involves the active construction and reconstruction of memories and may be affected by the information stored before and after the memory occurred.

2. *A schema is* an organized cluster of information about a particular topic. *Research has demonstrated that our schemas* can influence what we remember, that once a memory is formed it has the potential to be changed by new information, and how easily memories can become distorted.

3. *Source confusion is* a memory distortion that occurs when the true source of the memory is forgotten. *It can produce false memories because* one of the most easily forgotten parts of a memory is its source (how, when, or where it was acquired), and we are capable of confusing something we only heard about, read about, or even seen in a film, with something that really happened.

4. *The misinformation effect (one phenomenon that can reduce the accuracy of eyewitness testimony) refers to* a memory-distortion phenomenon in which a person's existing memories can be altered if the person is exposed to misleading information.

Concept Check 2

1. mood congruence
2. flashbulb
3. reconstructive
4. retrieval cue
5. recognition
6. misinformation effect
7. encoding specificity; context effect

Graphic Organizer 1

```
                                 1
                                 S E R I A L P O S I T I O N E F F E C T
              2                    |
              R E T R I E V A L C U E F A I L U R E
                             3     |
                             F L A S H B U L B M E M O R Y
     4                           | |
     T I P O F T H E T O N G U E E X P E R I E N C E
                               5 |
                               M O O D C O N G R U E N C E
                 6             |
                 R E C A L L
```

7. An organized cluster of information about a particular topic

Matching Exercise 2

1. context effect
2. retrieval
3. schema
4. serial position effect
5. source confusion
6. Elizabeth Loftus
7. cued recall

8. misinformation effect
9. retrieval cue
10. mood congruence
11. encoding specificity principle
12. cryptomnesia

True/False Test 2

1. F	5. T	9. F
2. F	6. T	10. T
3. T	7. T	11. T
4. T	8. T	

Forgetting: You *Forgot* the Plane Tickets?!

1. *Forgetting is the* inability to recall information that was previously available.

2. *The Ebbinghaus forgetting curve reveals two distinct patterns of memory: (a)* much of what we forget is lost relatively soon after we originally learned it; *(b)* the amount of forgetting eventually levels off, with information that is not quickly forgotten remaining quite stable in memory over long periods of time.

3. *Encoding failure refers to* the inability to recall specific information because of insufficient encoding for storage in long-term memory.

4. *Interference theory is the theory that* forgetting is caused by one memory competing with or replacing another memory. *The two basic types of interference affect memory in the following ways:* in retroactive interference, a new memory interferes with remembering an old memory (backward-acting memory interference); in proactive interference, an old memory interferes with remembering a new memory (forward-acting memory interference).

5. *Motivated forgetting refers to the idea that* we forget because we are motivated to forget, usually because a memory is unpleasant or disturbing. *There are two forms of motivated forgetting:* suppression (a conscious or deliberate effort to forget) and repression (unconscious motivation to forget).

6. *According to decay theory,* forgetting is due to normal metabolic processes that occur in the brain over time.

The Search for the Biological Basis of Memory

1. *Lashley and Thompson contributed to our understanding of the physical basis of memory by* demonstrating that memories have the potential to be both localized and distributed: very simple memories are localized in a specific area, and more complex memories appear to be distributed throughout the brain.

2. *When a new memory is formed, neurons change in two ways:* functionally, they increase the amount of neurotransmitters they produce, and structurally, they show an increase in the number of interconnecting branches between neurons as well as in the number of synapses on each branch.

3. *Amnesia refers to* severe memory loss. *Retrograde amnesia is* loss of memory, especially for episodic information (backward-acting amnesia). *Anterograde amnesia is* loss of memory caused by the inability to store new memories (forward-acting amnesia).

4. *The brain structures (and their functions) involved in normal memory are* the cerebellum (memories involving movement), amygdala (associates memories involving different senses and encodes the emotional aspects of memories), prefrontal cortex (memories of sequences of events), and the hippocampus (encodes and transfers new explicit memories to long-term memory).

Concept Check 3

1. proactive
2. encoding failure
3. suppression
4. retrograde
5. long-term
6. retroactive interference

Graphic Organizer 2

1. retroactive interference
2. proactive interference

Matching Exercise 3

1. suppression
2. anterograde amnesia
3. memory trace
4. amnesia
5. Richard F. Thompson
6. forgetting
7. decay theory
8. repression
9. interference theory
10. Hermann Ebbinghaus
11. encoding failure
12. infantile amnesia

True/False Test 3

1. T	5. F	9. F
2. F	6. T	10. T
3. T	7. T	11. T
4. T	8. T	12. T

Something to Think About

1. We are all vulnerable to forgetting, and sometimes the consequences can be serious. What can we do to improve memory? Fortunately, a number of strategies can help us to remember important information. You might begin your answer with a discussion of the fundamental processes of encoding, storage, and retrieval, then explain the function, capacity, and duration of each of the three stages of memory. Of course, no discussion of the topic of memory would be complete without mentioning Ebbinghaus's work on forgetting as well as the contributions of the various theories of forgetting to our understanding of memory. Finally, mention the ten most important strategies that could help improve memory, as described in the Application.

2. It is a real nightmare to contemplate the prospect of being falsely accused of a crime and having an eyewitness point at you and say very confidently, "Yes, that is the person. There's no doubt about it, he did it!" What can be done in such a situation? If you don't have an alibi, the jury is very likely to believe a confident eyewitness who, under oath, points a finger at the accused. First, you might consider hiring an expert witness, such as Elizabeth Loftus, to testify to the problems inherent in eyewitness testimony. Such testimony, based on scientific evidence, is difficult to refute. If your friend cannot afford the testimony of an expert witness, then we suggest he try to educate his defense lawyer about the relevant research findings in this important area of psychology. These include source confusion, the personal schema of the eyewitness, the power of the misinformation effect, evidence related to false memories, and relevant aspects of the encoding specificity principle. An additional source of information is a recent report published by the United Stated Department of Justice, which contains new guidelines for use of eyewitness evidence based on years of psychological research into eyewitness testimony (see textbook reference list for complete information about this report).

Progress Test 1

1. a	6. a	11. b
2. c	7. b	12. d
3. b	8. a	13. b
4. c	9. b	14. a
5. c	10. d	15. e

Progress Test 2

1. a	6. a	11. c
2. c	7. d	12. b
3. c	8. d	13. c
4. a	9. a	14. e
5. d	10. d	15. b

Progress Test 3

1. a	6. c	11. d
2. c	7. a	12. b
3. b	8. c	13. a
4. a	9. a	14. b
5. c	10. c	15. b

CHAPTER 7

Thinking, Language, and Intelligence

PREVIEW	Reading the section below first will give you a general sense of the chapter's contents and an initial introduction to some of the major concepts and terms. This will prime you for what you are about to read and help you to develop a "cognitive map" that will guide your study of the material in this chapter. Likewise, reading the **preview questions** at the beginning of each major section will improve your ability to understand, learn, and retain the information.

CHAPTER 7. . . AT A GLANCE

Chapter 7 combines thinking, language, and intelligence, three closely related cognitive functions. The section on thinking begins with discussions of the use of mental imagery and concept formation. This leads to a description of problem-solving strategies, followed by an explanation of two common obstacles to effective problem solving, functional fixedness and mental sets. The section concludes with a discussion of different decision-making models.

The next section, on our remarkable cognitive capacity for language, first explains the character of language, then explores the various ways in which language influences thought. Animal communication and the controversial debate over whether or not animals are capable of language finishes up this section.

Our ability to think and use language are aspects of what we call intelligence. Because the measurement of intelligence has been a controversial issue, this section provides some background into the development of intelligence testing and the contributions of various psychologists. The difference between aptitude tests and achievement tests is explained, and the requirements of standardization, reliability, and validity are described as a way of understanding the problems of testing.

The debate over the nature of intelligence centers on whether intelligence is a single, general ability or a cluster of different abilities, and on whether intelligence should be narrowly or broadly defined. Four theories regarding this issue are presented. The heredity-environment debate regarding the origins of intelligence is examined in detail.

Introduction: Thinking, Language, and Intelligence

Preview Questions

Consider the following questions as you study this section of the chapter.

- How is thinking defined, and what does it typically involve?
- What are mental images, and how do we manipulate them?
- What are concepts, and how are they formed?
- What is a prototype, and what role do prototypes play in concept formation?

*Read the section "Introduction: Thinking, Language, and Intelligence" and **write** your answers to the following:*

1. Thinking is defined as _____

   It typically involves _____

2. A mental image is _____

3. We manipulate mental images _____

   They are potentially subject to error and distortion because _____

4. Concepts are _____
   The two ways of forming concepts are _____

5. A prototype is _____

   The more closely an item matches a prototype,

Solving Problems and Making Decisions

Preview Questions

Consider the following questions as you study this section of the chapter.

- How is problem solving defined?
- What are four problem-solving strategies, and what are the advantages and/or disadvantages of each?
- What are functional fixedness and mental sets, and how do they interfere with problem solving?

*Read the section "Solving Problems and Making Decisions" and **write** your answers to the following:*

1. Problem solving is defined as _____

2. The trial-and-error strategy involves _____

3. An algorithm involves _____

4. A heuristic is a _____

5. Insight is the _____

6. Functional fixedness is _____

7. A mental set is _____

Decision-Making Strategies

Preview Questions

Consider the following questions as you study this section of the chapter.

- What are the single-feature, additive, and elimination by aspects models of decision making?
- Under what conditions is each strategy appropriate?
- When are the availability and representativeness heuristics used, and what potential problems are associated with each?

Read the section "Decision-Making Strategies" and **write** *your answers to the following:*

1. The single-feature model involves _____

   _____

   It is appropriate when _____

   _____

2. With the additive model, you first _____

   _____

   _____

   It is appropriate for _____

   _____

3. Using the elimination by aspects model, you

   _____

   _____

   _____

   It is appropriate when _____

   _____

4. The availability heuristic is a strategy _____

   _____

   _____

5. The representativeness heuristic is a strategy

   _____

   _____

   _____

After you have carefully studied the preceding sections, complete the following exercises.

Concept Check 1

Read the following and write the correct term in the space provided.

1. After a chimpanzee tries unsuccessfully to get bananas that are out of reach, she sits for a long time staring at them. Suddenly, she looks around the cage, picks up a stick, and uses it to pull the bananas within her reach, something she has never done before. Her solution to the banana problem is probably the result of

   _____ .

2. You learn that one of the Russell children is taking ballet classes; you immediately conclude that it is their one daughter rather than any of their three sons. You reached a possibly erroneous conclusion by using the

   _____ .

3. Dr. Mendleson studies how people manipulate mental representations to draw inferences and conclusions. Dr. Mendleson is most likely a _____ psychologist interested in people's _____ ability.

4. You are asked to decide which city is farther north, Edinburgh, Scotland, or Stockholm, Sweden, so you try to picture a map of Europe in your mind. You are using a

   _____ .

5. Marisa has learned the rules and features that define a square, a rectangle, and a right-angle triangle. Marisa has learned a _____ concept.

6. Henry had trouble recognizing that a seahorse is a fish because it does not closely resemble his _____ concept of fish.

7. In order to convert liters into U.S. gallons, Natalie multiplies the number of liters by 0.264178. She is using a(n) _____ to arrive at the correct answer.

8. Hilda is asked to complete the sequence "J, F, M, A, _, _, _, _, _, _, _, _." After trying a few different possibilities, she comes up with the correct answer—M, J, J, A, S, O, N, D (the first letter of the months of the year). It appears that Hilda is using a(n)

   _____ strategy to solve the problem.

9. Anatole is trying to decide which of two equally affordable and attractive cars to purchase, so he makes a list of the advantages and disadvantages of each using an arbitrary rating scale. Anatole is using the _____ model to help him make a decision.

Review of Terms and Concepts 1

Use the terms in this list to complete the Matching Test, then to help you answer the True/False items correctly.

cognition
thinking
mental image
concepts
formal concept
natural concept
prototype
problem solving
trial and error
algorithms
heuristic
subgoals
working backward

insight
functional fixedness
mental set
intuition
single-feature model
additive model
elimination by aspects
   model
availability heuristic
representativeness
   heuristic

Matching Exercise

Match the appropriate term with its definition or description.

1. _____ Decision-making model in which all the alternatives are evaluated one characteristic at a time, starting with the most important feature and scratching each alternative off the list of possible choices if it fails to meet the criterion.

2. _____ The manipulation of mental representations of information in order to draw inferences or conclusions.

3. _____ Most typical instance of a particular concept.

4. _____ Sudden realization of how a problem can be solved.

5. _____ Decision-making strategy in which the choice among many alternatives is simplified by basing the decision on a single feature.

6. _____ Strategy in which the likelihood of an event is estimated by comparing how similar it is to the typical prototype of the event.

7. _____ Problem-solving strategy that involves attempting different solutions and eliminating those that do not work.

8. _____ Mental category that is formed by learning the rules or features that define it.

9. _____ The mental activities involved in acquiring, retaining, and using knowledge.

10. _____ Mental category of objects or ideas based on properties that they share.

11. _____ Problem-solving strategy that involves following a general rule of thumb to reduce the number of possible solutions.

True/False Test

Indicate whether each statement is true or false by placing T or F in the blank space next to each item.

1. ___ Working backward is a common heuristic used to break a problem down into a series of smaller problems; as each subproblem is solved, you get closer to solving the larger problem.

2. ___ A mental representation of objects or events that are not physically present is called a mental image.

3. ___ Problem solving is thinking and behavior directed toward attaining a goal that is not readily available.

4. ___ The tendency to persist in solving problems with solutions that have worked in the past is called functional fixedness.

5. ___ The additive model of decision making involves generating a list of the most important factors, then using an arbitrary rating scale to rate each alternative on each factor, and finally adding the ratings together for comparison purposes.

6. ___ The availability heuristic is a strategy in which the likelihood of an event is estimated on the basis of how easily other instances of the event are available in memory.

7. ___ A natural concept is a mental category that is formed as a result of everyday experience.

8. ___ A useful heuristic in which you start at the end point and determine the steps necessary to reach your goal uses the analysis of subgoals.

9. ___ A mental set is the tendency to view objects as functioning only in their usual or customary manner.

10. ___ Intuition refers to the process of coming to a conclusion or making a judgment without conscious awareness.

11. ____ A problem-solving strategy that involves following a specific rule, procedure, or method that inevitably produces the correct solution is referred to as an algorithm.

Check your answers and review any areas of weakness before going on to the next section.

Language and Thought

Preview Questions

Consider the following questions as you study this section of the chapter.

- How is language defined?
- What are the five most important characteristics of language?
- In what ways does language influence thinking?
- Can animals use language?

Read the section "Language and Thought" and **write** *your answers to the following:*

1. Language is defined as _____

_____

2. The five most important characteristics of language are: _____
   (a) _____
   _____
   (b) _____
   _____
   (c) _____
   _____
   (d) _____
   _____
   (e) _____
   _____

3. An important way in which language can influence thought has to do with _____

_____

_____

_____

4. Animals communicate with each other and with other species, but _____

_____

_____

_____

Measuring Intelligence

Preview Questions

Consider the following questions as you study this section of the chapter.

- How is intelligence defined?
- What roles did Binet, Terman, and Wechsler play in the development of intelligence tests?

Read the section "Measuring Intelligence" and **write** *your answers to the following:*

1. Intelligence is defined as _____

_____

_____

2. Alfred Binet, along with psychiatrist Theodore Simon, devised _____

_____

_____

_____

3. Lewis Terman translated and adapted _____

_____

_____

_____

4. David Wechsler developed a new intelligence test, _____

_____

_____

_____

Principles of Test Construction: What Makes a Good Test?

Preview Questions

Consider the following questions as you study this section of the chapter.

- How do achievement tests differ from aptitude tests?

- What does it mean to standardize a test?
- What is the role of norms in standardization, and what is the normal curve?
- How are reliability and validity defined, and how are they determined?

*Read the section "Principles of Test Construction: What Makes a Good Test?" and **write** your answers to the following:*

1. Achievement tests are designed to _____
   _____

   Aptitude tests are designed to _____
   _____

2. Standardization refers to _____
   _____
   _____

3. The normal curve, or normal distribution, is
   _____
   _____

4. Reliability is defined as _____
   _____

   It is determined by _____
   _____

5. Validity is defined as _____
   _____

   It is determined by _____
   _____

_____

After you have carefully studied the preceding sections, complete the following exercises.

Concept Check 2

Read the following and write the correct term in the space provided.

1. A Norwegian visitor to England asks the hotel clerk, "Can you please my key to my room give me?" This visitor has apparently not yet mastered the _____ of the English language.

2. When Elinore's husband refers to her psychiatrist as a "headshrinker" during discussions with friends or family, he may be influencing their _____ perceptions of Elinore and her therapist.

3. Ten-year-old Jean performed at the same level as most 12-year-olds on Binet's test. Her _____ age is different from her _____ age.

4. According to his score on the Standard-Binet test, Marcel's mental age is identical to his chronological age. Marcel's IQ score is likely to be _____ .

5. When 25-year-old Dagmar applied for a position with the Department of Defense, she was given a test; she scored slightly above the norm on overall verbal ability but well above the norm in overall performance for her age group. The test Dagmar was given was a(n) _____ called the _____ .

6. The test and retest scores on the new Zander jealousy scale were highly similar but lacked predictive value; furthermore, it was not clear exactly what human attribute it was measuring. The Zander test was high in _____ but low in _____ .

Review of Terms, Concepts, and Names 2

Use the terms in this list to complete the Matching Test, then to help you answer the True/False items correctly.

language
linguistic relativity
  hypothesis
syntax
generative
displacement
animal cognition
  (comparative cognition)
intelligence
Alfred Binet
mental age
Lewis Terman
Stanford-Binet
  Intelligence Scale
intelligence quotient
  (IQ)

David Wechsler
Wechsler Adult
  Intelligence Scale
  (WAIS)
verbal score
performance score
achievement test
aptitude test
standardization
normal curve (normal
  distribution)
reliability
validity

Matching Exercise

Match the appropriate term/name with its definition or description.

1. _____ Every language's unique rules for combining words.

2. _____ The French psychologist who, along with French psychiatrist Théodore Simon, developed the first widely used intelligence test.

3. _____ The ability to communicate meaningfully about ideas, objects, and activities that are not physically present.

4. _____ Measure of intelligence in which an individual's mental level is expressed in terms of the average abilities of a given age group.

5. _____ Name of Lewis Terman's translation and revision of the Binet-Simon intelligence test.

6. _____ The ability of a test to measure what it is intended to measure.

7. _____ Characteristic of language that allows one to create an infinite number of new and different phrases and sentences.

8. _____ The study of animal learning, memory, thinking, and language.

9. _____ Bell-shaped distribution of individual differences in a normal population in which most scores cluster around the average score.

10. _____ The global capacity to think rationally, act purposefully, and deal effectively with the environment.

11. _____ System for combining arbitrary symbols to produce an infinite number of meaningful statements.

True/False Test

Indicate whether each item is true or false by placing T or F in the space next to each item.

1. ___ Lewis Terman was a French psychiatrist who, along with French psychologist Alfred Binet, developed the first widely used intelligence test, called the Binet-Terman IQ Test.

2. ___ David Wechsler was the American psychologist who developed the Wechsler Adult Intelligence Scale (WAIS), the most widely used intelligence scale.

3. ___ An aptitude test is designed to measure a person's level of knowledge, skill, or accomplishments in a particular area, such as mathematics or a foreign language.

4. ___ The intelligence quotient (IQ) is a global measure of intelligence derived by comparing an individual's score to that of others in the same age group.

5. ___ The *verbal score* on the WAIS reflects scores on subtests such as identifying missing parts in incomplete pictures, arranging pictures to tell a story, or arranging blocks to match a given pattern.

6. ___ Reliability refers to the ability of a test to produce consistent results when administered on repeated occasions under similar conditions.

7. ___ Standardization is the process of administering a test to a large, representative sample of people under uniform conditions for the purpose of establishing norms.

8. ___ An achievement test is designed to measure a person's capacity to benefit from education or training.

9. ___ The *performance score* on the WAIS represents scores on subtests of vocabulary, comprehension, knowledge of general information, and other similar tasks.

10. ___ The Wechsler Adult Intelligence Scale (WAIS) was designed as an achievement test but is now widely used as an aptitude test.

11. ___ The notion that differences among languages cause differences in the thoughts of their speakers is called the linguistic relativity hypothesis.

Check your answers and review any areas of weakness before going on to the next section.

The Nature of Intelligence

Preview Questions

Consider the following questions as you study this section of the chapter.

- What are the two key issues involved in the debate over the nature of intelligence?

- What is the *g* factor (general intelligence), and who first proposed the theory?

- What was Louis L. Thurstone's contribution to the debate about the nature of intelligence?
- Who proposed the idea of "multiple intelligences," and what are the eight distinct intelligences?
- What is the triarchic theory of intelligence, and who proposed it?

*Read the section "The Nature of Intelligence" and **write** your answers to the following:*

1. The two key issues involved in the debate over the nature of intelligence are:

   (a) _____

   _____

   (b) _____

   _____

2. The g factor (or general intelligence) is the notion _____

   _____

   It was proposed by _____

3. Louis L. Thurstone proposed the notion that

   _____

   _____

4. The idea of multiple intelligences was proposed by_____

   The eight intelligences are _____

   _____

   _____

   _____

5. The triarchic theory of intelligence proposes that_____

   _____

   It was developed by _____

The Roles of Genetics and Environment in Determining Intelligence

Preview Questions

Consider the following questions as you study this section of the chapter.

- What is the heredity-environment issue?
- How are twin studies used to measure genetic and environmental influences?

- What is heritability, and why can't heritability estimates be used to explain differences between groups?
- Are IQ tests culturally biased?

*Read the section "The Roles of Genetics and Environment in Determining Intelligence" and **write** your answers to the following:*

1. The basic heredity-environment issue is concerned with _____

   _____

   _____

   _____

2. Twin studies have been used because _____

   _____

   _____

3. Heritability is defined as _____

   _____

   Heritability estimates cannot be used to explain differences between groups because _____

   _____

   _____

   _____

4. It is virtually impossible to create a culture-free IQ test because _____

   _____

   _____

   _____

After you have carefully studied the preceding sections, complete the following exercises.

Concept Check 3

Read the following and write the correct term in the space provided.

1. Although Dr. Bowman recognizes that particular individuals might excel in specific areas, she believes that a factor, called general intelligence, or the g factor, is responsible for overall performance on mental ability tests. Her belief about the nature of intelligence is most consistent with the approach taken by psychologist

   _____ .

2. Jamal is a highly valued maintenance worker because of his almost uncanny ability to be able to fix almost any piece of equipment that breaks down. Jamal is demonstrating what Robert Sternberg would call _____ intelligence.

3. Selma is a very successful, highly motivated, goal-directed, creative graphic designer. These aspects of her intelligence are _____ (not likely/very likely) to be assessed and measured on a conventional intelligence test.

4. Dicky and Ricky are identical twins and have almost identical IQ scores despite the fact that they were separated at birth and raised separately. Fraternal twins Joel and Joanna were raised together but their IQ scores are much less similar than Dicky and Ricky's scores. This example provides the most support for the _____ side in the heredity-environment debate.

5. As compared with the scores of two randomly selected unrelated people of the same age, Joel and Joanna's IQ scores are much more similar. This finding provides most support for the _____ side in the heredity-environment debate.

6. Dr. Yokomoto, like the majority of experts on intelligence testing, is most likely to attribute the finding that Japanese and Chinese children outperform American children on mathematics achievement tests to _____ factors.

7. When Dr. Parsei, an expert on intelligence testing, was asked if a completely culture-free intelligence test could be designed, he replied that it _____ (was/was not) because group ability tests reflect the values, knowledge, and communication strategies of their culture of origin.

Graphic Organizer 2

Read the following statements and decide which psychologist is most associated with each.

Statement	Psychologist
1. I define intelligence as the global capacity to think rationally, act purposefully, and deal effectively with the environment; a good IQ test should have both verbal and performance scores representing subtests that measure a variety of abilities.	
2. My theory of intelligence emphasizes both universal aspects of intelligent behavior and the importance of adapting to the individual's particular social and cultural environment; there are essentially three forms of intelligence: analytical, creative, and practical intelligence.	
3. I'm not sure I have a fully developed theory of intelligence, but I do believe that we can help children do better in school if we devise tests that can identify those who need help and then provide that help. There is a great deal of variation in intelligence in any age group of children.	
4. I am convinced that a factor called general intelligence, or the *g* factor, is responsible for the overall performance on mental ability tests. Furthermore, I would go so far as to say that intelligence can be accurately expressed as a single number that reflects an individual's intellectual abilities.	
5. I disagree with those who say that intelligence is a single, general mental capacity. On the basis of my observations of what is valued in different cultures, I've concluded that there are multiple intelligences (at least seven), each independent of the other, and these must be viewed in the context of a particular culture.	
6. I tend to agree with statement 4 above. In addition, I believe that intelligence can best be expressed by a number I call the intelligence quotient, or IQ, which is derived by dividing the mental age by the chronological age and multiplying the result by 100.	

Review of Terms, Concepts, and Names 3

Use the terms in this list to complete the Matching Test, then to help you answer the True/False items correctly.

Charles Spearman
g factor (general
  intelligence)
L. L. Thurstone
primary mental abilities
Howard Gardner
Robert Sternberg
triarchic theory of
  intelligence

analytical intelligence
creative intelligence
practical intelligence
heredity
environment
identical twins
fraternal twins
heritability
creativity

Matching Exercise

Match the appropriate term/name with its definition or description.

1. _____ A contemporary American psychologist whose triarchic theory of intelligence includes three forms of intelligence (analytical, creative, and practical).

2. _____ The percentage of variation within a given population that is due to heredity.

3. _____ A factor of intelligence that is responsible for a person's overall performance on tests of mental ability.

4. _____ A group of cognitive processes used to generate useful, original, and novel ideas or solutions.

5. _____ American psychologist who advanced the theory that intelligence is composed of several primary mental abilities and cannot be accurately described by a general intelligence, or *g*, factor.

6. _____ Sternberg's type of intelligence that involves the ability to adapt to the environment and often reflects what is commonly described as street smarts.

7. _____ British psychologist who advanced the theory that a general intelligence factor, called the *g* factor, is responsible for overall intellectual functioning.

8. _____ A form of intelligence that involves the ability to deal with novel situations by drawing on existing skills and knowledge.

True/False Test

Indicate whether each item is true or false by placing T or F in the space next to each item.

1. ____ Howard Gardner is a contemporary American psychologist whose theory of intelligence states that there is not one intelligence but multiple intelligences, the importance of each being determined by cultural values.

2. ____ Identical twins develop from two different fertilized eggs and are 50 percent genetically similar to each other.

3. ____ Heredity refers to the traits, capacities, and intellectual potential that we inherit from our parents, grandparents, and great-grandparents.

4. ____ Analytical intelligence refers to the mental processes used in learning how to solve problems, that is, in picking a problem-solving strategy and applying it to solve problems.

5. ____ In the debate over what determines intelligence, environment refers to factors such as type of upbringing, nutritional and health standards, social and cultural factors, and other influences that may have an impact on intellectual development.

6. ____ Fraternal twins share exactly the same genes because they developed from a single fertilized egg that split into two.

7. ____ Sternberg's theory that there are three forms of intelligence—analytical, creative, and practical—is called the triarchic theory of intelligence.

8. ____ According to Thurstone, primary mental abilities are relatively independent elements of intelligence and include verbal comprehension, numerical ability, reasoning, and perceptual speed.

Check your answers and review any areas of weakness before going on to the next section.

Something to Think About

1. Many people mistakenly believe that creativity is restricted to a few gifted, genius-level, artistic people. What would you tell someone who wants to be creative but does not believe he or she possesses an artistic temperament?

2. People vary in their IQ test scores, but about 68 percent of scores on tests such as the WAIS-R are between 85 and 115, the range for normal intelligence. A friend comes up to you and says, "Wouldn't it be great if we all had above-average IQ scores? Just think how wonderful life would be and how happy and successful we'd be!" How might you enlighten your friend about IQ tests and IQ scores?

Check your answers and review any areas of weakness before doing the progress tests.

Progress Test 1

Review the complete chapter (including Concept Reviews and all the boxed inserts), review all your study notes, and then test yourself on the following progress test. Check your answers. If you make a mistake, review your notes, review the relevant section of the study guide, and, if necessary, go back and read the appropriate part of your textbook.

1. In applying for a job at O'Hare Airport, Lynda is given a test to see if she is suited to be an air traffic controller. This is an example of _____ testing.
   (a) intelligence   (c) aptitude
   (b) achievement   (d) motivational

2. When Aaron is asked to define *weapon*, he responds that it is anything you could use to beat someone with. Aaron is using the word *weapon* as a
   (a) natural concept.   (c) formal concept.
   (b) prototype.   (d) heuristic.

3. When Michelle is asked the same question as Aaron, she replies that a weapon is one of a variety of instruments, or objects, that can be used to defend, attack, hurt, maim, or kill. Furthermore, the term *weapon* can even refer to words in a phrase, as in "the pen is mightier than the sword." Michelle is using the word *weapon* as a
   (a) natural concept.   (c) formal concept.
   (b) prototype.   (d) heuristic.

4. When three-year-old Claudia is asked which letter of the alphabet comes before *G*, she recites the alphabet from the beginning until she arrives at the solution. Claudia is using _____ to solve the problem.
   (a) trial and error   (c) an algorithm
   (b) insight   (d) a heuristic

5. Louis forgot to bring his pillow when he went camping for the weekend, so he spent a very uncomfortable night. It didn't occur to Louis that he could use his down-filled jacket as a pillow. This example best illustrates
   (a) functional fixedness.
   (b) mental set.
   (c) the availability heuristic.
   (d) use of an algorithm.

6. When Vasilis is faced with the decision of which of two equally attractive apartments to rent, he makes a list of what is most important and gives each factor a numerical rating. It appears that Vasilis is using the _____ model of decision making.
   (a) elimination by aspects
   (b) additive
   (c) single-feature
   (d) heuristic

7. Jerome recently saw a TV special in which most of the psychologists interviewed were middle-aged males. When he took his first psychology class, he was surprised to find that his professor was a young female rather than an older, bearded male. Jerome's surprise is probably due to his use of the
   (a) availability heuristic.
   (b) representativeness heuristic.
   (c) single-feature model.
   (d) additive model.

8. When Heidi tells Hans that she is going to enter a foot race to raise funds to end the arms race, he has no trouble understanding that she is going to run in a race to generate support for an anti-weapons cause. Hans's correct interpretation best illustrates the importance of
   (a) syntax.   (c) generativity.
   (b) displacement.   (d) prototypes.

9. When asked what she does for a living, Krista always replies that she is a sanitary engineer rather than a garbage collector. Krista is probably aware of the effect of language on
   (a) functional fixedness. (c) social perception.
   (b) gender bias.   (d) income level.

10. Six-year-old Bruce's performance on an intelligence test is at a level characteristic of an average four-year-old. Bruce's mental age is
    (a) eight.   (c) six.
    (b) four.   (d) five.

11. Scott is a very bright ten-year-old with a mental age of thirteen. If tested on the Stanford-Binet Intelligence Scale, his IQ score would most likely be
    (a) 100.   (c) 150.
    (b) 77.   (d) 130.

12. Twenty-year-old Val has just taken a test that includes vocabulary, comprehension, general knowledge, object assembly, and other subtests. Val has completed the
    (a) WAIS.   (c) WISC.
    (b) WPPSI.   (d) Stanford-Binet.

13. In his research on very young black children adopted into white middle-class families, Dr. Wilson found that their IQ scores were several points above the average of both blacks and whites. Dr. Wilson, like most experts in this area, is most likely to conclude that
    (a) intelligence is determined primarily by heredity.
    (b) IQ scores cannot be improved by environmental factors.
    (c) improved diet and health standards are the crucial factor in improving IQ scores.
    (d) socioeconomic conditions, cultural values, and other such environmental factors can affect IQ scores.

14. Dr. Shong was initially puzzled by her patient's unusual symptoms and was unable to arrive at a clear diagnosis. However, by integrating both obvious and subtle cues she began to recognize a pattern in the patient's symptoms and, thus, was able to formulate a tentative hypothesis that enabled her to order the appropriate lab tests. In this instance, Dr. Shong appears to be using _____ to diagnose her patient's illness.
    (a) an algorithm
    (b) the single feature approach
    (c) the elimination by aspect technique
    (d) insight or intuition

15. All of the following are obstacles to logical thinking that can account for much of the persistence of unwarranted beliefs in pseudosciences *except*
    (a) the belief bias effect.
    (b) confirmation bias.
    (c) the underestimation effect.
    (d) the fallacy of positive instances.
    (e) the overestimation effect.

Progress Test 2

After you have checked your understanding of the material in Progress Test 1 and have done a complete chapter review with special focus on any areas of weakness, you are now ready to assess your knowledge of Progress Test 2. Check your answers. If you make a mistake, review your notes, the relevant section of the study guide, and, if necessary, the appropriate part of your textbook.

1. As part of his overall vocational assessment Steven took a test that measured his level of knowledge, skills, and accomplishments in particular areas such as mathematics and writing ability. Steven took a(n) _____ test.
   (a) aptitude   (c) intelligence
   (b) achievement   (d) motivational

2. When Katrina is asked to identify the letters of the alphabet that do not have curved lines, she tries to mentally picture each letter as she completes the task. Katrina is using
   (a) mental imagery.   (c) a formal concept.
   (b) a natural concept. (d) a prototype.

3. Shawn is asked to memorize a map of an island that has a hut, a lake, a tree, a beach, and a grassy area, all clearly marked at distinct locations. Later, he is asked to imagine a specific location, such as the hut; when a second location, the tree, is named, he has to press a button when he reaches the tree on the visual image in his mind. The results of this experiment will most likely reveal that the _____ the distance between the two points, the _____ time it will take to scan the mental image of the map.
   (a) greater; more
   (b) greater; less
   (c) shorter; more
   (d) All of the above are false; there is no relationship between distance and time taken to mentally scan points on a map.

4. When Earl is asked what object or objects come to mind in response to the word *vegetable*, he answers "potatoes and carrots." For Earl, potatoes and carrots are

(a) formal concepts.   (c) algorithms.
(b) prototypes.   (d) heuristics.

5. Dr. Naidu's research is concerned with the study of animal learning, memory, thinking, and language. Dr. Naidu is most likely interested in

(a) testing the linguistic relativity hypothesis.
(b) investigating the triarchic theory of intelligence.
(c) heritability and heritability estimates.
(d) animal cognition or comparative cognition.

6. When Elana got her new VCR, she spent hours trying different approaches to programming the machine rather than consulting the manual. Elana is using the _____ approach to problem solving.

(a) algorithm   (c) heuristic
(b) trial-and-error (d) insight

7. After spending weeks studying a variety of sources and materials, Terry still couldn't decide on a topic for her seminar presentation. However, when she was out for her daily jog, she suddenly had a flash of inspiration about her topic. Terry solved her problem

(a) through insight.
(b) by using an algorithm.
(c) through functional fixedness.
(d) by using the representativeness heuristic.

8. When his TV picture became fuzzy, Lloyd would bang the top of the TV set and the picture would clear. Recently, when he was playing a video on his new VCR, tracking problems created a fuzzy picture; Lloyd banged the top of the TV over and over but to no avail. Lloyd appears to be experiencing an obstacle to solving the problem called

(a) functional fixedness.
(b) subgoal analysis.
(c) a mental set.
(d) confirmation bias.
(e) prototypical male stupidity.

9. When writing term papers, assignments, and exams, Gary is very careful to use "he or she" in place of the masculine pronoun and "people" instead of "man." Gary is apparently aware of the relationship between language and

(a) prototypes.   (c) social perception.
(b) gender bias.   (d) functional fixedness.

10. Dr. Peerless has designed a test to measure the level of scientific knowledge in high school graduates. To establish a norm against which individual scores may be interpreted and compared, she is presently administering the test to a large representative sample of high school graduates. Dr. Peerless is in the process of

(a) establishing the test's reliability.
(b) establishing the test's validity.
(c) standardizing the test.
(d) determining the test's aptitude.

11. After completing the above process, Dr. Peerless needs to check whether her test measures what it was designed to measure. She does this by comparing scores on her test with the scores and grades obtained by students in high school science courses. In this instance, Dr. Peerless is in the process of

(a) establishing the test's reliability.
(b) establishing the test's validity.
(c) standardizing the test.
(d) determining the test's aptitude.

12. Arnie is very adept at dealing with novel situations by drawing on previous experience and can often find unusual ways to relate old information to solve new problems. Robert Sternberg would call this _____ intelligence.

(a) analytical   (c) creative
(b) practical   (d) motivational

13. As part of a bizarre experiment in a science fiction story, Dr. Igor places 100 genetically identical individual infants in different homes. Because they are all identical, the heritability of intelligence (that is, the percentage of variation within the group that is due to genetic factors) should be _____ percent.

(a) 0   (c) 65
(b) 50   (d) 100

14. According to In Focus 7.3, "Does a High IQ Score Predict Success in Life?," which of the following is true?

    (a) IQ scores reliably predict academic success.
    (b) Academic success is no guarantee of success beyond school.
    (c) Many different personality factors are involved in achieving success, such as motivation, emotional maturity, commitment to goals, creativity, and a willingness to work hard.
    (d) All of the above are true.

15. According to the Application, which of the following is *not* a way to increase your creative potential?

    (a) Focus almost exclusively on extrinsic motivation.
    (b) Choose the goal of creativity.
    (c) Try different approaches.
    (d) Acquire relevant knowledge.
    (e) Engage in problem finding.

Progress Test 3

After you have checked your understanding of the material in Progress Tests 1 and 2, and have done a complete chapter review with special focus on any areas of weakness, you are ready to further assess your knowledge on Progress Test 3. Check your answers. If you make a mistake, review your notes, the appropriate parts of the study guide, and, if necessary, the relevant sections of your textbook.

1. Adrian took the WAIS test. One aspect of his general cognitive ability that is *not* likely to have been measured is his

    (a) linguistic ability.
    (b) problem-solving ability.
    (c) general knowledge.
    (d) creativity.

2. Dr. Larch is a renowned researcher and theorist in the area of intelligence testing. Like most experts in his field, Dr. Larch is most likely to agree that

    (a) genetic factors, rather than environmental influences, are the primary cause of any IQ differences found between racial groups.
    (b) within a given racial group, the differences among people are due at least as much to environmental influences as they are to genetic influences.

    (c) the IQ of any individual, regardless of his or her race, is determined almost exclusively by genetic factors and is relatively uninfluenced by environmental influences.
    (d) the IQ of any given individual, regardless of his or her race, is determined almost exclusively by environmental factors and is relatively uninfluenced by genetics.

3. With little or no hesitation, Matthew was able to state that cats and dogs are both examples of the concept of mammal; he was slower to respond when asked whether dolphins and whales were also examples of mammals. This example suggests that

    (a) formal concepts have fuzzy boundaries and that cats and dogs are prototypes of the category.
    (b) natural concepts have fuzzy boundaries and that cats and dogs are prototypes of the category.
    (c) formal concepts have fuzzy boundaries and that dolphins and whales are prototypes of the category.
    (d) natural concepts have fuzzy boundaries and that dolphins and whales are prototypes of the category.

4. Tom created the novel sentence, "The faceless bureaucrat was finally faced with making a face-saving decision but could not face up to the fact that he was in a fatal face-off with his favorite facetious faculty." Tom's ability to do this illustrates the _____ nature of language.

    (a) syntactic
    (b) inflexible
    (c) generative
    (d) practical

5. Dr. Adatia, a cross-cultural psychologist, discovered that children of immigrant Buraku families living in the United States had IQ scores no different from other Japanese-Americans, but that the Burakumin in Japan had IQ scores 10 to 15 points lower than those of other Japanese. Dr. Adatia is most likely to conclude that

    (a) IQ scores are genetically determined.
    (b) social discrimination can affect IQ scores.
    (c) better nutrition is the main factor that influences IQ scores.
    (d) the U.S. educational system is better than that of Japan.

6. Dr. Bishop assesses the correlation between scores obtained on two halves of his new abstract reasoning test in order to measure the _____ of her test.
   - (a) reliability
   - (b) validity
   - (c) norms
   - (d) aptitude

7. Miguel is extremely adept at learning how to solve problems; that is, he is very good at picking problem-solving strategies and applying them to problems. Robert Sternberg would call this ability a form of
   - (a) analytical intelligence.
   - (b) creative intelligence.
   - (c) practical intelligence.
   - (d) general intelligence, or the *g* factor.

8. Dr. Welch believes that there are multiple independent intelligences that cannot be reflected in a single measure of mental ability and that each intelligence must be viewed within a cultural context. Dr. Welch's position is most consistent with the views of
   - (a) Charles Spearman.
   - (b) L. L. Thurstone.
   - (c) Howard Gardner.
   - (d) Robert Sternberg.

9. When Allison goes to graduate school, she plans to investigate aspects of the heredity-environment debate as it relates to intelligence. She is most likely to
   - (a) use animals, such as rats and pigeons, in her research.
   - (b) get involved in twin studies.
   - (c) study the language abilities of primates.
   - (d) explore creativity and intuition.

10. Maja is writing a paper for her course in comparative cognition. After reviewing all the relevant research on animal language, Maja is likely to conclude that
   - (a) only humans possess language capabilities.
   - (b) animals can communicate with each other but are not capable of mastering any aspect of language.
   - (c) some species have demonstrated an elementary understanding of syntax and certain other limited aspects of language.
   - (d) many animal species can "think," use language, and possess self-awareness.

11. Martin has had some difficulties in school and has fallen behind in academic achievement. His chronological age is ten and his IQ score on the Stanford-Binet is 70. Martin's mental age is therefore
   - (a) seven.
   - (b) ten.
   - (c) thirteen.
   - (d) five.

12. Cynthia always buys the brand of paper towels that is on sale whether or not it is the highest quality towel. Cynthia makes her decision about which paper towel to purchase based on the _____ model of decision making.
   - (a) single-feature
   - (b) additive
   - (c) elimination by aspects
   - (d) heuristic

13. Jan is orderly, neat, quiet, and shy. She enjoys reading in her spare time and is an avid chess player. Given this description, most people would guess that she is a librarian rather than a real estate agent. This tendency to classify Jan as a librarian illustrates the influence of
   - (a) the availability heuristic.
   - (b) belief perseverance.
   - (c) the representativeness heuristic.
   - (d) the elimination by aspects strategy.

14. According to Culture and Human Behavior 7.2, the linguistic relativity hypothesis (or Whorfian hypothesis)
   - (a) proposes that the differences among languages cause differences in the thoughts of their speakers.
   - (b) has been supported by the results of dozens of cross-cultural studies.
   - (c) accounts for the fact that the English language has more than a dozen words for *snow* but Eskimos have only one or two.
   - (d) holds that language does not determine cultural differences but instead language reflects cultural differences.

15. According to the Application, creativity refers
   - (a) to something that only a few very gifted people possess.
   - (b) to a group of cognitive processes used to generate useful, novel, and original ideas and solutions.
   - (c) only to artistic expression, with little or no practical value.
   - (d) to the ability to arrive at conclusions or make judgments without conscious awareness of the thought processes involved.

Answers

Introduction: Thinking, Language, and Intelligence

1. *Thinking is defined as* the manipulation of mental representations of information in order to draw inferences and conclusions. *It typically involves* the manipulation of mental images and concepts.

2. *A mental image is* a mental representation of objects or events that are not physically present.

3. *We manipulate mental images* in much the same way as we manipulate the actual objects they represent. *They are potentially subject to error and distortion because* mental images are not perfect duplicates of our actual sensory experience; instead they are memories of visual images and are actively constructed.

4. *Concepts are* mental categories of objects or ideas based on properties they share. *The two ways of forming concepts are* learning the rules or features that define the particular concept (formal concept) and as the result of everyday experiences (natural concept).

5. *A prototype is* the most typical instance of a particular concept. *The more closely an item matches a prototype,* the more quickly we can identify it as being an example of the concept.

Solving Problems and Making Decisions

1. *Problem solving is defined as* thinking and behavior directed toward attaining a goal that is not readily available.

2. *The trial-and-error strategy involves* attempting different solutions and eliminating those that do not work; it is useful when there is a limited range of possible solutions.

3. *An algorithm involves* following a specific rule, procedure, or method that inevitably produces the correct solution (such as mathematical formulas), but using an algorithm may not always be practical because of the amount of time it can take to solve some problems.

4. *A heuristic is a* general rule of thumb that reduces the number of possible solutions; while it tends to simplify problem solving, it is not guaranteed to solve a given problem.

5. *Insight is the* sudden realization of how a problem can be solved, but insights, intuitions, or hunches are likely to be accurate only in contexts in which you already have a broad base of knowledge and experience.

6. *Functional fixedness is* the tendency to view objects as functioning only in their usual or customary way; it may prevent us from seeing the full range of ways in which an object can be used.

7. *A mental set is* the tendency to persist in solving problems with solutions that have worked in the past; it may prevent us from coming up with new and possibly more effective solutions.

Decision-Making Strategies

1. *The single feature model involves* making a decision based on a single feature. *It is appropriate when* the decision is a minor one.

2. *Using the additive model, you first* generate a list of factors that are most important to you, next you rate each alternative using an arbitrary rating scale, and finally, you add up the ratings for each alternative. *It is appropriate for* complex decisions and useful in identifying the most acceptable choice from a range of possible decisions.

3. *Using the elimination by aspects model, you* evaluate all the alternatives one characteristic at a time (starting with what you consider to be the most important feature) and systematically eliminate all alternatives that don't meet that criterion until only the one choice that satisfies your criteria remains. *It is appropriate when* the decision is complex and there is a need to narrow down a range of choices with multiple features.

4. *The availability heuristic is a strategy* in which the likelihood of an event is estimated on the basis of how readily available other instances of the event are in memory.

5. *The representative heuristic is a strategy* in which the likelihood of an event is estimated by comparing how similar it is to the typical prototype of the event.

Concept Check 1

1. insight
2. representativeness heuristic
3. cognitive; thinking
4. mental image
5. formal
6. natural
7. algorithm
8. trial-and-error
9. additive

Matching Exercise 1

1. elimination by aspects model
2. thinking
3. prototype
4. insight
5. single-feature model
6. representativeness heuristic
7. trial and error
8. formal concept
9. cognition
10. concept
11. heuristic

True/False Test 1

1. F	5. T	9. F
2. T	6. T	10. T
3. T	7. T	11. T
4. F	8. F	

Language and Thought

1. *Language is defined as* a system for combining arbitrary symbols to produce an infinite number of meaningful statements.

2. *The five most important characteristics of language are: (a)* The purpose of language is to communicate and to do so language requires the use of symbols. *(b)* The meaning of these arbitrary symbols is shared by others. *(c)* Language is a highly structured system that follows rules for combining words (syntax). *(d)* Language is creative, allowing for the generation of an infinite number of new and different phrases and sentences (generative). *(e)* Language involves displacement, the ability to communicate meaningfully about ideas, objects, and activities that are not physically present.

3. *An important way in which language can influence thought has to do with* our social perception of others; when the nuances of words promote stereotypical thinking, language may encourage discrimination against women, the elderly, and members of racial or ethnic minorities.

4. *Animals communicate with each other and with other species, but* many psychologists question whether animals can learn to use language, and they caution against jumping to the conclusion that animals can think or that they possess self-awareness, on the basis of the few studies on animal cognition that demonstrated language ability in animals.

Measuring Intelligence

1. *Intelligence is defined as* the global capacity to think rationally, act purposefully, and deal effectively with the environment.

2. *Alfred Binet, along with psychiatrist Theodore Simon, devised* a series of tests to measure different elementary mental abilities, such as memory, attention, and the ability to understand similarities and differences; his research led to the concept of mental age.

3. *Lewis Terman translated and adapted* Binet's intelligence test (the Stanford-Binet Intelligence Scale) and developed the concept of the intelligence quotient, or IQ.

4. *David Wechsler developed a new intelligence test,* the Wechsler Adult Intelligence Scale (WAIS), which was designed specifically for adults, and its 11 subtest scores (measuring a variety of abilities) can be grouped to provide an overall verbal score and performance score. He also devised the WISC and WPPSI.

Principles of Test Construction: What Makes a Good Test?

1. *Achievement tests are designed to* measure a person's level of knowledge, skill, or accomplishment in a particular area. *Aptitude tests are designed to* assess a person's capacity to benefit from education or training.

2. *Standardization refers to* the administration of a test to a large, representative sample of people under uniform conditions for the purpose of establishing norms.

3. *The normal curve, or normal distribution, is* a bell-shaped distribution of individual differences in a normal population in which most scores cluster around the average.

4. *Reliability is defined as* the ability of a test to produce consistent results when administered on repeated occasions under similar conditions. *It is determined by* administering two similar, but not identical, versions of the test at different times, or by comparing the scores on one half of the test to the scores on the other half of the test.

5. *Validity is defined as* the ability of a test to measure what it is intended to measure. *It is determined by* demonstrating the predictive value of a test.

Concept Check 2

1. syntax
2. social
3. mental; chronological
4. 100
5. IQ test; WAIS
6. reliability; validity

Matching Exercise 2

1. syntax
2. Alfred Binet
3. displacement
4. mental age
5. Stanford-Binet Intelligence Scale
6. validity
7. generative
8. animal cognition (comparative cognition)
9. normal curve (normal distribution)
10. intelligence
11. language

True/False Test 2

1. F	5. F	9. F
2. T	6. T	10. F
3. F	7. T	11. T
4. T	8. F	

The Nature of Intelligence

1. *The two key issues involved in the debate over the nature of intelligence are: (a)* Is intelligence a singe, general ability, or is it better described as a cluster of different mental abilities? *(b)* Should the definition of intelligence be restricted to the mental abilities measured by IQ and other intelligence tests, or should it be defined more broadly?

2. *The g factor (or general intelligence) is the notion* of a general intelligence factor that is responsible for a person's overall performance on tests of mental ability. *It was proposed by* Charles Spearman.

3. *Louis L. Thurstone proposed the notion that* intelligence is a cluster of seven different primary mental abilities, each a relatively independent element of intelligence.

4. *The idea of multiple intelligences was proposed by* Howard Gardner. *The eight intelligences are* linguistic, logical-mathematical, musical, spatial, bodily-kinesthetic, interpersonal, intrapersonal, and naturalist intelligence.

5. *The triarchic theory of intelligence proposes that* there are three distinct forms of intelligence: analytic, creative, and practical. *It was developed by* Robert Sternberg.

The Roles of Genetics and Environment in Determining Intelligence

1. *The basic heredity-environment issue is concerned with* whether we inherit our intelligence from our parents (genes, or nature)), or whether our intellectual potential is primarily determined by our environment and upbringing (nurture). (Because of recent research by molecular biologists, the issue has become one of how environment influences gene expression).

2. *Twin studies have been used because* identical twins share exactly the same genes, and any differences between them must be due to environmental factors rather than to hereditary differences.

3. *Heritability is defined as* the percentage of variation within a given population that is due to heredity. *Heritability estimates cannot be used to explain differences between groups because* unless the environmental conditions of the two groups are identical, it is impossible to estimate the overall genetic differences between groups; even if intelligence were primarily determined by heredity, IQ differences between groups could still be due entirely to the environment (socioeconomic conditions, cultural values, and so on).

4. *It is virtually impossible to create a culture-free IQ test because* ability tests reflect the values, knowledge, and communication strategies of their culture of origin. Cultural differences in test-taking behavior may also affect results. Finally, the stereotype threat can cause students to perform as they think they are expected to perform.

Concept Check 3

1. Charles Spearman
2. practical
3. not likely
4. heredity
5. environment
6. environmental
7. was not

Graphic Organizer 2

1. David Wechsler
2. Robert Sternberg
3. Alfred Binet
4. Charles Spearman
5. Howard Gardner
6. Lewis Terman

Matching Exercise 3

1. Robert Sternberg
2. heritability
3. *g* factor (general intelligence)
4. creativity
5. L. L. Thurstone
6. practical intelligence
7. Charles Spearman
8. creative intelligence

True/False Test 3

1. T	4. T	7. T
2. F	5. T	8. T
3. T	6. F	

Something to Think About

1. Many people would like to be more creative. Fortunately, much can be done to increase our creative potential. The first thing to tell someone is that creativity is hard to define precisely but that most cognitive psychologists agree that creativity is a group of cognitive processes used to generate useful, original, and novel ideas and solutions. Creativity is not confined to artistic expression; as indicated in the definition, creativity involves usefulness as well as originality. Based on information in the Application, you could then conduct your own mini-workshop on creativity. You can summarize the workshop by using the letters of the word **CREATE** as an acronym: **C**hoose the goal of creativity; **R**einforce creative behavior; **E**ngage in problem finding; **A**cquire relevant knowledge; **T**ry different approaches; **E**xert effort and expect setbacks.

2. First, you could tell your friend that we can't all be above average. The distribution for intelligence will follow a normal, or bell-shaped, curve, with about 50 percent above average and 50 percent below average. Next, you could talk a little about the problems involved in defining intelligence. Not even the experts agree. Some think that performance on mental ability tests reflects a general intelligence, or *g* factor; others think there are three forms of intelligence; and some postulate multiple intelligences. Despite these disagreements, psychologists do agree that intelligence involves such elements as abstract thinking, problem solving, and the capacity to acquire knowledge. They also tend to agree that aspects of intelligent behavior such as creativity, motivation, goal-directed behavior, and adaptation to one's environment are not measured by conventional intelligence tests. Thus, IQ scores reflect the limitations of existing intelligence tests. Finally, according to In Focus Box 7.3, whereas IQ scores may predict academic success, success in school is no guarantee of success and happiness in life in general. Many different personality factors are involved in achieving success, such as motivation, emotional maturity, commitment to goals, creativity, and, perhaps most important of all, a willingness to work hard. None of these attributes are measured by traditional IQ tests.

Progress Test 1

1. c	6. b	11. d
2. a	7. a	12. a
3. c	8. a	13. d
4. c	9. c	14. d
5. a	10. b	15. c

Progress Test 2

1. b	6. b	11. b
2. a	7. a	12. c
3. a	8. c	13. a
4. b	9. b	14. d
5. d	10. c	15. a

Progress Test 3

1. d	6. a	11. a
2. b	7. a	12. a
3. b	8. c	13. c
4. c	9. b	14. a
5. b	10. c	15. b

Motivation
and Emotion

PREVIEW

Reading the section below first will give you a general sense of the chapter's contents and an initial introduction to some of the major concepts and terms. This will prime you for what you are about to read and help you to develop a "cognitive map" that will guide your study of the material in this chapter. Likewise, reading the **preview questions** at the beginning of each major section will improve your ability to understand, learn, and retain the information.

CHAPTER 8. . . AT A GLANCE

Chapter 8 is concerned with motivation and emotion. Motivation refers to the forces that act on or within an organism to initiate and direct behavior. Instinct theories, drive theories, incentive theories, and humanistic theories are introduced.

The motivation to eat is influenced by psychological, biological, social, and cultural factors. Set-point theory and the rate at which the body uses energy (basal metabolic rate, or BMR) are discussed in relation to the regulation of body weight. Factors influencing obesity, anorexia nervosa, and bulimia nervosa are examined Sexual motivation in humans and other animals is explored next. The four phases of the human sexual response cycle are presented, followed by a discussion of sexual orientation. Details of human sexuality in adulthood are presented, including the frequency and types of sexual behavior people engage in and people's fantasies about sexual activity. Curiosity, sensation seeking, and arousal motives are discussed next. Competence motivation and achievement motivation are compared, and the Thematic Apperception Test (TAT) is introduced.

Emotions, which serve many different functions in human behavior and relationships, have three basic components: subjective experience, physical arousal, and a behavioral or expressive response. Facial expressions for some basic emotions seem to be universal and innate, but expression is also influenced by cultural display rules.

The key theories of emotion—the James-Lange theory, Schachter and Singer's two-factor theory of emotion, and Richard Lazarus's cognitive-mediational theory—are examined. A synthesis is suggested by an interactive approach that emphasizes the idea that cognitive appraisals, physiological arousal, and behavioral expression all contribute to subjective emotional experiences.

Introduction: Motivation and Emotion

Preview Questions

Consider the following questions as you study this section of the chapter.

- How is motivation defined?
- What three characteristics are associated with motivation?
- How is emotion related to motivation?
- What four theories have historically been included in the study of motivation?
- How does each theory explain motivation, and what are the limits of each?

*Read the section "Introduction: Motivation and Emotion" and **write** your answers to the following:*

1. Motivation refers to _____

_____

2. The three characteristics associated with motivation are _____

_____

_____

3. Emotions are closely tied to motivational processes (and vice versa) because both topics involve _____

_____

4. According to the earliest theories of motivation, instinct theories, _____

_____

Limitations of these theories are _____

_____

5. According to drive theories, _____

_____

_____

Their limitations are _____

_____

_____

6. Incentive theories proposed that _____

_____

Their limitations are _____

_____

_____

7. Humanistic theories suggest that people are motivated to _____

_____

_____

_____

Limitations are _____

_____

_____

_____

_____

After you have carefully studied the preceding section, complete the following exercises.

Concept Check 1

Read the following and write the correct term in the space provided.

1. Amber is a graduate student studying the various forces acting on or within organisms that initiate and direct behavior. Her area of research is _____ .

2. When Trevor is hungry, he eats. The consumption of food serves to maintain

_____ .

3. Manuel is struggling to make enough money to feed and clothe himself and pay the rent. According to Maslow, it is _____ (likely/unlikely) that Manuel is close to reaching the goal of self-actualization.

4. Mrs. Lewis gives a gold star to any child in her class who gets 100 percent on the weekly spelling test. This example illustrates _____ theory.

5. Bruno the bear hibernates every winter. This behavior is an example of an

_____ .

6. When Bernice finished her first 10-mile race in less than 90 minutes, she felt totally exhilarated and overjoyed by having achieved her goal. Her intense feelings suggest that _____ are closely tied to motivation.

Review of Terms, Concepts, and Names 1

Use the terms in this list to complete the Matching Test, then to help you answer the True/False items correctly.

motivation	homeostasis
activation	drive
persistence	incentive theories
intensity	humanistic theories
emotion	hierarchy of needs
instinct theories	Abraham Maslow
drive theories	self-actualization

Matching Exercise

Match the appropriate term/name with its definition or description.

1. _____ The view that we are innately motivated to strive for a positive self-concept and the realization of our personal potential.

2. _____ The forces that act on or within an organism to initiate and direct behavior.

3. _____ Basic characteristic commonly associated with motivation that is seen in a person's continued efforts or determination to achieve a particular goal, often in the face of obstacles.

4. _____ American psychologist who developed a hierarchical model of human motivation in which basic needs must first be satisfied before people can strive for self-actualization.

5. _____ Impulse that activates behavior to reduce a need and restore homeostasis.

6. _____ View that some motives are innate and due to genetic programming.

7. _____ Maslow's levels of motivation that progress from basic physical needs to psychological needs to self-fulfillment needs.

True/False Test

Indicate whether each statement is true or false by placing T or F in the blank space next to each item.

1. ____ Incentive theories propose that behavior is motivated by the pull of external goals, such as rewards.

2. ____ *Self-actualization* is defined by Maslow as "the full use and exploitation of talents, capacities, and potentialities."

3. ____ Activation, one of the basic characteristics commonly associated with motivation, is seen in the greater vigor of responding that usually accompanies motivated behavior.

4. ____ Drive theories propose that behavior is motivated by the desire to reduce internal tension caused by unmet biological needs, such as hunger or thirst.

5. ____ Homeostasis refers to the notion that the body monitors and maintains internal states, such as body temperature and energy supplies, at relatively constant levels.

6. ____ Intensity, one of the basic characteristics commonly associated with motivation, is seen in the initiation or production of behavior.

7. ____ Emotion is a subjective and conscious psychological state that includes physiological arousal and an expressive response.

Check your answers and review any areas of weakness before going on to the next section.

The Motivation to Eat

Preview Questions

Consider the following questions as you study this section of the chapter.

- What four factors influence the motivation to eat?

- How do oral signals, stomach signals, CCK, insulin, and the hypothalamus seem to influence hunger and eating behavior?

- What is basal metabolic rate, and what factors influence it?

- How does set-point theory account for the regulation of body weight?

- What characterizes obesity, anorexia, and bulimia?

*Read the section "The Motivation to Eat" and **write** your answers to the following:*

1. The four factors that influence the motivation to eat are _____

    _____

2. Biologically, we are motivated to stop or start eating by the following: Oral signals influence eating behavior by _____

    _____

    Stomach signals _____

    _____

    _____

    Through a classical conditioning process, insulin levels _____

    _____

    The hypothalamus _____

    _____

    _____

3. The basal metabolic rate (BMR) is _____

    _____

    It is influenced by_____

    _____

4. Set-point theory suggests that _____

    _____

    _____

5. Obesity is defined as _____

    _____

6. Anorexia nervosa is _____

    _____

    _____

7. Bulimia nervosa is _____

    _____

    _____

After you have carefully studied the preceding section, complete the following exercises.

Concept Check 2

Read the following and write the correct term in the space provided.

1. Farah skipped lunch; later in the afternoon, while walking by the cafeteria, she smells french fries, and her mouth begins to water. At this time it is likely that her blood level of insulin is _____ (high/ low).

2. Farah is very responsive to food-related environmental stimuli even when she hasn't skipped a meal. Judith Rodin would classify her as a(n) _____ (external/nonexternal).

3. While Dr. Fleming was investigating the relationship between the brain and eating behavior, he discovered that rats would stop eating if he destroyed an area of their brain called the _____ hypothalamus, or

    _____ .

4. Although he leads a somewhat sedentary lifestyle, 35-year-old Joshua has been about the same weight, give or take a pound or two, since his late teens. His set-point weight is most likely maintained by his

    _____ , or

    _____ .

5. Despite trying many different weight-loss approaches, Roger is still about 30 percent above his "ideal" weight. According to most definitions, Roger would be classified as

    _____ .

6. Claire is a 15-year-old of average height who weighs only 85 pounds. She has lost 30 pounds over the past eight or nine months by eating very little and going to aerobics classes twice a day. Claire probably suffers from

    _____ .

Review of Terms and Concepts 2

Use the terms in this list to complete the Matching Test, then to help you answer the True/False items correctly.

satiation
oral signals
stomach signals
cholecystokinin (CCK)
insulin
externals/nonexternals
ventromedial
  hypothalamus (VMH)
lateral hypothalamus
  (LH)

basal metabolic rate
  (BMR)
set-point weight
set-point theory
obese
anorexia nervosa
bulimia nervosa

Matching Exercise

Match the appropriate term with its definition or description.

1. _____ Hormone that seems to play a role in signaling satiation, or fullness.

2. _____ The sensations involved in tasting and chewing food that contribute greatly to the subjective pleasure and satisfaction of eating.

3. _____ The rate at which the body uses energy for vital bodily functions when at rest.

4. _____ Judith Rodin's terms for people who are highly responsive to environmental food-related stimuli and for those who are less responsive to food cues.

5. _____ Area of the hypothalamus that, when damaged, causes an experimental animal to eat until it becomes obese.

6. _____ The particular weight that is set and maintained by increases or decreases in basal metabolic rate.

7. _____ Hormone secreted by the pancreas that helps regulate the metabolism of carbohydrates, fats, and starches in the body.

True/False Test

Indicate whether each statement is true or false by placing T or F in the blank space next to each item.

1. ____ Obesity is defined as weighing 20 percent or more above one's optimal body weight.

2. ____ Bulimia nervosa is an eating disorder characterized by the individual's refusal to maintain a minimally normal body weight, is extremely afraid of gaining weight or becoming fat, and a distorted perception of his or her body size.

3. ____ If the lateral hypothalamus (LH) is damaged, an experimental animal will stop eating.

4. ____ Satiation is the feeling of fullness and diminished desire to eat.

5. ____ The stomach has sensory receptors that detect the stretching of the stomach muscles as it accommodates food; these stomach signals are relayed to the brain, helping to trigger feelings of satiation.

6. ____ Anorexia nervosa is an eating disorder in which a person engages in binge eating and then purges the excessive food consumption by self-induced vomiting or, less often, by taking laxatives or enemas.

7. ____ Set-point theory is based on the well-established principle of homeostasis; increases or decreases in body weight are followed by corresponding changes in the body's basal metabolic rate.

Check your answers and review any areas of weakness before going on to the next section.

Sexual Motivation and Behavior

Preview Questions

Consider the following questions as you study this section of the chapter.

- What biological factors are involved in sexual motivation?

- What are the four stages of the human sexual response?

- What factors have been associated with sexual orientation?

- What characterizes the sexual behavior patterns of adults?

- What are sexual dysfunctions?

*Read the section "Sexual Motivation and Behavior" and **write** your answers to the following:*

1. In most non-human animals, sexual behavior is

_____

_____

2. In humans, sexual behavior is (refer to the major hormones involved in human sexual motivation) _____

_____

_____

_____

3. The four stages of the human sexual response cycle are _____

_____

_____

_____

4. Sexual orientation refers to _____

_____

The factors associated with sexual orientation are _____

_____

5. The most general conclusions about the sexual behavior patterns of adults are that_____

_____

_____

_____

_____

_____

6. Sexual dysfunction is a _____

_____

_____

_____

After you have carefully studied the preceding section, complete the following exercises.

Concept Check 3

Read the following and write the correct term in the space provided.

1. Mary and her husband James have just shared a fulfilling sexual experience. Unlike Mary, James is not likely to be able to experience another orgasm for a period of time; this is called the _____ period.

2. Mrs. Jacobson had her ovaries removed because of cancer and is now in perfect health. As a result of the operation, the level of the female sex hormone will _____ ; the level of her interest in sexual activity will _____ (increase/decrease/ stay the same).

3. Dr. Jamison surgically removed the testes of an experimental laboratory rat. It is very probable that the rat will experience a(n) _____ in sexual activity and interest.

4. Hamish, a 25-year-old medical student, is heterosexual; his brother Stuart, a 21-year-old philosophy major, is homosexual. The two brothers differ in their _____ .

5. In relation to the stages of the human sexual response, stage 2 is to _____ as stage 4 is to _____ .

6. Young Simon has a rather passive, weak father and a strong, assertive mother. Research on early life experiences and sexual orientation indicates that such atypical family relationships _____ (are/are not) one of the main causes of homosexuality.

7. Mr. and Mrs. Dempster are in their seventies and enjoy good health and an active lifestyle. If they are like many adults in their age range, they are very_____ (unlikely/likely) to have an interest in sex.

8. Shoran is writing a paper on sexual orientation and its determinants. After reading the relevant literature on the topic, she is likely to conclude that biological factors _____ (are/are not) correlated with homosexual orientation.

Review of Terms, Concepts, and Names 3

Use the terms in this list to complete the Matching Test, then to help you answer the True/False items correctly.

estrus	resolution phase
estrogen	refractory period
testosterone	sexual orientation
William H. Masters	heterosexual
Virginia E. Johnson	homosexual
excitement phase	bisexual
plateau phase	sexual dysfunction
orgasm	

Matching Exercise

Match the appropriate term/name with its definition or description.

1. _____ American behavioral scientist who, along with William H. Masters, conducted pioneering research in the field of human sexuality and sex therapy.

2. _____ The second stage in the human sexual response cycle in which physical arousal builds as pulse and breathing rates continue to rise; the penis becomes fully erect, the testes enlarge, the clitoris withdraws but remains sensitive, the vaginal entrance tightens, and vaginal lubrication continues.

3. _____ A consistent disturbance in sexual desire, arousal, or orgasm that causes psychological distress and interpersonal difficulties.

4. _____ A person who is sexually attracted to individuals of the other sex.

5. _____ For a male, a period of time following orgasm during which he is incapable of having another erection or orgasm.

6. _____ A person who is attracted to individuals of the same sex.

7. _____ American physician who, along with Virginia E. Johnson, conducted pioneering research in the field of human sexuality and sex therapy.

8. _____ The first stage in the human sexual response cycle that marks the beginning of sexual arousal and can occur in response to sexual fantasies or other sexually arousing stimuli, physical contact with another person, or masturbation.

True/False Test

Indicate whether each statement is true or false by placing T or F in the blank space next to each item.

1. ____ Estrus refers to the cyclical period during which a female non-human animal is fertile and receptive to male sexual advances.

2. ____ The fourth stage of the sexual response cycle, during which both sexes tend to experience a warm physical glow and sense of well-being and arousal returns to normal, is called the resolution phase.

3. ____ A bisexual is sexually attracted to individuals of both sexes.

4. ____ Testosterone, the female sex hormone produced by the ovaries, influences a woman's monthly reproductive cycle.

5. ____ Orgasm is the third and shortest phase of the sexual response cycle, during which blood pressure and heart rate reach their peak and muscles in the vaginal walls and uterus contract rhythmically, as do the muscles in and around the penis as the male ejaculates.

6. ____ Estrogen, the male sex hormone produced by the testes, is responsible for male sexual development.

7. ____ Sexual orientation is a person's emotional and erotic attraction toward members of the opposite sex, same sex, or both sexes.

Check your answers and review any areas of weakness before going on to the next section.

Arousal Motives: Curiosity and Sensation Seeking

Preview Questions

Consider the following questions as you study this section of the chapter.

- How does arousal theory account for people's motivation to maintain an optimal level of arousal?

- What factors influence curiosity and exploratory behavior?

- What is sensation seeking?

*Read the section "Arousal Motives: Curiosity and Sensation Seeking" and **write** your answers to the following:*

1. Arousal theory suggests that _____

   _____

   _____

2. Along with increasing arousal, curiosity and exploratory behavior may be motivated by

   _____

   _____

   _____

3. People who are high in sensation seeking are

   _____

   _____

Competence and Achievement Motivation

Preview Questions

Consider the following questions as you study this section of the chapter.

- How do competence motivation and achievement motivation differ?
- How is each type of motivation measured?
- What is self-efficacy?

*Read the section "Competence and Achievement Motivation" and **write** your answers to the following:*

1. Competence motivation is _____

   _____

   Achievement motivation is_____

   _____

2. Achievement motivation is most commonly measured by _____

   _____

   _____

3. Self-efficacy refers to _____

   _____

   _____

After you have carefully studied the preceding sections, complete the following exercises.

Concept Check 4

Read the following and write the correct term in the space provided.

1. Young Alec practices at the golf range for one or two hours most days because he plans to become a professional golfer. His goal and behavior suggest that Alec has a high level of _____ motivation.

2. Jasmine was very excited by her first trip to the zoo. She was particularly curious and a little nervous about what she would find in the reptile house. As Jasmine and her parents entered the reptile facility, she became more and more anxious, and when she saw the lizards and snakes, she burst into tears. It appears that the situation was moving faster than the _____ of Jasmine's curiosity and exploratory motive.

3. Roland loves the quiet routine of his life. He goes to work at the same time every day, meets his friends for bridge every Tuesday and Thursday evening, and works out at the gym on Monday, Wednesday, and Friday. Every year, he vacations at the same hotel in Aruba. Roland is likely to score very _____ (high/ low) on Marvin Zuckerman's Sensation Seeking Scale.

4. Yen Shih and her fellow students believe that it is unacceptable to express pride for personal achievements, but it is acceptable to feel pride in achievements that benefit others. Yen Shih most likely lives in a _____ culture.

5. Allison wants to prove to herself that she is capable of mastering basic mathematical concepts, so she enrolls in an algebra course and an introductory statistics course. Allison is demonstrating _____ motivation.

Graphic Organizer 1

Identify the theory associated with each of the following statements:

Statement	Theory
1. I believe that behavior is motivated by the desire to reduce internal tension caused by unmet biological needs that push us to behave in certain ways.	
2. I emphasize the importance of psychological and cognitive components in human motivation and believe that we are innately driven to strive for a positive self-concept and the realization of our personal potential.	
3. I take my lead from Charles Darwin, and although my ideas may not be popular today, I strongly believe that we are motivated to engage in certain behaviors because of genetic programming.	
4. We do what we do because of the pull of external goals, such as rewards. I think that learning theorists have it right when they say reinforcement is a key factor in motivation.	
5. How do we explain curiosity and exploratory behavior? I believe that we are motivated to maintain an optimal level of arousal. When arousal is too low, we try to increase it by seeking out stimulating experiences; when it is too high, we seek to reduce arousal in a less stimulating environment.	

Review of Terms and Concepts 4

Use the terms in this list to complete the Matching Test, then to help you answer the True/False items correctly.

arousal theory
sensation seeking
competence motivation
achievement motivation

Thematic Apperception
   Test (TAT)
self-efficacy

Matching Exercise

Match the appropriate term with its definition or description:

1. _____ The degree to which a person is subjectively convinced of his or her ability to effectively meet the demands of a situation.

2. _____ The view that people are motivated to maintain an optimal level of arousal, which is neither too high nor too low.

3. _____ Motivated behavior directed toward demonstrating ability and exercising control in a situation.

4. _____ Being motivated to experience high levels of arousal associated with varied and novel activities.

5. _____ Motivated behavior directed toward excelling, succeeding, or outperforming others at some task.

6. _____ Test in which a person is asked to make up a story about each of a series of ambiguous pictures; the story is coded in terms of its achievement themes and imagery.

Check your answers and review any areas of weakness before going on to the next section.

Emotion

Preview Questions

Consider the following questions as you study this section of the chapter.

- How is emotion defined, and what are the three components of emotion?

- How do emotions and mood differ?
- How do culture and individual differences influence emotional experience?
- What physical changes are associated with different emotions?
- What are display rules, and how do they affect facial expressions?

*Read the section "Emotion" and **write** your answers to the following:*

1. Emotion is defined as _____

    _____

    _____

2. Emotions tend to _____

    _____

    _____

    Moods involve _____

    _____

3. Cross-cultural research has shown that ____

    _____

    _____

    _____

4. The physiological component of emotions such as anger and fear involves _____

    _____

    _____

    _____

5. Display rules are _____

    _____

    _____

Explaining Emotions: Key Theories

Preview Questions

Consider the following questions as you study this section of the chapter.

- What is the James-Lange theory of emotion, and how did Cannon refute the James-Lange theory?
- What is the facial feedback hypothesis?
- How does the two-factor theory account for emotions, and what aspects of the theory have been supported by research?

- What is the cognitive-mediational theory of emotion?

*Read the section "Explaining Emotions: Key Theories" and **write** your answers to the following:*

1. The James-Lange theory of emotions states that _____

    _____

2. Walter Cannon criticized the James-Lange theory on a number of grounds:

    (a) _____

    _____

    (b) _____

    _____

    (c) _____

    _____

    (d) _____

    _____

3. According to the facial feedback hypothesis,

    _____

    _____

4. Schachter and Singer's two-factor theory of emotion suggests that _____

    _____

    _____

5. Richard Lazarus's cognitive-mediational theory emphasizes _____

    _____

    _____

    _____

6. The interactive approach to emotion suggests that _____

    _____

    _____

    _____

After you have carefully studied the preceding sections, complete the following exercises.

Concept Check 5

Read the following and write the correct term in the space provided.

1. Since the end of the semester, Ellen had been feeling very contented and relaxed. When she received her transcript in the mail and discovered that she had received an A+ in statistics, she was overjoyed. Ellen's two different states (contentment and joy) illustrate the difference between _____ and

   _____ .

2. Walking to the parking lot late at night, Camellia suddenly hears footsteps behind her. Her heartbeat and blood pressure increase, her muscles tense, her mouth goes dry, and she begins to perspire. These physiological reactions were activated by her _____ nervous system.

3. Mr. Hashimoto is very careful to hide his true feelings and control his facial expressions when in the presence of his company's chief executive officers. This example illustrates the

   _____ of his culture.

4. Whenever she feels a bit gloomy, Danica sings the song "Pretend you're happy when you're blue" ; if she follows the advice of the song, she actually experiences an elevation in her mood. This example is consistent with the

   _____ of emotion.

5. When Harbinder first rode on the High Peak ski lift, he looked down at the steep slopes beneath him and became aware of his high level of physiological arousal. Suddenly, he felt fearful. Harbinder's experience is best explained by the _____ theory of emotion.

Graphic Organizer 2

Identify the emotion (relaxation, alarm, annoyance, boredom, astonishment) associated with each of the following descriptions and indicate where it should go on the matrix below.

1. Natasha receives an A+ in her third-year history course and can hardly believe it.

   _____

2. In the middle of the night, Harry, who lives alone, is startled out of a deep sleep by strange noises coming from the basement.

   _____

3. During his three o'clock calculus class Nathan finds the topic totally uninteresting and starts losing his concentration. _____

4. On Saturday Dawn sleeps in and spends most of the morning propped up on comfortable pillows reading a romantic novel.

   _____

5. Five minutes after the meter has expired Dhillon arrives at his car only to find he has been given a $20 ticket. _____

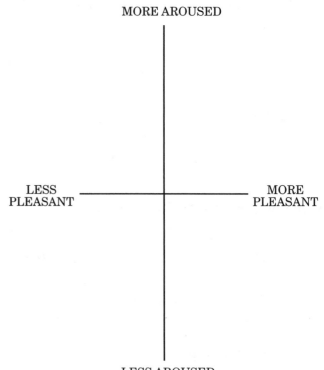

MORE AROUSED

LESS
PLEASANT   MORE
                                     PLEASANT

LESS AROUSED

Review of Terms, Concepts, and Names 5

Use the terms in this list to complete the Matching Test, then to help you answer the True/False items correctly.

emotion
mood
basic emotions
mixed emotions
interpersonal
    engagement
sympathetic nervous
    system
nonverbal behavior
display rules
William James

James-Lange theory of
    emotion
Walter B. Cannon
facial feedback
    hypothesis
two-factor theory of
    emotion
Richard Lazarus
cognitive-mediational
    theory of emotion
interactive approach to
    emotion

Matching Exercise

Match the appropriate term/name with its definition or description:

1. _____ View that expressing a specific emotion, especially facially, causes the subjective experience of that emotion.

2. _____ American psychologist who proposed the cognitive-mediational theory of emotion.

3. _____ Distinct psychological state that involves subjective experience, physical arousal, and a behavioral or expressive response.

4. _____ Schachter and Singer's theory that emotion is a result of the interaction of physiological arousal and the cognitive label that we apply to explain the arousal.

5. _____ Universal emotions that are biologically determined products of evolution; they include anger, happiness, sadness, fear, disgust, surprise, anxiety, shame, and interest.

6. _____ A third dimension, added by the Japanese to the two basic dimensions of emotion (pleasantness and arousal), that describes the degree to which each emotion involves relationships with others.

7. _____ Emotional expressions such as gestures, changes in posture, and facial expressions that don't rely on language or spoken communication.

8. _____ Approach to emotion that emphasizes the notion that cognitive appraisals, physiological arousal, and behavioral expression all contribute to subjective emotional expression.

True/False Test

Indicate whether each item is true or false by placing T or F in the space next to each item.

1. ____ Walter B. Cannon was an American psychologist who developed an influential theory of emotion called the two-factor theory of emotion.

2. ____ The cognitive-mediational theory of emotion is Lazarus's theory that emotions result from the cognitive appraisal of the effect of a situation on personal well-being.

3. ____ Display rules are social and cultural rules that regulate the expression of emotions, particularly facial expressions.

4. ____ The James-Lange theory suggests that emotions arise from the perception and interpretation of bodily changes.

5. ____ Arousal of the sympathetic nervous system gears you up for action, affecting many bodily activities such as heartbeat, blood pressure, respiration, perspiration, and blood-sugar levels.

6. ____ In more complex situations we may experience mixed emotions; these very different emotions are experienced simultaneously or in rapid succession.

7. ____ William James was an American psychologist who developed an influential theory of emotion called the facial feedback hypothesis.

8. ____ A mood is intense but rather short lived, is likely to have a specific cause, tends to be directed toward some particular object, and will motivate a person to take some sort of action.

Check your answers and review any areas of weakness before going on to the next section.

Something to Think About

1. Many Americans are obsessed with achieving, or at least getting closer to, the socially desirable goal of thinness. Approximately one-third of all American women and one-fifth of all American males are trying to lose weight, and the weight-loss industry is a $30 billion a year enterprise. Based on what you have read in your text, what advice would you give to a friend who is trying to lose weight?

2. Just about everyone experiences a relationship problem at one time or another. Most frequently, problems tend to arise in intimate relationships between men and women. Imagine that you are a therapist and a couple comes to you for help in resolving their ongoing interpersonal conflicts. Based on what you have discovered in this chapter, what advice would you give them?

Check your answers and review any areas of weakness before doing the progress tests.

Progress Test 1

Review the complete chapter (including Concept Reviews and the boxed inserts), review all your study notes, and then test yourself on the following progress test. Check your answers. If you make a mistake, review your notes, review the relevant section of the study guide, and, if necessary, go back and read the appropriate part of your textbook.

1. It is an innate characteristic of the European cuckoo to lay her eggs in other birds' nests. This behavior is an example of
   (a) an instinct.
   (b) a drive.
   (c) incentive motivation.
   (d) homeostasis.

2. Mrs. Kim talks proudly about her daughter Koko, who studies hard and earns good grades in college, and about how Koko intends to go to medical school and become a brain surgeon. Mrs. Kim is referring to Koko's
   (a) motivation.   (c) instincts.
   (b) extrinsic desires.   (d) drive.

3. About ten or fifteen minutes into his weightlifting routine Scott usually begins to perspire heavily. His body's tendency to maintain a steady temperature through the cooling action of sweating is a function of
   (a) instinct.
   (b) incentive motivation.
   (c) homeostasis.
   (d) self-actualization.

4. Tim buys a lottery ticket every Friday with the expectation that he is going to win some money. His behavior illustrates
   (a) instinct.
   (b) incentive motivation.
   (c) drive.
   (d) self-actualization.

5. Nicole feels that she has all the material possessions she needs in life and is now determined to devote all her energy to her art. According to Maslow's hierarchy of needs, Nicole is probably striving
   (a) to fulfill her fundamental biological need to paint.
   (b) to fulfill her basic safety needs.
   (c) toward the realization of her personal potential.
   (d) toward the realization of her social needs.

6. Dr. Dorfman destroys the lateral hypothalamus of one rat and the ventromedial hypothalamus of a second rat. It is very probable that the first rat will _____ and the second rat will _____ .
   (a) eat until it becomes obese; stop eating
   (b) have a decreased rate of metabolism; have an increased rate of metabolism
   (c) have an increased rate of metabolism; have a decreased rate of metabolism
   (d) stop eating; eat until it becomes obese

7. After her fourth piece of pizza, Mary feels quite full. Her satiation is due, at least in part, to increased levels of the hormone
   (a) insulin.
   (b) testosterone.
   (c) cholecystokinin (CCK).
   (d) estrogen.

8. Whenever he sees Amanda, Richard's heart beats faster and he gets a trembling feeling inside. Richard now thinks that he must be in love with Amanda. Which theory of emotion is represented in this example?

   (a) James-Lange theory
   (b) drive theory
   (c) two-factor theory
   (d) cognitive-mediational theory

9. Mr. Jackson is about thirty-five pounds overweight. Compared to people who are not overweight, Mr. Jackson is likely to have

   (a) higher metabolism.
   (b) lower metabolism.
   (c) the same metabolism.
   (d) all of the above; there is no relationship between weight and metabolism.

10. Erin has been diagnosed with bulimia nervosa. The main characteristic of her eating disorder is

    (a) being 15 to 20 percent below the ideal body weight.
    (b) a distorted self-perception about body shape and body weight.
    (c) binge eating and purging by self-induced vomiting and occasionally by using laxatives or enemas.
    (d) an obsession with food and a denial of being hungry.

11. Jill is independent, open-minded, and unconventional; she loves the outdoors and includes among her many interests skydiving, downhill skiing, white water kayaking, and hang-gliding. Jill is likely to be classified as

    (a) a sensation seeker.
    (b) shy and timid.
    (c) an external.
    (d) a nonexternal.

12. As part of his overall vocational assessment Bertram took the Thematic Apperception Test (TAT). His score on this test is most likely to reveal his level of

    (a) competence motivation.
    (b) achievement motivation.
    (c) self-efficacy.
    (d) emotionality.

13. When Willard's relationship ended, he felt pretty confused and experienced a combination of relief, sadness, nostalgia, anger, and jealousy. Willard's experience illustrates

    (a) basic emotions.
    (b) mixed emotions.
    (c) mood fluctuations.
    (d) interpersonal engagement.

14. Some people claim that subliminal self-help tapes will quickly and easily produce changes in our motivation, learning ability, attitudes, and other behaviors. According to Science Versus Pseudoscience 8.3,

    (a) all these claims have been supported by empirical evidence.
    (b) subliminal self-help tapes are effective but only for highly suggestible people.
    (c) because university and college bookstores sell subliminal self-help tapes, they probably work for improving study habits and passing exams.
    (d) there is no scientific support for the claims made by promoters of subliminal self-help tapes.

15. One of the most pervasive gender stereotypes is that women are more emotional than are men. Culture and Human Behavior 8.4 concludes that

    (a) women are more emotionally expressive compared to men.
    (b) males and females do not differ in their experience of emotion.
    (c) men mask their emotions more so than do women.
    (d) all of the above are true.

Progress Test 2

After you have checked your understanding of the material in Progress Test 1 and reviewed the chapter with special focus on any areas of weakness, you are ready to assess your knowledge of Progress Test 2. Check your answers. If you make a mistake, review your notes, the relevant section of the study guide, and, if necessary, the appropriate part of your textbook.

1. After her husband died, sixty-eight-year-old Mrs. Jaspers started dating seventy-year-old Sidney. At their age

   (a) it is very unlikely that they will engage in sexual activity.
   (b) they will want to get married almost immediately.
   (c) dating fills their needs for companionship and sexual intimacy.
   (d) all of the above are true.

2. Dr. Spearpoint believes that emotions arise from the perception and interpretation of bodily changes. His views are most consistent with

 (a) the James-Lange theory.
 (b) incentive theory.
 (c) the facial feedback hypothesis.
 (d) the two-factor theory.

3. If he's feeling sad or unhappy, Milton "puts on a happy face." When he does this, his mood often improves. This result is best predicted by the

 (a) cognitive-mediational theory.
 (b) two-factor theory.
 (c) instinct theory.
 (d) facial feedback hypothesis.

4. Both Javid and Jamal received a 10 percent pay raise to their base salary of $15 an hour. Javid is very happy, but Jamal is disappointed. Their different emotional reactions to the same pay raise reflect their different interpretations of the event. This example illustrates the _____ theory of emotion.

 (a) James-Lange
 (b) incentive
 (c) two-factor
 (d) cognitive-mediational

5. After reviewing the major theories of motivation, Zomobia decided that a key problem with _____ theories was that they merely described and labeled behaviors rather than actually explaining them.

 (a) drive
 (b) instinct
 (c) incentive
 (d) humanistic

6. Jasbir has a term paper to write so she heads for the library to do the necessary research. Despite an initial failure to locate material related to her topic, Jasbir continues her catalogue search for many hours until she comes up with sufficient relevant information. She writes, rewrites, and edits her paper until she feels it is almost perfect. Jasbir is demonstrating which basic characteristic commonly associated with motivation?

 (a) activation
 (b) persistence
 (c) intensity
 (d) all of the above

7. Dr. Zascow thinks that emotion is best conceptualized as a dynamic system in which cognitive appraisals, physiological arousal, and behavioral expression all contribute to subjective emotional experience. Dr. Zascow's view is most consistent with the

 (a) integrative approach to emotion.
 (b) cognitive-mediational theory of emotion.
 (c) two-factor theory of emotion.
 (d) James-Lange theory of emotion.

8. While writing a term paper for her motivation course, Cara notes that the majority of people do not experience or achieve self-actualization, despite the claim that it is a goal common to all people. She decides that this is an important limitation of

 (a) instinct theories.
 (b) drive theories.
 (c) incentive theories.
 (d) humanistic theories.

9. Barney and Bailey are identical twins. Barney is gay. Therefore, there is

 (a) about a 50 percent chance that Bailey will also be homosexual.
 (b) almost 100 percent chance that Bailey will also be homosexual.
 (c) about a 20 percent chance that Bailey will also be homosexual.
 (d) no way to predict Bailey's sexual orientation because there is no correlation between genetic factors and sexual behavior.

10. About six months ago, fifteen-year-old Kirsten went on a drastic weight-loss diet that caused her to drop from 115 to 85 pounds. Although she is dangerously underweight and undernourished, she continues to think she looks fat. Kirsten probably suffers from

 (a) obesity.
 (b) a very high metabolic rate.
 (c) bulimia nervosa.
 (d) anorexia nervosa.

11. Shortly after eating lunch, Marty is daydreaming in class. Imagining the taste and smell of his favorite pizza, he starts to feel hungry. In this instance, his feelings of hunger are probably caused by

 (a) increased levels of insulin.
 (b) decreased levels of insulin.
 (c) increased levels of cholecystokinin (CCK).
 (d) satiation.

12. Safana is writing a term paper on human sexuality. Her library research is likely to indicate that the normal order of the four stages in the human sexual response cycle is
    (a) excitement, resolution, plateau, and orgasm.
    (b) excitement, orgasm, plateau, and resolution.
    (c) plateau, excitement, resolution, and orgasm.
    (d) excitement, plateau, orgasm, and resolution.

13. Merv is in his early twenties. If he is typical of people his age, his basic metabolic rate (BMR) has _____ since he was a child.
    (a) decreased
    (b) increased
    (c) remained relatively the same
    (d) done any of the above (there is no relationship between age and BMR)

14. According to In Focus 8.2, which of the following is true?
    (a) Sexual fantasies are psychologically unhealthy.
    (b) Male and female sexual fantasies are almost identical in content and frequency.
    (c) Sexual fantasies are a sign of sexual frustration and dissatisfaction with a relationship.
    (d) All of the above are true.
    (e) None of the above are true.

15. According to the Application, a key ingredient in successful intimate relationships is
    (a) suppressing one's true emotions.
    (b) resolving conflict.
    (c) stonewalling.
    (d) flooding.

Progress Test 3

After you have checked your understanding of the material in Progress Tests 1 and 2, and have done a complete chapter review with special focus on any areas of weakness, you are ready to further assess your knowledge on Progress Test 3. Check your answers. If you make a mistake, review your notes, the appropriate parts of the study guide, and, if necessary, the relevant sections of your textbook.

1. Pat experiences very intense positive emotions and is generally considered to be a very emotionally expressive person. It is likely that Pat
   (a) also tends to experience very intense negative emotions.
   (b) is very unpopular as compared with people who are emotionally inhibited.
   (c) almost never experiences negative emotions.
   (d) is very low in both achievement and competence motivation.

2. Five-year-old Nemanja was excited and very curious about the various animals he saw when he was taken to the zoo for the first time. His exploratory behavior was quickly inhibited, however, when he was suddenly startled and frightened by a loud roar from the lion's enclosure. His initial curiosity rapidly gave way to extreme fear and withdrawal. Nemanja's behavior is best explained by _____ theory.
   (a) drive
   (b) incentive
   (c) arousal
   (d) instinct

3. The desire to drink when thirsty is to _____ theory as the desire to avoid boredom is to _____ theory.
   (a) humanistic; drive
   (b) arousal; incentive
   (c) drive; arousal
   (d) self-actualization; homeostasis

4. During a discussion of motivational theories, Harland pointed out that people often engage in behaviors that serve to increase tension and physiological arousal. Harland's observation most strongly argues against which theory of motivation?
   (a) instinct theory
   (b) drive theory
   (c) arousal theory
   (d) humanistic theory

5. Cyril has a strong need for privacy and independence; he has an accurate perception of himself, other people, and external reality; and he appreciates the simple pleasures in life. According to Maslow, Cyril is probably
   (a) a sensation-seeker.
   (b) an external.
   (c) a nonexternal.
   (d) self-actualized.

6. Dennis and Kathy have a warm, stable, and loving relationship. If they are like most American adults in a similar situation, they are
   (a) likely to be fundamentally happy with their relationship.
   (b) probably conservative and traditional in their sexual practices and preferences.
   (c) likely to have more active sexual lives than single people do.
   (d) all of the above.

7. Thirty-year-old Ali is very similar to his parents in physical appearance. Like both his mother and father, Ali is of short stature, heavy set, broad shouldered, and overweight. The fact that Ali's adult weight resembles that of his parents illustrates the influence of _____ on weight regulation and metabolism.
   (a) genetic factors
   (b) age
   (c) gender
   (d) environmental factors

8. Wilda is a diplomat and was trained in the customs, language, and religions of Slakia, where she is now posted. It is very unlikely that Wilda needed special training to correctly interpret her hosts' expressions of emotion as revealed by their
   (a) songs.
   (b) dancing.
   (c) facial expressions.
   (d) eating etiquette.

9. Tasleem is about 30 percent heavier than her optimal body weight. If she is like most obese people, she probably differs from nonobese people in the daily regulation of her eating behavior by
   (a) being highly responsive to external cues associated with food.
   (b) physiologically reacting to food-related stimuli with greater insulin production.
   (c) having a generally higher body level of insulin.
   (d) all of the above.

10. When Moira was preparing for her first solo landing in a single-engine plane, she experienced a number of physiological reactions such as a racing heart, sweaty palms, and tension in her muscles. These physiological reactions were activated by her _____ nervous system.
    (a) central   (c) skeletal
    (b) sympathetic   (d) parasympathetic

11. When Ulricke lost twelve pounds on a diet, her weight fell below her set-point weight. She is likely to experience a(n) _____ in hunger and a(n) _____ in her basal metabolic rate.
    (a) increase; increase   (c) increase; decrease
    (b) decrease; decrease   (d) decrease; increase

12. After working in the garden all afternoon on a hot day, Mrs. Ulman is very thirsty and drinks a big glass of iced tea. Her motivation to drink to reduce her feeling of thirst can best be explained by
    (a) instinct theory.
    (b) drive theory.
    (c) incentive motivation.
    (d) humanistic theory.

13. Laureen is a lesbian. It is very probable that
    (a) her sexual orientation was determined before adolescence and before any sexual activity occurred.
    (b) she experienced some early childhood sexual abuse by a member of the opposite sex.
    (c) her father was overly domineering and her mother was ineffectual and provided her with a poor feminine role model.
    (d) her first sexual experience occurred in childhood with a member of the same sex.

14. In order to break the vicious circle of flooding-stonewalling-flooding, the Application suggests that couples should
    (a) become aware of the gender differences in handling emotion.
    (b) call a time-out whenever either one begins to feel overwhelmed or in danger of flooding.
    (c) spend the time-out period thinking about ways to resolve the conflict, not about ways to mount a more effective counterattack.
    (d) recognize that males need to try to stop avoiding conflict and females should try to raise issues in need of resolution in a calm manner and without personal attack.
    (e) do all of the above.

15. According to research by David Buss (Culture and Human Behavior 8.1)
    (a) mutual attraction and love are the most important factors in selecting a mate in all cultures studied.
    (b) men are more likely than women to value youth and physical attractiveness in a potential mate.
    (c) women value financial security, access to material resources, and high status and education in a potential mate.
    (d) all of the above are true.

Answers

Introduction: Motivation and Emotion

1. *Motivation refers to* the forces that act on or within an organism to initiate and direct behavior.

2. *The three characteristics associated with motivation are* activation (the initiation of behavior), persistence (continued efforts to achieve a goal), and intensity (the vigor of responding).

3. *Emotions are closely tied to motivational processes (and vice versa) because both topics involve* the complex interaction of physical, behavioral, cognitive, and social factors.

4. *According to the earliest theories of motivation, instinct theories,* people are motivated to engage in certain behaviors because of genetic programming. *Limitations of these theories are* that they merely describe and label behaviors rather than actually explaining them.

5. *According to drive theories,* behavior is motivated by the desire to reduce internal tension caused by unmet biological needs such as hunger and thirst. *Their limitations are* that people engage in behaviors that are not a reflection of internal drives (we sometimes eat when we are not hungry or don't eat when we are hungry) and that many behaviors are directed toward increasing tension and physiological arousal.

6. *Incentive theories proposed that* behavior is motivated by the pull of external goals, such as rewards. *Their limitations are* that many behaviors are not primarily motivated by any kind of external incentive, we sometimes engage in behaviors for their own sake, such as helping others or satisfying curiosity.

7. *Humanistic theories suggest that people are motivated to* satisfy a progression of needs, beginning with the most basic physiological needs and steadily moving upward as the needs associated with each level are met to the ultimate goal of self-actualization, the realization of personal potential. *Limitations are* concepts such as self-actualization are vague, difficult to define, and hard to test scientifically; the initial research was based on a limited sample with questionable reliability; and finally, most people do not experience or achieve self-actualization, despite the claim that this is an inborn goal in all people.

Concept Check 1

1. motivation
2. homeostasis
3. unlikely
4. incentive
5. instinct
6. emotions

Matching Exercise 1

1. humanistic theories
2. motivation
3. persistence
4. Abraham Maslow
5. drive
6. instinct theories
7. hierarchy of needs

True/False Test 1

1. T	3. F	5. T	7. T
2. T	4. T	6. F	

The Motivation to Eat

1. *The four factors that influence the motivation to eat are* psychological, biological, social, and cultural factors.

2. *Biologically, we are motivated to stop or start eating by the following: Oral signals influence eating behavior by* maintaining or slowing down eating behavior once it has begun. *Stomach signals* trigger the release of cholecystokinin (CCK) into the bloodstream; CCK appears to magnify the feeling of satiation by slowing the rate at which the stomach empties and by heightening the sensitivity of stretch receptors in the stomach. *Through a classical condition-*

ing process, insulin levels are increased before we eat, which leads us to experience more hunger. *The hypothalamus* detects various signals (oral, stomach, and CCK), and then initiates or suppresses eating behavior.

3. *The basal metabolic rate (BMR) is* the rate at which the body uses energy for vital bodily functions when at rest. *It is influenced by* gender, weight, age, and genetics.

4. *Set-point theory suggests that* each of us has a particular weight that the body is naturally set to maintain by increasing or decreasing BMR; this weight is based on the well-established principle of homeostasis.

5. *Obesity is defined as* weighing 20 percent or more above one's optimal body weight.

6. *Anorexia nervosa is* an eating disorder in which the individual refuses to maintain a minimally normal body weight, is extremely afraid of gaining weight or becoming fat, and has a distorted perception about the size of his or her body.

7. *Bulimia nervosa is* an eating disorder in which a person engages in binge eating and then purges the excessive food consumption by self-induced vomiting or, less often, by taking laxatives or enemas.

Concept Check 2

1. high
2. external
3. lateral; LH
4. basal metabolic rate; BMR
5. obese
6. anorexia nervosa

Matching Exercise 2

1. cholecystokinin (CCK)
2. oral signals
3. basal metabolic rate (BMR)
4. externals/nonexternals
5. ventromedial hypothalamus (VMH)
6. set-point weight
7. insulin

True/False Test 2

1. T	4. T	6. F
2. F	5. T	7. T
3. T		

Sexual Motivation and Behavior

1. *In most non-human animals, sexual behavior is* biologically determined and triggered by hormonal changes in the female.

2. *In humans, sexual behavior is (refer to the major hormones involved in human sexual motivation)* not limited to a woman's fertile period. Even without the female sex hormone estrogen, women show little or no drop in sexual interest. Men, on the other hand, with a significant decrease in testosterone may lose interest in sexual activity—although some do not.

3. *The four stages of the human sexual response cycle are* excitement, plateau, orgasm, and resolution as described by Masters and Johnson in the 1950s and 1960s. Most men experience only one intense orgasm, while women are capable of multiple orgasms.

4. *Sexual orientation refers to* the direction of a person's emotional and erotic attraction toward members of the opposite sex, the same sex, or both sexes. *The factors associated with sexual orientation are* psychological, biological (genetics), social, and cultural.

5. *The most general conclusions about the sexual behavior patterns of adults are that* the development of sexual behavior follows a predictable sequence of events from infancy through adolescence; most people spend their adult years involved in a stable sexual relationship; married and cohabiting couples have more active sex lives than do single people; most Americans are fundamentally happy with the relationship they have with their sexual partner; and most Americans are very conservative and traditional in their sexual practices and preferences and are not inclined toward kinky or unusual sexual practices.

6. *Sexual dysfunction is a* consistent disturbance in sexual desire, arousal, or orgasm that causes psychological distress and interpersonal difficulties.

Concept Check 3

1. refractory
2. decrease; stay the same
3. decrease
4. sexual orientation
5. plateau; resolution
6. are not

7. likely

8. are

Matching Exercise 3

1. Virginia E. Johnson
2. plateau phase
3. sexual dysfunction
4. heterosexual
5. refractory period
6. homosexual
7. William H. Masters
8. excitement phase

True/False Test 3

1. T	4. F	6. F
2. T	5. T	7. T
3. T		

Arousal Motives: Curiosity and Sensation Seeking

1. *Arousal theory suggests that* people are motivated to maintain an optimal level of arousal that is neither too high nor too low.

2. *Along with increasing arousal, curiosity and exploratory behavior may be motivated by* the urge to understand the environment. We don't explore haphazardly; instead, we pace the rate at which we expose ourselves to increasing complexity and novelty.

3. *People who are high in sensation seeking are* motivated to experience high levels of arousal associated with varied and novel activities that often involve some degree of physical or social risk. Sensation seeking may be an innate tendency.

Competence and Achievement Motivation

1. *Competence motivation is* striving to be capable. *Achievement motivation is* striving to excel or outperform others.

2. *Achievement motivation is most commonly measured by* the Thematic Apperception Test (TAT), which consists of a series of ambiguous pictures about which the person being tested has to make up a story.

3. *Self-efficacy refers to* the degree to which a person is subjectively convinced of his or her ability to effectively meet the demands of a situation.

Concept Check 4

1. achievement
2. pace
3. low
4. collectivistic
5. competence

Graphic Organizer 1

1. drive theory
2. humanistic theory
3. instinct theory
4. incentive theory
5. arousal theory

Matching Exercise 4

1. self-efficacy
2. arousal theory
3. competence motivation
4. sensation seeking
5. achievement motivation
6. Thematic Apperception Test (TAT)

Emotion

1. *Emotion is defined as* a psychological state involving three distinct components: subjective experience, physical arousal, and a behavioral or expressive response.

2. *Emotions tend to* be intense, rather short lived, have a specific cause, be directed to a particular object, and motivate a person to take some form of action. *Moods involve* a milder emotional state that is more global and pervasive, such as gloominess or contentment, and lasts for a few hours or days.

3. *Cross-cultural research has shown that* people from different cultures tend to arrange emotions in much the same way as Americans, with general agreement among cultures regarding the subjective experience of different basic emotions such as joy, anger, fear, disgust, and sadness.

4. *The physiological component of emotions such as anger and fear involves* the activation of the sympathetic division of the autonomic nervous system, which gears you for action, affecting heart rate, blood pressure, respiration, perspiration, and other bodily activities (the flight-or-fight response).

5. *Display rules are* social and cultural rules that regulate the expression of emotions, particularly facial expressions; because the rules can vary greatly from culture to culture, the expression of various emotions may also vary depending on the culture and its display rules.

Explaining Emotions: Key Theories

1. *The James-Lange theory of emotions states that* emotions arise from the perception and interpretation of bodily changes.

2. *Walter Cannon criticized the James-Lange theory on a number of grounds:* (a) Bodily reactions are similar for many emotions, yet our subjective experience of various emotions is very different. (b) Our emotional reaction to a stimulus is often faster than our physiological reaction, but the subjective experience of emotion is often virtually instantaneous. (c) When physiological changes are artificially induced, people do not necessarily report feeling a related emotion. (d) People cut off from feeling bodily changes do experience true emotions (the perception of physical arousal does not seem to be essential to the experience of emotion).

3. *According to the facial feedback hypothesis,* expressing a specific emotion, especially facially, causes us to subjectively experience that emotion.

4. *Schachter and Singer's two-factor theory of emotion suggests that* emotion is a result of the interaction of physiological arousal and the cognitive label that we apply to explain the arousal, and if one of these factors in absent, emotion will not be experienced.

5. *Richard Lazarus's cognitive-mediational theory emphasizes that* the most important aspect of an emotional experience is our cognitive interpretation, or appraisal, of the emotion-causing stimulus and that all other components of emotion, including physiological arousal, follow from the initial cognitive appraisal.

6. *The interactive approach to emotion suggests that* cognitive appraisals, physiological arousal, and behavioral expression all contribute to subjective emotional experience.

Concept Check 5

1. mood; emotion

2. sympathetic

3. display rules

4. facial feedback hypothesis

5. James-Lange theory

Graphic Organizer 2

1. astonish-ment

2. alarm

3. boredom

4. relaxation

5. annoyance

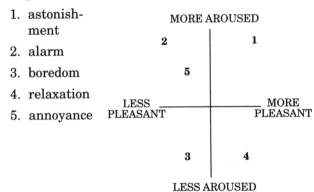

Matching Exercise 5

1. facial feedback hypothesis

2. Richard Lazarus

3. emotion

4. two-factor theory of emotion

5. basic emotions

6. interpersonal engagement

7. nonverbal behavior

8. interactive approach to emotion

True/False Test 5

1. F	4. T	7. F
2. T	5. T	8. F
3. T	6. T	

Something to Think About

1. Losing weight and keeping it off is a big problem for many people. You might begin your discussion by noting that our motivation to eat is influenced by psychological, biological, social, and cultural factors. For example, biologically, hunger and satiation are regulated by oral sensations, stomach signals, CCK, and insulin. Psychologically, some people are more strongly influenced by food-related external stimuli. Socially, women, in particular, are affected by society's ideal of thinness. Next, describe the role of BMR in relation to weight regulation. In addition, set-point theory and the principle of homeostasis will help your friend to understand why some people keep a relatively constant weight and why some are obese.

   Applying the above to losing weight, note that obese people do not necessarily eat more than nonobese people. Instead, they may be highly responsive to external cues associated with food; they also produce more insulin; and they operate with higher body levels of insulin. Moreover, obese people gain weight more easily than nonobese people, and dieting may sharply reduce their metabolic rate and keep it low for long periods of time.

The best advice for someone trying to lose weight is to modify his or her eating patterns and follow a regular exercise program. It's an uphill battle, and, despite the gloomy statistics, many people have successfully kept weight off by following this advice.

2. Resolving conflicts is a key ingredient in successful intimate relationships. Men and women differ significantly in the way they communicate, especially when they are trying to deal with emotional issues and interpersonal conflicts. These fundamental differences can sabotage conflict resolution. There is hope, however. John Gottman's research provides evidence of a number of constructive ways for overcoming these communication differences.

First, conflict can play a key role in a healthy, happy relationship; a couple's relationship will grow if the couple successfully reconciles the inevitable differences that occur. Men and women react differently to conflict, particularly if it involves strong emotions. Typically, men have learned to suppress and contain their emotions, whereas women tend to be more comfortable with emotional expression. During emotional conflicts, people may experience flooding (the feeling of being overwhelmed emotionally); in reaction to this intense physiological arousal, they may engage in stonewalling (withdrawing to contain their uncomfortable emotions). Men tend to get more physiologically aroused during relationship conflicts than do women and are therefore more likely to engage in stonewalling. Women tend to experience stonewalling as disapproval and rejection and typically react by flooding. And that's how the vicious circle of flooding-stonewalling-flooding begins.

A number of things can be done to break this vicious circle. First, both parties need to become aware of the gender differences in han-

dling emotion. Men need to remember that women experience stonewalling as rejection, disapproval, and abandonment, and women need to accept men's need to temporarily withdraw from the situation. Second, calling for a 20- to 30-minute time-out period during a conflict is a good idea so long as both parties use the time to think about ways to resolve the conflict, rather than rehearsing or preparing vengeful comments and counterattack strategies. Third, men need to make a conscious effort to embrace, rather than avoid, the problem; sidestepping the issue won't make it go away. If the woman didn't care about the relationship, she wouldn't keep confronting her partner; generally, she wants both people to resolve the issue together. Fourth, women should try raising the issue in a more calm and less emotionally confrontational manner. Frame the problem in the context of maintaining a loving relationship and avoid personal attacks. Finally, tell the couple to buy, read, and discuss John Gottman's book—together!

Progress Test 1

1. a	6. d	11. a
2. a	7. c	12. b
3. c	8. c	13. b
4. b	9. a	14. d
5. c	10. c	15. d

Progress Test 2

1. c	6. d	11. a
2. a	7. a	12. d
3. d	8. d	13. a
4. d	9. a	14. e
5. b	10. d	15. b

Progress Test 3

1. a	6. d	11. c
2. c	7. a	12. b
3. c	8. c	13. a
4. b	9. d	14. e
5. d	10. b	15. d

CHAPTER

9

Lifespan Development

PREVIEW	Reading the section below first will give you a general sense of the chapter's contents and an initial introduction to some of the major concepts and terms. This will prime you for what you are about to read and help you to develop a "cognitive map" that will guide your study of the material in this chapter. Likewise, reading the **preview questions** at the beginning of each major section will improve your ability to understand, learn, and retain the information.

CHAPTER 9 . . . AT A GLANCE

Chapter 9 examines the scope of developmental psychology and major themes such as the stages of lifespan development, the nature of change, and the interaction between heredity and environment. The first two sections explain genetic contributions to development and describe the stages of prenatal development.

Development during infancy and childhood and the capacities and capabilities of the newborn are explored, including social and personality development, with special attention paid to the nature of temperament and the concept of attachment. This is followed by a description of the stages of language development and gender-role development. The section concludes with a detailed analysis of Piaget's theory of cognitive development and an examination of Vygotsky's information-processing model.

Adolescence is defined as a distinctive stage of development, with important changes in physical, sexual, and social development. Erikson's theory of psychosocial development and Kohlberg's theory of the development of moral reasoning are discussed next.

The final sections describe the three phases of adult development as well as the contributions of genetics, environment, and the individual's lifestyle. Love and work are the key themes that dominate adult development. Late adulthood does not necessarily involve a steep decline in physical and cognitive functioning. In discussing dying and death, which can occur at any point in the lifespan, the text outlines Kübler-Ross's five-stage model of dying, noting that dying is an individual process, much as any other during the lifespan.

Introduction: Your Life Story

Preview Questions

Consider the following questions as you study this section of the chapter.

- What do developmental psychologists study?
- What are the major themes in developmental psychology?

Read the section "Introduction: Your Life Story" and **write** *your answers to the following:*

1. Developmental psychology is the _____
   _____
   _____

2. The major themes in developmental psychology
   are _____
   _____
   _____
   _____
   _____

Genetic Contributions to Your Life Story

Preview Questions

Consider the following questions as you study this section of the chapter.

- What are chromosomes, DNA, and genes, and what role do they play in determining each individual's unique genetic makeup?
- What role does the environment play in the relationship between genotype and phenotype?
- How do dominant and recessive genes differ, and what are sex-linked recessive characteristics?

Read the section "Genetic Contributions to Your Life Story" and **write** *your answers to the following:*

1. Chromosomes are_____
   _____

2. DNA (deoxyribonucleic acid) is _____
   _____

3. Genes are _____
   _____
   _____

4. Genotype refers to the _____
   _____

   Phenotype refers to the _____
   _____

5. We inherit from our biological parents _____
   _____
   _____

6. In a pair of genes, the dominant gene is _____
   _____
   _____

   A recessive gene is _____
   _____

7. The sex chromosomes are _____
   _____
   _____

   Sex-linked recessive characteristics are traits
   determined by _____
   _____

Prenatal Development

Preview Questions

Consider the following questions as you study this section of the chapter.

- What happens to the single-cell zygote during prenatal development?
- What are the three stages of prenatal development?
- What are teratogens?

Read the section "Prenatal Development" and **write** *your answers to the following:*

1. During prenatal development, the single-cell
   zygote _____
   _____

2. The three stages of the prenatal stage are _____
   _____
   _____
   _____

3. Teratogens are _____
   _____
   _____
   _____

After you have carefully studied the preceding sections, complete the following exercises.

Concept Check 1

Read the following and write the correct term in the space provided.

1. Dr. Dalliwhal's research focuses on the relationship between various teratogens and birth defects. Dr. Dalliwhal is most likely a _____ psychologist.

2. From the day Franco was born, people have always responded very positively to his good looks. Now that he is growing older, it is clear that he is developing a socially confident and outgoing personality. This best illustrates the interaction of _____ and _____ .

3. Paul and Paula are brother and sister; in terms of chromosomes, Paul received a(n) _____ from his mother and a(n) _____ from his father, and Paula received a(n) _____ from her mother and a(n) _____ from her father.

4. It is now six weeks since Jennifer conceived. The human organism she is carrying is called a(n) _____ ; after the eighth week, it will be called a(n) _____ .

5. When Myra became pregnant, she decided that she would not drink any alcohol because she did not want to risk causing abnormal development or birth defects in her unborn child. Myra is aware that alcohol is a _____ .

Graphic Organizer 1

There is a dominant gene (D) for "dimples" and a recessive gene (r) for "no dimples." The following matrix shows the four possible combinations. Decide which combinations (genotype) will result in "dimples" or "no dimples" (phenotype).

	Dominant (D)	Recessive (r)
Dominant (D)	Cell 1 DD	Cell 2 Dr
Recessive (r)	Cell 3 Dr	Cell 4 rr

Cell 1: The genotype DD results in the phenotype of _____ .

Cell 2: The genotype Dr results in the phenotype of _____ .

Cell 3: The genotype Dr results in the phenotype of _____ .

Cell 4: The genotype rr results in the phenotype of _____ .

Review of Terms and Concepts 1

Use the terms in this list to complete the Matching Test, then to help you answer the True/False items correctly.

developmental psychology
critical period
nature-nurture issue
chromosome
deoxyribonucleic acid (DNA)
gene
genotype
phenotype
dominant gene
dominant characteristics
recessive gene
recessive characteristics
sex chromosomes
sex-linked recessive characteristics
prenatal stage
zygote
germinal period (zygotic period)
embryo
embryonic period
teratogens
fetal period
fetus

Matching Exercise

Match the appropriate term with its definition or description.

1. _____ The stage of development before birth; divided into the germinal, embryonic, and fetal periods.

2. _____ The basic unit of heredity that directs the development of a particular characteristic; the individual unit of DNA instructions on a chromosome.

3. _____ The branch of psychology that studies how people change over the life-span.

4. _____ Traits determined by reces-sive genes located on the X chromosome; in males, these characteristics require only one recessive gene to be expressed.

5. _____ Harmful agents or sub-stances that can cause malformations or defects in an embryo or a fetus.

6. _____ Long, threadlike structure composed of twisted parallel strands of DNA; found in the nucleus of the cell.

7. _____ In a pair of genes, the gene containing genetic instructions that will not be expressed unless paired with another recessive gene.

8. _____ The first two weeks of pre-natal development.

9. _____ Cluster of cells that develop from the single-cell zygote by the end of the two-week germinal period.

10. _____ Traits whose expression requires two identical recessive genes, like those for light hair and being dimple-free.

11. _____ Chromosomes designated as X or Y that determine biological sex; the 23rd pair of chromosomes in humans.

True/False Test

Indicate whether each statement is true or false by placing T or F in the blank space next to each item.

1. ____ The fetus is the name given to the growing organism at the beginning of the third month.

2. ____ A critical period during development is a time during which the child is maximally sensi-tive to environmental influences.

3. ____ Deoxyribonucleic acid (DNA) is the chemi-cal basis of heredity; carries genetic instruc-tions in the cell.

4. ____ The fetal period is the second period of pre-natal development, extending from the third week through the eighth week.

5. ____ At conception, chromosomes from the bio-logical mother and father combine to form a single cell called the fertilized egg, or zygote.

6. ____ In a pair of genes, the gene containing genetic instructions that will be expressed whether paired with another dominant gene or with a recessive gene is called the dominant gene.

7. ____ The embryonic period is the third and longest period of prenatal development, extend-ing from the eighth week until birth.

8. ____ An important theme in developmental psy-chology is the interaction between heredity and environment; traditionally called the nature-nurture issue.

9. ____ The genotype refers to observable traits or characteristics of an organism determined by the interaction of genetic and environmental factors.

10. ____ Traits such as freckles, dark eyes, dark hair, and dimples are referred to as dominant characteristics because they require only one member of a gene pair to be present in order for the trait to be displayed.

11. ____ Phenotype refers to the underlying genetic makeup of a particular organism, including the genetic instructions for traits that are not actu-ally displayed.

Check your answers and review any areas of weakness before going on to the next section.

Development During Infancy and Childhood: Physical Development

Preview Questions

Consider the following questions as you study this section of the chapter.

- What reflexes and sensory capabilities are physically helpless infants equipped with that enhance their chances for survival?

- How do the sensory capabilities of the newborn promote the development of relationships with caregivers?

- How does the brain develop after birth?

*Read the section "Development During Infancy and Childhood" and **write** your answers to the following:*

1. Newborn infants enter the world equipped with

Their senses of vision, hearing, smell, and touch are _____

_____

2. The infant's sensory capabilities promote the development of relationships with caregivers, as evidenced by the fact that they _____

_____

_____

_____

_____

3. After birth, a number of changes take place in the infant's brain: _____

_____

_____

Development During Infancy and Childhood: Social and Personality Development

Preview Questions

Consider the following questions as you study this section of the chapter.

- What is temperament, and what is attachment?
- What temperamental patterns have been identified?
- How is attachment measured?
- What is the basic premise of attachment theory?

*Read the section "Social and Personality Development" and **write** your answers to the following:*

1. Temperament refers to _____

_____

Attachment is the _____

_____

2. The three broad temperamental patterns are

_____

3. Attachment is measured using a procedure called the _____
In this technique _____

_____

_____

_____

4. The basic premise of attachment theory is

_____

_____

_____

_____

_____

Development During Infancy and Childhood: Language Development

Preview Questions

Consider the following questions as you study this section of the chapter.

- How does a biological predisposition to learn language function in language development?
- How is language development encouraged by caregivers?
- What are the stages of language development?

*Read the section "Language Development" and **write** your answers to the following:*

1. According to Noam Chomsky _____

_____

_____

_____

2. Language development is encouraged by _____

_____

3. The stages of language development are _____

_____

_____

_____

After you have carefully studied the preceding sections, complete the following exercises.

Concept Check 2

Read the following and write the correct term in the space provided.

1. Dr. Snow is interested in the abilities of newborn children. While testing visual perception, she is likely to find that newborns will look longer at the image of a(n) _____ compared to other visual patterns.

2. In order to determine whether a child is securely or insecurely attached, researchers are likely to use _____ .

3. Kathy gave birth to a normal, healthy, eight-and-half-pound baby. In terms of brain development, the baby's brain weighs _____ (25 percent/50 percent/75 percent/100 percent) of its adult weight.

4. As Kathy's baby develops, it becomes apparent that she readily adapts to new experiences, displays positive moods and emotions, and has regular sleeping and eating patterns. She is likely to be classified as a temperamentally _____ baby.

5. Kathy and her husband are consistently warm, responsive, and sensitive to their infant's needs, and the baby has developed the expectation that her needs will be met. It is very probable that the baby will form a(n) _____ attachment to her parents.

6. When Kathy tells 12-month-old Kaila to "Bring Mommy the dolly," Kaila immediately does so, even though she cannot say the words "bring," "Mommy," or "dolly." This suggests that Kaila's _____ vocabulary is larger than her _____ vocabulary.

Review of Terms, Concepts, and Names 2

Use the terms in this list to complete the Matching Test, then to help you answer the True/False items correctly.

infancy
rooting reflex
sucking reflex
grasping reflex
temperament
easy temperament
difficult temperament
slow-to-warm-up
  temperament
attachment
secure attachment
insecure attachment

Strange Situation
Mary Ainsworth
Noam Chomsky
motherese (infant-
  directed speech)
cooing and babbling
  stage
one-word stage
comprehension
  vocabulary
production vocabulary
two-word stage

Matching Exercise

Match the appropriate term/name with its definition or description.

1. _____ The first two years of life.

2. _____ Measure of attachment devised by Mary Ainsworth, typically used with infants who are between one and two years old.

3. _____ Automatic response elicited by touching a newborn's lips.

4. _____ Temperamental category for babies who have a low activity level, who withdraw from new situations and people, and who adapt to new experiences very gradually.

5. _____ Universal style of speech used with babies and characterized by very distinct pronunciation, a simplified vocabulary, short sentences, a high pitch, and exaggerated intonation and expression.

6. _____ Biologically programmed stage in language development that occurs between about three months of age and nine months of age.

7. _____ Emotional bond that forms between infants and their caregiver(s), especially parents.

8. _____ Words that are understood by an infant or child.

9. _____ Form of attachment that may develop when parents are neglectful, inconsistent, or insensitive to their infant's moods or behaviors and reflects an ambivalent or detached emotional relationship between infant and mother.

10. _____ Universal stage in language development, starting around two years of age, in which infants combine two words to construct simple "sentences" that reflect the first understanding of grammar.

True/False Test

Indicate whether each statement is true or false by placing T or F in the blank space next to each item.

1. ____ Noam Chomsky is the psychologist who devised the Strange Situation procedure to measure attachment; contributed to attachment theory.

2. ____ Production vocabulary refers to the words that an infant or child can speak.

3. ____ An infant's response to having his or her palms touched is called the rooting reflex.

4. ____ Babies with a difficult temperament tend to be intensely emotional, are irritable and fussy, cry a lot, and have irregular sleeping and eating patterns.

5. ____ During the one-word stage, babies use a single word and vocal intonation to stand for an entire sentence.

6. ____ Secure attachment is likely to develop when parents are consistently warm, responsive, and sensitive to their infant's needs.

7. ____ Mary Ainsworth is the American linguist who proposed that people have an innate understanding of the basic principles of language, which is called a universal grammar.

8. ____ Babies with an easy temperament readily adapt to new experiences, generally display positive moods and emotions, and have regular sleeping and eating patterns.

9. ____ Touching the newborn's cheek elicits the grasping reflex; the infant turns toward the source of the touch and opens the mouth.

10. ____ Temperament is the inborn predisposition to consistently behave and react in a certain way.

Check your answers and review any areas of weakness before going on to the next section.

Development During Infancy and Childhood: Gender-Role Development

Preview Questions

Consider the following questions as you study this section of the chapter.

- What are gender, gender roles, and gender identity?
- What is the social learning theory of gender-role development?
- What is the gender schema theory of gender-role development?
- How do these two theories explain the development of gender roles?

Read the section "Gender-Role Development" and **write** *your answers to the following:*

1. Gender refers to _____
   _____

   Gender roles are _____
   _____

   Gender identity is _____

2. According to social learning theory _____
   _____
   _____

3. Gender schema theory contends that _____
   _____
   _____

Development During Infancy and Childhood: Cognitive Development

Preview Questions

Consider the following questions as you study this section of the chapter.

- What are Piaget's four stages of cognitive development, and what are the characteristics of each stage?
- What are the main criticisms of Piaget's theory?

Read the section "Cognitive Development" and **write** *your answers to the following:*

1. The four stages (and their characteristics) in Piaget's theory are
   (a) _____
   _____
   _____
   (b) _____
   _____
   _____
   (c) _____
   _____
   _____
   (d) _____
   _____
   _____

2. Piaget's theory has been criticized because ____

   _____

   _____

   _____

   _____

3. The information-processing model of cognitive development views cognitive development as

   _____

   _____

   _____

   _____

After you have carefully studied the preceding sections, complete the following exercises.

Concept Check 3

Read the following and write the correct term in the space provided.

1. Four-year-old Tiborg is not completely egocentric, and five-year-old Natasha exhibits some understanding of conservation. Observations such as these suggest that Piaget may have _____ (overestimated/underestimated) the cognitive abilities of infants and children.

2. Eight-year-old Nadia has the ability to think logically about visible and tangible objects and situations. She is in the _____ stage of cognitive development.

3. Young Adrienne attempts to retrieve her toy bear after her father hides it under a blanket. This suggests that Adrienne has developed a sense of _____ .

4. When Mrs. Goodley cut Janet's hot dog into eight pieces and Simon's into six pieces, Simon started to cry and complained that he wasn't getting as much hot dog as Janet. Piaget would say that Simon doesn't understand the principle of _____ .

5. Three-year-old Rita calls all unfamiliar four-legged animals "doggies." She appears to be _____ these new experiences into

her existing concept of a dog.

6. Piaget would call Rita's mental representation or concept of dog a _____ .

7. During a tutorial devoted to the pros and cons of genetic engineering, Vasilis raised some important issues about the ownership of fertilized eggs and whether destroying them constitutes taking a life. Piaget would say that Vasilis is in the _____ operational stage of cognitive development.

8. Liam describes his girlfriend as gentle, caring, empathetic, and very feminine. Liam is referring to his girlfriend's _____ .

9. Sheila contends that children actively develop cognitive categories for masculinity and femininity and that these mental representations influence how children perceive, interpret, and remember relevant aspects of what is appropriate for boys and girls. Sheila's views are most consistent with _____ theory.

Review of Terms, Concepts, and Names 3

Use the terms in this list to complete the Matching Test, then to help you answer the True/False items correctly.

gender
gender roles
gender identity
social learning theory
gender schema theory
schemas (gender)
cognitive processes
Jean Piaget
qualitative difference in thinking
sensorimotor stage
object permanence
schemas
preoperational stage
operations
symbolic thought
egocentrism
irreversibility
centration
conservation
concrete operational stage
formal operational stage
information-processing model of cognitive development
Lev Vygotsky

Matching Exercise

Match the appropriate term/name with its definition or description.

1. _____ The ability to use words, images, and symbols to represent the world.

2. _____ The mental functions used in thinking, remembering, and processing information.

3. _____ The understanding that an object continues to exist even when it can no longer be seen.

4. _____ Piaget's fourth stage of cognitive development, which lasts from adolescence through adulthood and is characterized by the ability to think logically about abstract principles and hypothetical situations.

5. _____ Swiss child psychologist whose influential theory proposed that children progress through distinct stages of cognitive development.

6. _____ The model that views cognitive development as a continuous process over the lifespan and that studies the development of basic mental processes such as attention, memory, and problem solving.

7. _____ Piaget's term for the mental representations of the world that children acquire as their memories improve and as they gain an understanding of object permanence.

8. _____ Piaget's first stage of cognitive development, from birth to about age two; the period during which the infant explores the environment and acquires knowledge through sensing and manipulating objects.

9. _____ In Piaget's theory, the inability to take another person's perspective or point of view.

10. _____ The cultural, social, and psychological meanings that are associated with masculinity and femininity.

11. _____ In gender schema theory, the mental categories or representations of masculinity and femininity.

12. _____ Theory that gender roles are acquired through the basic processes of learning, including reinforcement, punishment, and modeling.

True/False Test

Indicate whether each statement is true or false by placing T or F in the blank space next to each item.

1. ____ In Piaget's theory, the word *operations* refers to logical, mental activities.

2. ____ Lev Vygotsky was the Russian psychologist who stressed the importance of social and cultural influences on cognitive development.

3. ____ In Piaget's theory, the concrete operational stage is the second stage of cognitive development, which lasts from about age two to age seven and is characterized by increasing use of symbols and prelogical thought processes.

4. ____ In Piaget's theory, irreversibility is the inability to reverse a sequence of events or logical operations mentally.

5. ____ In Piaget's theory, centration refers to the understanding that two equal quantities remain equal even though the form or appearance is rearranged, as long as nothing is added or subtracted.

6. ____ According to Piaget, as children advance to a new stage, their thinking is qualitatively different from that used in the previous stage; each new stage represents a fundamental shift in *how* children think and understand the world.

7. ____ In Piaget's theory, the tendency to focus on only one aspect of a situation and ignore other important aspects of the situation is called conservation.

8. ____ Gender identity refers to the behaviors, attitudes, and personality traits that are designated as either masculine or feminine in a given culture.

9. ____ In Piaget's theory, the preoperational stage is the third stage of cognitive development, which lasts from about age seven to adolescence and is characterized by the ability to think logically about concrete objects and situations.

10. ____ Gender schema theory states that gender-role development is influenced by the formation of schemas, or mental representations, of masculinity and femininity.

11. ____ Gender role refers to people's psychological sense of being male or female.

Check your answers and review any areas of weakness before going on to the next section.

Adolescence

Preview Questions

Consider the following questions as you study this section of the chapter.

- How is adolescence defined, and what physical developments occur during this period?

- What characterizes relationships between parents and peers in adolescence?
- How do adolescents begin the process of identity formation?
- What is Erikson's psychosocial theory of life-span development?
- What are the stages and levels in Kohlberg's theory of moral development?
- What are some criticisms of Kohlberg's theory?

*Read the section "Adolescence" and **write** your answers to the following:*

1. Adolescence is _____
   _____

2. The physical changes of adolescence include
   _____
   _____

3. The relationship between parents and their adolescent children is _____
   _____
   _____

4. Identity refers to _____
   _____
   _____

5. Adolescents begin the process of identity formation by _____
   _____
   _____

6. According to Erikson's psychosocial theory of lifespan development _____
   _____

   The key psychosocial conflict facing adolescents is _____

7. Kohlberg's levels (and stages) of moral development include _____
   _____
   _____
   _____
   _____
   _____

8. Criticisms of Kohlberg's theory are
   _____
   _____
   _____
   _____

After you have carefully studied the preceding section, complete the following exercises.

Concept Check 4

Read the following and write the correct term in the space provided.

1. Delbert resists stealing cookies from the cookie jar because he is afraid his mother will punish him if he does. According to Kohlberg's theory, Delbert is demonstrating stage _____ of the _____ level of moral reasoning.

2. When she was almost thirteen, Mandy had her first menstrual period, called _____ , which indicates that she has reached the stage of adolescence called _____ .

3. Adam is fifteen and has gained both height and weight, some body hair, and a deeper voice during the past year. These changes are referred to as the _____ .

4. When her daughter chided her about driving slowly, Mrs. Estafani replied that she would not drive faster than the posted speed limit because responsible, law abiding citizens should always obey traffic laws. According to Kohlberg's theory of moral development, Mrs. Estafani is probably at stage _____ of the _____ level of moral development.

5. Seventeen-year-old Brendan questions his parents' values but is not sure that his peer group's standards are totally correct either. His confusion about what is really important in life suggests that Brendan is struggling with the problem of _____ .

Graphic Organizer 2

For each of the following, identify the appropriate stage of Piaget's theory and the stage and level of Kohlberg's theory.

Statement	Theory	Stage/Level
1. Jeremy refuses to pay taxes and risks going to jail because he does not believe in supporting a government that spends so many tax dollars on weapons of mass destruction. Jeremy enjoys discussing his position and is very articulate in developing logical arguments.	Piaget	
	Kohlberg	
2. Mary is convinced that her older sister Natalie has more soda than she does after her mother poured Natalie's can of soda into a long, thin glass and hers into a short, fat one. Despite being tempted to take a big drink out of Natalie's glass when she is in the washroom, Mary refrains because she thinks she might get punished.	Piaget	
	Kohlberg	
3. While playing a game of cards with his friends, Mark insists that everyone should have a chance to be dealer because that is the fair thing to do. Mark is also able to explain the rules to everyone by dealing a couple of practice hands; later, he has difficulty trying to explain the game to his Dad without using the cards.	Piaget	
	Kohlberg	
4. During a discussion with her therapist, Mrs. Bradshaw is asked to describe her husband. Among other things, she notes that he is very law abiding, always drives with extreme care, and frequently boasts that he has never received a ticket. He never completed high school because he couldn't handle all that abstract, hypothetical stuff and is fairly content working as a custodian in an office building.	Piaget	
	Kohlberg	

Review of Terms, Concepts, and Names 4

Use the terms in this list to complete the Matching Test, then to help you answer the True/False items correctly.

adolescence
puberty
primary sex
   characteristics
secondary sex
   characteristics
adolescent growth spurt
menarche
identity
Erik Erikson
identity diffusion

moratorium period
integrated identity
moral reasoning
Lawrence Kohlberg
preconventional level
conventional level
postconventional level
ethic of individual rights
   and justice
ethic of care and
   responsibility

Matching Exercise

Match the appropriate term/name with its definition or description.

1. _____ The stage of adolescence in which an individual reaches sexual maturity and becomes physiologically capable of sexual reproduction.

2. _____ A female's first menstrual period, which occurs during puberty.

3. _____ Carol Gilligan's categorization of women's moral development and reasoning, based on her research that showed women tended to stress the importance of maintaining interpersonal relationships and responding to the needs of others, rather than focusing primarily on individual rights.

4. _____ Period of accelerated growth during puberty, involving rapid increases in height and weight.

5. _____ In Erikson's theory, the period following identity diffusion during which the adolescent experiments with different roles, values, and beliefs.

6. _____ Transitional stage between late childhood and the beginning of adulthood, during which sexual maturity is reached.

7. _____ Kohlberg's level of moral reasoning that begins in late childhood and continues through adolescence and adulthood; characterized by moral reasoning that emphasizes social roles, rules, and obligations.

8. _____ The aspect of cognitive development related to the way an individual reasons about moral decisions.

9. _____ A person's self-definition or description, including the values, beliefs, and ideals that guide the individual's behavior.

True/False Test

Indicate whether each item is true or false by placing T or F in the space next to each item.

1. ____ Erik Erikson was the German-born American psychoanalyst who proposed an influential theory of psychosocial development throughout the lifespan.

2. ____ Secondary sex characteristics are the sexual organs that are directly involved in reproduction, such as the uterus, ovaries, penis, and testicles.

3. ____ In Erikson's theory, the adolescent's path to successfully achieving an identity begins with identity diffusion, which is characterized by little sense of commitment to the various issues he or she has to grapple with and the social demands made on him or her.

4. ____ The ethic of individual rights and justice is Carol Gilligan's term for the ethic that she believes is the basis for Kohlberg's theory and that she suggests is a more common perspective for males.

5. ____ Following the moratorium period, during which the adolescent experiments with different roles, values, and beliefs, he or she may then choose among alternatives and make commitments and gradually arrive at an integrated identity.

6. ____ Lawrence Kohlberg was the American psychologist who proposed an influential theory of moral development.

7. ____ In Kohlberg's theory, the preconventional level is characterized by moral reasoning that reflects self-chosen ethical principles that are universally applied.

8. ____ Primary sex characteristics are sexual characteristics that develop during puberty and are not directly involved in reproduction but differentiate between sexes, such as male facial hair and female breast development.

Check your answers and review any areas of weakness before going on to the next section.

Adult Development

Preview Questions

Consider the following questions as you study this section of the chapter.

- What physical changes take place in adulthood?
- What general patterns of social development occur?
- How does the transition to parenthood affect adults?

*Read the section "Adult Development" and **write** your answers to the following:*

1. The physical changes that take place during adulthood include _____

   _____

   _____

   _____

2. According to Erikson, the primary psychosocial task of middle adulthood is _____

   _____

3. The most general pattern of social development includes _____

   _____

   _____

4. In relation to having children, marital satisfaction _____

   _____

Late Adulthood and Aging

Preview Questions

- What cognitive changes take place in late adulthood?
- What factors can influence social development during this period?

Read the section "Late Adulthood and Aging" and **write** *your answers to the following:*

1. Regarding mental abilities in late adulthood

   _____

   _____

   _____

2. According to the activity theory of aging _____

   _____

   _____

   _____

3. According to Erikson, the psychosocial task of late adulthood is _____

The Final Chapter: Dying and Death

Preview Question

- How did Kübler-Ross describe the stages of dying, and how valid is her theory?

Read the section "The Final Chapter: Dying and Death" and **write** *your answers to the following:*

1. According to Kübler-Ross's theory of dying and death, the five stages are _____

   _____

   _____

   _____

   _____

2. Problems with Kübler-Ross's theory are that

   _____

   _____

After you have carefully studied the preceding sections, complete the following exercises.

Concept Check 5

Read the following and write the correct term in the space provided.

1. Forty-eight-year-old Dr. Gretinger has three grown children, a thriving dental practice, and is very involved in local community activities. Dr. Gretinger is in the _____ stage of life and, according to Erikson, has achieved the psychosocial task of

   _____ .

2. Compared with their grandparents, Mr. and Mrs. Belmont's children are likely to marry for the first time at _____ (an earlier/a later) age.

3. David, a sixty-five-year-old retired civil servant, feels that his life has been unproductive and ultimately meaningless. David is in the _____ stage of life and, according to Erikson, is experiencing

   _____ .

4. Andrew, a forty-five-year-old accountant, has just learned he has a terminal illness. According to Kübler-Ross, as soon as Andrew gets over his initial denial, he will experience

   _____ .

5. Sarah is a twenty-five-year-old, white, middle-class, well-educated, moderately religious person. If she is typical, she will marry someone very _____ (different from/similar to) herself.

6. The last of the Sandwells' four children has just left home to pursue a career with NASA. If the Sandwells are like most parents whose children have left home, they are likely to experience a steady _____ (decline/increase) in marital satisfaction.

Graphic Organizer 3

Identify the theorist related to each of the following statements.

Statement	Theorist
1. I believe that social and cultural influences are the most important factors in cognitive development.	
2. I study attachment, and I have devised a measure of attachment called the Strange Situation.	
3. In my view people have an innate understanding of the basic principles of language, which I call a "universal grammar."	
4. I believe that development continues throughout the lifespan and that individuals pass through eight distinct stages during which they are faced with resolving important psychosocial conflicts.	
5. My primary interest is in how children develop intellectually and cognitively, and my theory proposes that children progress through four distinct stages in succession, each stage characterized by a qualitatively different way of thinking from the previous stage.	
6. The primary goal of my research has been to map out the development of moral reasoning in humans; it is my view that there are three levels, each consisting of two stages, and that humans progress through these stages in sequence, until reaching the highest level.	

Review of Terms and Concepts 5

Use the terms in this list to complete the Matching Test, then to help you answer the True/False items correctly.

menopause
early adulthood
middle adulthood
late adulthood
generativity
activity theory of aging

authoritarian parenting
   style
permissive parenting
   style
authoritative parents
induction

Matching Exercise

Match the appropriate term/name with its definition or description.

1. _____ Discipline technique that combines parental control with explaining why a behavior is prohibited.

2. _____ The natural cessation of menstruation and the end of reproductive capacity in women.

3. _____ Baumrind's term for a parenting style in which parents are extremely tolerant and not demanding.

4. _____ Stage of adulthood, roughly from the forties to the mid-sixties, when physical strength and endurance gradually decline.

5. _____ Psychosocial theory that life satisfaction in late adulthood is highest when people maintain the level of activity they displayed earlier in life.

True/False Test

Indicate whether each item is true or false by placing T or F in the space next to each item.

1. ____ In Erikson's theory, the primary psychosocial task of middle adulthood in which the person contributes to future generations through children, career, and other meaningful activity is called generativity.

2. ___ Early adulthood refers to the stage of development during the twenties and thirties when physical strength typically peaks.

3. ___ Authoritarian parenting style is Baumrind's term for parents who set clear standards for their children's behavior but are also responsive to the children's needs and wishes.

4. ___ Late adulthood refers to the stage of development from the mid-sixties on, when physical stamina and reaction time tend to decline further and faster.

5. ___ According to Baumrind, authoritative parents are demanding and unresponsive toward their children's needs or wishes.

Check your answers and review any areas of weakness before going on to the next section.

Something to Think About

1. A popular and controversial topic in any discussion of raising children is the effect of day care on a child's development. Discussions like this can become quite heated, with people holding strong views on both sides of the debate. On the basis of what you have read in this chapter, what light could you shed on this controversial topic?

2. You may be planning to have a family one day if you haven't already done so. For most people this is quite a responsibility and a lot of work. Unlike many other areas in life, no formal training is available or required for the job of parent. You, however, are fortunate because you are taking an introductory psychology course and have learned a few things about child development. What advice would you give to people who are planning to have a family?

Check your answers and review any areas of weakness before doing the progress tests.

Progress Test 1

Review the complete chapter (including Concept Reviews and the boxed inserts), review all your study notes, and then test yourself on the following progress test. Check your answers. If you make a mistake, review your notes, review the relevant sec-

tion of the study guide, and, if necessary, go back and read the appropriate part of your textbook.

1. When Thomas was conceived, he was a single fertilized egg called a(n)
   (a) zygote.   (c) fetus.
   (b) embryo.   (d) infant.

2. When Thomas was growing up, it became apparent that he was red-green color-blind. This disorder
   (a) is probably a sex-linked recessive characteristic.
   (b) is more common in males than females.
   (c) has to do with the 23rd pair of chromosomes.
   (d) is all of the above.

3. In her research, Dr. Joacim found that a pregnant mother's use of a certain chemical substance caused harm to the fetus. The chemical substance could be classified as
   (a) deoxyribonucleic acid.
   (b) a chromosome.
   (c) a phenotype.
   (d) a teratogen.

4. Kalbiar has dimples, which is a dominant characteristic determined by a single pair of genes. Kalbiar's genotype
   (a) could be a dimples/no dimples combination.
   (b) could be a no dimples/no dimples combination.
   (c) could be expressed phenotypically as no dimples, depending on the amount of sunlight she was exposed to.
   (d) could be all of the above.

5. When Mrs. Euland touched her newborn's lips, he produced an automatic response called the _____ reflex.
   (a) rooting   (c) grasping
   (b) sucking   (d) greedy

6. It has become apparent to Mr. and Mrs. Euland that their baby has a low activity level, tends to withdraw from new situations and people, and adapts to new experiences very gradually. The baby would be classified as a(n) _____ baby.
   (a) easy   (c) slow-to-warm-up
   (b) difficult   (d) securely attached

7. When two-year old Kerry was tested in the Strange Situation, she did not explore the environment even when her mother was present. She appeared very anxious, and she became extremely distressed when her mother left the room. Kerry is a(n)
   (a) insecurely attached infant.
   (b) securely attached infant.
   (c) conventional infant.
   (d) concrete operational infant.

8. When she was almost eleven months old, Jessica said "ba ba" when she pointed at her bottle and "ma ma" when she pointed at her Mom. Jessica is in the _____ stage of language development.
   (a) cooing
   (b) babbling
   (c) one-word
   (d) two-word

9. When Neil's mother hides his favorite toy under a blanket, Neil acts as though it no longer exists and makes no attempt to retrieve it. Neil is in Piaget's _____ stage, and his behavior suggests that he _____ .
   (a) sensorimotor; has developed object permanence
   (b) preoperational; has not developed object permanence
   (c) concrete operational; is capable of reversible thinking
   (d) formal operational; understands the principle of conservation

10. In a term paper on child development, Sima made the case that children actively develop categories for masculinity and femininity and suggested that these mental representations influence how children perceive, interpret, and remember relevant aspects of what is appropriate for girls and boys. Sima's position is most consistent with the _____ theory of gender-role development.
    (a) gender schema
    (b) evolutionary
    (c) activity
    (d) social learning

11. Danielle has switched college majors four times and does not know what she wants to do after she gets her degree. Erikson would suggest that Danielle has not achieved
    (a) an integrated identity.
    (b) a sense of generativity.
    (c) the conventional level of moral reasoning.
    (d) the concrete operational stage of development.

12. Preconventional morality is to postconventional morality as _____ is to _____ .
    (a) social approval; ethical principle
    (b) self-interest; social approval
    (c) self-interest; ethical principle
    (d) social approval; self-interest

13. Gordon, a fifty-year-old lawyer, has just learned from his physician that he has only one year to live. According to Kübler-Ross, his first reaction to hearing the news is likely to be
    (a) "No, it's not possible, there's obviously been some mix-up, some terrible mistake."
    (b) "Life is not worth living any more."
    (c) "Why me? This is very unfair and makes me mad."
    (d) "Well, that's the way it goes, I guess."

14. According to the Application, a parenting style in which parents set clear standards for their children's behavior but are also responsive to the children's needs and wishes is called
    (a) authoritarian.
    (b) permissive-indulgent.
    (c) permissive-indifferent.
    (d) authoritative.

15. According to Culture and Human Behavior 9.1, infants typically sleep in their own bed and in a separate room from their parents in
    (a) all cultures.
    (b) all Western cultures.
    (c) the United States.
    (d) all Latin cultures.

Progress Test 2

After you have checked your understanding of the material in Progress Test 1 and have done a complete chapter review with special focus on any areas of weakness, you are ready to assess your knowledge of Progress Test 2. Check your answers. If you make a mistake, review your notes, the relevant section of the study guide, and, if necessary, the appropriate part of your textbook.

1. Dr. Strayer is conducting longitudinal research on factors that correlate with getting older. She is likely to find that
   (a) intelligence declines sharply with age.
   (b) there is severe memory impairment as people reach late adulthood.
   (c) most people maintain their intellectual abilities as they age.
   (d) no matter how much older people practice their mental skills, they still do very poorly on intellectual tasks.

2. Mr. Danzig is a sixty-eight-year-old retired accountant. If he is typical of people his age, he is probably living
   (a) in his own home.
   (b) in a nursing home.
   (c) with his grown-up children.
   (d) in a mental health facility.

3. Aldred believes that gender roles develop as a result of young children observing others modeling particular gender-appropriate behaviors and that children are rewarded when they behave accordingly and are punished when they don't. Aldred's view is most consistent with the _____ theory of gender-role development.
   (a) attachment
   (b) gender schema
   (c) social learning
   (d) evolutionary

4. Miguel is a twenty-five-year-old, college-educated middle-class engineer. Like his Mexican parents, he is a devout Catholic. If Miguel is like most people, he will probably marry someone who is
   (a) completely different from him in every way as long as she is Catholic.
   (b) very much like he is.
   (c) much older than he is.
   (d) much richer than he is.

5. Mrs. Grant is forty-nine years old and has recently ceased to menstruate. Mrs. Grant has experienced
   (a) moratorium.   (c) induction.
   (b) menopause.   (d) centration.

6. Late adulthood is to _____ as adolescence is to _____ .
   (a) ego integrity; generativity
   (b) generativity; intimacy
   (c) intimacy; ego integrity
   (d) ego integrity; integrated identity

7. Mr. Gates believes in law and order, obeys all rules and regulations, and has respect for authorities just because they are authorities. Mr. Gates is likely at Kohlberg's _____ level of moral reasoning.
   (a) conventional   (c) concrete operational
   (b) preconventional   (d) formal operational

8. Sixteen-year-old Jade is reading books about different religions and philosophies and is trying out different approaches to how one should live one's life. Jade is in Erikson's
   (a) moratorium period.
   (b) generativity stage.
   (c) ego integrity period.
   (d) formal operational stage.

9. The Atwells have two teenage children. If they are like most parents, their relationship with their kids
   (a) is very negative and getting worse.
   (b) is full of fights, arguments, anger, and hostility.
   (c) is just about as positive as it was when the children were younger.
   (d) was positive at first but has deteriorated as the children aged.

10. Marcel is researching a paper for his child development course and discovers the work of Lev Vygotsky. In summarizing Vygotsky's contribution to developmental psychology, Marcel is likely to note that the theorist emphasized
    (a) genetic factors.
    (b) clearly defined biological stages of cognitive development.
    (c) clearly defined biological stages of moral development.
    (d) social and cultural factors in cognitive development.

11. Kelly is five years old and has a good imagination. Recently, for example, she used a discarded box as a make-believe castle and made up a very interesting dialogue between the "king" and "queen" of her castle. This illustrates
    (a) centration.   (c) symbolic thought.
    (b) conservation.   (d) object permanence.

12. In the Strange Situation procedure, little Anthony used his mother as a safe base from which to explore the environment, showed distress when she left the room, and greeted her warmly when she returned. Anthony would be classified as a(n)
    (a) difficult baby.
    (b) securely attached baby.
    (c) insecurely attached baby.
    (d) slow-to-warm-up baby.

13. During a class debate on the issue of whether war is ever justified, Dominique argued that it is never justified because war involves killing people and killing people is against the law. Dominique is in the conventional stage of
    (a) Kohlberg's model of moral development.
    (b) Piaget's model of cognitive development.
    (c) Erikson's model of psychosocial development.
    (d) Chomsky's model of language development.

14. According to Critical Thinking 9.2, putting young children in a high-quality day-care facility
    (a) is detrimental to their physical health.
    (b) severely disrupts the attachment process.
    (c) has no detrimental effect on the children.
    (d) is detrimental to their psychological health.

15. According to the Application, psychologist Diana Baumrind has described a number of basic parenting styles. In her research, she found that children of _____ parents were likely to be moody, unhappy, fearful, withdrawn, unspontaneous, and irritable.
    (a) permissive-indulgent
    (b) permissive-indifferent
    (c) authoritative
    (d) authoritarian

Progress Test 3

After you have checked your understanding of the material in Progress Tests 1 and 2, and have done a complete chapter review with special focus on any areas of weakness, you are ready to further assess your knowledge on Progress Test 3. Check your answers. If you make a mistake, review your notes, the appropriate parts of the study guide, and, if necessary, the relevant sections of your textbook.

1. In looking back at his life, seventy-year-old Redner experiences regret, dissatisfaction, and disappointment about his accomplishments. According to Erikson, Redner, who is in late adulthood, is experiencing _____ and has failed to achieve a sense of

    _____ .

    (a) inferiority; generativity
    (b) despair; ego integrity
    (c) stagnation; ego identity
    (d) isolation; intimacy

2. Nine-year-old Adam has acquired the mental operations to comprehend such things as conservation and reversibility and can solve tangible problems in a logical manner. Adam is in Piaget's _____ stage of development.
    (a) sensorimotor   (c) concrete operational
    (b) preoperational   (d) formal operational

3. Piaget is to cognitive development as Erikson is to _____ development.
    (a) moral   (c) emotional
    (b) physical   (d) psychosocial

4. Despite the fact that he uses only one word utterances when he attempts to talk, one-year-old Vincent immediately does what he is told when his mother says, "Bring Mommy the teddy bear, Vincent." This suggests that
    (a) Vincent's comprehension vocabulary is much larger than his production vocabulary.
    (b) Vincent is in the embryonic stage of language development.
    (c) Vincent has a sex-linked recessive characteristic that has retarded his development.
    (d) Vincent's production vocabulary is much larger than his comprehension vocabulary.

5. When Kiran was born, his brain was about 25 percent of its adult weight; during infancy, it reached about 75 percent of its adult weight. This increase in weight is due to the fact that
    (a) millions of new neurons were formed daily during this period.
    (b) the number of dendrites increased dramatically and the axons of many neurons acquired myelin.
    (c) neurons grew bigger in size and the dendrites acquired a white fatty covering called myelin.
    (d) the number of new neurons increased dramatically and the original neurons increased in size and weight.

6. Nine months after conception, baby Tracy is born. The stages of her prenatal development, from first to last, were
    (a) embryonic, fetal, germinal.
    (b) fetal, embryonic, germinal.
    (c) germinal, embryonic, fetal.
    (d) germinal, fetal, embryonic.

7. Mrs. Hoff uses very distinct pronunciation, a simplified vocabulary, short sentences, a high pitch, and exaggerated intonation and expression whenever she interacts with her baby. This is an example of
   (a) motherese, or infant-directed speech.
   (b) a sex-linked recessive characteristic.
   (c) an insecurely attached mother.
   (d) cooing and babbling.

8. Michael has red-green color blindness, which is a sex-linked recessive characteristic, but his sister Eileen has normal color vision. It is likely that
   (a) Eileen has the recessive gene for red-green color blindness on each of her X chromosomes.
   (b) Michael has the recessive gene for red-green color blindness on each of his X chromosomes.
   (c) Eileen has the recessive gene for red-green color blindness on each of her Y chromosomes.
   (d) Michael has the recessive gene for red-green color blindness on the X chromosome of his XY chromosomes.

9. During Mr. Guerno's seventieth birthday party his grandchildren had a chance to ask him about some of his many adventures and travels. It was apparent while listening to his colorful stories that their grandfather had lived a very meaningful life and was very satisfied with his many accomplishments. Mr. Guerno is in the _____ stage of life and has achieved what Erikson called _____ .
   (a) middle adulthood; generativity
   (b) late adulthood; ego integrity
   (c) middle adulthood; initiative
   (d) late adulthood; ego identity

10. When he was thirteen, Kyle experienced several physical changes: His testicles started to enlarge, his height and weight increased, and his voice deepened. Kyle has experienced
   (a) menarche.
   (b) puberty.
   (c) ego identity.
   (d) generativity.

11. Young Allison doesn't understand that adding together one and three is the same as adding together three and one. Allison is demonstrating _____ and is in Piaget's _____ stage of development.
   (a) conservation; concrete operational
   (b) egocentrism; preoperational
   (c) centration; sensorimotor
   (d) irreversibility; preoperational

12. Fourteen-year-old Jason has the ability to reason abstractly and think logically even about hypothetical situations. Jason is in Piaget's _____ stage of cognitive development.
   (a) sensorimotor
   (b) preoperational
   (c) concrete operational
   (d) formal operational

13. When Oliver played with dolls and domestic toys, his mother would show her disapproval; when he played with toy vehicles and building blocks, his mother would respond in a positive manner. As Oliver grew older, he played less and less with dolls, dollhouses, and domestic toys and more and more with stereotypical "boys'" toys. This description of gender-role development illustrates
   (a) gender schema theory.
   (b) attachment theory.
   (c) social learning theory.
   (d) evolutionary theory.

14. According to Culture and Human Behavior 9.3
   (a) the level of conflict between parents and adolescents tends to be higher in Chinese families compared with European-American families.
   (b) although the level of conflict may vary, parent-adolescent conflict is a common dimension of family life in all cultures.
   (c) regardless of which culture they belonged to, adolescents showed a high level of respect for parental authority, a strong sense of family obligation, and a keen desire for harmony within the family.
   (d) there is significantly less parent-adolescent conflict in individualistic cultures compared to collectivistic culture.

15. According to the Application, which of the following is *not* recommended for raising psychologically healthy children?
    (a) Work with your children's temperamental qualities.
    (b) Use induction to teach as you discipline.
    (c) Let your children know that you love them.
    (d) Strive to be an authoritarian parent.
    (e) Listen to your children.

Answers

Introduction: Your Life Story

1. *Developmental psychology is the* study of how people change physically, mentally, and socially over the lifespan.

2. *The major themes in developmental psychology are* the common patterns of growth and development people share and how they differ in terms of social, occupational, and interpersonal accomplishment; the abrupt age-related stages people go through over the lifespan and those aspects of development that reflect gradually unfolding changes; and the nature of the interaction between heredity (nature) and environment (nurture) throughout development.

Genetic Contributions to Your Life Story

1. *Chromosomes are* long, threadlike structures composed of twisted parallel strands of DNA; they are found in the nucleus of the cell.

2. *DNA (deoxyribonucleic acid) is* the chemical basis of heredity and carries genetic instructions in the cell.

3. *Genes are* the basic units of heredity that direct the development of a particular characteristic; each gene is a unit of DNA instructions pertaining to some characteristic such as eye or hair color, height, or handedness.

4. *Genotype refers to the* underlying genetic make-up of a particular organism, including the genetic instructions for traits that are not actually displayed. *Phenotype refers to the* observable traits or characteristics of an organism as determined by the interaction of genetics and environmental factors.

5. *We inherit from our biological parents* a genetic potential, the expression of which can be influenced by environmental conditions.

6. *In a pair of genes, the dominant gene is* the gene that contains genetic instructions that will

be expressed whether paired with another dominant gene or with a recessive gene. *A recessive gene is* the gene that contains genetic instructions that will not be expressed unless paired with another recessive gene.

7. *The sex chromosomes are* chromosomes designated as X or Y that determine biological sex; they are the 23rd pair of chromosomes in humans. *Sex-linked recessive characteristics are traits determined by* recessive genes located on the X chromosome; in males, these characteristics require only one recessive gene to be expressed.

Prenatal Development

1. *During prenatal development, the single-cell zygote* undergoes division and differentiation into body organs, eventually developing into a full-term fetus.

2. *The three stages of the prenatal stage are* the germinal period (the first two weeks), the embryonic period (from the third to eighth week), and the fetal period (from the ninth week until birth).

3. *Teratogens are* harmful agents or substances that can cross the placenta and cause malformations or defects in an embryo or fetus. The greatest vulnerability to teratogens is during the embryonic stage.

Concept Check 1

1. developmental
2. nature (heredity); nurture (environment)
3. X; Y; X; X
4. embryo; fetus
5. teratogen

Graphic Organizer 1

Cell 1: dimples
Cell 2: dimples
Cell 3: dimples
Cell 4: no dimples

Matching Exercise 1

1. prenatal stage
2. gene
3. developmental psychology
4. sex-linked recessive characteristics
5. teratogens

6. chromosome

7. recessive gene

8. germinal period (zygotic period)

9. embryo

10. recessive characteristics

11. sex chromosomes

True/False Test 1

1. T	5. T	9. F
2. T	6. T	10. T
3. T	7. F	11. F
4. F	8. T	

Development During Infancy and Childhood: Physical Development

1. *Newborn infants enter the world equipped with* the rooting reflex, the sucking reflex, and the grasping reflex. *Their senses of vision, hearing, smell, and touch are* keenly attuned to people, and this ability helps them differentiate between their mothers and other people.

2. *The infant's sensory capabilities promote the development of relationships with caregivers is evidenced by the fact that they* stare at human faces longer than other images, make eye contact with adults who position themselves close to the newborn (6 to 12 inches), respond with increased alertness to the sound of human voices, and quickly become sensitized to the scent of their mothers.

3. *After birth, a number of changes take place in the infant's brain:* during infancy, the brain will go from being 25 percent of its adult weight to 75 percent; the number of dendrites will increase dramatically during the first two years; and the axons of many neurons will acquire myelin.

Development During Infancy and Childhood: Social and Personality Development

1. *Temperament refers to* the inborn predispositions to consistently behave and react in a certain way. *Attachment is the* emotional bond that forms between the infant and his or her caregivers, especially the parents.

2. *The three broad temperamental patterns are* easy, difficult, and slow-to-warm-up.

3. *Attachment is measured using a procedure called the* Strange Situation. *In this technique* the baby and mother are brought into an unfamiliar room with a variety of toys, and a few

minutes later a stranger enters. The mother stays with the child for a few moments, then departs and returns a short time later, she spends a little time with the child, and then departs and returns again. Observers record the infant's behavior through a one-way mirror.

4. *The basic premise of attachment theory is that* an infant's ability to thrive physically and psychologically depends in part on the quality of attachment. When parents are consistently warm, responsive, and sensitive to their infant's needs, the infant develops a secure attachment; if parents are neglectful, inconsistent, or insensitive, an infant may suffer insecure attachment.

Development During Infancy and Childhood: Language Development

1. *According to Noam Chomsky,* all children are born with a biological predisposition to learn language, and, in effect, they possess a universal grammar, which allows them to easily extract grammatical rules from what they hear.

2. *Language development is encouraged by* the use of infant-directed speech (motherese) that adults instinctively use with babies.

3. *The stages of language development are* the cooing and babbling stage, the one-word stage (in which comprehension vocabulary is usually much larger than production vocabulary), the two-word stage, and finally, fully developed language comprehension and production.

Concept Check 2

1. human face

2. the Strange Situation

3. 25 percent

4. easy

5. secure

6. comprehension; production

Matching Exercise 2

1. infancy

2. Strange Situation

3. sucking reflex

4. slow-to-warm-up temperament

5. motherese (infant-directed speech)

6. cooing and babbling stage

7. attachment

8. comprehension vocabulary

9. insecure attachment

10. two-word stage

True/False Test 2

1. F	5. T	9. F
2. T	6. T	10. T
3. F	7. F	
4. T	8. T	

Development During Infancy and Childhood: Gender Role Development

1. *Gender refers to* the cultural, social, and psychological meanings that are associated with masculinity or femininity. *Gender roles are* the behaviors, attitudes, and personality traits that are designated as either masculine or feminine in a given culture. *Gender identity is* a person's psychological sense of being either male or female.

2. *According to social learning theory,* gender roles are acquired through the basic processes of learning, including reinforcement, punishment, and modeling.

3. *Gender schema theory contends that* children actively develop mental categories, or schemas, for masculinity and femininity, and these mental representations influence gender-role development.

Development During Infancy and Childhood: Cognitive Development

1. *The four stages (and their characteristics) in Piaget's theory are*

   (a) the sensorimotor stage, from birth to about age two, during which the infant explores the environment and acquires knowledge through sensing and manipulating objects. The development of object permanence is characteristic of this stage.

   (b) the preoperational stage, from about age two to age seven, during which the use of symbols and prelogical thought processes increase. Characteristics of this stage include the increasing use of symbolic thought, the tendency for egocentrism, irreversibility, centration, and the development of conservation.

   (c) the concrete operational stage, from about age seven to adolescence, during which the child develops the ability to think logically about concrete objects and situations. Characteristics of this stage are the tendency to be less egocentric in their thinking, the ability to reverse mental problems, and an understanding of the principle of conservation.

   (d) the formal operational stage, from adolescence through adulthood, during which the person acquires the ability to think logically about abstract principles and hypothetical situations. This stage is characterized by more systematic and logical problem solving abilities.

2. *Piaget's theory has been criticized because* he underestimated the cognitive abilities of infants and children, confusing motor-skill limitations with cognitive-skill limitations; his notion that the stages unfold universally has not been supported by research; and he underestimated the impact of the social and cultural factors on cognitive development.

3. *The information-processing model of cognitive development views cognitive development as* a continuous process over the lifespan. Researchers in this area focus on the development of basic mental processes, such as attention, memory, and problem solving.

Concept Check 3

1. underestimated
2. concrete operational
3. object permanence
4. conservation
5. assimilating
6. schema
7. formal
8. gender role
9. gender schema

Matching Exercise 3

1. symbolic thought
2. cognitive processes
3. object permanence
4. formal operational stage
5. Jean Piaget
6. information-processing model of cognitive development
7. schemas
8. sensorimotor stage
9. egocentrism
10. gender
11. (gender) schemas

12. social learning theory

True/False Test 3

1. T
2. T
3. F
4. T
5. F
6. T
7. F
8. F
9. F
10. T
11. F

Adolescence

1. *Adolescence is* the transitional stage between late childhood and the beginning of adulthood, during which sexual maturity is reached.

2. *The physical changes of adolescence include the* attainment of puberty, the development of primary and secondary sex characteristics, the adolescent growth spurt, and for females the first menstrual period (menarche).

3. *The relationship between parents and their adolescent children is* generally positive, but relationships with friends and peers become increasingly important.

4. *Identity refers to* a person's definition or description of himself or herself, including the values, beliefs, and ideals that guide the individual's behavior.

5. *Adolescents begin the process of identity formation by* evaluating themselves on several different dimensions, such as social acceptance by peers, academic and athletic abilities, personal appearance, and romantic appeal.

6. *According to Erikson's psychosocial theory of lifespan development,* each of the eight stages of life is associated with a particular psychosocial conflict that can be resolved in either a positive or negative direction. *The key psychosocial conflict facing adolescents is* identity versus identity diffusion.

7. *Kohlberg's levels (and stages) of moral development include* the preconventional level (stage 1: punishment and obedience and stage 2: mutual benefit), the conventional level (stage 3: interpersonal expectations and stage 4: law and order), and the postconventional level (stage 5: legal principles and stage 6: universal moral principles).

8. *Criticisms of Kohlberg's theory are* that it reflects a male perspective and does not accurately depict the development of moral reasoning in women, that it is based on the ethic of individual rights and justice, and that aspects of moral reasoning in other cultures do not appear to be reflected in the theory.

Concept Check 4

1. 1; preconventional
2. menarche; puberty
3. adolescent growth spurt
4. 4; conventional
5. identity

Graphic Organizer 2

1. Piaget: formal operational stage; Kohlberg: postconventional level, stage 6
2. Piaget: preoperational stage; Kohlberg: preconventional level, stage 1
3. Piaget: concrete operational stage; Kohlberg: preconventional level, stage 2
4. Piaget: concrete operational stage; Kohlberg: conventional level, stage 4

Matching Exercise 4

1. puberty
2. menarche
3. ethic of care and responsibility
4. adolescent growth spurt
5. moratorium period
6. adolescence
7. conventional level
8. moral reasoning
9. identity

True/False Test 4

1. T
2. F
3. T
4. T
5. T
6. T
7. F
8. F

Adult Development

1. *The physical changes that take place during adulthood include* genetically influenced changes such as menopause (the cessation of menstruation) and thinning, graying hair; environmentally influenced changes such as the formation of wrinkles, a decrease in the efficiency of various body organs, and a decline in physical strength and endurance.

2. *According to Erikson, the primary psychosocial task of middle adulthood is* generativity versus stagnation.

3. *The most general pattern of social development includes* love and work, which involves forming

a long-term committed relationship, becoming parents, and pursuing a career or careers. However, there is great variability in the path to intimacy.

4. *In relation to having children, marital satisfaction* tends to decline after the first child is born and to increase after children leave home.

Late Adulthood and Aging

1. *Regarding mental abilities in late adulthood,* there is not necessarily a steep decline in physical or cognitive abilities; mental abilities only begin to decline at around age 60, and these declines can be minimized or eliminated with an active and mentally stimulating lifestyle.

2. *According to the activity theory of aging,* life satisfaction in late adulthood is highest when you maintain your previous level of activity, either by continuing old activities or by finding new ones.

3. *According to Erikson, the psychosocial task of late adulthood is* ego integrity versus despair.

The Final Chapter: Dying and Death

1. *According to Kübler-Ross's theory of death and dying, the five stages are* denial (people deny that death is imminent); anger (people feel and express indignation and rage); bargaining (people try to work out a deal with doctors, relatives, or God); depression (people become despondent about their fate); and acceptance (people realize what lies ahead and resign themselves to their fate).

2. *Problems with Kübler-Ross's theory are that* dying individuals do not progress through a predictable sequence of stages. Dying is as individual a process as living; people cope with the prospect of dying much as they have coped with other stresses in their lives.

Concept Check 5

1. middle adulthood; generativity
2. a later
3. late adulthood; despair
4. anger
5. similar to
6. increase

Graphic Organizer 3

1. Lev Vygotsky
2. Mary D. Salter Ainsworth

3. Noam Chomsky
4. Erik Erikson
5. Jean Piaget
6. Lawrence Kohlberg

Matching Exercise 5

1. induction
2. menopause
3. permissive parenting style
4. middle adulthood
5. activity theory of aging

True/False Test 5

1. T   4. T
2. T   5. F
3. F

Something to Think About

1. Most psychologists today agree that the *quality* of the child-care arrangements is the key factor in promoting secure attachment in early childhood and preventing problems in later childhood. In fact, many studies have found that children who experience high-quality day care tend to be more sociable, better adjusted, and more academically competent than children who experience poor-quality day care. In addition, some researchers have found that grade school children enrolled in high-quality day care from infancy experience no negative effects of their day-care experience. Research in Sweden has supported these findings.

    High-quality day care is characterized by a number of key factors: caregivers should be warm and responsive, developmentally appropriate activities and a variety of play materials should be available, caregivers should have some training and education in child development, low staff turnover is important, and the ratio of caregivers to children should be low.

2. A short discussion of the various stages of cognitive, psychosocial, and moral development would be appropriate. Raising psychologically healthy children is possible if parents adopt some of the strategies suggested by the experts. Psychologist Diana Baumrind has described three basic parenting styles: authoritarian, permissive, and authoritative. Research has shown that the authoritative style produces the best

results. Can parents learn to be authoritative in their parenting style? The Application has a number of practical suggestions: let your children know that you love them, listen to your children, use induction to teach as you discipline, work with your children's temperamental qualities, and understand your child's age-related cognitive abilities and limitations.

Although all children inherit genetic predispositions from both parents, research has shown that environmental factors, such as the social and cultural influences, educational experiences, and parenting style have very powerful effects on a child's development.

Progress Test 1

1. a	6. c	11. a
2. d	7. a	12. c
3. d	8. c	13. a
4. a	9. b	14. d
5. b	10. a	15. c

Progress Test 2

1. c	6. d	11. c
2. a	7. a	12. b
3. c	8. a	13. a
4. b	9. c	14. c
5. b	10. d	15. d

Progress Test 3

1. b	6. c	11. d
2. c	7. a	12. d
3. d	8. d	13. c
4. a	9. b	14. b
5. b	10. b	15. d

Personality

PREVIEW	Reading the section below first will give you a general sense of the chapter's contents and an initial introduction to some of the major concepts and terms. This will prime you for what you are about to read and help you to develop a "cognitive map" that will guide your study of the material in this chapter. Likewise, reading the **preview questions** at the beginning of each major section will improve your ability to understand, learn, and retain the information.

CHAPTER 10 . . . AT A GLANCE

Chapter 10 focuses on the four major perspectives on personality. Freud's psychoanalysis stresses the unconscious, the importance of sex and aggression, and the influences of early childhood experiences. The major defense mechanisms, as well as the psychosexual stages of development and the various conflicts associated with each, are examined. The contributions of Freud's early followers, the neo-Freudians, are explored, and criticisms of Freud's theory are discussed.

Carl Rogers's humanistic theory and his optimistic view of human nature are examined, including his ideas about the self-concept, unconditional positive regard, the actualizing tendency, and the fully functioning person.

The social cognitive perspective stresses the role of conscious thought processes, goals, self-regulation, and reciprocal determinism. The influence of self-efficacy on behavior, performance, motivation, and persistence is explored. The notion that the interaction of multiple factors determines personality and behavior is examined.

The trait perspective focuses on measuring and describing individual differences. Cattell initially suggested sixteen basic personality factors, then Eysenck proposed three. The five-factor model is the current view of the number of source traits. The text concludes that traits are generally stable across time and across situations.

Behavioral genetics research uses twin and adoption studies to measure the relative influences of genetics and environment. Personality factors that appear to have a genetic basis are identified. The final section examines projective tests and self-report inventories, as well as their strengths and weaknesses.

Introduction: What Is Personality?

Preview Questions

Consider the following questions as you study this section of the chapter.

- How is personality defined, and what is a personality theory?
- What are the four major theoretical perspectives on personality?

*Read the section "Introduction: What Is Personality?" and **write** your answers to the following:*

1. Personality is defined as _____
   _____

2. A personality theory is _____
   _____
   _____

3. The four basic perspectives on personality (and the main emphasis of each) are _____
   _____
   _____
   _____
   _____
   _____
   _____

The Psychoanalytic Perspective on Personality

Preview Questions

Consider the following questions as you study this section of the chapter.

- Who was the founder of psychoanalysis, and what did he consider to be the main factors that influenced personality development?
- What were some of the key influences on Freud's thinking?

*Read the section "The Psychoanalytic Perspective on Personality" and **write** your answers to the following:*

1. Psychoanalysis—Freud's theory of personality—stresses _____
   _____
   _____

2. Some of the key factors in the development of Freud's ideas were _____
   _____
   _____
   _____
   _____

The Psychoanalytic Perspective on Personality: Freud's Dynamic Theory of Personality

Preview Questions

Consider the following questions as you study this section of the chapter.

- How do we access unconscious mental processes?
- What are the three basic structures of personality, and what are their functions?
- What are the main defense mechanisms, and what role do they play?

*Read the section "The Psychoanalytic Perspective: Freud's Dynamic Theory of Personality" and **write** your answers to the following:*

1. The content of the unconscious can surface in disguised form in _____
   _____

2. The three basic structures of personality (and their functions) are _____
   _____
   _____
   _____
   _____
   _____

3. The two main ego defense mechanisms (and the roles they play) are _____

_____

_____

_____

_____

The Psychoanalytic Perspective: Personality Development

Preview Questions

Consider the following questions as you study this section of the chapter.

- What are the five psychosexual stages of personality development?
- What are the core conflicts of the oral, anal, and phallic stages, and what are the consequences of fixation?
- What role does the Oedipus complex play in personality development?

Read the section "The Psychoanalytic Perspective: Personality Development" and **write** *your answers to the following:*

1. The psychosexual stages are age-related development periods _____

_____

_____

2. The five psychosexual stages are _____

_____

_____

3. If the developmental conflict of a particular stage is not resolved_____

_____

_____

4. The Oedipus complex refers to _____

_____

_____

5. Identification (which is one result of the Oedipus complex) is an ego defense mechanism that _____

_____

_____

After you have carefully studied the preceding sections, complete the following exercises.

Concept Check 1

Read the following and write the correct term in the space provided.

1. Wilma typically responds to stress and stressful situations in a very agitated, panic-stricken manner. Gloria, on the other hand, usually stays calm and handles things in a careful and thoughtful manner. The reactions of Wilma and Gloria indicate that each has a distinctive

_____ .

2. Colleen, who is suffering from some puzzling physical and psychological symptoms that don't appear to have any physiological cause, has decided to seek help from a Freudian psychoanalyst. The therapist is most likely to use

_____ in an attempt to explore Colleen's unconscious.

3. During a heated argument, David inadvertently called his wife Joanne by his mother's name. From the psychoanalytic perspective, this "Freudian slip" reveals something about David's

_____ (conscious/preconscious/ unconscious) motivation.

4. Amelia had a very strange dream in which she was with a very handsome man on a train traveling through the Swiss Alps. The train kept going in and out of tunnels and going faster and faster as it made its way through the mountains. According to Freudian theory, the

_____ (manifest/latent) content of the dream should give some clue as to what is going on in Amelia's unconscious.

5. When two-year-old Tyler was told that he would get no dessert unless he finished eating all his vegetables, he turned the plate upside down and said he hated his Mom and Dad. Freud would have said that Tyler was responding to the demands of the _____ .

6. Kato found a wallet containing $200 in cash. For just a moment he was tempted to keep the money, but the thought of doing so made him feel guilty and anxious, and he immediately took the wallet to the lost-and-found office. According to Freud, Kato's good deed was motivated by his _____ .

7. Leslie sometimes thinks that the real reason her husband became a psychotherapist was to provide himself with a socially acceptable way to indulge his excessive inquisitiveness about other people's private lives. Leslie is suggesting that her husband is using a special form of displacement called _____ .

8. Nine-year-old Danny looks up to his father and, when he grows up, wants to be an engineer just like him. Freud would suggest that Danny is exhibiting signs of the process of _____ .

Graphic Organizer 1

Read the following and match each one with the appropriate stage of psychosexual development:

Description	Stage
1. Sixteen-year-old Graham has started going steady with Julie and is experiencing all the sensations of being in love.	
2. Five-year-old Annette has become very competitive with her mother for her father's affections and quite defiantly states that she is "Going to marry Daddy when I grow up!"	
3. Vivian is eight years old and does not like boys very much. In fact, she plays with her girlfriends almost exclusively.	
4. It seems that no matter what Marie gives her baby to play with, she immediately puts it in her mouth.	
5. Darcy is not quite two but seems to take great pleasure in refusing to obey his parents and by asserting his control and independence. His favorite word is "No!"	

Review of Terms, Concepts, and Names 1

Use the terms in this list to complete the Matching Test, then to help you answer the True/False items correctly.

personality	unconscious	superego	fixation
personality theory	id	ego defense mechanisms	Oedipus complex
Sigmund Freud	Eros	repression	castration anxiety
psychoanalysis	libido	displacement	identification
catharsis	Thanatos	psychosexual stages	penis envy
free association	pleasure principle	oral stage	latency stage
conscious	ego	anal stage	genital stage
preconscious	reality principle	phallic stage	

Matching Exercise

Match the appropriate term/name with its definition or description.

1. _____ In Freud's theory, the psychological and emotional energy associated with expressions of sexuality; the sex drive.

2. _____ An individual's unique and relatively consistent patterns of thinking, feeling, and behaving.

3. _____ In Freud's theory, the partly conscious self-evaluative, moralistic component of personality that is formed through the internalization of parental and societal rules.

4. _____ In Freud's theory, a child's unconscious sexual desire for the opposite-sex parent, usually accompanied by hostile feelings toward the same-sex parent.

5. _____ Latin for "I"; in Freud's theory, the partly conscious rational component of personality that regulates thoughts and behavior and is most in touch with the demands of the external world.

6. _____ Level of awareness that contains information that is not currently in conscious awareness but is easily accessible.

7. _____ The first psychosexual stage of development, during which the infant derives pleasure through the activities of sucking, chewing, and biting.

8. _____ In psychoanalytic theory, the ego defense mechanism that involves unconsciously shifting the target of an emotional urge to a substitute target that is less threatening or dangerous.

9. _____ Austrian neurologist who founded psychoanalysis and emphasized the role of unconscious determinants of behavior and early childhood experiences in the development of personality and psychological problems.

10. _____ The second psychosexual stage of development, during which the infant derives pleasure through elimination and acquiring control of elimination.

11. _____ Theory that attempts to describe and explain individual similarities and differences.

12. _____ Latin for "the it"; in Freud's theory, the completely unconscious, irrational component of personality that seeks immediate satisfaction of instinctual urges and drives; ruled by the pleasure principle.

13. _____ The fourth psychosexual stage of development, during which the sexual urges of male and female children become repressed; outwardly, children express a strong desire to associate with same-sex peers, a preference that strengthens the child's sexual identity.

14. _____ Sigmund Freud's theory of personality, which emphasizes unconscious determinants of behavior, sexual and aggressive instinctual drives, and the enduring effects of early childhood experiences on later personality development.

15. _____ In psychoanalytic theory, largely unconscious distortions of thought or perception that act to reduce anxiety.

16. _____ In Freud's theory, age-related developmental periods in which the child's sexual urges are expressed through different areas of the body and the activities associated with those areas.

True/False Test

Indicate whether each statement is true or false by placing T or F in the blank space next to each item.

1. ____ The final psychosexual stage of development, during which the person directs sexual urges toward socially acceptable substitutes and away from morally and socially prohibited ones, is called the phallic stage.

2. ____ As the Oedipus complex unfolds, the little boy feels affection for his mother and hostility and jealousy toward his father but realizes that his father is more physically powerful than he is; the boy experiences castration anxiety, or the fear that his father will punish him by castrating him.

3. ____ Fixation occurs if the child is frustrated or overindulged in his or her attempts to resolve the conflict associated with a stage, and the individual will continue to seek pleasure through behaviors that are similar to those associated with that psychosexual stage.

4. ____ In Freud's theory, the death instinct, reflected in aggressive, destructive, and self-destructive actions, is called Eros.

5. ___ In psychoanalytic theory, repression refers to the unconscious exclusion of anxiety-provoking thoughts, feelings, and memories from conscious awareness; the most fundamental ego defense mechanism.

6. ___ The term *unconscious* is used in Freud's theory to describe thoughts, feelings, wishes, and drives that are operating below the level of conscious awareness.

7. ___ Catharsis is a phenomenon that occurs when puzzling physical and psychological problems disappear after a person expresses pent-up emotions associated with traumatic events that may have been related to his or her problems.

8. ___ As part of the resolution of her Oedipus complex, the little girl discovers that little boys have a penis and that she does not; she experiences a sense of loss, or deprivation, that Freud termed *penis envy*.

9. ___ The genital stage is the third psychosexual stage of development; during this stage, the child's pleasure seeking is focused on his or her genitals.

10. ___ In psychoanalytic theory, identification is an ego defense mechanism that involves reducing anxiety by modeling the behavior and characteristics of another person.

11. ___ The reality principle refers to the awareness of environmental demands and the capacity to accommodate them by postponing gratification until the appropriate time or circumstances exist.

12. ___ In Freud's theory, Thanatos refers to the self-preservation, or life, instinct, reflected in the expression of basic psychological urges that perpetuate the existence of the individual as well as the species.

13. ___ Free association is a psychoanalytic technique in which the patient spontaneously reports all thoughts, feelings, and mental images as they come to mind.

14. ___ All thoughts, feelings, and sensations that a person is aware of at any given moment represent the conscious level of awareness.

15. ___ The pleasure principle refers to the motive to obtain pleasure and avoid tension or discomfort; the most fundamental human motive and the guiding principle of the id.

Check your answers and review any areas of weakness before going on to the next section.

The Psychoanalytic Perspective: The Neo-Freudians

Preview Questions

Consider the following questions as you study this section of the chapter.

- What are the similarities and differences in the approaches taken by Freud and the neo-Freudians?
- What are the key ideas of Jung, Horney, and Adler?

*Read the section "The Psychoanalytic Perspective: The Neo-Freudians" and **write** your answers to the following:*

1. The neo-Freudians followed Freud in stressing

_____

However, they developed independent personality theories, because they disagreed with Freud on three key points: (a) _____

_____

(b) _____

_____

(c) _____

2. Carl Jung emphasized _____

_____

_____

3. Karen Horney stressed _____

_____

_____

4. Alfred Adler believed _____

_____

_____

The Psychoanalytic Perspective: Evaluating Freud and the Psychoanalytic Perspective on Personality

Preview Questions

Consider the following questions as you study this section of the chapter.

- What are three criticisms of Freud's theory and, more generally, the psychoanalytic perspective?
- Which Freudian ideas have been substantiated by empirical research?

*Read the section "Evaluating Freud and the Psychoanalytic Perspective on Personality" and **write** your answers to the following:*

1. Although Sigmund Freud's ideas have had a profound and lasting effect on psychology and on society, the main criticisms of Freud's theory and psychoanalysis are

   (a) _____

   _____

   (b) _____

   _____

   _____

   (c) _____

   _____

   _____

2. Several of Freud's ideas have been substantiated by empirical evidence, including

   _____

   _____

   _____

   _____

After you have carefully studied the preceding sections, complete the following exercises.

Concept Check 2

Read the following and write the correct term in the space provided.

1. Wilfred suffered a lot of physical hardship and abuse as a child; as an adult, he lacks confidence, can't hold a job for long, and feels that nothing is really worth striving for. Adler would have said that Wilfred suffers from feelings of

   _____ .

2. In a class discussion, Louanne disputed Freud's assumption that women are inferior to men and that they suffer from penis envy; instead, she suggested that men suffer from womb envy and feel inadequate because they are incapable of bearing children. Louanne's views are most consistent with those of personality theorist

   _____ .

3. During a lecture on personality, Dr. Shornagel suggested that the deepest aspect of the individual psyche is a part inherited from previous generations, which contains universally shared experiences and ideas called archetypes. Dr. Shornagel is describing the

   _____ , which is

   central to _____ theory of personality.

4. Terry has an excessive need to exert power over people; his competitiveness and need to feel superior to others stem from the feeling he had as a child of being isolated and helpless in a potentially hostile world. Horney would have suggested that Terry is attempting to deal with

   _____ .

5. Frank is very sociable and outgoing and has a keen interest in sports and outdoor activities. Jung would probably describe Frank as a(n)

   _____ personality type.

Review of Terms, Concepts, and Names 2

Use the terms in this list to complete the Matching Test, then to help you answer the True/False items correctly.

neo-Freudians	basic anxiety
Carl Jung	womb envy
collective unconscious	Alfred Adler
archetypes	striving for superiority
introvert	feelings of inferiority
extravert	inferiority complex
Karen Horney	superiority complex

Matching Exercise

Match the appropriate term/name with its definition or description.

1. _____ German-born American psychoanalyst who emphasized the role of social relationships and culture in personality; sharply disagreed with Freud's characterization of female psychological development, especially his notion that women suffer from penis envy; key ideas included basic anxiety.

2. _____ In Jung's theory, the inherited mental images of universal human instincts, themes, and preoccupations that are the main components of the collective unconscious.

3. _____ In Adler's theory, the desire to improve oneself, master challenges, and move toward self-perfection and self-realization, considered to be the most fundamental human motive.

4. _____ Fundamental emotion that Horney described as the feeling a child has of being isolated and helpless in a potentially hostile world.

5. _____ Adler's term for the personality characteristic that people who are unable to compensate for specific weaknesses develop; a general sense of inadequacy, weakness, and helplessness.

6. _____ In Jung's theory, the basic personality type that focuses attention and energy toward the outside world.

7. _____ In Jung's theory, the hypothesized part of the unconscious mind that is inherited from previous generations and that contains universally shared ancestral experiences and ideas.

True/False Test

Indicate whether each statement is true or false by placing T or F in the blank space next to each item.

1. ____ The term *neo-Freudians* was given to the early followers of Freud who developed their own theories yet still recognized the importance of many of Freud's basic notions, such as the influence of unconscious processes and early childhood experiences.

2. ____ Alfred Adler was an Austrian physician who broke with Freud and developed his own psychoanalytic theory of personality, which emphasized social factors and motivation toward self-improvement and self-realization, and overcoming feelings of inferiority.

3. ____ According to Adler's theory, people can overcompensate for their feelings of inferiority and develop a superiority complex, which is characterized by exaggeration of one's accomplishments and importance in an effort to cover up weaknesses and limitations.

4. ____ Horney used the term *womb envy* to describe the envy that men feel about women's capacity to bear children.

5. ____ In Jung's theory, the introvert is a basic personality type that focuses attention inward.

6. ____ Carl Jung was the Swiss psychiatrist who broke with Freud to develop his own psychoanalytic theory of personality, which stressed striving toward psychological harmony and included the key ideas of the collective unconscious and archetypes.

7. ____ According to Adler's theory, striving for superiority arises from universal feelings of inferiority that are experienced during infancy and childhood, when the child is helpless and dependent on others.

Check your answers and review any areas of weakness before going on to the next section.

The Humanistic Perspective on Personality

Preview Questions

Consider the following questions as you study this section of the chapter.

- What is the focus of the humanistic perspective?

- What role do the self-concept, the actualizing tendency, and unconditional positive regard play in Rogers's personality theory?

- What are the key strengths and weaknesses of the humanistic perspective?

*Read the section "The Humanistic Perspective on Personality" and **write** your answers to the following:*

1. The humanistic perspective emphasizes

_____

_____

2. The actualizing tendency is _____

_____

3. The self-concept is _____

_____

_____

4. Conditional positive regard is_____

_____

_____

Unconditional positive regard is _____

_____

_____

5. The fully functioning person experiences _____

_____

6. The humanistic perspective has been criticized on two particular points: _____

_____

_____

_____

The Social Cognitive Perspective on Personality

Preview Questions

Consider the following questions as you study this section of the chapter.

- What is the focus of the social cognitive perspective?
- What is the principle of reciprocal determinism, and what is the role of self-efficacy beliefs in personality, according to this perspective?
- What are the key strengths and weaknesses of the social cognitive perspective?

*Read the section "The Social Cognitive Perspective on Personality" and **write** your answers to the following:*

1. The social cognitive perspective stresses _____

_____

_____

2. Bandura's social cognitive theory emphasizes

_____

_____

_____

3. Reciprocal determinism suggests that human functioning and personality _____

_____

4. Self-efficacy is _____

_____

5. Key strengths of the social cognitive perspective are _____

_____

_____

_____

_____

6. Some weaknesses of the social cognitive perspective are that _____

_____

_____

_____

_____

The Trait Perspective on Personality

Preview Questions

Consider the following questions as you study this section of the chapter.

- What is the focus of trait theories, and what are three influential trait theories?
- How are traits defined, and what is the difference between surface traits and source traits?
- How is the expression of personality traits affected by situational demands?
- What is the focus of behavioral genetics?
- To what degree are personality traits inherited?
- What are the key strengths and weaknesses of the trait perspective?

*Read the section "The Trait Perspective on Personality" and **write** your answers to the following:*

1. Trait theories focus on _____

_____

2. Traits are _____

_____

Surface traits are _____

_____

Source traits are _____

_____

3. Cattell believed that _____

_____

4. Hans Eysenck proposed that _____

_____

_____

5. According to the five-factor model _____

_____

_____

6. The field of behavioral genetics studies ____

_____

7. Factors that seem to have a significant genetic component are _____

_____

_____

_____

8. The trait perspective is useful in _____

_____

9. Some criticisms of the trait theories are ____

_____

_____

_____

_____

After you have carefully studied the preceding sections, complete the following exercises.

Concept Check 3

Read the following and write the correct term in the space provided.

1. Dunja is confident in her ability to service her own car but is less sure of her ability to bake cakes and cookies. According to Bandura, Dunja's different beliefs about her own abilities are her _____ beliefs.

2. Eileen is consistently cheerful, optimistic, talkative, and impulsive. These traits, which are inferred from her observable behavior, are referred to as _____ traits.

3. Navi is viewed by her family and friends as a flexible, creative, spontaneous, open, caring person who likes and is liked by most people. Carl Rogers would probably describe her as a(n) _____ person.

4. Alfred believes that from an early age we develop a set of perceptions and beliefs about ourselves, our nature, and our personal qualities and are motivated to act in accordance with these perceptions. Alfred's belief about personality development is most consistent with

_____

theory.

5. Dr. Bhatt is concerned with describing, classifying, and measuring the numerous ways in which individuals may differ from one another. Her approach is most characteristic of the _____ perspective on personality.

6. Whenever her son misbehaves, Rochelle's disciplinary strategy is to make sure he clearly understands that his behavior is not acceptable while taking care to reassure him that he is loved and valued. Rachel is using Rogers's concept of _____ .

7. Dr. Lavalle studies the effects of heredity on behavior. In his research, he studies identical and fraternal twins who were separated at birth, identical and fraternal twins raised together, and the similarities and differences between adopted children and their adoptive and biological parents. Dr. Lavalle works in the field of _____ .

Graphic Organizer 2

Read the following statements and match the personality theorist and theory/perspective associated with each:

Statement	Theorist	Theory/ Perspective
1. I believe that people can be classified into four basic types: introverted-neurotic, introverted-stable, extraverted-neurotic, and extraverted-stable.		
2. It is my belief that people have an innate drive to maintain and enhance themselves. This actualizing tendency is the most basic human motive, and all other motives, whether biological or social, are secondary.		
3. I reduced Allport's 4,000 terms to 171, and then, by using factor analysis, I eventually came up with 16 personality factors that represent the essential source of human personality.		
4. My theory of personality stresses the influence of unconscious mental processes, the importance of sexual and aggressive instincts, and the enduring effects of early childhood experiences on personality.		
5. For me the most fundamental human motive is striving for superiority, which arises from universal feelings of inferiority. Depending on how people deal with these feelings, they may develop either an inferiority complex or a superiority complex.		
6. My research suggests that human functioning is caused by the interaction of behavioral, cognitive, and environmental factors, a process I call reciprocal determinism.		
7. For me the impact of social relationships and the nature of the parent-child interaction are the main determinants of personality. Different patterns of behavior develop as people try to deal with their basic anxiety. Males have an additional problem to deal with, womb envy.		
8. I am most well known for my theory of motivation and the notion of a hierarchy of needs. I also identified the qualities most associated with self-actualized people.		
9. It is apparent to me, from my observations of different cultures and my own patients, that the deepest part of the individual psyche is the collective unconscious, which contains universal archetypes. Personality can be described on two basic dimensions, introversion and extraversion.		

Review of Terms, Concepts, and Names 3

Use the terms in this list to complete the Matching Test, then to help you answer the True/False items correctly.

humanistic psychology
Abraham Maslow
Carl Rogers
actualizing tendency
self-concept
positive regard
conditional positive
   regard
incongruence
unconditional positive
   regard
fully functioning person
congruence
Albert Bandura
self-efficacy
social cognitive theory

reciprocal determinism
self-system
trait theory
trait
surface trait
source traits
Raymond Cattell
Hans Eysenck
introversion
extraversion
neuroticism
stability
psychoticism
five-factor model of
   personality
behavioral genetics

Matching Exercise

Match the appropriate term/name with its definition or description.

1. _____ A relatively stable, enduring predisposition to consistently behave in a certain way.

2. _____ People's beliefs about their ability to meet the demands of a specific situation; feelings of self-confidence or self-doubt.

3. _____ Contemporary American psychologist who is best known for his research on observational learning and his social cognitive theory of personality.

4. _____ In Rogers's theory, the innate drive to maintain and enhance the human organism.

5. _____ Trait theory of personality that identifies five basic source traits (extraversion, neuroticism, agreeableness, conscientiousness, and openness to experience) as the fundamental building blocks of personality.

6. _____ American psychologist who was one of the founders of humanistic psychology and emphasized the study of healthy personality development; developed a hierarchical theory of motivation based on the idea that people will strive for self-actualization, the highest motive, only after more basic needs have been met.

7. _____ In Eysenck's theory, a third dimension of personality; a person high on this trait is antisocial, cold, hostile, and unconcerned about others, whereas a person low on this trait is warm and caring toward others.

8. _____ In Rogers's theory, the term for the sense of being loved and valued by other people, especially one's parents.

9. _____ Bandura's theory of personality, which emphasizes the importance of observational learning, conscious cognitive processes, social experiences, self-efficacy beliefs, and reciprocal determinism.

10. _____ Theory of personality that focuses on identifying, describing, and measuring individual differences in attributes.

11. _____ In Eysenck's theory, the dimension of personality that describes people who direct their energies outward toward the environment and other people; a person high on this dimension would be outgoing and sociable, enjoying new experiences and stimulating environments.

12. _____ American psychologist who was one of the founders of humanistic psychology; developed a theory of personality and form of psychotherapy that emphasized the inherent worth of people, the innate tendency to strive toward one's potential, and the importance of the self-concept in personality development.

13. _____ Theoretical viewpoint on personality that generally emphasizes the inherent goodness of people, human potential, self-actualization, the self-concept, and healthy personality development.

14. _____ Albert Bandura's model that explains human functioning and personality as caused by the interaction of behavioral, cognitive, and environmental factors.

15. _____ In Eysenck's theory, a personality dimension in which the person directs his or her energies inward, toward inner, self-focused experiences; a person high on this dimension might be quiet, solitary, and reserved, avoiding new experiences.

True/False Test

Indicate whether each statement is true or false by placing T or F in the blank space next to each item.

1. ____ Behavioral genetics is an interdisciplinary field that studies the effects of genes and heredity on behavior.

2. ___ In Rogers's theory, people are in a state of congruence when their feelings and experiences are denied and distorted because they contradict or conflict with their self-concept.

3. ___ Raymond Cattell was a British-born American psychologist who developed a trait theory that identifies 16 essential source traits or personality factors; also developed the widely used self-report personality test, the Sixteen Personality Factor Questionnaire (16PF).

4. ___ Personality characteristics or attributes that can easily be inferred from observable behavior are called source traits.

5. ___ In Rogers's theory, the sense that you will be valued and loved only if you behave in a way that is acceptable to others is called conditional positive regard.

6. ___ Self-concept is the set of perceptions and beliefs that you hold about yourself.

7. ___ In Eysenck's theory, neuroticism refers to a person's predisposition to become emotionally upset.

8. ___ In Rogers's theory, the fully functioning person has a flexible, constantly evolving self-concept and is realistic, open to new experiences, and capable of changing in response to new experiences.

9. ___ Unconditional positive regard, in Rogers's theory, is the sense that you will be valued and loved even if you don't conform to the standards and expectations of others.

10. ___ A surface trait is the most fundamental dimension of personality; these broad basic traits are hypothesized to be universal and relatively few in number.

11. ___ In Rogers's theory, people are in a state of incongruence when their sense of self (their self-concept) is consistent with their emotions and experiences.

12. ___ Hans Eysenck was a German-born British psychologist who developed a trait theory of personality that identifies the three basic dimensions of personality as neuroticism, extraversion, and psychoticism.

13. ___ In Eysenck's theory, stability reflects a person's predisposition to be emotionally even.

14. ___ Cognitive skills, abilities, and attitudes that emerge through developmental experiences involving the interaction of behavioral, cognitive, and environmental factors represent the person's self-system.

Check your answers and review any areas of weakness before going on to the next section.

Assessing Personality: Psychological Tests

Preview Questions

Consider the following questions as you study this section of the chapter.

- What are projective tests and self-report inventories, and how are they used to measure personality?
- What are the key strengths and weaknesses of projective tests and self-report inventories?

*Read the section "Assessing Personality: Psychological Tests" and **write** your answers to the following:*

1. A psychological test is _____
   _____
   _____

2. A projective test is _____
   _____
   _____

3. A self-report inventory is _____
   _____
   _____

4. Projective tests provide qualitative data but their weaknesses are that _____
   _____
   _____
   _____

5. The strengths of self-report inventories are that
   _____
   _____
   _____

6. Problems with self-report inventories are that
   _____
   _____
   _____

After you have carefully studied the preceding section, complete the following exercises.

Concept Check 4

Read the following and write the correct term in the space provided.

1. Michelle was given a psychological test in which she was asked to look at a series of cards with ambiguous scenes and make up stories for each one. She was told to give as much detail as possible about what the characters are feeling and how the story ends. Michelle was given a(n) _____ test called the

   _____ .

2. When Roger was assessed for his suitability to be a police officer, he was given a 500-item test that was used to evaluate his mental health. The test he was given was most likely the

   _____ .

3. Mr. and Mrs. Sheldrake want to get some idea of how their son is going to do in high school. The test that is best at predicting their son's high school grades is the

   _____ .

4. In his psychoanalytic practice, Dr. Coles tries to understand his client's unconscious conflicts, motives, psychological defenses, and personality traits. It is very probable that Dr. Coles uses a(n) _____ test called the

   _____ .

5. Dr. Cera sees a lot of married couples in his counseling practice. In an effort to help them resolve their conflicts, he frequently administers a test to each partner, which generates a profile of their personality characteristics. Dr. Cera most likely uses the

   _____ .

Review of Terms and Concepts 4

Use the terms in this list to complete the Matching Test, then to help you answer the True/False items correctly.

psychological test
projective test
Rorschach Inkblot Test
Thematic Apperception
  Test (TAT)
self-report inventory

Minnesota Multiphasic
  Personality Inventory
  (MMPI)
California Personality
  Inventory (CPI)

Sixteen Personality
  Factor Questionnaire
  (16PF)

graphology
possible selves

Matching Exercise

Match the appropriate term with its definition or description.

1. _____ Type of psychological test in which a person's responses to standardized questions are compared with established norms.

2. _____ Projective test that uses inkblots, developed by Swiss psychiatrist Hermann Rorschach in 1921.

3. _____ Self-report inventory that assesses personality characteristics in normal populations.

4. _____ Test that assesses a person's abilities, aptitudes, interests, or personality, based on a systematically obtained sample of behavior.

5. _____ Self-report inventory developed by Raymond Cattell that generates a personality profile with ratings on 16 trait dimensions.

True/False Test

Indicate whether each statement is true or false by placing T or F in the blank space next to each item.

1. ____ A projective test is a type of personality test that involves a person's interpreting an ambiguous image and is used to assess unconscious motives, conflicts, psychological defenses, and personality traits.

2. ____ Possible selves refers to an aspect of the self-concept that includes images of the selves that you hope, fear, or expect to become in the future.

3. ____ The Minnesota Multiphasic Personality Inventory (MMPI) is a projective personality test that involves creating stories about each of a series of ambiguous scenes.

4. ____ The Thematic Apperception Test (TAT) is a self-report inventory that assesses personality characteristics and psychological disorders; used to assess both normal and disturbed populations.

5. ____ Graphology is a pseudoscience that claims to assess personality as well as social and occu-

pational attributes based on a person's distinctive handwriting, doodles, and drawing style.

Check your answers and review any areas of weakness before going on to the next section.

Something to Think About

1. The use of psychological tests has been and will continue to be an interesting topic of discussion for most people. Almost everyone has heard of the famous inkblot test, but not everyone knows its purpose or its limitations. Considering what you have learned about psychological tests in this chapter, what would you tell someone about the inkblot test and psychological tests in general?

2. The history of astrology can be traced back over 4,000 years. Astrology's basic premise is that the positions of the planets and stars at the time and place of your birth determine your personality and destiny. Today, belief in astrological predictions remains widespread. Indeed, you probably know a number of people who, even if they are not true believers, at least read their daily horoscope in the paper. How might you enlighten these people about scientific research on astrology?

Check your answers and review any areas of weakness before completing the progress tests.

Progress Test 1

Review the complete chapter (including Concept Reviews and the boxed inserts), review all your study notes, and then test yourself on the following progress test. Check your answers. If you make a mistake, review your notes, review the relevant section of the study guide, and, if necessary, go back and read the appropriate part of your textbook.

1. Marvin is angry and upset after an argument with his boss. At home that evening he is harshly and unreasonably critical of his son for not getting all his homework assignments completed. According to Freud, Marvin is using an ego defense mechanism called
   (a) identification.   (c) rationalization.
   (b) repression.   (d) displacement.

2. Seven-year old Salvatore prefers to play with his male friends and does not like playing with girls very much. Salvatore is probably in the _____ stage of psychosexual development.
   (a) anal   (c) latency
   (b) phallic   (d) genital

3. Although Tim has many fond memories of his college days, he only vaguely remembers the girl he was engaged to but who left him suddenly for another man. Tim's unconscious forgetting is an ego defense mechanism called
   (a) identification.   (c) displacement.
   (b) sublimation.   (d) repression.

4. Every time two-year-old Kate is given a bath, she plays with her genital area. If her parents chastise or punish her, she is likely to experience frustration, which could lead to an unresolved developmental conflict called
   (a) fixation.   (c) displacement.
   (b) undoing.   (d) denial.

5. Zachary considers himself to be an outgoing, fun-loving type of person, and he goes to a lot of parties. Sondra, on the other hand, thinks of herself as fairly quiet and shy, and enjoys being by herself, reading a book and listening to classical music. In Jung's theory, Zachary's and Sondra's different behaviors reflect
   (a) the two basic personality types, the extravert and the introvert.
   (b) the two important archetypes, the hero and the nurturing mother.
   (c) a superiority complex and an inferiority complex.
   (d) penis envy and womb envy.

6. Read the example in question 5 again. According to social cognitive theory, the different personalities of Zachary and Sondra reflect the interaction of behavioral, cognitive, and environmental factors, a process Bandura called
   (a) identification.
   (b) striving for superiority.
   (c) the actualizing tendency.
   (d) reciprocal determinism.

7. As part of a research project, Jasbinder was given the same psychological test three times at two-month intervals by three different therapists. Her results on the tests were all very different. It is most probable that she was given the
   (a) MMPI.   (c) CPI.
   (b) 16PF.   (d) TAT.

8. The actualizing tendency and the self-concept are to _____ as reciprocal determinism and self-efficacy are to _____ .
   (a) Abraham Maslow; Hans Eysenck
   (b) Alfred Adler; Albert Bandura
   (c) Raymond Cattell; Carl Jung
   (d) Carl Rogers; Albert Bandura

9. When asked to describe her husband, Mrs. Roech said that he is prone to exaggerating his accomplishments and importance, seems unaware of the reality of his limitations, and tends to overcompensate for his feelings of inferiority and weakness. Adler would probably have said that Mr. Roech has
   (a) an inferiority complex.
   (b) an extraverted personality.
   (c) a superiority complex.
   (d) an anal fixation.

10. Katrina thinks of herself as fairly laid back, easygoing, and relatively calm. She believes that she is above average academically and intellectually and sees herself as very conscientious at work and caring and loving with her family. Carl Rogers's term for Katrina's perceptions and beliefs about herself would be
    (a) self-efficacy.   (c) self-system.
    (b) self-concept.   (d) possible selves.

11. Miguel is giving a lecture on the five-factor model of personality. Which of the following personality dimensions is *not* likely to be included in his talk?
    (a) anal retentiveness
    (b) extraversion
    (c) neuroticism
    (d) agreeableness
    (e) openness to experience

12. Dr. Markowitz studies the effects of heredity on behavior. One of his areas of research focuses on similarities and differences in identical twins who were separated at birth or early infancy and raised by different families. Dr. Markowitz is most probably a(n)
    (a) psychoanalyst.
    (b) humanistic psychologist.
    (c) social cognitive psychologist.
    (d) behavioral geneticist.

13. Zintyre was very impressed when told by an astrologer that, "You are gregarious, outgoing, and fond of travel. You tend to react negatively to authority figures, and you have had a num-

ber of confrontations as a result. You enjoy good food and good wine and you don't suffer fools gladly." According to Science and Pseudoscience 10.4, which of the following is true?
   (a) The astrologer probably has an extraordinary gift for accurately assessing personality.
   (b) The astrologer is probably operating at chance level in assessing personality.
   (c) The astrologer is using a proven scientific method in his personality assessment of Zintyre.
   (d) Zintyre is probably extremely accurate in assessing the accuracy of the astrologer's personality description.

14. According to the Application, the term *possible selves* refers to
    (a) the unconscious part of the mind that motivates our behavior.
    (b) the major symptom of a fixated personality.
    (c) the aspect of the self-concept that includes images of the selves that you hope, fear, or expect to become in the future.
    (d) delusional thought processes.

15. According to the Critical Thinking 10.1, which of the following is true?
    (a) Freud's view of human nature was deeply pessimistic.
    (b) Rogers's view of human nature was deeply pessimistic.
    (c) Freud believed that humans are positive, forward-moving, constructive, realistic, and trustworthy.
    (d) Rogers believed that the essence of human nature is destructive but that societal, religious, and cultural restraints make people behave in good and moral ways.

Progress Test 2

After you have checked your understanding of the material in Progress Test 1 and have done a complete chapter review with special focus on any areas of weakness, you are ready to assess your knowledge of Progress Test 2. Check your answers. If you make a mistake, review your notes, the relevant section of the study guide, and, if necessary, the appropriate part of your textbook.

1. Nathan chews the end of his pen, bites his nails, overeats, smokes cigarettes, and talks incessantly. According to Freud, Nathan has

probably fixated at the _____ stage of psychosexual development due to some unresolved conflict.

(a) oral
(b) anal
(c) phallic
(d) genital

2. Dr. Jivraj, like many contemporary trait theorists, believes that the 16 trait model is too complex, and that the three-dimensional trait theory is too limited. Instead, he favors a model in which five basic dimensions represent the structural organization of personality traits. These five factors are

(a) extraversion, neuroticism, agreeableness, conscientiousness, and openness to experience.
(b) submissiveness, apprehensiveness, dominance, sociability, and venturesomeness.
(c) inferiority, superiority, introversion, extraversion, and actualizing tendencies.
(d) self-efficacy, self-concept, reciprocal determining tendencies, defensiveness, and openness to experience.

3. Shelly was often rejected by her parents; as a result, she mistrusts other people and treats them with hostility, which leads to their rejection of her. This cycle of rejection, mistrust, hostility, and further rejection illustrates what Bandura called

(a) self-efficacy.
(b) identification.
(c) displacement.
(d) reciprocal determinism.

4. During a class discussion of various perspectives on personality, Sasha points to all the evidence that human beings are destructive and aggressive. He points to the millions who died in two world wars and the ongoing killings and massacres that continue in many parts of the world today. Sasha's observation about basic human nature supports the _____ perspective and is a criticism of the _____ perspective.

(a) humanistic; psychoanalytic
(b) trait; social cognitive
(c) social cognitive; trait
(d) psychoanalytic; humanistic

5. Dr. Sheenan is a clinical psychologist who wants to assess the extent to which a client is suffering from depression, delusions, and other mental health problems. Dr. Sheenan is most likely to use the

(a) 16PF.
(b) CPI.
(c) MMPI.
(d) TAT.

6. When Cindy was given the Rorschach Inkblot Test, she reported seeing a number of inanimate objects and some animal figures and tended to concentrate on very small details in each inkblot. Her therapist observed her behavior, gestures, and reactions as she responded to each card. It is most probable that her therapist is

(a) interested in her unconscious conflicts, motives, and psychological defenses.
(b) assessing her suitability for a particular occupation, such as police officer or pilot.
(c) trying to generate a personality profile based on a number of personality traits.
(d) trying to predict how she will perform academically when she goes to college.

7. Lukasz was given a forced-choice personality test in which he was required to respond to each item by choosing one of three alternatives. The results generated a personality profile with ratings on a number of trait dimensions that helped Lukasz decide which career path he should pursue. Lukasz was most likely given the

(a) Thematic Apperception Test (TAT).
(b) Minnesota Multiphasic Personality (MMPI).
(c) California Personality Inventory (CPI).
(d) Sixteen Personality Factor Questionnaire (16PF).

8. Five-year-old Dunstan has recently become very possessive of his mother and appears to be jealous of his father. He is sometimes openly hostile, telling his father, "Don't kiss my Mommy!" According to Freud, Dunstan is in the _____ stage of psychosexual development and showing manifestations of

_____ .

(a) oral; fixation
(b) anal; fixation
(c) phallic; the Oedipus complex
(d) latency; the Oedipus complex

9. Wendy believes that the most fundamental human motive is striving for superiority. She thinks that this drive arises from global feelings of inferiority and that human personality and behavior reflect our attempts to compensate for or overcome our perceived weaknesses. Which personality theorist is most likely to agree with Wendy's views?
   (a) Freud   (c) Horney
   (b) Jung   (d) Adler

10. David is very quiet, pessimistic, anxious, and moody and becomes emotionally upset very easily. In terms of Eysenck's four basic personality types, he would be classified as
    (a) introverted-neurotic.
    (b) introverted-stable.
    (c) extraverted-neurotic.
    (d) extraverted-stable.

11. In a term paper on Carl Jung's theory of personality, Justin quoted Jung as saying that the _____ contains "the whole spiritual heritage of mankind's evolution, born anew in the brain structure of every individual."
    (a) personal preconscious
    (b) collective conscious
    (c) personal unconscious
    (d) collective unconscious

12. Ursula's therapist instructs her to relax, close her eyes, and state aloud whatever thoughts come to mind no matter how trivial, silly, or absurd they seem. The therapist is using a technique called
    (a) free association.
    (b) displacement.
    (c) unconditional positive regard.
    (d) repression.

13. Leanne studies very hard, but she always feels that she hasn't studied enough. If she takes a break to socialize with her friends, she starts feeling guilty and anxious. Freud would say that Leanne has a
    (a) strong superego.   (c) weak superego.
    (b) strong id.   (d) weak id.

14. According to In Focus 10.3, which of the following is true?
    (a) Any two randomly chosen people of the same age, sex, and culture will likely have absolutely no similarities.
    (b) Some similarities between separated identical twins may be genetically influenced.
    (c) Personality is almost completely determined by genes.
    (d) Personality is almost completely determined by environmental factors.

15. According to Science Versus Pseudoscience 10.5, graphologists' claims that handwriting reveals temperament, personality traits, intelligence, and reasoning ability
    (a) have been empirically tested and supported by numerous scientific studies.
    (b) have not been supported by scientific research.
    (c) should be believed because thousands of U.S. companies have used graphologists to assist in hiring new employees.
    (d) have much greater validity and reliability than similar claims made by astrologers.

Progress Test 3

After you have checked your understanding of the material in Progress Tests 1 and 2, and have done a complete chapter review with special focus on any areas of weakness, you are ready to further assess your knowledge on Progress Test 3. Check your answers. If you make a mistake, review your notes, the appropriate parts of the study guide, and if necessary, the relevant sections of your textbook.

1. During a class reunion Adeil reminisced with some of his high school friends about their last year at school and had no problem recalling many of the fun times they had together. In terms of Freud's theory of personality, Adeil's ability to recall these events would suggest that they are stored at the _____ level of awareness.
   (a) unconscious   (c) latency
   (b) conscious   (d) preconscious

2. Researchers conducting twin and adoption studies are likely to conclude that
   (a) in general, the influence of environmental factors on personality traits is at least equal to the influence of genetic factors.
   (b) certain personality traits, such as extraversion and neuroticism, are significantly influenced by genetics.
   (c) identical twins are more alike early in life, but as they grow up, leave home, and encounter different experiences and environments, their personalities become more different.
   (d) all of the above are true.

3. Juan is a very experienced car mechanic who believes he can fix just about any problem in any make of car or truck. According to Bandura, Juan's confidence in his ability to handle mechanical problems is his
   (a) self-concept.
   (b) superiority complex.
   (c) self-efficacy.
   (d) actualizing tendency.

4. When Romwaldo was given the results of his psychological test, he was told that he scored high on the extraverted-stable dimension and that he has a tendency to be sociable, outgoing, talkative, and responsive. This description of Romwaldo's source and surface traits is most consistent with
   (a) Hans Eysenck's view of personality.
   (b) Rorschach's theory of personality.
   (c) Alfred Adler's model of personality.
   (d) Carl Rogers's humanistic approach to personality.

5. The pleasure principle is to _____ as the reality principle is to _____ .
   (a) the oral stage; the anal stage
   (b) Thanatos; Eros
   (c) the id; the ego
   (d) the ego; the superego

6. When Kaysone was researching a term paper for her history of psychology course, she was intrigued by the ideas of neo-Freudian Alfred Adler. She noted that for Adler the most fundamental human motive was _____ , which arises from universal _____ .
   (a) driven by basic anxiety; feelings of womb and penis envy.
   (b) the need to achieve psychological growth, self-realization, and psychic harmony; archetypes in the collective unconscious
   (c) sexual and aggressive in nature; feelings of guilt and anxiety repressed in the unconscious
   (d) striving for superiority; feelings of inferiority.

7. Dr. Selnick believes in the importance of unconscious psychological conflicts, sexual and aggressive drives, and the formative influence of early childhood experiences. Dr. Selnick's views are most consistent with the _____ perspective.
   (a) psychoanalytic   (c) social cognitive
   (b) humanistic   (d) trait

8. Raffi is shown a series of cards with ambiguous scenes and is told to make up a story about each one, describing the characters' feelings and their motives. Raffi has been given the
   (a) Thematic Apperception Test (TAT).
   (b) Rorschach Inkblot Test.
   (c) California Personality Inventory (CPI).
   (d) Minnesota Multiphasic Personality Inventory (MMPI).

9. Sheldon has frequently been rebellious, inconsiderate, and self-centered. His parents are consistent in disciplining him for his inappropriate behaviors while communicating to him that they value and love him. The person most likely to agree with their parenting approach and use of unconditional positive regard is
   (a) Sigmund Freud.   (c) Joseph Breuer.
   (b) Carl Rogers.   (d) Carl Jung.

10. Dr. Welch is a clinical psychologist who uses the MMPI and the 16PF. If asked to identify the key strength of these tests, he is most likely to note that
    (a) they provide a wealth of qualitative information about the individual.
    (b) scoring relies on the examiner's subjective judgment and clinical experience and expertise.
    (c) they accurately measure the individual's unconscious motives and conflicts.
    (d) they are standardized and objectively scored.

11. When Professor Mainprize was going through a very painful divorce, he tended to mark student papers very harshly and to make the exams difficult. A psychoanalyst would be most likely to view the professor's treatment of his students as an example of
    (a) identification.   (c) displacement.
    (b) repression.   (d) reaction formation.

12. Dr. Sharma stresses the importance of identifying, measuring, and describing individual differences in terms of various personality characteristics. His views are most representative of the _____ perspective on personality.
    (a) psychoanalytic   (c) social cognitive
    (b) humanistic   (d) trait

13. According to the Application section, which of the following is false?
    (a) A person's self-concept is a multifaceted system of related images and ideas.
    (b) Possible selves influence our behavior in important ways.
    (c) We're often unaware of how possible selves we've mentally constructed influence our beliefs, actions, and self-evaluations.
    (d) A person's self-concept is a singular mental self-image.

14. According to Critical Thinking 10.2, which of the following is true?
    (a) Freud viewed aggression as a universal, unconscious, human instinct.
    (b) Bandura believed that the essence of human nature is aggressive but that societal, religious, and cultural restraints make people behave in nonaggressive ways.
    (c) Freud believed human aggression, like other human behavior, is driven by conscious, rational goals and motives.

(d) Bandura viewed aggression as a universal, unconscious, human instinct.

15. Science versus Pseudoscience 10.4, which discusses astrology and personality, concluded that
    (a) the position of the planets and stars at the time and place of your birth determines your personality and destiny.
    (b) today, virtually nobody believes in astrological interpretations and predictions.
    (c) science has not been able to refute the claims, predictions, and interpretations of astrology.
    (d) neither popular nor serious astrology has any reliable basis in scientific fact.

Answers

Introduction: What Is Personality?

1. *Personality is defined as* an individual's unique and relatively consistent pattern of thinking, feeling, and behaving.

2. *A personality theory is* an attempt to describe and explain how people are similar, how they are different, and why every individual is unique.

3. *The four basic perspectives on personality (and the main emphasis of each) are* the psychoanalytic perspective, which emphasizes the importance of unconscious processes and the influence of early childhood experience; the humanistic perspective, which represents an optimistic look at human nature, emphasizing the self and the fulfillment of a person's unique potential; the social cognitive perspective, which emphasizes learning and conscious cognitive processes, including the importance of beliefs about the self, goal-setting, and self-regulation; and the trait perspective, which emphasizes the description and measurement of specific personality differences among individuals.

The Psychoanalytic Perspective on Personality

1. *Psychoanalysis—Freud's theory of personality— stresses* the influence of unconscious mental processes, the importance of sexual and aggressive instincts, and the enduring effects of early childhood experiences on later personality development.

2. *Some of the key factors in the development of Freud's ideas were* his collaboration with Joseph Breuer on the cause of hysteria, the concept of catharsis; the development of free association to study the unconscious; the impor-

tance of dreams and their interpretation; and the impact war had on culture and society.

The Psychoanalytic Perspective: Freud's Dynamic Theory of Personality

1. *The content of the unconscious can surface in disguised form in* free association, dreams, slips of the tongue, and what, on the surface, appear to be accidents.

2. *The three basic structures of personality (and their functions) are* the id (the completely unconscious, irrational component of personality that seeks immediate satisfaction of instinctual urges and is ruled by the pleasure principle); the ego (the partly conscious rational component of personality that regulates thoughts and behavior, that is most in touch with the real world, and that is governed by the reality principle); and the superego (the partly conscious, self-evaluative, moralistic component of personality that is formed through the internalization of parental and societal rules).

3. *The two main ego defense mechanisms (and the roles they play) are* repression (the unconscious exclusion of anxiety-provoking thoughts, feelings, and memories from conscious awareness, which is involved in all other ego defense mechanisms) and displacement (unconscious shifting of the target of an emotional urge to a substitute target that is less threatening or dangerous). Other ego defense mechanisms include sublimation, rationalization, projection, reaction formation, denial, undoing, and regression.

The Psychoanalytic Perspective: Personality Development

1. *The psychosexual stages are age-related development periods* in which the child's sexual urges are expressed through different areas of the body and the activities associated with these areas.

2. *The five psychosexual stages are* the oral stage, the anal stage, the phallic stage, the latency stage, and the genital stage.

3. *If the developmental conflict of a particular stage is not resolved* the result may be fixation, and the person will continue to seek pleasure through behaviors that are similar to those associated with that psychosexual stage.

4. *The Oedipus complex refers to* a child's unconscious sexual desire for the opposite-sex parent, usually accompanied by hostile feelings toward the same-sex parent.

5. *Identification (which is one result of the Oedipus complex) is an ego defense mechanism that* involves reducing anxiety by modeling the behavior and characteristics of another person.

Concept Check 1

1. personality
2. free association
3. unconscious
4. latent
5. id
6. superego
7. sublimation
8. identification

Graphic Organizer 1

1. genital
2. phallic
3. latency
4. oral
5. anal

Matching Exercise 1

1. libido
2. personality
3. superego
4. Oedipus complex
5. ego
6. preconscious
7. oral stage
8. displacement
9. Sigmund Freud
10. anal stage
11. personality theory
12. id
13. latency stage
14. psychoanalysis
15. ego defense mechanisms
16. psychosexual stages

True/False Test 1

1.	F	6.	T	11.	T
2.	T	7.	T	12.	F
3.	T	8.	T	13.	T
4.	F	9.	F	14.	T
5.	T	10.	T	15.	T

The Psychoanalytic Perspective: The Neo-Freudians

1. *The neo-Freudians followed Freud in stressing* the importance of the unconscious and early childhood. *However, they developed independent personality theories, because they disagreed with Freud on three key points: (a)* They took issue with Freud's belief that behavior was primarily motivated by sexual desires. *(b)* They disagreed with Freud's contention that personality is fundamentally determined by early childhood experiences; instead, they believed that personality can also be influenced by experiences throughout the lifespan. *(c)* They departed from Freud's generally pessimistic view of human nature and society.

2. *Carl Jung emphasized* psychological growth and self-realization. He proposed the existence of the collective unconscious, which contains archetypes of universal human instincts, themes, and preoccupations. He was the first to describe two basic personality types: introverts and extraverts.

3. *Karen Horney stressed* the role of social relationships in protecting against basic anxiety; she objected to Freud's views of female development, particularly his idea of penis envy (she proposed that males have womb envy).

4. *Alfred Adler believed* that the most fundamental human motive was to strive for superiority, which arose from universal feelings of inferiority. He proposed the notions of the inferiority complex and the superiority complex.

The Psychoanalytic Perspective: Evaluating Freud and the Psychoanalytic Perspective on Personality

1. *Although Sigmund Freud's ideas have had a profound and lasting effect on psychology and on society, the main criticisms of Freud's theory and psychoanalysis are:*

   (a) Freud's theory relies wholly on data derived from a relatively small sample of patients and from his self-analysis. He did not take notes during his private therapy sessions, and so we have only Freud's interpretations of the cases;

   this problem has to do with the ability to objectively evaluate the evidence.

   (b) Many psychoanalytic concepts, because they are so vague and ambiguous, are very difficult to measure or confirm scientifically. In addition, because even seemingly contradictory information can be used to support Freud's theory, psychoanalytic concepts are often impossible to disprove. Psychoanalysis is also better at explaining past behavior than at predicting future behavior.

   (c) Many people feel that Freud's theories reflect a sexist view of women; Freud's theory uses male psychology as a prototype, and women are essentially viewed as a deviation from the norm of masculinity.

2. *Several of Freud's ideas have been substantiated by empirical evidence, including* the idea that much of mental life is unconscious; that early childhood experiences have a critical influence on interpersonal relationships and psychological adjustment in adulthood; and that people differ significantly in the degree to which they are able to regulate their impulses, emotions, and thoughts toward adaptive and socially acceptable ends.

Concept Check 2

1. inferiority
2. Karen Horney
3. collective unconscious; Jung's
4. basic anxiety
5. extravert

Matching Exercise 2

1. Karen Horney
2. archetypes
3. striving for superiority
4. basic anxiety
5. inferiority complex
6. extravert
7. collective unconscious

True/False Test 2

1.	T	4.	T	7.	T
2.	T	5.	T		
3.	T	6.	T		

The Humanistic Perspective on Personality

1. *The humanistic perspective emphasizes* free will, self-awareness, and psychological growth.

2. *The actualizing tendency is* the innate drive to maintain and enhance the human organism.

3. *The self-concept is* the set of perceptions and beliefs that you hold about yourself, including your nature, your personal qualities, and your typical behavior.

4. *Conditional positive regard is* the sense that you will be loved and valued only if you behave in a way that is acceptable to others; this can cause a person to deny or distort aspects of experience, leading to a state of incongruence with regard to the self-concept. *Unconditional positive regard is* the sense that you will be valued and loved even if you don't conform to the standards and expectations of others; this leads to a state of congruence, where your sense of self is consistent with your emotions and experiences.

5. *The fully functioning person experiences* congruence, the actualizing tendency, and psychological growth.

6. *The humanistic perspective has been criticized on two particular points*: first, humanistic theories are hard to validate or test scientifically; second, according to many psychologists, the humanistic perspective's view of human nature is too optimistic.

The Social Cognitive Perspective on Personality

1. *The social cognitive perspective stresses* the role of conscious thought processes, self-regulation, and the importance of situational influences.

2. *Bandura's social cognitive theory emphasizes* the importance of observational learning, conscious cognitive processes, social experiences, self-efficacy beliefs, and reciprocal determinism.

3. *Reciprocal determinism suggests that human functioning and personality* are caused by the interaction of behavioral, cognitive, and environmental factors.

4. *Self-efficacy is* the belief that people have about their ability to meet the demands of a specific situation (feelings of self-confidence or self-doubt); self-efficacy influences behavior, performance, motivation, and persistence.

5. *Key strengths of the social cognitive perspective are* that it is grounded in empirical, laboratory research; it is built on research in learning, cognitive psychology, and social psychology rather than on clinical impressions. Unlike the vague psychoanalytic and humanistic concepts, the concepts of social cognitive theory are scientifically testable; they can be operationally defined and measured.

6. *Some weaknesses of the social cognitive perspective are that* real-life, everyday situations are not adequately captured in the typical laboratory research situation because they are more complex, with multiple factors converging to affect behavior and personality. Other psychologists argue that the social cognitive perspective ignores unconscious conflicts and emotions.

The Trait Perspective on Personality

1. *Trait theories focus on* measuring and describing individual differences.

2. *Traits are* relatively stable, enduring predispositions to consistently behave in certain ways. *Surface traits are* personality characteristics or attributes that can easily be inferred from observing behavior. *Source traits are* the most fundamental dimensions of personality and are thought to be universal and relatively few in number.

3. *Cattell believed that* there are 16 basic personality factors (he developed the 16PF test).

4. *Hans Eysenck proposed that* there are three personality dimensions, introversion-extraversion, neuroticism-stability, and psychoticism.

5. *According to the five-factor model,* there are five basic personality dimensions: extraversion, neuroticism, agreeableness, conscientiousness, and openness to experience.

6. *The field of behavioral genetics studies* the effects of genes and heredity on behavior.

7. *Factors that seem to have a significant genetic component are* extraversion, neuroticism, openness to experience, and conscientiousness, but the influence of environmental factors on personality traits is at least as equal to the influence of genetic factors.

8. *The trait perspective is useful in* describing individual differences and in predicting behavior.

9. *Some criticisms of the trait theories are that* they don't really explain human personality, or how or why individual differences develop, and they generally fail to address other important personality factors, such as the basic motives that drive human personality, the role of unconscious mental processes, how beliefs about the self influence personality, or how psychological change and growth occur.

Concept Check 3

1. self-efficacy
2. surface
3. fully functioning
4. social cognitive
5. trait
6. unconditional positive regard
7. behavioral genetics

Graphic Organizer 2

1. Hans Eysenck; trait
2. Carl Rogers; humanistic
3. Raymond Cattell; trait
4. Sigmund Freud; psychoanalytic
5. Alfred Adler; psychoanalytic (neo-Freudian)
6. Albert Bandura; social cognitive
7. Karen Horney; psychoanalytic (neo-Freudian)
8. Abraham Maslow; humanistic
9. Carl Jung; psychoanalytic (neo-Freudian)

Matching Exercise 3

1. trait
2. self-efficacy
3. Albert Bandura
4. actualizing tendency
5. five-factor model of personality
6. Abraham Maslow
7. psychoticism
8. positive regard
9. social cognitive theory
10. trait theory
11. extraversion
12. Carl Rogers
13. humanistic psychology

14. reciprocal determinism
15. introversion

True/False Test 3

1. T	6. T	11. F
2. F	7. T	12. T
3. T	8. T	13. T
4. F	9. T	14. T
5. T	10. F	

Assessing Personality: Psychological Tests

1. *A psychological test is* a test that assesses a person's abilities, aptitudes, interests, or personality, based on a systematically obtained sample of behavior.

2. *A projective test is* a type of personality test that involves the client's interpreting an ambiguous image; it is used to assess unconscious motives, conflicts, psychological defenses, and personality traits. The Rorschach Inkblot Test, and the Thematic Apperception Test are examples.

3. *A self-report inventory is* a type of psychological test in which a person's responses to standardized questions are compared to established norms. The MMPI, the CPI, and the 16PF are examples.

4. *Projective tests provide qualitative data but their weaknesses are that* responses may be affected by the examiner or the situation, scoring is very subjective, results may be inconsistent, and they do not predict behavior well.

5. *The strengths of self-report inventories are that* they are objectively scored, they differentiate among people on particular personality characteristics, they have high reliability, validity, and predictive value.

6. *Problems with self-report inventories are that* people do not always respond honestly or accurately, people can successfully fake responses and answer in socially desirable ways, and some people may respond in a set way to all questions.

Concept Check 4

1. projective; Thematic Apperception Test (TAT)
2. MMPI
3. CPI

4. projective; Rorschach Inkblot Test

5. 16PF

Matching Exercise 4

1. self-report inventory

2. Rorschach Inkblot Test

3. California Personality Inventory (CPI)

4. psychological test

5. Sixteen Personality Factor Questionnaire (16PF)

True/False Test 4

1. T	3. F	5. T
2. T	4. F	

Something to Think About

1. In any discussion of psychological testing it is always a good idea to point out the important characteristics of a good test, namely, reliability and validity. In terms of personality testing, you should first describe the two categories of tests, projective tests and self-report inventories.

   The famous Rorschach Inkblot Test is, of course, a projective test. In other words, it is assumed that people will project their unconscious feelings, motives, drives, thoughts, and so on in their responses to the series of inkblots. Similarly, the Thematic Apperception Test (TAT) gives subjects an opportunity to project unconscious information into the stories they make up about ambiguous scenes. Both tests developed out of the psychoanalytic approaches to personality, and scoring involves the subjective interpretations of the examiner. A brief discussion of Freud's theory as it relates to personality would probably be in order. A review of the most damaging criticisms of psychoanalysis may shed light on the topic, and the issue of the validity and reliability of projective tests should not be overlooked. Despite the criticisms, projective tests are widely used and can provide a wealth of qualitative data about an individual.

   Self-report inventories are used by clinical psychologists to evaluate both normal and abnormal populations in a variety of settings and for a variety of purposes. The most common are the MMPI, the CPI, and the 16PF. These are often called objective personality tests because they are standardized and objectively scored and measured against established norms. Self-report inventories are far more reli-

able and valid than are projective tests. These tests do have some drawbacks, including a person's ability to fake responses and answer in a socially desirable manner, some people's tendency to answer in a set way to all questions, and the fact that people are not always the best judges of their own behavior.

   Personality tests are generally useful strategies that can provide insights about the psychological makeup of a person. However, no personality test, by itself, is likely to provide a definitive description of a given individual. In addition, because people can and often do change over time, any personality test provides a profile of the person only at the time of the test.

2. Many people believe in astrology, and a large number consult professional astrologers to find out what they should do and what lies ahead of them in the future. Belief in astrology is not restricted to any class or group of individuals. People from all walks of life, from senior managers to assembly line workers, from government leaders to junior clerks, consult their horoscopes on a regular basis. As is the case with many strongly held beliefs, it is often difficult to get true believers in astrology to listen to any information that might contradict what they feel is a valid point of view. It is always important to be aware of this and to respect their right to believe whatever they wish. However, if the opportunity does arise to have an open-minded discussion, presenting the results of Shawn Carlson's (1985) carefully designed study could be useful. Remember, a panel of astrological advisers were involved in helping Carlson design the study, and thirty of the top American and European astrologers were involved. All the participating astrologers agreed beforehand that Carlson's study was a fair test of astrological claims. Although the astrologers who approved the design predicted that 50 percent was the minimum effect they would expect to see, the results showed that astrologers performed at a chance level. In other words, anybody simply guessing would have done as well as the astrologers. Carlson's results are consistent with those of many other researchers. A careful review of the scientific research on astrology came to the conclusion that astrology has absolutely no reliable basis in scientific fact and cannot stand up to any valid statistical test. Of course, if the astrologers had any real insight from their

reading of the planets, they could easily have foreseen the outcome of Carlson's study!

Progress Test 1

1. d	6. d	11. a
2. c	7. d	12. d
3. d	8. d	13. b
4. a	9. c	14. c
5. a	10. b	15. a

Progress Test 2

1. a	6. a	11. d
2. a	7. d	12. a
3. d	8. c	13. a
4. d	9. d	14. b
5. c	10. a	15. b

Progress Test 3

1. d	6. d	11. c
2. d	7. a	12. d
3. c	8. a	13. d
4. a	9. b	14. a
5. c	10. d	15. d

CHAPTER

11

Social Psychology

PREVIEW

Reading the section below first will give you a general sense of the chapter's contents and an initial introduction to some of the major concepts and terms. This will prime you for what you are about to read and help you to develop a "cognitive map" that will guide your study of the material in this chapter. Likewise, reading the **preview questions** at the beginning of each major section will improve your ability to understand, learn, and retain the information.

CHAPTER 11 . . . AT A GLANCE

Chapter 11 discusses social psychology—the scientific study of the way individuals think, feel, and behave in social situations—as broadly divided into two major research areas: social cognition and social influence. The chapter first explores person perception, including the factors that influence our perceptions of others. This is followed by a discussion of the process of attribution, including three important attributional biases and the influence of culture on attributional processes.

Once we form impressions of people, we tend to interpret their behavior in terms of our attitudes about them. The conditions under which attitudes determine behavior are identified. The role of cognitive dissonance in behavior and cognition is explored. In discussing prejudice, the text describes such cognitive influences as stereotypes, in-groups, out-groups, the out-group homogeneity effect, in-group bias, and ethnocentrism.

Conformity occurs when people change their behavior, attitudes, or beliefs in response to real or imagined group pressure. The original experimental design and the results of Stanley Milgram's research on a type of conformity called obedience are presented in detail. Conditions that influence people to obey and to resist obeying authority figures are identified.

Latané and Darley's research on helping behavior, bystander intervention, and diffusion of responsibility is discussed, and their model, which identifies the factors that increase and decrease the likelihood of bystander intervention, is presented.

Introduction: Social Psychology

Preview Questions

Consider the following questions as you study this section of the chapter.

- What is social psychology?
- What is meant by social cognition and social influence?

*Read the section "Introduction: Social Psychology" and **write** your answers to the following:*

1. Social psychology is _____

2. Social cognition refers to _____

3. Social influence focuses on _____

Person Perception: Forming Impressions of Other People

Preview Questions

Consider the following questions as you study this section of the chapter.

- What is person perception?
- What four principles does the mental process of forming judgments of others follow?
- How do social categories, implicit personality theories, and physical attractiveness influence person perception?

*Read the section "Person Perception: Forming Impressions of Other People" and **write** your answers to the following:*

1. Person perception refers to _____

2. The four basic principles of person perception are
   (a) _____
   (b) _____
   (c) _____
   (d) _____

3. In combination, these four basic principles underscore that person perception is _____

4. Social categorization is_____

   Its advantages and disadvantages are _____

5. An implicit personality theory is _____

   Like social categories, implicit personality theories are useful _____

Attribution: Explaining Behavior

Preview Questions

Consider the following questions as you study this section of the chapter.

- How is attribution defined?
- What are the fundamental attribution error, blaming the victim, the just-world hypothesis, the actor–observer discrepancy, and the self-serving bias?

*Read the section "Attribution: Explaining Behavior" and **write** your answers to the following:*

1. Attribution is _____

2. The fundamental attribution error is the tendency to _____

3. Blaming the victim is the tendency to _____

4. The just-world hypothesis is _____

5. The actor–observer discrepancy is the tendency to _____

    _____

6. The self-serving bias is the tendency to _____

    _____

    _____

After you have carefully studied the preceding sections, complete the following exercises.

Concept Check 1

Read the following and write the correct term in the space provided.

1. Adam got an A in his philosophy class and concluded that he had quite a talent for writing coherently and thinking logically. When he got a C in his sociology class, he expressed dissatisfaction with the course content, the teaching ability of the professor, and the quality and clarity of the exams. This best illustrates the

    _____ .

2. Rachel has just learned that her neighbor's teenage son, Brad, was involved in an automobile accident at a nearby intersection. She said to her husband, "Well, Brad's recklessness has finally got him into trouble!" Rachel's comment suggests that she has made the

    _____ .

3. When Allen observed Mark miss what looked to him like an easy point, Allen concluded that Mark was not a skilled basketball player. Later, in an identical position, Allen also failed to score. However, this time he concluded that it was the strong opposing team that prevented him from scoring. It would appear that Allen is committing the_____ .

4. When Cheryl first met Charles, who is an archivist in the university library, she concluded that he was probably very quiet, introverted, and introspective. She was later surprised to learn that he was the lead singer in a heavy metal band. Cheryl's surprise is probably the result of using a(n)

    _____

    to make judgments about the traits and characteristics associated with certain types of people.

5. After learning about some interesting social psychology phenomena in his introductory class, Patrick decided he would like to test one of the concepts by facing the back instead of the front while riding the elevator. Much to his surprise, he found that he could not carry out his plan. After a second or two, he was overcome with embarrassment and ended up facing the front like everyone else. Patrick's behavior was governed by the _____ of the situation.

6. Grover does not support any charities because he believes that people who are poor, hungry, or homeless did something to deserve their situation. Grover's explanatory style is called

    _____ ; it probably reflects his strong need to believe the world is fair, an assumption called the

    _____ .

Graphic Organizer 1

The following statements represent attributional processes. Decide which is (A) the fundamental attribution error, (B) the actor–observer discrepancy, or (C) the self-serving bias, and decide whether the attribution is to the self or to others or to both and whether it is internal (INT) or external (EXT).

Statement	Process	Attribution
1. I got an A in biology because I'm smart; I got a C in chemistry because the professor was disorganized, couldn't teach, and gave exams that were grossly unfair.		
2. My sister had a fender-bender because she is a typical female driver; when I had a fender-bender, it was because the other driver was an idiot.		
3. I don't care what he said about his car breaking down; he was fifteen minutes late for the first class, so he must be one of those inconsiderate professors who is more concerned with his research than with his students.		

Review of Terms and Concepts 1

Use the terms in this list to complete the Matching Test, then to help you answer the True/False items correctly.

social psychology
social cognition
social influence
person perception
social norms
social categorization
implicit personality
   theory
attribution

fundamental attribution
   error
blaming the victim
just-world hypothesis
actor–observer
   discrepancy
self-serving bias
self-effacing bias
   (modesty bias)

Matching Exercise

Match the appropriate term with its definition or description.

1. _____ The "rules," or expectations, for appropriate behavior in a particular social situation.

2. _____ Mental process of inferring the causes of people's behavior, including one's own. Also used to refer to the explanation made for a particular behavior.

3. _____ Tendency to attribute successful outcomes of one's own behavior to internal causes and unsuccessful outcomes to external, situational causes.

4. _____ Branch of psychology that studies how people think, feel, and behave in social situations.

5. _____ Network of assumptions or beliefs about the relationships among various types of people, traits, and behaviors.

6. _____ Tendency to attribute one's own behavior to external, situational causes while attributing the behavior of others to internal, personal causes; especially likely to occur with regard to behaviors that lead to negative outcomes.

7. _____ Tendency to blame an innocent victim of misfortune for having somehow caused the problem or for not having taken steps to avoid or prevent it.

True/False Test

Indicate whether each statement is true or false by placing T or F in the blank space next to each item.

1. ____ The effect that situational factors and other people have on an individual's behavior is called social cognition.

2. ____ The fundamental attribution error refers to the tendency to attribute the behavior of others to internal, personal characteristics while ignoring or underestimating the effects of external, situational factors; an attributional bias that is common in individualistic cultures.

3. ___ The mental processes we use to form judgments and draw conclusions about the characteristics and motives of others are called person perception.

4. ___ Social categorization refers to the mental process of classifying people into groups (or categories) on the basis of their shared characteristics.

5. ___ Social influence is the study of the mental processes people use to make sense of their social environment; it includes the study of person perception, attribution, attitudes, and prejudice.

6. ___ The self-effacing bias (modesty bias) involves blaming failure on internal, personal factors while attributing success to external, situational factors; more common in collectivistic cultures than in individualistic cultures.

7. ___ People have a tendency to blame the victim because they have a strong need to believe that the world is fair and that we get what we deserve and deserve what we get; this is called the just-world hypothesis.

Check your answers and review any areas of weakness before going on to the next section.

The Social Psychology of Attitudes

Preview Questions

Consider the following questions as you study this section of the chapter.

- How is the term *attitude* defined, and what are its three components?
- Under what conditions are attitudes most likely to determine behavior?
- What is cognitive dissonance, and how does it affect behavior?

*Read the section "The Social Psychology of Attitudes" and **write** your answers to the following:*

1. An attitude is defined as _____

   _____

2. The three components of an attitude are

   (a) _____

   (b) _____

   (c) _____

3. You are most likely to behave in accordance with your attitudes in any of five conditions:

   (a) _____

   (b) _____

   (c) _____

   (d) _____

   (e) _____

4. Cognitive dissonance is _____

   _____

   It commonly occurs in situations in which

   _____

   _____

   _____

   _____

5. Cognitive dissonance can also change _____

   _____

6. Cognitive dissonance also operates when you have to choose _____

   _____

   _____

   _____

   _____

Understanding Prejudice

Preview Questions

Consider the following questions as you study this section of the chapter.

- How is prejudice defined?
- What are in-groups, out-groups, the out-group homogeneity effect, the in-group bias, and ethnocentrism?
- How can prejudice be overcome, and what are the three steps that help reduce prejudice?

*Read the section "Understanding Prejudice" and **write** your answers to the following:*

1. Prejudice is defined as _____

   _____

2. A stereotype is _____

   _____

   _____

3. An in-group is _____

_____

An out-group is _____

_____

4. The out-group homogeneity effect refers to ____

_____

The in-group bias is _____

_____

5. Ethnocentrism is the belief _____

_____

_____

6. Psychologist Muzafer Sherif demonstrated that

_____

_____

7. Prejudice reduction at the individual level involves three steps:

(a) _____

_____

(b) _____

_____

(c) _____

_____

After you have carefully studied the preceding sections, complete the following exercises.

Concept Check 2

Read the following and write the correct term in the space provided.

1. In Zeegland, where Majib grew up, women manage all the household finances, make all the major decisions regarding the family, and earn most of the family income. The men, on the other hand, tend to spend their time "hanging out" and trying to impress each other with the way they dress. Majib's belief that all women are naturally more assertive and domineering than men reflects her _____ about gender.

2. In a discussion about gun control laws, Jerrilee said, "In my opinion, easy access to guns is the major contributing factor to the high homicide rate in the United States." This statement reflects the _____ component of Jerrilee's attitude about gun control.

3. At lunch one day, a group of fine arts majors happened to sit next to a group of engineering students. During a discussion after lunch, one of the fine arts students remarked, "Boy, those engineering students are all alike. They are so loud, pushy, and aggressive, and, unlike us, they haven't got a scrap of creativity among them!" This statement reflects the

_____

effect.

4. During a sociology class, the instructor mentioned that the Heckawe tribe considers chopped-up earthworms, sheep's eyeballs, water buffalo testicles, and live caterpillars to be delicacies. Later, while having a hamburger and fries for lunch, a student remarked that the Heckawe diet was disgusting and repulsive. Another suggested that the tribe would someday become civilized and maybe even start eating good food "just like us." These remarks illustrate a form of in-group bias called

_____

5. Sylvester was having a tough time deciding which computer to buy: the model Z5000 Spartan or its equivalent, the LX5000 MBI. With a toss of a coin, he chose the Z5000 Spartan. Initially, he was worried about his choice; however, after talking with many enthusiastic Z5000 Spartan owners, he is now very pleased that he chose the better of the two options. It is very likely that Sylvester experienced _____ when he purchased his PC, and his subsequent behavior was an attempt to _____ this unpleasant state of psychological tension.

Graphic Organizer 2

The following statements reflect attitudes about certain topics. Decide which component—cognitive, affective, or behavioral— is represented by each statement.

Statement	Component
1. I believe that the automobile is the single most destructive element on this planet.	
2. I consistently recycle paper, plastic, soda cans, glass, and other waste.	
3. I vote for antigun control advocates and give them my full support.	
4. I get really angry when I see people carelessly throwing their litter on the ground.	
5. I don't want to contribute to the pollution of our city, so I ride my bicycle or take public transportation.	
6. I am very happy when I see women doing well in what used to be male-dominated occupations.	
7. In my opinion, a woman's place is in the home, raising the kids and doing housework.	
8. I get really upset when motorists are rude and inconsiderate.	
9. I believe that the automobile is the greatest invention ever and that we need to elect politicians who will promise to build more roads and freeways.	

Review of Terms, Concepts, and Names 2

Use the terms in this list to complete the Matching Test, then to help you answer the True/False items correctly.

attitude
cognitive dissonance
prejudice
stereotype
in-group
out-group
out-group homogeneity
   effect

in-group bias
ethnocentrism
discrimination
Muzafer Sherif
jigsaw classroom
   technique

Matching Exercise

Match the appropriate term/name with its definition or description.

1. _____ American social psychologist who is best known for his "Robbers Cave" experiments to study prejudice, conflict resolution, and group processes.

2. _____ The belief that one's own culture or ethnic group is superior to all others and the related tendency to use one's own culture as a standard by which to judge other cultures.

3. _____ Learned tendency to evaluate some object, person, or issue in a particular way; such evaluations may be positive, negative, or ambivalent.

4. _____ A social group to which one belongs.

5. _____ Unpleasant state of psychological tension or arousal that occurs when two thoughts or perceptions are inconsistent; typically results from awareness that attitudes and behavior are in conflict.

6. _____ A social group to which one does not belong.

True/False Test

Indicate whether each statement is true or false by placing T or F in the blank space next to each item.

1. ___ Prejudice is a negative attitude toward people who belong to a specific social group.

2. ___ When prejudice is displayed behaviorally, it is called discrimination.

3. ___ The out-group homogeneity effect refers to the tendency to judge the behavior of in-group members favorably and out-group members unfavorably.

4. ___ A stereotype is a cluster of characteristics that are associated with all members of a specific social group, often including qualities that are unrelated to the objective criteria that define the group.

5. ___ The jigsaw classroom technique is a teaching technique that stresses cooperative, rather than competitive, learning situations.

6. ___ The in-group bias refers to the tendency to see members of out-groups as very similar to one another.

Check your answers and review any areas of weakness before going on to the next section.

Conformity: Following the Crowd

Preview Questions

Consider the following questions as you study this section of the chapter.

- What is social influence, and how is conformity defined?

- Which psychologist first studied conformity, and what did he find?

- Why do people conform, and what factors influence the degree to which people conform?

- How does culture affect conformity?

*Read the section "Conformity: Following the Crowd" and **write** your answers to the following:*

1. Social influence is _____
_____
_____

2. Conformity is the tendency to _____
_____
_____

3. In studying the degree to which people would conform to the group even when the group opinion was clearly wrong, Asch found that _____
_____
_____

4. We conform to the larger group for two basic reasons:
(a) _____
_____
(b) _____
_____

5. In a cross-cultural meta-analysis, British psychologists found that _____
_____
_____

Obedience: Just Following Orders

Preview Questions

Consider the following questions as you study this section of the chapter.

- How is obedience defined?

- What was the basic procedure in Milgram's original obedience experiment, and what were the results?

- What aspects of the experimental situation increased the likelihood of obedience?

- What factors did Milgram later discover that decreased the level of obedience?

*Read the section "Obedience: Just Following Orders" and **write** your answers to the following:*

1. Obedience is defined as _____
_____

2. The basic design of Milgram's obedience experiment was as follows: _____
_____
_____
_____

3. In contrast to predictions, the results of Milgram's original experiment showed that
_____
_____

4. Aspects of the experimental situation that had a strong impact on the subjects' willingness to continue obeying the experimenter's orders were _____
_____
_____
_____
_____
_____
_____
_____

5. Some of the situational factors that made people less willing to obey were _____
_____
_____
_____
_____
_____

Helping Behavior: Coming to the Aid of Strangers

Preview Questions

Consider the following questions as you study this section of the chapter.

- What factors increase or decrease the likelihood that people will help others?

- What is the bystander effect, and what causes it?

- What factors decrease the likelihood that people will help others?

*Read the section "Helping Behavior: Coming to the Aid of Strangers" and **write** your answers to the following:*

1. According to Latané and Darley's general model, six factors affect the likelihood of bystander intervention:

   (a) _____
   _____

   (b) _____
   _____

   (c) _____
   _____

   (d) _____
   _____

   (e) _____
   _____

   (f) _____

2. The bystander effect refers to _____
   _____
   _____

3. There are two reasons for the bystander effect:

   (a) _____
   _____
   _____

   (b) _____
   _____

4. Factors that decrease the likelihood of helping behavior are

   (a) _____
   _____

   (b) _____
   _____

   (c) _____
   _____

   (d) _____
   _____

After you have carefully studied the preceding sections, complete the following exercises.

Concept Check 3

1. Trent hates to wear ties but wears one to his sister's wedding to avoid the disapproval of his family. Trent's behavior illustrates the importance of _____ social influence.

2. Harold is a subject in a replication of Milgram's obedience experiment. If he is like most of the subjects in the experiment, he _____ (will/will not) administer high levels of shock to the learner.

3. If Harold was allowed to act as his own authority and freely choose the shock level, it is very _____ (likely/unlikely) that he will use a shock over 150 volts, the first point at which the learner is likely to protest.

4. At the end of a music concert featuring his favorite group, Jamal joined everyone else in giving the group a standing ovation. Jamal's behavior _____ (is/is not) an example of conformity.

5. Carmichael was elated when he won $1,000 in the lottery. Later that day, he gladly volunteered to spend a few hours on the weekend to help collect food for the local food bank. This illustrates the "_____" effect.

6. While about twenty subjects were filling out a questionnaire in a classroom, an odorless vapor started seeping into the room from one of the heating vents. The room slowly began to fill with the vapor, yet nobody stopped what they were doing, and nobody went to report the incident. This bystander effect occurred because the presence of other people creates a(n) _____ .

Graphic Organizer 3

Describe the main research findings of the following social psychologists. (For example, Zimbardo's grasshopper study showed how behavior can change attitude through the process of cognitive dissonance.)

Researcher	Main Research Findings
1. Asch	
2. Sherif	
3. Milgram	
4. Latané and Darley	

Review of Terms, Concepts, and Names 3

Use the terms in this list to complete the Matching Test, then to help you answer the True/False items correctly.

conformity
Solomon Asch
normative social
    influence
informational social
    influence
Stanley Milgram
obedience

Bibb Latané
John M. Darley
"feel good, do good"
    effect
bystander effect
diffusion of
    responsibility
persuasion

Matching Exercise

Match the appropriate term/name with its definition or description.

1. _____ American social psychologist who is best known for his controversial investigation of destructive obedience to an authority.

2. _____ The tendency to adjust one's behavior, attitudes, or beliefs to group norms in response to real or imagined group pressure.

3. _____ Contemporary American social psychologist who, along with co-researcher John M. Darley, is best known for his pioneering studies of bystander intervention in emergency situations.

4. _____ Performance of an action in response to the direct orders of an authority or person of higher status.

5. _____ American social psychologist who is best known for his pioneering studies of conformity.

6. _____ Contemporary American social psychologist who, along with co-researcher Bibb Latané, is best known for his pioneering studies of bystander intervention in emergency situations.

True/False Test

Indicate whether each item is true or false by placing T or F in the space next to each item.

1. ____ Persuasion is the deliberate attempt to influence the attitudes or behavior of another person in a situation in which that person has some freedom of choice.

2. ____ The bystander effect refers to the phenomenon in which the greater the number of people present, the less likely each individual is to help someone in distress.

3. ____ The phenomenon in which the presence of other people makes it less likely that any individual will help someone in distress because the obligation to intervene is shared among all the onlookers is called diffusion of responsibility.

4. ____ Source of behavior that is motivated by the desire to gain social acceptance and approval is called informational social influence.

5. ____ The "feel good, do good" effect refers to the fact that when people feel good, successful, happy, or fortunate, they are more likely to help others.

6. ____ Source of behavior that is motivated by the desire to be correct is called normative social   . influence.

Check your answers and review any areas of weakness before going on to the next section.

Something to Think About

1. People often ask, "Why are so many people reluctant to help others who are in distress and need help?" The most usual responses are that people suffer from apathy and that big cities alienate and depersonalize people. What would you say if someone asked you that question?

2. We are subjected to a wide variety of situations and stimuli that are designed to influence our attitudes or behavior. The most obvious of these are media advertisements, but we regularly encounter many other more subtle sources of attempted influence. These attempts to influence us all use techniques of persuasion. Imagine that you are hired by a company, and management wants you to write a brief summary of the factors that are most powerful in changing people's attitudes or behaviors. What would you put in your report?

Check your answers and review any areas of weakness before completing the progress tests.

Progress Test 1

Review the complete chapter (including Concept Reviews and the boxed inserts), review all your study notes, and then test yourself on the following progress test. Check your answers. If you make a mistake, review your notes, review the relevant section of the study guide, and, if necessary, go back and read the appropriate part of your textbook.

1. Dr. Lopez is a social psychologist who studies the mental processes people use to make sense of their social environment, including such topics as person perception, attribution, attitudes, and prejudice. His specific area of research is called
   (a) social cognition.
   (b) perception.
   (c) social influence.
   (d) personality.

2. About a dozen students were sitting in a small research laboratory room filling out a questionnaire when they heard a crash followed by groaning from the room next door. While many of them appeared to notice, nobody went to inform the researcher, who said he would be in his office just down the hall. This example illustrates
   (a) the actor–observer discrepancy.
   (b) diffusion of responsibility.
   (c) obedience.
   (d) informational social influence.

3. Michael, who is an accountant, often wonders why people are surprised when they find out that he is also a skydiving instructor on the weekends. The most obvious explanation is that people form cognitive schemas for different types of people and occupations. The use of these types of assumptions is called
   (a) the fundamental attribution error.
   (b) ethnocentrism.
   (c) implicit personality theory.
   (d) the self-serving bias.

4. In her field research, Dr. Safarian observes that people generally do not sit next to strangers on trains. She also notices a similar pattern in movie theaters, airport lounges, and cafeterias. Dr. Safarian is documenting the effects of _____ on behavior.
   (a) stereotypes
   (b) ethnocentrism
   (c) prejudice
   (d) social norms

5. Sally did very poorly on her last math test. If her fifth-grade teacher concludes that Sally did poorly because she is not motivated to do well in school, the teacher may be committing the
   (a) fundamental attribution error.
   (b) actor–observer discrepancy.
   (c) self-serving bias.
   (d) social categorization error.

6. When Allison landed a big contract for her firm, she accepted the credit for her hard work and smart "wheeling and dealing." When she failed to get the contract in another situation, she blamed the sneaky and dishonest tactics of the competition. This illustrates
   (a) informational social influence.
   (b) the self-serving bias.
   (c) the self-effacing bias.
   (d) the actor–observer discrepancy.

7. During a discussion on fast food and fast-food outlets, Reginald stated, "Fast food is great. I just love southern fried chicken, fries, coleslaw, and milkshakes." This statement represents the _____ component of Reginald's positive attitude toward fast-food restaurants.
   (a) cognitive   (c) behavioral
   (b) affective   (d) ambivalent

8. Faced with the equally attractive choice of either a baconburger or a cheeseburger, Jill finally decided on the cheeseburger. Shortly after she made her choice, she decided that the cheeseburger was a healthier choice and probably had fewer calories than the baconburger. Her tendency to emphasize the positive aspects of her choice and the negative aspects of the choice she rejected is an example of
   (a) diffusion of responsibility.
   (b) conformity.
   (c) prejudice.
   (d) cognitive dissonance.

9. One of Manfred's college classmates was from Turkey, and he loved turkey sandwiches, turkey pizza, turkey burgers, and turkey sausages. Manfred now believes that the main diet of all people from Turkey is centered around meals made from turkey meat, and he has little doubt why the country is called Turkey. Manfred's beliefs about the culture of Turkey reflect
   (a) ethnic stereotyping.
   (b) ethnocentrism.
   (c) informational social influence.
   (d) in-group bias.

10. Jackson joined the Alpine cross-country ski club because he couldn't afford the cost of downhill skiing. Many members of his club think that downhill skiing is destroying the natural environment, and they often make derogatory remarks about downhillers. Since joining the club, Jackson has changed his attitude about downhill skiing; he now promotes the benefits of cross-country skiing and joins his new buddies in categorizing all downhill skiers as self-centered, uncaring destroyers of the environment. This example illustrates

   (a) the out-group homogeneity effect.
   (b) in-group bias.
   (c) stereotyping.
   (d) all of the above.

11. Greg, who is a new faculty member, is on a college committee concerned with student evaluation. Greg disagrees with the proposal to institute a collegewide percentage system for grading. The other five members have already stated that they are in favor of the proposal. Greg decides that it would be in his best interests to go along with his colleagues and not risk antagonizing them, so he votes in favor of the proposed policy. This example best illustrates

   (a) obedience.
   (b) informational social influence.
   (c) in-group bias.
   (d) normative social influence.

12. All the members of the MacGregor household are enthusiastic supporters of the new community recycling program. They consistently sort their garbage by placing paper, plastic, glass, and aluminum in their respective bins. The actions of the MacGregors best illustrates the _____ component of attitudes.

   (a) emotional
   (b) behavioral
   (c) biological
   (d) cognitive

13. Just moments after dozens of people get off a crowded bus, a badly dressed man stumbles and falls on the sidewalk near the bus stop. Research on bystander intervention would suggest that

   (a) he will get immediate help from many people.
   (b) the presence of others will decrease the diffusion of responsibility.
   (c) if one person stops to help him, other people are likely to help as well.
   (d) no one in the crowd will perceive that he may need help.

14. According to Critical Thinking 11.2, which of the following is true of Milgram's experiment?

   (a) Two-thirds of the subjects completely obeyed the experimenter's destructive demands and progressed to the full 450-volt level.
   (b) Milgram was criticized because he failed to debrief the subjects after the experiment was over.
   (c) Less than 1 percent of the subjects obeyed the experimenter's destructive demands and progressed to the full 450-volt level.
   (d) The vast majority of Milgram's subjects experienced long-term traumatic reactions, such as depression, decreased self-esteem, and psychotic episodes.

15. According to the Application, which of the following is correct?

   (a) Persuasion refers to the deliberate attempt to influence the attitudes or behaviors of another person in a situation in which the person has some freedom of choice.
   (b) Persuasion techniques are not effective in manipulating people in any way.
   (c) Professional persuaders can easily manipulate and change the attitudes and behaviors of the vast majority of people.
   (d) Because of the flexible nature of social norms, the vast majority of people can resist conforming to any societal standards.

Progress Test 2

After you have checked your understanding of the material in Progress Test 1 and have done a complete chapter review with special focus on any areas of weakness, you are ready to assess your knowledge of Progress Test 2. Check your answers. If you make a mistake, review your notes, the relevant section of the study guide, and, if necessary, the appropriate part of your textbook.

1. Jake lost his job two months ago when his company downsized its operations; despite his efforts, he has not yet found another job. One of his neighbors stated that Jake is just like most unemployed people—irresponsible, unmotivated, and basically lazy. The neighbor has committed the
   (a) self-serving bias.
   (b) actor–observer discrepancy.
   (c) social categorization error.
   (d) fundamental attribution error.

2. When their town was threatened by a flood, two families who had been enemies for years ended up working together to try to save the town from the overflowing river. Generalizing from Sherif's findings, you might conclude that this act of cooperative behavior may lead to
   (a) increased antagonism once the danger has passed.
   (b) an increase in cognitive dissonance.
   (c) reduced conflict and increased harmony between the two families.
   (d) diffusion of responsibility.

3. Liliana thinks that people her parents' age are old-fashioned, critical, intolerant, and unconcerned about important social issues. Liliana is assuming that people in a particular age category have certain characteristics, even though these qualities may be unrelated to the objective criteria that define this particular age group. This example illustrates
   (a) the just-world hypothesis.
   (b) stereotyping.
   (c) ethnocentrism.
   (d) the self-effacing (modesty) bias.

4. When Rachel found out that she had straight As in all her courses, she was elated. Later that day, when she was asked if she could donate some money to the restore-the-church fund, she readily made a donation, even though she is not religious and does not go to church. This illustrates
   (a) cognitive dissonance.
   (b) the "feel good, do good" effect.
   (c) conformity.
   (d) informational social influence.

5. Studying the mental processes people use to make sense of their social situations is to _____ as studying the effects of situational factors and other people on an individual's behavior is to _____ .
   (a) social influence; social cognition
   (b) social perception; social categorization
   (c) social cognition; social influence
   (d) social categorization; social perception

6. When Inge was first elected to the student finance committee, she was asked to make a decision on some important financial matter with which she was not familiar. All the other members of the committee stated that they were going to vote against the proposal. Inge voted with the group because she assumed that they must have the correct information. This example illustrates
   (a) the bystander effect.
   (b) normative social influence.
   (c) informational social influence.
   (d) diffusion of responsibility.

7. Martha is a subject in a replication of Milgram's original obedience experiment that involves female subjects only. Compared with a similar study involving only male subjects,
   (a) at least 60 percent of the females will refuse to continue with the experiment at the 300-volt level.
   (b) a much higher percentage of the females will obey the experimenter and progress to the 450-volt level.
   (c) only about 10 percent of the female subjects will obey the experimenter and progress to the 450-volt level.
   (d) the results of the all-female replication will be the same as the all-male condition.

8. In the study described in question 7, if the experimenter leaves the room and gives the directions over the phone, it is very likely that
   (a) the level of compliance will be the same as if the experimenter was in the room.
   (b) the level of compliance will be greater than if the experimenter was in the room.
   (c) the level of compliance will be significantly lower than if the experimenter was in the room.
   (d) none of the subjects will follow the experimenter's instructions and progress to the 450-volt level.

9. Quincy has reviewed the literature on conformity and obedience for a term paper. He is most likely to conclude that
   (a) virtually nobody is capable of resisting group or authority pressure.
   (b) all people are innately predisposed to be cruel and aggressive.
   (c) conformity and obedience are not necessarily bad in and of themselves and are important for an orderly society.
   (d) all of the above are true.

10. Jorge thought that either horse, Con Brio or White Lightening, had an equal chance of winning the next race and was debating which one to bet on. After he placed his money on Con Brio, however, he felt very confident that he had backed the winner. This example illustrates the effect of
    (a) cognitive dissonance.
    (b) the self-serving bias.
    (c) conformity.
    (d) social influence.

11. Jenny got 90 percent on her biology midterm exam, Jean got 60 percent, and Jackie got 75 percent. On the basis of their scores on the exam, Jackie thinks to herself that Jenny must be really intelligent and that Jean must be a little slow. Which of the following is true?
    (a) Jackie has made an attribution.
    (b) Jackie's assessment of her classmates' intelligence is accurate.
    (c) Jackie's evaluation reflects the in-group bias.
    (d) Jackie's assessment of her classmates' intelligence reflects her prejudice.

12. During a discussion about gun control laws, Marylou said, "I believe it is every American's fundamental right to own a gun and that the government has no right to pass laws banning the ownership of guns under any circumstances." This statement reflects the _____ component of Marylou's attitude about guns and gun-control laws.
    (a) cognitive   (c) behavioral
    (b) affective   (d) dissonant

13. Yoko was late for work because the traffic was particularly heavy. When she arrived at the office, she apologized to her boss, insisting that it was her fault for being late; if she were less lazy, it wouldn't have happened. This example of blaming an accidental occurrence on an internal, personal disposition rather than on situational factors is called the
    (a) self-serving bias.
    (b) fundamental attribution error.
    (c) actor–observer discrepancy.
    (d) self-effacing bias (modesty bias).

14. According to Culture and Human Behavior 11.1, collectivistic and individualistic cultures differ in their attributional biases. In general, compared with members of individualistic cultures, how likely are members of collectivistic cultures to commit the fundamental attribution error?
    (a) more likely
    (b) less likely
    (c) just as likely
    (d) All of the above are equally likely.

15. A number of persuasion techniques are used by professional marketers. According to the Application, which of the following is *not* one of those techniques?
    (a) the door-in-the-face technique
    (b) the that's-not-all technique
    (c) the foot-in-the-mouth technique
    (d) the low-ball technique
    (e) the foot-in-the-door technique

Progress Test 3

After you have checked your understanding of the material in Progress Tests 1 and 2, and have done a complete chapter review with special focus on any areas of weakness, you are ready to further assess your knowledge on Progress Test 3. Check your answers. If you make a mistake, review your notes, the appropriate parts of the study guide, and, if necessary, the relevant sections of your textbook.

1. Dr. Saroya is a social psychologist whose research interests focus on how our behavior is affected by situational factors and other people, and in particular why we conform to group norms and why we help or don't help strangers. The basic area of social psychology that Dr. Saroya studies is called
   (a) social cognition.
   (b) social perception.
   (c) social influence.
   (d) social categorization.

2. When Ruby got on the subway, she quickly looked around and decided it would be safer to sit next to the middle aged, well-dressed woman than the man with bright orange hair and earrings. Ruby has engaged in the process of
   (a) blaming the victim.
   (b) person perception.
   (c) ethnocentrism.
   (d) cognitive dissonance.

3. When Mr. Denbridge was asked to donate to a fund to help people infected with hepatitis B and the HIV virus, he responded that he would not help these people because they caused their own misfortunes. It appears that Mr. Denbridge is
   (a) blaming the victim.
   (b) demonstrating the out-group homogeneity effect.
   (c) responding to normative social influence.
   (d) reducing his cognitive dissonance.

4. During a tour of a Latin America country, Susanne was surprised to find that almost everyone took a long three-hour break in the middle of the day. She concluded that, compared with the United States, this country was not doing well economically because everyone was lazy, lacked motivation, and spent too much time sleeping. Susanne's conclusion reflects a form of in-group bias called
   (a) ethnocentrism.
   (b) the self-effacing bias.
   (c) the self-serving bias.
   (d) the actor–observer discrepancy.

5. In her fifth grade class, Miss Tausig uses a technique for improving cooperation that involves students working together in small, ethnically diverse groups on a mutual project. Miss Tausig is using the
   (a) out-group homogeneity procedure.
   (b) jigsaw classroom technique.
   (c) normative social influence technique.
   (d) actor–observer discrepancy technique.

6. Vince suggests that his sister's aggressive behavior results from her insecurity. Vince's explanation for his sister's behavior is an example of
   (a) stereotyping.
   (b) the bystander effect.
   (c) an attribution.
   (d) cognitive dissonance.

7. Kyle is in sixth grade and, like most children in his school, he believes that his school is better than all the other schools in town. This best illustrates
   (a) in-group bias.
   (b) ethnic stereotyping.
   (c) cognitive dissonance.
   (d) the fundamental attribution error.

8. Seeing a skier wipe out on a steep section of the run, Jenny comments, "A klutz like that shouldn't be allowed on the slopes!" Later, when Jenny wipes out in the same place, she blames the icy conditions. This is an example of
   (a) the self-serving bias.
   (b) the actor–observer discrepancy.
   (c) social categorization.
   (d) stereotyping.

9. Pietro notices that when there are empty seats on the bus, nobody ever sits beside a stranger, but when the bus is crowded, people sit beside strangers all the time. He noticed that the same thing happens in movie theaters, the cafeteria, and even the classroom. Pietro's observation suggests that people's behavior in these situations is governed by
    - (a) prejudice.
    - (b) social categorization.
    - (c) stereotypes.
    - (d) social norms.

10. Fraser loves wearing sandals or thongs and hates wearing shoes. However, when he went out to dinner with his girlfriend's family, he wore shoes because he did not want to evoke their disapproval. Fraser's behavior best illustrates the importance of
    - (a) informational social influence.
    - (b) normative social influence.
    - (c) diffusion of responsibility.
    - (d) obedience.

11. While Lyle was alone in a classroom filling out a questionnaire, an odorless vapor started seeping slowly into the room from one of the heating vents. In this situation, it is very likely that Lyle will leave the room and report the strange odor to someone. If Lyle was in the room with a large group of other people who were also filling out questionnaires, it is much less likely that he would report the vapor. The difference in Lyle's behavior is best explained by
    - (a) the bystander effect.
    - (b) the just-world hypothesis.
    - (c) altruism.
    - (d) cognitive dissonance.

12. When Maryjane steps into the elevator, she quickly looks at the other passengers and decides that the gray-haired man with the beard must be a professor at the college. Maryjane has engaged in the process of
    - (a) prejudicial thinking.
    - (b) discrimination.
    - (c) social categorization.
    - (d) ethnocentrism.

13. During cross-examination, a witness repeatedly offers his opinion in answer to the lawyer's questions, so the judge orders him to confine his answers to a simple "yes" or "no." Following the judge's rebuke, the witness stops offering his opinions. This example best illustrates
    - (a) obedience.
    - (b) conformity.
    - (c) persuasion.
    - (d) prejudice.

14. According to Critical Thinking 11.2, which of the following is true of Milgram's research?
    - (a) It created a controversy that led to the establishment of ethical safeguards by the American Psychological Association and the federal government regarding experiments involving human subjects.
    - (b) It was criticized for causing the subjects emotional stress, tension, and loss of dignity.
    - (c) It demonstrated, much to everyone's surprise, that the majority of subjects would obey an authority figure even if it apparently meant hurting another person.
    - (d) All of the above are true.

15. According to Culture and Human Behavior 11.1, which of the following is true of the self-effacing bias (modesty bias)?
    - (a) It refers to the tendency to blame an innocent victim of misfortune for having somehow caused the problem or for not having taken steps to avoid or prevent it.
    - (b) It involves blaming failure on internal, personal factors while attributing success to external, situational factors.
    - (c) It refers to the tendency to assume that the world is fair and that therefore people get what they deserve and deserve what they get.
    - (d) It involves attributing successful outcomes of one's own behavior to internal causes and unsuccessful outcomes to external, situational causes.

Answers

Introduction: Social Psychology

1. *Social psychology is* the branch of psychology that studies how people think, feel, and behave in social situations.

2. *Social cognition refers to* the study of the mental processes people use to make sense out of their social environment.

3. *Social influence focuses on* the study of the effects of situational factors and other people on an individual's social behavior.

Person Perception: Forming Impressions of Other People

1. *Person perception refers to* the mental processes we use to form judgments and draw conclusions about the characteristics and motives of others; it is an active and subjective process that always occurs in some interpersonal context.

2. *The four basic principles of person perception are (a)* Your reactions to others are determined by your perceptions of them, not by who or what they really are. *(b)* Your goals in a particular situation determine the amount and kind of information you collect about others. *(c)* In every situation, how you expect people to act in that situation partly determines how you evaluate them (you make reference to the social norms for the appropriate behavior in a particular social situation). *(d)* Your self-perception also influences how you perceive others and how you act on your perceptions.

3. *In combination, these four basic principles underscore that person perception is* not a one-way process in which we objectively survey other people, then logically evaluate their characteristics. Instead, the context, our self-perceptions, and the perception we have of others all interact.

4. *Social categorization is* the mental process of classifying people into groups (or categories) on the basis of their shared characteristics. This is mostly automatic and spontaneous and occurs outside of conscious awareness. *Its advantages and disadvantages are* that it ignores a person's unique qualities. On the other hand, it is natural and adaptive.

5. *An implicit personality theory is* a network of assumptions or beliefs about the relationships among various types of people, traits, and behaviors. *Like social categories, implicit personality theories are useful* as mental shortcuts in perceiving other people; however, they are not always accurate and in some instances can be dangerously misleading.

Attribution: Explaining Behavior

1. *Attribution is* the mental process of inferring the causes of people's behavior, including one's own (also refers to the explanation made for a particular behavior).

2. *The fundamental attribution error is the tendency to* attribute the behavior of others to internal, personal characteristics, while ignoring or underestimating the effects of external, situational factors.

3. *Blaming the victim is the tendency to* blame an innocent victim of misfortune for having somehow caused the problem or for not having taken steps to avoid or prevent it.

4. *The just-world hypothesis is* the assumption that the world is fair and that therefore people get what they deserve and deserve what they get.

5. *The actor–observer discrepancy is the tendency to* attribute one's own behavior to external, situational causes, while attributing the behavior of others to internal, personal causes, especially when the outcome is likely to be negative.

6. *The self-serving bias is the tendency to* attribute successful outcomes of our own behavior to internal causes and unsuccessful outcomes to external, situational causes.

Concept Check 1

1. self-serving bias
2. fundamental attribution error
3. actor–observer discrepancy
4. implicit personality theory
5. social norms
6. blaming the victim; just-world hypothesis

Graphic Organizer 1

1. C; INT for own success; EXT for own failure
2. B; EXT for self; INT for other
3. A; INT for other

Matching Exercise 1

1. social norms
2. attribution
3. self-serving bias
4. social psychology
5. implicit personality theory
6. actor–observer discrepancy
7. blaming the victim

True/False Test 1

| 1. F | 3. T | 5. F | 7. T |
| 2. T | 4. T | 6. T | |

The Social Psychology of Attitudes

1. *An attitude is defined as* a learned tendency to evaluate some object, person, or issue in a particular way; such evaluations may be positive, negative, or ambivalent.

2. *The three components of an attitude are (a)* cognitive (your thoughts and conclusions about a given topic or object); *(b)* affective (your feelings or emotions about a given topic or object); and *(c)* behavioral (your attitude is reflected in your actions).

3. *You are most likely to behave in accordance with your attitudes when (a)* your attitudes are extreme or are frequently expressed; *(b)* your attitudes have been formed through direct experience; *(c)* you are very knowledgeable about the subject; *(d)* you have a vested interest in the subject; and *(e)* you anticipate a favorable outcome or response from others.

4. *Cognitive dissonance is* an unpleasant state of psychological tension or arousal (dissonance) that occurs when two thoughts or perceptions (cognitions) are inconsistent. *It commonly occurs in situations in which* you become uncomfortably aware that your behavior and your attitudes conflict with each other. If you can easily change your behavior to make it consistent with your attitude, then any dissonance can be quickly and easily resolved. When your behavior cannot be easily changed, you will tend to change your attitude to make it consistent with your behavior.

5. *Cognitive dissonance can also change* the strength of an attitude so that it is consistent with some behavior you've already performed.

6. *Cognitive dissonance also operates when you have to choose* between two basically equal alternatives; each choice has desirable and undesirable features, creating dissonance. Once you make a choice, however, you immediately bring your attitudes more closely into line with that commitment, reducing the dissonance; you emphasize the negative features of the choice you rejected and the positive features of the choice you made.

Understanding Prejudice

1. *Prejudice is defined as* a negative attitude toward people who belong to a specific social group.

2. *A stereotype is* a cluster of characteristics that are associated with all members of a specific social group, often including qualities that are unrelated to the objective criteria that define the group.

3. *An in-group is* a social group to which one belongs. *An out-group is* a social group to which one does not belong.

4. *The out-group homogeneity effect refers to* the tendency to see members of out-groups as very similar to one another. *The in-group bias is* the tendency to judge the behavior of in-group members favorably and out-group members unfavorably.

5. *Ethnocentrism is the belief* that one's own culture or ethnic group is superior to all others and the related tendency to use one's own culture as a standard by which to judge other cultures.

6. *Psychologist Muzafer Sherif demonstrated that* prejudice an be overcome when rival groups cooperate to achieve a common goal.

7. *Prejudice reduction at the individual level involves three steps: (a)* Individuals must decide that prejudiced responses are wrong and consciously reject prejudice and stereotyped thinking. *(b)* They must internalize their nonprejudiced beliefs so that those beliefs become an integral part of their personal self-concept. *(c)* Individuals must learn to inhibit automatic prejudicial reactions and deliberately replace them with nonprejudiced responses that are based on their personal standards.

Concept Check 2

1. stereotype
2. cognitive
3. out-group homogeneity
4. ethnocentrism
5. cognitive dissonance; reduce

Graphic Organizer 2

1. cognitive
2. behavioral
3. behavioral
4. affective
5. behavioral
6. affective
7. cognitive
8. affective
9. cognitive

Matching Exercise 2

1. Muzafer Sherif
2. ethnocentrism
3. attitude
4. in-group
5. cognitive dissonance
6. out-group
7. prejudice

True/False Test 2

1. T	3. F	5. T
2. T	4. T	6. F

Conformity: Following the Crowd

1. *Social influence is* the study of the effects of situational factors and other people on an individual's behavior.

2. *Conformity is the tendency to* adjust one's behavior, attitudes, or beliefs to group norms in response to real or imagined group pressure.

3. *In studying the degree to which people would conform to the group even when the group opinion was clearly wrong, Asch found that* the vast majority conformed with the group judgment on at least one of the critical trials in the line judgment task.

4. *We conform to the larger group for two basic reasons: (a).* normative social influence (we want to be liked and accepted by the group; *(b)* informational social influence (we want to be right; when we're uncertain or doubt our own judgment, we may look to the group as a source of accurate information).

5. *In a cross-cultural meta-analysis, British psychologists found that* conformity is generally higher in collectivistic cultures than in individualistic cultures.

Obedience: Just Following Orders

1. *Obedience is defined as* the performance of an action in response to the direct orders of an authority or person of higher status.

2. *The basic design of Milgram's obedience experiment was as follows:* the subject (the teacher) thought he was delivering ever-increasing levels of electric shock to another person (the learner); if the teacher protested that he wished to stop, he was instructed by the experimenter to continue with the experiment.

3. *In contrast to predictions, the results of Milgram's original experiment showed that* most of the subjects (two-thirds) obeyed the experimenter and progressed to the maximum shock level.

4. *Aspects of the experimental situation that had a strong impact on the subjects' willingness to continue obeying the experimenter's orders were* the subjects had a previously well-established mental framework to obey; the context or situation influenced them (they believed the experiment would advance scientific knowledge and may have felt that defying the experimenter's orders would make them appear arrogant, rude, disrespectful, or uncooperative); the gradual, repetitive escalation of the task; the experimenter's behavior and reassurances (the experimenter took responsibility for the learner's well-being); and the physical and psychological separation from the learner.

5. *Some of the situational factors that made people less willing to obey were* when the buffers that separated the teacher from the learner were lessened or removed, such as when both of them were put in the same room; when subjects (teachers) were allowed to act as their own authority and freely choose the shock level, 95 percent of them did not go beyond 150 volts; and if the teacher observed two other teachers rebel and refuse to continue, then the obedience rate dropped to 10 percent.

Helping Behavior: Coming to the Aid of Strangers

1. *According to Latané and Darley's general model, six factors affect the likelihood of bystander intervention: (a)* We tend to be more helpful when we're feeling good, successful, happy or fortunate (the feel good, do good effect). *(b)* We tend to be more helpful when we're feeling guilty, such as after telling a lie or inadvertently causing an accident. *(c)* Seeing others who are willing to help increases the likelihood that we will help. *(d)* We're more likely to help people who are perceived as deserving, such as people who are in need through no fault of their own. *(e)* Knowing how to help contributes greatly to the decision to help someone else. *(f)* Any sort of personal relationship (even the most minimal social interaction, such as making eye contact or engaging in small talk) increases the likelihood that one person will help another.

2. *The bystander effect refers to* the phenomenon in which the greater the number of people present, the less likely each individual is to help someone in distress.

3. *There are two reasons for the bystander effect: (a)* The presence of other people creates a diffusion of responsibility, which means that the responsibility to intervene is shared (or diffused) among the other onlookers (because no one person feels all the pressure to respond, each bystander becomes less likely to help).

(b) Each of us is motivated to some extent by the desire to behave in a socially acceptable way (normative social influence) and to appear correct (informational social influence), and consequently we often rely on the reactions of others to help us define the situation and guide our responses.

4. *Factors that decrease the likelihood of helping behavior are (a)* the presence of other people (if other people are present, helping behavior declines, a phenomenon called the *bystander effect*); *(b)* being in a big city or a very small town (people are less likely to help a stranger in very big cities [300,000 people or more] or in very small towns [5,000 people or less], but you are more likely to get help in towns with populations in between these two extremes); *(c)* when situations are vague or ambiguous and people are not certain that help is needed, such as in domestic disputes or a lovers' quarrel; and, *(d)* as a general rule, we tend to weigh the costs as well as the benefits in deciding whether to help others (when the cost of helping outweighs the benefit, we tend not to help).

Concept Check 3

1. normative
2. will
3. unlikely
4. is not
5. feel good, do good
6. diffusion of responsibility

Graphic Organizer 3

1. Naive subjects yielded to group pressure in the line-judging task even though the group opinion was wrong.
2. The Robbers Cave study helped clarify the conditions that produce intergroup conflict and harmony and led to the use of the jigsaw classroom technique to promote cooperative behavior.
3. Dramatic illustration of the pressure to obey an authority figure's request to shock another person in a mock learning experiment.
4. Showed the conditions under which people are more likely to help a stranger in distress as well as the factors that decrease helping behavior.

Matching Exercise 3

1. Stanley Milgram
2. conformity
3. Bibb Latané
4. obedience
5. Solomon Asch
6. John M. Darley

True/False Test 3

1. T	4. F
2. T	5. T
3. T	6. F

Something to Think About

1. Why is it that people do not help others who are in obvious distress? What prevents bystanders from intervening? In some instances, such as in the Kitty Genovese case, people could easily help by simply making a phone call, but often they don't. Latané and Darley have developed a model that addresses the question of why people don't intervene. Some of the most obvious factors, if intervention is to occur, are that people have to notice the event or incident, they need to believe it is a situation in which help is needed, they should feel some sense of responsibility to help, and, finally, knowing how to deal with the situation is useful.

   Latané and Darley's final model identifies six specific factors that increase the likelihood that bystanders will help: (1) the "feel good, do good" effect, (2) feeling guilty, (3) seeing others who are willing to help, (4) perceiving others as deserving help, (5) knowing how to help, and (6) a personal relationship with the person who needs help.

   A number of factors decrease the likelihood of bystanders helping: (1) the presence of others, called the bystander effect, and the resulting diffusion of responsibility; (2) being in a big city or a very small town; (3) a vague or ambiguous situations; and (4) when the personal costs for helping outweigh the benefits. In a discussion of this issue it is important to be able to explain and give examples of each factor.

2. The summary in the Application "The Persuasion Game" provides the information you need to answer this question. First, define persuasion, then paraphrase the main strategies

that professional persuaders use to manipulate people's attitudes and behaviors. These include the role of reciprocity, the door-in-the-face technique, the that's-not-all technique, the rule of commitment, the foot-in-the-door technique, and the low-ball technique. You might also want to integrate material from the chapter, such as the role of cognitive dissonance in changing cognitions and behavior, and various aspects of conformity and obedience research. Finally, you should discuss the ways in which people can defend themselves against professional persuasion techniques—for example, sleeping on it, playing the devil's advocate, and paying attention to gut feelings.

Progress Test 1

1. a	6. b	11. d
2. b	7. b	12. b
3. c	8. d	13. c
4. d	9. a	14. a
5. a	10. d	15. a

Progress Test 2

1. d	6. c	11. a
2. c	7. d	12. a
3. b	8. c	13. d
4. b	9. c	14. b
5. c	10. a	15. c

Progress Test 3

1. c	6. c	11. a
2. b	7. a	12. c
3. a	8. b	13. a
4. a	9. d	14. d
5. b	10. b	15. b

CHAPTER

12

Stress, Health, and Coping

<table>
<tr>
<td>PREVIEW</td>
<td>Reading the section below first will give you a general sense of the chapter's contents and an initial introduction to some of the major concepts and terms. This will prime you for what you are about to read and help you to develop a "cognitive map" that will guide your study of the material in this chapter. Likewise, reading the preview questions at the beginning of each major section will improve your ability to understand, learn, and retain the information.</td>
</tr>
</table>

CHAPTER 12 . . . AT A GLANCE

Chapter 12 deals with the effects of stress on health and the ways in which people cope with stress. Health psychologists study stress and other psychological factors that influence health, illness, and treatment and are guided by the biopsychosocial model. The life events approach to stress first developed in the 1960s is critically examined. More recently, researchers have focused on the importance of daily hassles, conflict, and social and cultural factors as sources of stress.

The physical effects of stress are discussed. Walter Cannon's fight-or-flight response and Hans Selye's three-stage general adaptation syndrome are described. Ader and Cohen's research on conditioning the immune system and its influence on the foundation of psychoneuroimmunology are presented along with research findings on the effects of stress on the immune system.

Psychological factors can also influence our response to stress. People's sense of personal control and their explanatory style—optimistic or pessimistic—are important in determining how a person responds to stress. The text notes that chronic negative emotions are related to the development of some chronic diseases and that Type A behavior patterns can predict the development of heart disease, with the most critical component being hostility. The role of social support in how people deal with stressful situations is explored.

The final section covers coping strategies. Depending on the situation, people use problem-focused or emotion-focused coping. Culture affects the choice of coping strategies; individualistic and collectivistic coping strategies are compared and contrasted.

Introduction: What Is Stress?

Preview Questions

Consider the following questions as you study this section of the chapter.

- How is stress defined, and what is the main focus of health psychology?
- What is the biopsychosocial model?

*Read the section "Introduction: What Is Stress?" and **write** your answers to the following:*

1. Stress is defined as _____

_____

_____

2. Health psychologists focus on_____

_____

_____

3. The biopsychosocial model is _____

_____

_____

What Is Stress?: Sources of Stress

Preview Questions

Consider the following questions as you study this section of the chapter.

- What are stressors, and what are some of the most important sources of stress?
- What is the life events approach, and what problems are associated with this approach?
- What are daily hassles and conflict, and how do they contribute to stress?
- How can social and cultural factors become sources of stress?

*Read the section "What Is Stress?: Sources of Stress" and **write** your answers to the following:*

1. Stressors are _____

_____

2. Early stress researchers Holmes and Rahe believed that _____

_____

_____

3. Several problems with the life events approach have been pointed out:

(a) _____

_____

(b) _____

_____

(c) _____

_____

(d) _____

_____

4. Daily hassles are _____

_____

_____

5. Conflict is the _____

_____

6. The three basic types of conflict are:

(a) _____

_____

(b) _____

_____

(c) _____

_____

7. Social factors that are a source of stress include

_____

_____

8. In terms of culture, stress can result when

_____

_____

After you have carefully studied the preceding sections, complete the following exercises.

Concept Check 1

Read the following and write the correct term in the space provided.

1. Dr. Woodworth studies stress, how psychological factors influence health, illness, treatment, and health-related behaviors. Dr. Woodworth is a _____ psychologist.

2. If Dr. Woodworth is like most psychologists in his specialty area, he adheres to the theory that health and illness are determined by the complex interaction of biological, psychological, and social factors. In other words, he is guided by the _____ model.

3. In the past year, Frank has been divorced, moved twice, and started a new relationship. In addition, he has received a promotion and a big raise at work but now has many more responsibilities. His score on the Social Readjustment Rating scale is likely to be _____ (high/low); according to the scale's developers, Homes and Rahe, Frank has a(n) _____

(increased/decreased) likelihood of developing serious physical or psychological problems.

4. According to Richard Lazarus, Frank's major life events may create a ripple effect and generate a host of _____ that may accumulate to cause even greater stress.

5. Janet can only take one course this semester because of work commitments. She is torn between two courses she really wants to take, each of which fits her work schedule. Janet is probably experiencing an _____ conflict.

Graphic Organizer 1

Read the following descriptions and decide which type of stress-producing conflict is involved: approach-approach, avoidance-avoidance, or approach-avoidance. In addition, label each one as producing either a high, medium, or low level of stress.

Description	Type of Conflict/ Level of Stress (low/medium/high)
1. Lyndle wants to maintain a high grade-point average and needs to study hard before his exam tomorrow, but he has been asked by his girlfriend to go with her to a party this evening.	
2. A rat in the start box of a Y-shaped maze with two separate goal boxes at the end of each prong will receive an equally desirable food pellet in each one.	
3. Annalee is very happy to be doing well on her diet but now has to decide whether to go for lunch with her friends at her favorite Greek taverna or stay in the lunchroom and eat her low-calorie snack.	
4. In order to be able to borrow the family car for the evening, Jason has to decide between doing two equally unappealing chores, the family laundry or washing and waxing the bathroom and kitchen floors.	
5. Virginia entered her name in a contest and was overwhelmed when she won a seven-day Caribbean cruise. She has to decide between a seven-day eastern Caribbean cruise or a seven-day western Caribbean cruise.	
6. Melvin is overweight and out of shape and is given a choice of two daily exercise regimens by his doctor, one involving 40 minutes of running, riding an exercise bike, and weightlifting and the other involving 40 minutes of rowing machine, step-up machine, and weightlifting.	

Review of Terms, Concepts, and Names 1

Use the terms in this list to complete the Matching Test, then to help you answer the True/False items correctly.

stressors
stress
health psychology
biopsychosocial model
Social Readjustment
  Rating Scale
Richard Lazarus
daily hassles

conflict
approach-approach
  conflict
avoidance-avoidance
  conflict
approach-avoidance
  conflict
acculturative stress

Matching Exercise

Match the appropriate term/name with its definition or description.

1. _____ American psychologist who helped promote the cognitive perspective in the study of emotion and stress; developed the cognitive appraisal model of stress and coping with coresearcher Susan Folkman.

2. _____ Basic type of conflict in which you're faced with a choice between two equally appealing outcomes. As a rule, these conflicts are usually easy to resolve and don't produce much stress.

3. _____ Situation in which a person feels pulled between two or more opposing desires, motives, or goals.

4. _____ Everyday minor events that annoy and upset people.

5. _____ The branch of psychology that studies how psychological factors influence health, illness, and medical treatment as well as health-related behaviors.

6. _____ Model that guides the work of health psychologists. According to this model, health and illness are determined by the complex interaction of biological, psychological, and social factors.

True/False Test

Indicate whether each statement is true or false by placing T or F in the blank space next to each item.

1. ____ Stress refers to events or situations that are perceived as harmful, threatening, or challenging.

2. ____ The Social Readjustment Rating Scale was developed by Thomas Holmes and Richard Rahe in an attempt to measure the amount of stress people experienced as a function of life events that are likely to require some level of adaptation.

3. ____ An approach-avoidance conflict has a single goal with both desirable and undesirable aspects. When faced with this conflict, people often vacillate, or repeatedly go back and forth in their minds, unable to decide to approach or avoid the goal.

4. ____ Stressors refer to negative emotional states that occur in response to events that are perceived as taxing or exceeding a person's resources or ability to cope.

5. ____ An avoidance-avoidance conflict involves choosing between two unappealing or undesirable outcomes. People often delay making a decision when faced with this conflict, or they may bail out altogether.

6. ____ The stress that results from the pressure of adapting to a new culture is called acculturative stress.

Check your answers and review any areas of weakness before going on to the next section.

Physical Effects of Stress: The Mind–Body Connection

Preview Questions

Consider the following questions as you study this section of the chapter.

- How can stress contribute to health problems both directly and indirectly?

- What is the fight-or-flight response, and what role do catecholamines play?

- What is the general adaptation syndrome, and what endocrine pathways are involved?

*Read the section "Physical Effects of Stress: The Mind–Body Connection" and **write** your answers to the following:*

1. Stress can indirectly affect a person's health by

_____

_____

2. High levels of stress can also interfere with

_____

_____

3. Stress can directly affect physical health by

_____

_____

4. The fight-or-flight response refers to _____

_____

_____

_____

5. Catecholamines are _____

_____

_____

6. The general adaptation syndrome is _____

_____

_____

_____

7. Selye found that prolonged stress activates a

_____

_____

_____

Physical Effects of Stress: Stress and the Immune System

Preview Questions

Consider the following questions as you study this section of the chapter.

- What is the immune system, and what is its function?
- What did the work of Ader and Cohen demonstrate, and what new interdisciplinary field was created?
- What is psychoneuroimmunology, and how does the immune system interact with the nervous system?
- What kinds of stressors affect immune system functioning?

*Read the section "Physical Effects of Stress: Stress and the Immune System" and **write** your answers to the following:*

1. The elements of the immune system are _____

_____

_____

The function of this system is _____

_____

_____

2. Psychologist Robert Ader and immunologist Nicholas Cohen demonstrated that _____

_____

_____

3. Psychoneuroimmunology is _____

_____

_____

4. The three main findings of psychoneuroimmunological research are:

(a) _____

_____

(b) _____

_____

(c) _____

_____

5. Extremely stressful events reduce _____

_____

_____

_____

6. Psychologist Janice Kiecolt-Glaser, immunologist Ronald Glaser, and others have found that

_____

_____

_____

After you have carefully studied the preceding sections, complete the following exercises.

Concept Check 2

Read the following and write the correct term in the space provided.

1. When Hans was hiking on a trail in the wilderness, he unexpectedly encountered a large brown bear and her two cubs. Hans froze in his tracks, and his heartbeat, blood pressure, and pulse increased dramatically. Fortunately, the bear and the cubs took off into the bush. The rapidly occurring chain of internal physical reactions that Hans experienced was described by Walter Cannon as the

   _____ response.

2. The physiological changes that Hans experienced when he was startled resulted from his sympathetic nervous system stimulating the adrenal medulla to secrete hormones called

   _____ .

3. After overcoming the initial shock of finding her new car badly damaged by a hit-and-run driver, Wilma phones the police and becomes actively involved in seeking witnesses to the incident. At this point it is most likely that Wilma is in the _____ stage of the general adaptation syndrome.

4. Dr. Laslo believes that there is an interaction among psychological processes, the nervous and endocrine systems, and the immune system and that each system influences and is influenced by the other systems. It is very likely that Dr. Laslo works in the new interdisciplinary field called _____ .

5. When Georgia was under a lot of stress, she became ill due to a viral infection. In response to this infection, the most important elements in her immune system, called

   _____ , will try to defend against the foreign invader.

Review of Terms, Concepts, and Names 2

Use the terms in this list to complete the Matching Test, then to help you answer the True/False items correctly.

fight-or-flight response
Walter Cannon
catecholamines
Hans Selye
general adaptation
  syndrome
alarm stage
resistance stage

exhaustion stage
corticosteroids
immune system
lymphocytes
Robert Ader
psychoneuroimmunology
Janice Kiecolt-Glaser

Matching Exercise

Match the appropriate term/name with its definition or description.

1. _____ American psychologist who made several important contributions to psychology, especially in the study of emotions; he described the fight-or-flight response, which involves the sympathetic nervous system and the endocrine system.

2. _____ Specialized white blood cells that are responsible for immune defenses.

3. _____ Hormones, including adrenaline and noradrenaline, secreted by the adrenal medulla that cause rapid physiological arousal.

4. _____ Canadian endocrinologist who was a pioneer in stress research; defined stress as "the nonspecific response of the body to any demand placed on it" and described a three-stage response to prolonged stress that he called the general adaptation syndrome.

5. _____ Hormones released by the adrenal cortex that play a key role in the body's response to long-term stressors.

6. _____ The first stage of the general adaptation syndrome, during which intense arousal occurs as the body mobilizes internal physical resources to meet the demands of the stress-producing event.

7. _____ Body system that produces specialized white blood cells that protect the body from viruses, bacteria, and tumor cells.

True/False Test

Indicate whether each statement is true or false by placing T or F in the blank space next to each item.

1. ___ Robert Ader is the American psychologist who, with immunologist Nicholas Cohen, first demonstrated that immune system responses could be classically conditioned; helped establish the new interdisciplinary field of psychoneuroimmunology.

2. ___ The rapidly occurring chain of internal physical reactions that prepare people to either fight or take flight from an immediate threat is called the general adaptation syndrome.

3. ___ In the resistance stage of the general adaptation syndrome, the body actively tries to resist or adjust to the continuing stressful situation.

4. ___ Janice Kiecolt-Glaser is the American psychologist who, with immunologist Ronald Glaser, conducted extensive research on the effect of stress on the immune system.

5. ___ The fight-or-flight response is Hans Selye's term for the three-stage progression of physical changes that occur when an organism is exposed to intense and prolonged stress.

6. ___ Psychoneuroimmunology is an interdisciplinary field that studies the interconnections among psychological processes, nervous and endocrine system functions, and the immune system.

7. ___ In the exhaustion stage of the general adaptation syndrome, the symptoms of the alarm stage reappear, only this time irreversibly; as the body's energy reserves become depleted, adaptation begins to break down, leading to exhaustion, physical disorders, and, potentially, death.

Check your answers and review any areas of weakness before going on to the next section.

Individual Factors That Influence the Response to Stress

Preview Questions

Consider the following questions as you study this section of the chapter.

- What are the psychological factors that can affect our response to stress?

- How do feelings of control, explanatory style, and negative emotions influence stress and health?

- What is Type A behavior, and what role does hostility play in its relationship to health?

Read the section "Individual Factors That Influence the Response to Stress" (up to "Social Factors") and ***write*** *your answers to the following:*

1. Psychological factors that influence responses to stressful events include _____
   _____
   _____
   _____
   _____

2. According to psychologist Martin Seligman, how people characteristically explain _____
   _____
   _____
   _____

3. Explanatory style is related to health consequences in that _____
   _____
   _____

4. Two effects of chronic negative emotions on health are that_____
   _____
   _____
   _____

5. Type A behavior pattern refers to _____
   _____
   _____

   The critical component (and the strongest predictor of cardiac disease) in this type of behavior pattern is _____
   _____
   _____

6. High levels of hostility are associated with
   _____
   _____
   _____
   _____

Individual Factors That Influence the Response to Stress: Social Factors

Preview Questions

Consider the following questions as you study this section of the chapter.

- What is meant by social support, and how does it benefit health?
- How can social supports sometimes increase stress?
- What gender differences have been found in the effects of social support?

*Read the section "Individual Factors That Influence the Reaction to Stress: Social Factors" and **write** your answers to the following:*

1. Social support refers to _____

   _____

2. Social support may benefit our health and improve our ability to cope with stressors by

   (a) _____

   _____

   (b) _____

   _____

   (c) _____

   _____

3. Conversely, relationships with others can also be a significant source of stress for two reasons:

   (a) _____

   _____

   (b) _____

   _____

4. Some of the main gender differences in social support are:

   (a) _____

   _____

   (b) _____

   _____

   (c) _____

   _____

   (d) _____

Coping: How People Deal with Stress

Preview Questions

Consider the following questions as you study this section of the chapter.

- How is *coping* defined?
- What are the two basic forms of coping, and when is each typically used?
- What are some of the most common coping strategies, and how does culture affect coping style?

*Read the section "Coping: How People Deal with Stress" and **write** your answers to the following:*

1. Coping refers to _____

   _____

2. The two basic types of coping (and their uses) are _____

   _____

   _____

   _____

3. Problem-focused coping strategies include

   (a) _____

   _____

   (b) _____

   _____

4. Emotion-focused coping strategies include

   (a) _____

   _____

   (b) _____

   _____

   (c) _____

   _____

   (d) _____

   _____

   (e) _____

   _____

5. In terms of coping strategy, members of individualistic cultures tend to

   _____

   _____

   _____

   _____

Members of collectivistic cultures tend to

_____

_____

_____

_____

_____

*After you have carefully studied the preceding
sections, complete the following exercises.*

Concept Check 3

*Read the following and write the correct term in the
space provided.*

1. When Marie turned down Massimo's offer to go
   out for dinner on Friday night, he was very disappointed. Upon reflection, however, he decided
   that Marie was really not his type anyway, and
   he'd be better off going out with someone else.
   Massimo's rationalization of the situation
   reflects a(n) _____ explanatory
   style.

2. When asked by her therapist to describe her
   husband, Cheryl said that he was very competitive and ambitious, he was always very busy,
   and any demands made on his time angered
   and irritated him. Cheryl's description suggests
   that her husband may have a(n) _____
   behavior pattern.

3. Irene constantly complains about her health,
   her job, and in general everything about her
   life. She tends to dislike most of the people she
   meets and always seems to be in a grouchy
   mood. It appears that Irene suffers from
   _____ emotions.

4. Masayuki is a member of a group of engineers
   in a large industrial plant in Tokyo. When
   things get stressful, Masayuki tries to control
   the outward expression of his emotions and
   endeavors to accept the situation with maturity,
   serenity, and flexibility. Masayuki is using a(n)
   _____ coping strategy, which is
   more characteristic of collectivistic cultures
   than of individualistic cultures.

5. Shortly after he lost his job and his relationship
   with his girlfriend ended, Jim went to visit his
   family. Unfortunately, being with his family
   made him feel worse. The only time he felt better was when he was with the family dog. It is
   possible that Jim perceived his family as being
   _____ and the dog as being
   _____ and unconditionally supportive.

6. Although Lambert was very disappointed when
   he didn't even come close to winning his first
   mountain bike race, he concluded that all his
   training and the knowledge he gained from the
   experience were beneficial. Lambert is using a
   very constructive emotion-focused strategy
   called _____ .

Graphic Organizer 2

*Read the following statements and decide which researcher(s)
is (are) most likely to have expressed these views:*

Statement	Researcher(s)
1. I believe that when we are faced with danger or any threatening or stress-producing situation we have an immediate physical reaction that involves the sympathetic nervous system and the endocrine system and the release of catecholamines. I call these internal physical changes the fight-or-flight response.	
2. When we published the results of our research, we realized that we were challenging the prevailing scientific view that the immune system operates independently of the brain and psychological processes. However, our results, which demonstrated that the immune response in rats could be classically conditioned, have been replicated by many other researchers.	
3. We were two of the earliest researchers to study stress. In an attempt to measure the amount of stress people experienced, we developed the Social Readjustment Rating Scale. Our view at the time was that any changes, either positive or negative, would cause stress and that high levels of stress, as measured by life change units, would lead to the development of serious physical and psychological problems.	
4. My research on stress, which I define as the nonspecific response of the body to any demand, led me to postulate a three-stage model to prolonged stress, called the general adaptation syndrome. I believe that the stress response involves the hypothalamus, pituitary gland, adrenal cortex, and release of hormones such as ACTH and corticosteroids.	
5. My view is that what causes us problems in the long run is not so much the major life events, which do cause stress, but the cumulative effect of daily hassles that annoy, irritate, and upset people. I have developed a scale to measure these hassles. The number of daily hassles is a better predictor of physical illness and symptoms than the number of major life events experienced.	
6. In my view, it is the way people characteristically explain their failures and defeats that determines who will persist and who will not. I think there are two basic types of explanatory style, an optimistic explanatory style and a pessimistic explanatory style. Those who use a pessimistic explanatory style experience more stress than those who use an optimistic explanatory style.	
7. We are a husband-and-wife team who collected immunological and psychological data from medical students, who face three-day exam periods several times each academic year. We have consistently found that even the rather commonplace stress of exams adversely affects the immune system.	

Review of Terms, Concepts, and Names 3

Use the terms in this list to complete the Matching Test, then to help you answer the True/False items correctly.

Martin Seligman
optimistic explanatory
   style
pessimistic explanatory
   style
Type A behavior pattern
Type B behavior pattern
social support
stress contagion effect
coping
problem-focused coping

emotion-focused coping
confrontive coping
planful problem solving
escape-avoidance
seeking social support
distancing
denial
positive reappraisal
emotional support
tangible support
informational support

Matching Exercise

Match the appropriate term/name with its definition or description.

1. _____ Behavioral and cognitive responses used to contend with stressors; involves efforts to change circumstances, or one's interpretation of circumstances, to make them more favorable and less threatening.

2. _____ Problem-focused coping strategy in which the person relies on aggressive or risky efforts to change the situation.

3. _____ American psychologist who conducted research on explanatory style and the role it plays in stress, health, and illness.

4. _____ Emotion-focused coping strategy in which the person shifts his or her attention away from the stressor and toward other activities.

5. _____ Behavioral and emotional style characterized by a sense of time urgency, hostility, and competitiveness.

6. _____ Category of social support that includes the expression of concern, empathy, and positive regard.

7. _____ Gender difference in the effects of social support that results from women becoming upset about negative life events that happen to other people.

8. _____ Resources provided by other people in times of need, including emotional support, tangible support, and informational support.

9. _____ Emotion-focused coping strategy that involves turning to friends, relatives, or other people for emotional, tangible, or informational support.

10. _____ Emotion-focused coping strategy that involves the refusal to acknowledge that the problem exists.

True/False Test

Indicate whether each item is true or false by placing T or F in the space next to each item.

1. ____ An optimistic explanatory style involves accounting for negative events or situations with internal, stable, and global explanations.

2. ____ The Type B behavior pattern is a behavioral and emotional style characterized by a relatively relaxed and laid-back approach to situations and problems.

3. ____ Informational social support involves direct assistance, such as providing transportation, lending money, or helping with meals, child care, or household tasks.

4. ____ Emotion-focused coping efforts are aimed primarily at relieving or regulating the emotional impact of a stressful situation.

5. ____ The most constructive emotion-focused coping strategy is positive reappraisal, which involves not only minimizing the negative emotional aspects of the situation but also trying to create positive meaning by focusing on personal growth.

6. ____ A pessimistic explanatory style involves accounting for negative events or situations with external, unstable, and specific explanations.

7. ____ An emotion-focused coping strategy in which the individual acknowledges the stressor but attempts to minimize or eliminate its emotional impact is called distancing.

8. ____ Problem-focused coping efforts are aimed primarily at directly changing or managing a threatening or harmful stressor.

9. ____ A problem-focused coping strategy that involves efforts to rationally analyze the situation, identify potential solutions, and then implement them is called planful problem solving.

10. ____ Tangible social support involves offering helpful suggestions and advice to a person in distress.

Check your answers and review any areas of weakness before going on to the next section.

Something to Think About

It sometimes seems that everyone you meet is stressed out. There are things to be done, deadlines to be met, social and family obligations, financial pressures, work-related problems, and so on. How can people cope with all this stress? Is there anything that can be done? Fortunately, there are several strategies for coping with stress. What advice would you give someone who is experiencing stress?

Check your answers and review any areas of weakness before completing the progress tests.

Progress Test 1

Review the complete chapter (including Concept Reviews and the boxed inserts), review all your study notes, and then test yourself on the following progress test. Check your answers. If you make a mistake, review your notes, review the relevant section of the study guide, and, if necessary, go back and read the appropriate part of your textbook.

1. Natasha experienced a great deal of anxiety when she had three exams on the same day. In this situation the exams are _____ and her response is called _____ .
   (a) stress; stressor
   (b) the biological component; the cognitive component
   (c) stressors; stress
   (d) the social component; the biological component

2. Dr. Turnbull uses the biopsychosocial model to guide his research into how psychological factors influence health, illness, and treatment. Dr. Turnbull is most likely a
   (a) developmental psychologist.
   (b) health psychologist.
   (c) psychoneuroimmunologist.
   (d) psychiatrist.

3. Donald scored 300 points on the Social Readjustment Rating Scale. What does that mean?
   (a) It is absolutely certain that Donald will develop physical and psychological problems.
   (b) It is impossible to accurately predict whether Donald will develop physical and psychological problems.
   (c) Donald has probably experienced very few daily hassles during the past year.
   (d) Donald's subjective appraisal of the events in his life during the previous year will have no bearing on his health and well-being.

4. Del got up late and nicked himself three times while shaving. When he poured his coffee, he found that there was no cream in the fridge; then, as he was tying his shoe laces, one of them broke. Richard Lazarus would call these incidents
   (a) major life events.   (c) minor life events.
   (b) daily hassles.   (d) life change units.

5. To earn money so that he can buy a ticket to a rock concert, Ken has to either wash and wax the two family cars or wash and wax the kitchen and bathroom floors. In trying to decide between these two equally unappealing choices, Ken is likely to experience an _____ conflict.
   (a) approach-avoidance
   (b) approach-approach
   (c) avoidance-avoidance
   (d) escape-avoidance

6. Yui is leaving Japan to work and live in the United States and is very excited about the move. When Yui arrives and starts work in the United States, she is likely to
   (a) be much more relaxed and laid back than she was in Japan.
   (b) experience increased levels of stress due to the acculturation process.
   (c) become physically and psychologically ill within weeks.
   (d) adapt to the new environment without experiencing any stress whatsoever.

7. When Nibras was chased and attacked by a dog during his regular morning run, he experienced the classic symptoms of the fight-or-flight response. According to Walter Cannon, it is likely that his sympathetic nervous system stimulated his adrenal medulla to secrete hormones called

   (a) catecholamines.   (c) corticosteroids.
   (b) ACTH.   (d) lymphocytes.

8. After overcoming the initial shock of having his house broken into and many of his personal possessions stolen, Vincent calls the police for help and starts thinking of ways to help catch the burglar and retrieve his belongings. At this point, Vincent is most likely in the _____ stage of the general adaptation syndrome.

   (a) alarm   (c) exhaustion
   (b) resistance   (d) denial

9. When Claudia became ill because of a viral infection, her immune system kicked into high gear to defend her by producing

   (a) lymphocytes.   (c) catecholamines.
   (b) corticosteroids.   (d) noradrenaline.

10. Dr. Blackman studies the interconnections among psychological processes, the nervous and endocrine systems, and the immune system. Like other specialists in the field of psychoneuroimmunology, Dr. Blackman is aware that researchers have discovered that

    (a) the central nervous system and the immune system are directly linked.
    (b) the surfaces of lymphocytes contain receptor sites for neurotransmitters and hormones, including catecholamines and cortisol.
    (c) lymphocytes themselves produce neurotransmitters and hormones.
    (d) all of the above are true.

11. When Darcy was taking his statistics exam, he was very anxious and nervous. According to researchers such as Janice Kiecolt-Glaser, the stress of exams

    (a) adversely affects the immune system.
    (b) has no effect on the immune system.
    (c) has a beneficial effect on the immune system.
    (d) does none of the above.

12. Whenever anything goes wrong in his life, Dean typically feels that it must be something about him that causes the problem; he also believes that no amount of personal effort will improve his situation. Martin Seligman would say that Dean has

    (a) a Type A behavior pattern.
    (b) an optimistic explanatory style.
    (c) a Type B behavior pattern.
    (d) a pessimistic explanatory style.

13. After his third month of low sales, Allen is called into the sales manager's office and told that he had better start meeting his quota or he will be laid off. The manager appears to be coping with the problem of low sales by using a(n) _____ strategy called _____ .

    (a) problem-focused; confrontive coping
    (b) emotion-focused; escape-avoidance
    (c) problem-focused; planful problem solving
    (d) emotion-focused; distancing

14. According to Culture and Human Behavior 12.1, which of the following is not a pattern of acculturation?

    (a) integration   (d) marginalization
    (b) assimilation   (e) disembarkation
    (c) separation

15. Critical Thinking 12.3, which discusses personality and disease, points out that psychologists and other scientists are cautious in reaching conclusions about the connection between personality and health for which of the following reasons?

    (a) Many studies investigating the role of psychological factors in disease are correlational.
    (b) Personality factors might indirectly lead to disease via poor health habits.
    (c) It may be that the disease influences a person's emotions, rather than the other way around.
    (d) All of the above factors are true.

Progress Test 2

After you have checked your understanding of the material in Progress Test 1 and have done a complete chapter review with special focus on any areas of weakness, you are ready to assess your knowledge of Progress Test 2. Check your answers. If you make a mistake, review your notes, the relevant section of the study guide, and, if necessary, the appropriate part of your textbook.

1. When Janeen was caught in a large traffic jam, she experienced a severe headache. In this case, the traffic jam is to _____ as her headache is to _____ .
   (a) fight; flight
   (b) stressor; stress
   (c) flight; fight
   (d) stress; stressor

2. For his birthday, Liam has to decide between a pair of skis and a mountain bike. In trying to decide between these two equally attractive alternatives, Liam is likely to experience an _____ conflict.
   (a) approach-avoidance
   (b) approach-approach
   (c) avoidance-avoidance
   (d) escape-avoidance

3. Fifty-five-year-old Maxwell is a very impatient and competitive defense lawyer who feels that he must be the best in his field. In addition, he has a reputation for being hostile toward judges and prosecuting attorneys. Maxwell is likely to be classified as having a(n)
   (a) Type A behavior pattern.
   (b) pessimistic explanatory style.
   (c) Type B behavior pattern.
   (d) optimistic explanatory style.

4. In the above example, it is very likely that Maxwell is at high risk for developing heart disease. The component of his behavior that is most likely to contribute to health problems is his
   (a) impatience.
   (b) competitiveness
   (c) achievement orientation.
   (d) hostility.

5. Heloise is an emergency room nurse. Whenever she has a particularly hectic and stressful shift, she and some of the other nurses find themselves making fun of the patients and the doctors. Heloise is using an emotion-focused coping strategy called
   (a) confrontive coping.
   (b) denial.
   (c) distancing.
   (d) positive reappraisal.

6. Madge wants advice on how to cope with the stress of returning to college after being out of school for a number of years. She would be best advised to approach her classes
   (a) with a sense of personal control and optimism.
   (b) with a realistic but pessimistic attitude.
   (c) using an emotion-focused coping strategy called distancing.
   (d) using an emotion-focused coping strategy called denial.

7. Whenever Beth experiences problems in her relationship with her fiancee, she typically talks to her family about her troubles. Beth is using a(n) _____ strategy called _____ .
   (a) problem-focused; confrontive coping
   (b) emotion-focused; distancing
   (c) problem-focused; planful problem solving
   (d) emotion-focused; seeking social support

8. While researching a paper for her psychology class, Joyce came across the research of Ader and Cohen on conditioning and immune system functioning. She is likely to conclude that their work was important for which of the following reasons?
   (a) It challenged the prevailing scientific view that the immune system operates independently of the brain and psychological processes.
   (b) It demonstrated that humans could be conditioned to salivate just like Pavlov's dogs.
   (c) Before their research was published, everyone believed that there was a strong interconnectedness among psychological processes, nervous and endocrine system functions, and the immune system.
   (d) It proved conclusively that the immune system could not be classically conditioned.

9. After a bank was robbed, the bank tellers and the customers got up off the floor, where they had been held at gunpoint. Because it was such a frightening experience, they are likely to have experienced a rapidly occurring chain of internal physical reactions called

    (a) daily hassles.
    (b) the fight-or-flight response.
    (c) the general adaptation syndrome.
    (d) the stress contagion effect.

10. Following the bank robbery, the people who were very frightened probably experienced increased activation of the sympathetic nervous system, stimulation of the adrenal medulla, and the release of hormones called

    (a) lymphocytes.   (c) testosterone.
    (b) catecholamines.   (d) estrogen.

11. During her final year of medical training, Lissette was under constant pressure; she never seemed to get enough sleep, was anxious and nervous most of the time, and experienced many physical symptoms and disorders. As a result of this prolonged stress, it is likely that her hypothalamus, pituitary gland, and adrenal cortex will work together to release stress-related hormones called

    (a) lymphocytes.   (c) corticosteroids.
    (b) catecholamines.   (d) acetylcholine.

12. Gregory was very disappointed when he wasn't accepted to the graduate program at State University. Upon reflection, however, he decided that the preparations he made in putting his application together and the knowledge he gained from the interview were very beneficial experiences. Gregory is using a(n) _____ strategy called _____ .

    (a) problem-focused; confrontive coping
    (b) emotion-focused; positive reappraisal
    (c) problem-focused; planful problem solving
    (d) emotion-focused; escape-avoidance

13. According to the Application, which of the following is *not* recommended for helping someone in distress?

    (a) Express affection for the person, whether by a warm hug or simply a pat on the arm.
    (b) Be a good listener and show concern and interest.
    (c) Ask questions that encourage the person under stress to express his or her feelings and emotions.
    (d) Give advice that the person has not asked for.
    (e) Be willing to invest time and attention in helping.

14. In Focus 12.2, which discusses the relationship between stress and the common cold, concludes that

    (a) stress reduces the effectiveness of the immune system and its ability to fight off viruses, bacteria, and other foreign invaders.
    (b) factors such as health-compromising behaviors provide the underlying stress-illness connection.
    (c) highly stressed people get sick more often because they interact with more people than do people with little stress.
    (d) all of the above are true.

15. According to Culture and Human Behavior 12.1, the term *acculturative stress* refers to the

    (a) coping strategies used by immigrants.
    (b) stress that results from the pressure of adapting to a new culture.
    (c) stress-producing events and situations that occur when people leave home and move to a different city.
    (d) final stage of the general adaptation syndrome.

Progress Test 3

After you have checked your understanding of the material in Progress Tests 1 and 2, and have done a complete chapter review with special focus on any areas of weakness, you are ready to further assess your knowledge on Progress Test 3. Check your answers. If you make a mistake, review your notes, the appropriate parts of the study guide, and, if necessary, the relevant sections of your textbook.

1. Richard Lazarus is to _____ as Hans Selye is to _____ .

    (a) daily hassles; the general adaptation syndrome
    (b) the fight-or-flight response; the cognitive appraisal model
    (c) classically conditioning the immune system; the general adaptation syndrome
    (d) daily hassles; life event units

2. When Argento encountered a wild cougar on the hiking trail, he experienced acute stress. Which of the following would Walter Cannon consider the correct sequence involved in Argento's fight-or-flight response?
   (a) pituitary; hypothalamus; ACTH release, sympathetic nervous system.
   (b) secretion of corticosteroids, ACTH release, perspiration, cognitive appraisal.
   (c) hypothalamus, sympathetic nervous system, adrenal medulla, secretion of catecholamines
   (d) perspiration, ACTH release, respiration, parasympathetic nervous system, secretion of catecholamines

3. If Dr. Penman is like most researchers in the field of psychoneuroimmunology he is likely to hold the view that
   (a) it is impossible to classically condition the immune system.
   (b) the immune system works independently of other body systems.
   (c) there are interconnections between the endocrine system and the immune system functions, but psychological processes operate independently.
   (d) there are interconnections among psychological processes, nervous and endocrine system functions, and the immune system.

4. Rita and Richard both have a large network of social relationships, including close friends and family members. Compared with Richard, Rita may be potentially vulnerable to some of the problematic aspects of social support because
   (a) women are less likely than men to serve as providers of support.
   (b) women, in general, are more likely than men to suffer from the stress contagion effect.
   (c) women tend to rely on a close personal relationship with their spouse and place less importance on relationships with other people.
   (d) women are less likely than men to become upset about what happens to their friends and relatives.

5. Reena has a very successful accounting practice and frequently works sixty hours or more a week. She has to manage her time efficiently in order to keep up with the demands of her career and family life. Despite all the pressure, Reena loves her job, is always kind and considerate to her employees, and has a very cheerful personality. Which of the following is most likely to be true of Reena?
   (a) Because of her very stressful lifestyle, she is likely to have very high levels of corticosteroids.
   (b) She is at a very high risk for coronary disease and other health problems.
   (c) She is very likely to develop coronary disease because of her Type A behavior pattern.
   (d) Because she is low in hostility, her risk of developing coronary disease is no higher than that of anyone else.

6. Forty-year-old Lannie is a widow, lives alone, has very few friends, and rarely interacts with other people except at work. Research suggests that compared with people who have many social contacts and relationships, social isolation such as Lannie's is correlated with
   (a) higher-than-normal levels of catecholamines.
   (b) poor health and higher death rates.
   (c) lower-than-normal levels of corticosteroids.
   (d) good health and lower death rates.

7. In replicating Ader and Cohen's original research, Dr. Andrews and his colleagues also found that the suppression of the immune system was influenced by
   (a) Type A behavior.
   (b) the general adaptation syndrome.
   (c) classical conditioning.
   (d) aerobic exercise.

8. Kari is a very laid-back, easygoing mail carrier. She loves her job because it allows her to meet people and get daily exercise. Kari is likely to be classified as having a
   (a) Type A behavior pattern.
   (b) high risk of heart disease.
   (c) Type B behavior pattern.
   (d) stress contagion syndrome.

9. Jacob was one of the unsuccessful candidates for a job, and naturally he was disappointed. However, in his habitual manner, he thought that he would have better luck next time, especially if he took some additional training to make himself more qualified for the position. Martin Seligman would say that Jacob has a(n)

   (a) Type A behavior pattern.
   (b) optimistic explanatory style.
   (c) problem-focused coping style.
   (d) pessimistic explanatory style.

10. Helga, a college student, was offered a new job. On the plus side, the higher salary and increased benefits are appealing; on the down side, she will have to work longer hours, take on extra responsibilities, and have a longer commute to work. She needs the extra money but she also needs to keep her high GPA at college. Helga is likely experiencing a type of conflict called _____ conflict.

    (a) approach-approach
    (b) avoidance-avoidance
    (c) escape-avoidance
    (d) approach-avoidance

11. Anders, a fifty-two-year-old insurance salesman, is unexpectedly called into the sales manager's office and told that he is going to be laid off because the company is downsizing. Which stage of the general adaptation syndrome is Anders likely experiencing?

    (a) alarm stage   (c) exhaustion stage
    (b) resistance stage   (d) denial stage

12. Dr. Chambers has a very busy clinical practice. To clear his mind of all the problems he faces each day and to cope with the high level of stress, he goes to the gym for a workout four or five times a week. Dr. Chambers is using a(n) _____ coping strategy called _____ .

    (a) emotion-focused; escape-avoidance
    (b) problem-focused; denial
    (c) emotion-focused; wishful thinking
    (d) problem-focused; confrontive coping

13. When Lester was having personal and academic problems in college, he went to see one of the counselors, who provided some helpful suggestions to improve his study habits and advised him to enroll in a remedial course to improve his writing skills. According to the Application, the type of social support that Lester received is called _____ support.

    (a) emotional   (c) informational
    (b) tangible   (d) confrontive

14. According to In Focus 12.4, which of the following strategies is recommended for minimizing stress?

    (a) Exercise regularly.
    (b) Avoid or minimize stimulants.
    (c) Regularly practice a relaxation technique.
    (d) All of the above are recommended.

15. Having moved to the United States from China two years ago, Mi-Ling feels equally comfortable with her new American friends and with her Chinese relatives. According to Culture and Human Behavior 12.1, Mi-Ling has adopted the acculturation pattern of

    (a) assimilation.   (c) marginalization.
    (b) separation.   (d) integration.

Answers

Introduction: What Is Stress?

1. *Stress is defined as* a negative emotional state occurring in response to events that are perceived as taxing or exceeding a person's resources or ability to cope.

2. *Health psychologists focus on* how psychological factors influence health, illness, medical treatments, and health-related behaviors.

3. *The biopsychosocial model is* the belief that physical health and illness are determined by the complex interactions of biological, psychological, and social factors.

What Is Stress?: Sources of Stress

1. *Stressors are* events or situations that are perceived as harmful, threatening, or challenging.

2. *Early stress researchers Holmes and Rahe believed that* any change, whether positive or negative, that required you to adjust your behavior or lifestyle would cause stress (they developed the Social Readjustment Rating Scale in an attempt to measure the amount of stress people experienced).

3. *Several problems with the life events approach have been pointed out: (a)* The link between scores on the Social Readjustment Rating Scale and the development of physical and psychological problems is relatively weak. *(b)* Most people don't develop physical or mental problems as a result of major life events. *(c)* The Social Readjustment Rating Scale does not take into account a person's subjective appraisal of an event, response to that event, or ability to cope with the event (it assumes that a given life event will have the same impact on virtually everyone). *(d)* The life events approach assumes change in itself, whether good or bad, produces stress (research has shown that health is most adversely affected by negative life events, especially when they are unexpected or uncontrollable, whereas positive or desirable events are much less likely to affect health adversely).

4. *Daily hassles are* everyday minor events that annoy and upset people. The frequency of daily hassles is linked to psychological distress and physical symptoms: The number of daily hassles people experience is a better predictor of physical illness and symptoms than the number of major life events experienced.

5. *Conflict is the* feeling of being pulled between two or more opposing desires, motives, or goals.

6. *The three basic types of conflict are (a)* approach-approach conflict (a win-win situation in which the choice is between two equally appealing outcomes); *(b)* avoidance-avoidance conflict (in which the choice is between two unappealing or undesirable outcomes); and *(c)* approach-avoidance conflict (a very stressful situation in which the goal has both desirable and undesirable aspects).

7. *Social factors that are a source of stress include* crowding, crime, unemployment, poverty, racism, inadequate health care, and substandard housing (people in the lowest socioeconomic levels of society tend to have the highest levels of psychological distress, illness, and death).

8. *In terms of culture, stress can result when* cultures clash; for refugees, immigrants, and their children, adapting to a new culture can be extremely stress-producing.

Concept Check 1

1. health
2. biopsychosocial
3. high; increased
4. daily hassles
5. approach-approach

Graphic Organizer 1

1. approach-avoidance; high
2. approach-approach; low
3. approach-avoidance; high
4. avoidance-avoidance; medium
5. approach-approach; low
6. avoidance-avoidance; medium

Matching Exercise 1

1. Richard Lazarus
2. approach-approach conflict
3. conflict
4. daily hassles
5. health psychology
6. biopsychosocial model

True/False Test 1

1. F	3. T	5. T
2. T	4. F	6. T

Physical Effects of Stress: The Mind–Body Connection

1. *Stress can indirectly affect a person's health by* prompting behavior that jeopardizes physical well-being; people under chronic stress are more likely to use alcohol, coffee, and cigarettes than are people under less stress.

2. *High levels of stress can also interfere with* cognitive abilities, such as attention, concentration, and memory; in turn, such disruptions can increase the likelihood of accidents and injuries.

3. *Stress can directly affect physical health by* altering body functions, leading to symptoms, illness, or disease (for example, stress can cause neck and head muscles to contract and tighten, resulting in stress-induced headaches).

4. *The fight-or-flight response refers to* a rapidly occurring chain of internal physical reactions that prepare people to either fight or take flight from an immediate threat (involves both the sympathetic nervous system and the endocrine system).

5. *Catecholamines are* hormones secreted by the adrenal medulla that cause rapid physiological arousal (they include adrenaline and noradrenaline).

6. *The general adaptation syndrome is* Selye's term for the three-stage progression of physical changes that occur when an organism is exposed to intense and prolonged stress; the three stages are alarm, resistance, and exhaustion.

7. *Selye found that prolonged stress activates a* second endocrine pathway that involves the hypothalamus, the pituitary gland, and the secretion of a hormone called adrenocorticotropic hormone (ACTH), which in turn stimulates the adrenal cortex to release stress-related hormones called corticosteroids, the most important being cortisol.

Physical Effects of Stress: Stress and the Immune System

1. *The elements of the immune system are* the bone marrow, the spleen, the thymus, and lymph nodes. Most important are the lymphocytes, which are manufactured in the bone marrow. *The function of this system is* to detect and battle foreign invaders, such as bacteria, viruses, and tumor cells.

2. *Psychologist Robert Ader and immunologist Nicholas Cohen demonstrated that* the immune system response in rats could be classically conditioned; their research helped establish a new interdisciplinary field called psychoneuroimmunology.

3. *Psychoneuroimmunology is* the scientific study of the interconnections among psychological processes (psycho-), the nervous system (-neuro-), and the immune system (-immunology).

4. *The three main findings of psychoneuroimmunological research are (a)* The central nervous system and the immune system are directly linked; the sympathetic nervous system fibers go into virtually every organ of the immune system, directly influencing the production and functioning of lymphocytes. *(b)* The surfaces of lymphocytes contain receptor sites for neurotransmitters and hormones, including catecholamines and cortisol. *(c)* Lymphocytes themselves produce neurotransmitters and hormones, which in turn influence the nervous and endocrine systems.

5. *Extremely stressful events reduce* immune system functioning. Thus, common negative life events, such as the end or disruption of important interpersonal relationships and chronic stressors that continue for years, can diminish immune system functioning.

6. *Psychologist Janice Kiecolt-Glaser, immunologist Ronald Glaser, and others have found that* even the rather commonplace stress of exams adversely affects the immune system and that brief exposure to a psychological stressor, such as performing a frustrating task for 30 minutes or less, can temporarily alter immune system responses.

Concept Check 2

1. fight-or-flight
2. catecholamines
3. resistance
4. psychoneuroimmunology
5. lymphocytes

Matching Exercise 2

1. Walter Cannon
2. lymphocytes
3. catecholamines
4. Hans Selye
5. corticosteroids
6. alarm stage
7. immune system

True/False Test 2

1. T   5. F
2. F   6. T
3. T   7. T
4. T

Individual Factors That Influence the Response to Stress

1. *Psychological factors that influence responses to stressful events include* people's appraisal of the event and their resources for coping with it;

having a sense of control over the stressful situation; and being able take steps to minimize or avoid the stressor (in contrast, feeling a lack of control over events produces all the landmarks of the stress response: Levels of catecholamines and corticosteroids increase, and the effectiveness of immune system decreases).

2. *According to psychologist Martin Seligman, how people characteristically explain* their failures and defeats makes the difference: People who have an optimistic explanatory style tend to use external, unstable, and specific explanations for negative events; people who have a pessimistic explanatory style use internal, stable, and global explanations for negative events.

3. *Explanatory style is related to health consequences in that* Explanatory style in early adulthood predicts physical health status decades later; those with optimistic explanatory styles have significantly better health than those with pessimistic explanatory styles.

4. *Two effects of chronic negative emotions on health are that* people who are habitually anxious, depressed, angry, and hostile are more likely to develop diseases such as arthritis or heart disease, and people who are tense, angry, and unhappy experience more stress than happier people (they also report more frequent and intense daily hassles and react much more intensely to the stressful events they encounter).

5. *The Type A behavior pattern refers to* a behavioral and emotional style characterized by a sense of time urgency, hostility, and competitiveness. *The critical component (and the strongest predictor of cardiac disease) in this type of behavior pattern is* hostility, which refers to the tendency to feel anger, annoyance, and contempt and to hold negative beliefs about human nature in general.

6. *High levels of hostility are associated with* suspiciousness, mistrust, cynicism, and pessimism; an increased likelihood of dying from all natural causes, including cancer; increased blood pressure, heart rate, and the production of stress-related hormones; more intense reactions to stressors and a tendency to create more stress; and more severe negative life events and daily hassles than other people.

Individual Factors That Influence the Response to Stress: Social Factors

1. *Social support refers to* the resources provided by other people in times of need.

2. *Social support may benefit our health and improve our ability to cope with stressors by* (a) modifying our appraisal of a stressor's significance, including the degree to which we perceive it as threatening or harmful (simply knowing that support and assistance are readily available may make the situation seem less threatening); (b) decreasing the intensity of physical reactions to a stressor; and (c) making us less likely to experience negative emotions (in contrast, loneliness and depression are unpleasant emotional states that increase levels of stress hormones and negatively affect immune system functioning).

3. *Conversely, relationships with others can also be a significant source of stress for two reasons:* (a) Negative interactions with other people are more effective in creating psychological distress than positive interactions are in improving well-being. (b) When people are perceived as being judgmental, their presence may increase the individual's physical reaction to a stressor.

4. *Some of the main gender differences in social support are:* (a) Women are more likely than men to serve as providers of support, which can be a very stressful role. (b) Women may be more likely to suffer from the stress contagion effect, becoming upset about negative life events that happen to other people whom they care about. (c) Men are more likely to be distressed only by negative events that happen to their immediate family—their wives and children. (d) Men generally tend to rely heavily on a close relationship with their spouse, placing less importance on relationships with other people (women, in contrast, are more likely to list close friends along with their spouses as confidants).

Coping: How People Deal with Stress

1. *Coping refers to* behavioral and cognitive responses used to deal with stressors; it involves efforts to change circumstances, or our interpretations of circumstances, to make them more favorable and less threatening.

2. *The two basic types of coping (and their uses) are* problem-focused coping (aimed at managing or changing a threatening or harmful stressor) and emotion-focused coping (aimed at relieving or regulating the emotional impact of the stressful situation).

3. *Problem-focused coping strategies include (a)* confrontive coping (relying on aggressive or risky efforts to change the situation) and *(b)* planful problem solving (rationally analyzing the situation, identifying potential solutions, and then implementing them).

4. *Emotion-focused coping strategies include (a)* escape-avoidance (shifting attention away from the stressor and toward other activities, with the basic goal of escaping or avoiding the stressor and neutralizing distressing emotions), *(b)* seeking social support (turning to friends, relatives, or other people for emotional, tangible, or informational support), *(c)* distancing (acknowledging the stressor while attempting to minimize or eliminate its emotional impact), *(d)* denial (the refusal to acknowledge that the problem even exists), and *(e)* positive reappraisal (minimizing the negative emotional aspects of the situation but also trying to create positive meaning by focusing on personal growth).

5. *In terms of coping strategies, members of individualistic cultures tend to* emphasize personal autonomy and personal responsibility in dealing with problems (they are less likely to seek social support in stressful situations than are members of collectivistic cultures) and to favor problem-focused strategies, such as confrontive coping and planful problem solving. *Members of collectivistic cultures tend to* be more oriented toward their social group, family, or community and to seek help with their problems; they also place greater emphasis on controlling personal reactions to a stressful situation rather than trying to control the situation itself.

Concept Check 3

1. optimistic

2. Type A

3. chronic negative

4. emotion-focused

5. judgmental; nonjudgmental

6. positive reappraisal

Graphic Organizer 2

1. Walter Cannon

2. Robert Ader and Nicholas Cohen

3. Thomas Holmes and Richard Rahe

4. Hans Selye

5. Richard Lazarus

6. Martin Seligman

7. Janice Kiecolt-Glaser and Ronald Glaser

Matching Exercise 3

1. coping

2. confrontive coping

3. Martin Seligman

4. escape-avoidance

5. Type A behavior pattern

6. emotional support

7. stress contagion effect

8. social support

9. seeking social support

10. denial

True/False Test 3

1. F	5. T	9. T
2. T	6. F	10. F
3. F	7. T	
4. T	8. T	

Something to Think About

A good place to start in giving advice to someone is to explain what stressors are and what the stress reaction is. Identifying potential sources of stress, from major life events to daily hassles, is useful, and noting how our subjective cognitive appraisal of stressors influences our reactions is also important. It is also helpful to know about physical reactions and psychological and social factors that influence our response to stress.

People vary a great deal in the way they respond to distressing events. Psychologists have identified several different factors that influence an individual's response to stressful events. Having a sense of control reduces the impact of stressors and decreases feelings of anxiety and depression. The type of explanatory style we use—optimistic, pessimistic, or, as in most cases, somewhere in between—can also have an effect on our health.

People with a pessimistic explanatory style tend to have poorer physical health, whereas people with an optimistic, confident, and generally positive outlook have better immune system responses and better physical health. Furthermore, chronically grouchy people experience more stress, have more frequent and intense daily hassles, and generally react with far greater distress to stressful events.

Many different strategies can be used to deal with stress, some of which are more adaptive than others. Having good social support is beneficial, but so too are the types of strategies that we adopt to cope with distressing events. Problem-focused and emotion-focused coping strategies are two that the text discusses in detail. In addition, we can minimize the impact of stressors by exercising regularly, avoiding or minimizing stimulants such as coffee, tea, or cigarettes, and by regularly practicing a relaxation technique such as meditation or progressive muscle relaxation. Stress is an unavoidable part of life and can influence both our physical and psychological well-being. How we choose to cope with stress can reduce and minimize its destructive effects.

Progress Test 1

1. c	6. b	11. a
2. b	7. a	12. d
3. b	8. b	13. a
4. b	9. a	14. e
5. c	10. d	15. d

Progress Test 2

1. b	6. a	11. c
2. b	7. d	12. b
3. a	8. a	13. d
4. d	9. b	14. a
5. c	10. b	15. b

Progress Test 3

1. a	6. b	11. a
2. c	7. c	12. a
3. d	8. c	13. c
4. b	9. b	14. d
5. d	10. d	15. d

CHAPTER

13

Psychological Disorders

PREVIEW   Reading the section below first will give you a general sense of the chapter's contents and an initial introduction to some of the major concepts and terms. This will prime you for what you are about to read and help you to develop a "cognitive map" that will guide your study of the material in this chapter. Likewise, reading the **preview questions** at the beginning of each major section will improve your ability to understand, learn, and retain the information.

CHAPTER 13 . . . AT A GLANCE   Chapter 13 begins by addressing the distinction between normal and abnormal behavior and the criteria for diagnosing psychological disorders, according to DSM-IV.

Anxiety is a common experience for all people, but only when it becomes maladaptive is it considered a disorder. The prevalence, course, and possible causes of anxiety disorders, including generalized anxiety disorder, panic disorder, phobias, posttraumatic stress disorder, and obsessive-compulsive disorder, are discussed.

Mood disorders involve serious, persistent disturbances in emotions that cause psychological discomfort and/or impair the ability to function. The symptoms of major depression and bipolar disorder are identified, and the course and potential causes of these mood disorders are discussed.

Personality disorders are characterized by inflexibility and maladaptive personality traits. Antisocial personality disorder and borderline personality disorder are discussed in terms of symptoms, causation, and treatment.

Dissociative experiences involve a disruption in awareness, memory, and personal identity. The symptoms and possible causes of dissociative amnesia, dissociative fugue, and dissociative identity disorder (DID) are examined.

The main symptoms of schizophrenia are identified. Positive symptoms represent excesses in normal functioning, and negative symptoms reflect deficits or decreases in normal functioning. Three subtypes of schizophrenia are discussed, and the course and prevalence of the disorder are presented. Various theories of the causes of schizophrenia are explored, and the conclusion is reached that no single factor has emerged as causing this psychological disorder.

Introduction: Understanding Psychological Disorders

Preview Questions

Consider the following questions as you study this section of the chapter.

- What is psychopathology, and what characterizes psychological disorders?
- What is DSM-IV, and how was it developed?
- How prevalent are psychological disorders?

*Read the section "Introduction: Understanding Psychological Disorders" and **write** your answers to the following:*

1. Psychopathology is _____

   _____

2. A psychological, or mental, disorder can be defined as _____

   _____

   _____

3. DSM-IV stands for _____

   _____

   _____

   This manual describes _____

   _____

   _____

   _____

4. The National Comorbidity Survey found that psychological disorders were more common than previously thought, which can be interpreted to mean _____

   _____

   _____

   _____

Anxiety Disorders

Preview Questions

Consider the following questions as you study this section of the chapter.

- What are the main symptoms of anxiety disorder, and how does pathological anxiety differ from normal anxiety?

- What characterizes generalized anxiety disorder and panic disorder?
- What are the phobias, and how have they been explained?

*Read the section "Anxiety Disorders" (up to "Posttraumatic Stress Disorder") and **write** your answers to the following:*

1. Anxiety is defined as _____

   _____

   _____

   It is often adaptive and normal because _____

   _____

   _____

2. In the anxiety disorders, the anxiety is _____

   _____

3. The three features that distinguish normal anxiety from pathological anxiety are

   (a) _____

   _____

   (b) _____

   _____

   (c) _____

   _____

4. Generalized anxiety disorder is characterized by _____

   _____

5. A panic attack is _____

   _____

6. A panic disorder is _____

   _____

7. A phobia is _____

   A specific phobia is _____

   _____

8. Phobias are assumed by some to involve various forms of learning such as _____

   _____

   _____

   _____

   _____

   _____

Anxiety Disorders: Posttraumatic Stress Disorder and Obsessive-Compulsive Disorder

Preview Questions

Consider the following questions as you study these sections of the chapter.

- How is posttraumatic stress disorder (PTSD) defined?
- What are the main characteristics of PTSD, and what causes the disorder?
- What is obsessive-compulsive disorder, and what causes it?

*Read the sections "Anxiety Disorders: Posttraumatic Stress Disorder" and "Obsessive-Compulsive Disorders" and **write** your answers to the following:*

1. Posttraumatic stress disorder (PTSD) is _____

   _____

2. The three core symptoms that characterize PTSD are:

   (a) _____

   _____

   (b) _____

   _____

   (c) _____

   _____

3. Factors that influence the likelihood of developing posttraumatic stress disorder are:

   (a) _____

   _____

   (b) _____

   _____

   (c) _____

   _____

4. Obsessive-compulsive disorder is _____

   _____

   Obsessions are _____

   _____

   _____

   Compulsions are _____

   _____

   _____

5. People with obsessive-compulsive disorder commonly experience _____

   _____

   _____

6. Two biological factors that seem to be involved in obsessive-compulsive disorder are _____

   _____

   _____

   _____

   _____

After you have carefully studied the preceding sections, complete the following exercises.

Concept Check 1

Read the following and write the correct term in the space provided.

1. Dr. Janz is a psychiatrist who assesses and treats patients in a mental institution. Dr. Sloane is a clinical psychologist who works with a similar population of patients in a mental health clinic. Dr. Janz is likely to describe his patients as suffering from _____ disorders, whereas Dr. Sloane is more likely to use the term _____ disorder when referring to his patients' problems.

2. Seventeen-year-old Brad has a shaven head, and he has rings in his nose, ears, and navel. Shortly after purchasing a new pair of jeans, he cut and tore horizontal slits across the thigh and knee areas of each leg. In our present culture, Brad would be classified as

   _____ .

3. Mr. and Mrs. Jefferson want to hire a new housekeeper. Mr. Jefferson suggests that the best person would be someone who has an excessive dislike and fear of dirt, germs, and insects and who deals with anxiety about contamination by using a very thorough cleaning, washing, and disinfecting routine. Mrs. Jefferson thinks that any person fitting that description might have a problem called

   _____ disorder.

4. Mr. Alviro suffers from intense anxiety most of the time. He is nervous and worried and is overly concerned about a wide range of life circumstances with little or no justification. Mr. Alviro probably suffers from _____ disorder.

5. Maurice is very quiet and introverted. He is painfully shy in the presence of other people and has dropped many courses at college simply because they involved oral presentations. He can't get a job because he is intensely afraid and anxious about being interviewed. Maurice would probably be classified as having

_____ .

6. Mr. Ng frequently recalls the horrors he and his family experienced in his native Cambodia. He suffers from sleep disturbances and is often awakened by terrifying nightmares. Mr. Ng is experiencing _____ disorder.

7. Ever since the sudden death of her husband, Mrs. Baxter has experienced a number of terrifying and unexpected episodes in which her heart suddenly starts to pound hard for no apparent reason; she typically feels a choking sensation, has trouble breathing, and starts to sweat and tremble. Mrs. Baxter is probably experiencing _____ .

Graphic Organizer 1

List the main symptoms of each of the following anxiety disorders:

Generalized Anxiety Disorder	Panic Disorder	Phobias

Posttraumatic Stress Disorder	Obsessive-Compulsive Disorder

Review of Terms and Concepts 1

Use the terms in this list to complete the Matching Test, then to help you answer the True/False items correctly.

psychopathology
psychological disorder
  (mental disorder)
DSM-IV
anxiety
anxiety disorders
generalized anxiety
  disorder
panic attack
panic disorder

phobia
specific phobia
agoraphobia
social phobia
posttraumatic stress
  disorder (PTSD)
obsessive-compulsive
  disorder
obsessions
compulsions

Matching Exercise

Match the appropriate term with its definition or description.

1. _____ The scientific study of the origins, symptoms, and development of psychological disorders.

2. _____ Abbreviation for the *Diagnostic and Statistical Manual of Mental Disorders*, fourth edition, the book published by the American Psychiatric Association that describes the specific symptoms and diagnostic guidelines for different psychological disorders.

3. _____ Anxiety disorder in which the symptoms of anxiety are triggered by intrusive, repetitive thoughts and urges to perform certain actions.

4. _____ Unpleasant emotional state characterized by physical arousal and feelings of tension, apprehension, and worry.

5. _____ Irrational fear triggered by a specific object or situation.

6. _____ Anxiety disorder in which chronic and persistent symptoms of anxiety develop in response to an extreme physical or psychological trauma.

7. _____ Anxiety disorder involving the extreme and irrational fear of experiencing a panic attack in a public situation and being unable to escape or get help.

8. _____ Anxiety disorder characterized by an extreme or irrational fear of a specific object or situation that interferes with the ability to function in daily life.

True/False Test

Indicate whether each statement is true or false by placing T or F in the blank space next to each item.

1. ___ Compulsions refer to repeated, intrusive, and uncontrollable irrational thoughts or mental images that cause extreme anxiety and distress.

2. ___ A psychological (or mental) disorder is a pattern of behavioral and psychological symptoms that cause significant personal distress, impair the ability to function in one or more important areas of daily life, or both.

3. ___ Generalized anxiety disorder is characterized by excessive, global, and persistent symptoms of anxiety; also called free-floating anxiety.

4. ___ Panic disorder is an anxiety disorder in which the person experiences frequent and unexpected panic attacks.

5. ___ Obsessions refer to repetitive behaviors or mental acts that are performed to prevent or reduce anxiety.

6. ___ Social phobia is an anxiety disorder involving the extreme and irrational fear of being embarrassed, judged, or scrutinized by others in social situations.

7. ___ Anxiety disorders are a category of psychological disorders in which extreme anxiety is the main diagnostic feature and causes significant disruptions in the person's cognitive, behavioral, and interpersonal functioning.

8. ___ A panic attack is a sudden episode of extreme anxiety that rapidly escalates in intensity.

Check your answers and review any areas of weakness before going on to the next section.

Mood Disorders: Emotions Gone Awry

Preview Questions

Consider the following questions as you study this section of the chapter.

- What are mood disorders?
- What characterizes major depression, and what is dysthymic disorder?
- What is seasonal affective disorder (SAD)?

- How is bipolar disorder defined?
- What characterizes a manic episode, and what is cyclothymic disorder?
- How prevalent is bipolar disorder, and what factors contribute to mood disorders?

*Read the section "Mood Disorders: Emotions Gone Awry" and **write** your answers to the following:*

1. Mood disorders are _____

   _____

   _____

2. Major depression is characterized by _____

   _____

   _____

3. Dysthymic disorder is _____

   _____

   _____

4. Seasonal affective disorder is a mood disorder in which _____

   _____

5. Bipolar disorder is defined as _____

   _____

   _____

6. A manic episode is a_____

   _____

   _____

7. Cyclothymic disorder is a mood disorder characterized by_____

   _____

8. Multiple factors appear to be involved in the development of mood disorders. These include

   _____

   _____

   _____

Personality Disorders: Maladaptive Traits

Preview Questions

Consider the following questions as you study this section of the chapter.

- What are the main characteristics of personality disorder?
- What characterizes the behavior of someone with an antisocial or borderline personality disorder?

*Read the section "Personality Disorders: Maladaptive Traits" and **write** your answers to the following:*

1. Personality disorder is characterized by_____

   _____

   _____

   _____

2. The antisocial personality is characterized by

   _____

   _____

3. Borderline personality disorder is characterized by_____

   _____

The Dissociative Disorders: Fragmentation of the Self

Preview Questions

Consider the following questions as you study this section of the chapter.

- How is a dissociative experience defined, and what are dissociative disorders?
- What are dissociative amnesia and dissociative fugue?
- What is dissociative identity disorder (DID), and what is thought to cause it?

*Read the section "The Dissociative Disorders: Fragmentation of the Self" and **write** your answers to the following:*

1. The dissociative experience is _____

   _____

2. Dissociative disorders are _____

   _____

3. Dissociative amnesia is a disorder involving

   _____

   Dissociative fugue is _____

   _____

4. Dissociative identity disorder (DID) involves

   _____

   _____

5. According to one theory, DID is caused by _____

   _____

   _____

   _____

After you have carefully studied the preceding sections, complete the following exercises.

Concept Check 2

Read the following and write the correct term in the space provided.

1. Ursula is generally happy about her move to northern Canada six years ago, but at regular intervals since then she has suffered episodes of depression during the fall and winter months. Ursula is probably suffering from _____ disorder.

2. Laura suffers from a mood disorder. Her therapist has taken a family history and found that Laura's mother and two sisters also suffer from the same problem. Although her therapist is aware that multiple factors may be involved in her problem, he is most likely to conclude that Laura may have a(n) _____ predisposition for the disorder.

3. Dr. Markoff has prescribed lithium for Sandro's mood disorder. It is most likely that Sandro suffers from _____ disorder.

4. Nedzad has a chronic disorder involving moderate but frequent mood swings that are not severe enough to qualify as bipolar disorder or major depression. He is perceived as being very moody, unpredictable, and inconsistent; taken together, these symptoms may indicate _____ disorder.

5. Marion Einer, a fifth-grade schoolteacher in Jersey City, disappeared a few days after her husband left her. One year later, she was discovered working as a waitress in a cocktail lounge in San Diego. Calling herself Faye Bartell, she claimed to have no recollection of her past life and insisted that she had never been married. This example illustrates

   _____ .

6. When Vanessa goes to a movie, she tends to become totally absorbed in the plot and loses all track of time and place; she is also often momentarily disoriented when she leaves the theater. These episodes represent

   _____ .

7. Karlson recently survived an airplane crash. Although he escaped from the burning plane with very few injuries, three of his friends were killed in the crash. Karlson is unable to recall any details from the time of the accident until a week later. Karlson has experienced

   _____ .

8. Dr. Rendell studies people who typically disregard and violate the rights of others and who appear to have no remorse or conscience about their destructive behaviors. Her colleague Dr. Gideon studies people who have a personality disorder characterized by instability of interpersonal relationships, self-image, and emotions and marked impulsivity. Dr. Rendell studies _____ personality disorder, and Dr. Gideon studies _____ personality disorder.

Graphic Organizer 2

List the main symptoms of the mood disorders:

Major Depression	Bipolar Disorder
1.	1.
2.	2.
3.	3.
4.	
5.	
6.	
Dysthymic Disorder	**Cyclothymic Disorder**
1.	1.

Review of Terms and Concepts 2

Use the terms in this list to complete the Matching Test, then to help you answer the True/False items correctly.

mood disorders
major depression
dysthymic disorder
seasonal affective
  disorder (SAD)
bipolar disorder
manic episode
cyclothymic disorder
personality disorder

antisocial personality
  disorder (psychopath
  or sociopath)
borderline personality
  disorder
dissociative experience
dissociative disorders
dissociative amnesia
dissociative fugue
dissociative identity
  disorder (DID)

Matching Exercise

Match the appropriate term with its definition or description.

1. _____ Personality disorder characterized by a pervasive pattern of disregarding and violating the rights of others; such individuals are also referred to as psychopaths or sociopaths.

2. _____ Often called manic depression, this mood disorder involves periods of incapacitating depression alternating with periods of extreme euphoria and excitement.

3. _____ Mood disorder in which episodes of depression typically recur during fall and winter and disappear during spring and summer.

4. _____ Mood disorder characterized by extreme and persistent feelings of despondency, worthlessness, and hopelessness, causing impaired emotional, cognitive, behavioral, and physical functioning.

5. _____ Sudden, rapidly escalating emotional state characterized by extreme euphoria, excitement, physical energy, and rapid thoughts and speech.

6. _____ Break or disruption in consciousness during which awareness, memory, and personal identity become separated or divided.

7. _____ Inflexible, maladaptive patterns of thoughts, emotions, behavior, and interpersonal functioning that are stable over time and across situations; they deviate from the expectations of the individual's culture.

8. _____ Formerly called *multiple personality disorder*; dissociative disorder involving extensive disruptions along with the presence of two or more distinct identities, or "personalities."

True/False Test

Indicate whether each statement is true or false by placing T or F in the blank space next to each item.

1. _____ Mood disorders are a category of mental disorders in which significant and chronic disruption in mood is the predominant symptom, causing impaired cognitive, behavioral, and physical functioning.

2. ____ Dissociative fugue involves the inability to recall information but does not involve sudden, unexpected travel from home.

3. ____ Dissociative amnesia involves sudden and unexpected travel away from home, extensive amnesia, and identity confusion.

4. ____ Cyclothymic disorder involves chronic, low-grade feelings of depression that produce subjective discomfort but do not seriously impair the ability to function and are not severe enough to qualify as major depression.

5. ____ Dissociative disorders are a category of psychological disorders in which extreme and frequent disruptions of awareness, memory, and personal identity impair the ability to function.

6. ____ Borderline personality disorder is characterized by instability of interpersonal relationships, self-image, and emotions, as well as by marked impulsivity.

7. ____ Dysthymic disorder is a milder but chronic form of bipolar disorder in which the person experiences moderate but frequent mood swings.

Check your answers and review any areas of weakness before going on to the next section.

Schizophrenia: A Different Reality

Preview Questions

Consider the following questions as you study this section of the chapter.

- How is schizophrenia characterized?
- How do positive and negative symptoms differ?
- What are the main subtypes of schizophrenia?
- What factors have been implicated in the development of schizophrenia?

- What evidence points to the involvement of genetic factors and brain abnormalities in the development of schizophrenia?
- How do environmental factors affect the development of schizophrenia?

*Read the section "Schizophrenia: A Different Reality" and **write** your answers to the following:*

1. Schizophrenia is a psychological disorder that involves _____

   _____

2. Positive symptoms include _____

   _____

   _____

   _____

   _____

   Negative symptoms reflect _____

   _____

   _____

3. The four subtypes of schizophrenia are

   (a) _____

   _____

   (b) _____

   _____

   (c) _____

   _____

   (d) _____

   _____

4. Evidence that genetic factors are involved in the development of schizophrenia comes from

   _____

5. The idea that schizophrenia is the result of abnormal brain chemistry is supported largely by two pieces of indirect evidence:

   (a) _____

   _____

   (b) _____

   _____

6. Environmental and psychological factors implicated in the development of schizophrenia include _____

_____

_____

_____

After you have carefully studied the preceding section, complete the following exercises.

Concept Check 3

Read the following and write the correct term in the space provided.

1. Franko and Alberto are identical twins. Franko has developed schizophrenia. The probability that Alberto will also develop schizophrenia is about _____ percent.

2. Dr. Hansen is conducting research on the viral infection theory. He is likely to find that people born in the winter and spring months, when upper respiratory infections are most common, are _____ (more/less) likely to suffer from schizophrenia than those born at other times of the year.

3. Derrick hears voices that tell him to be careful because he is being watched by aliens. Kirk believes that he is a famous rock star. Derrick suffers from _____ , and Kirk suffers from _____ .

4. Quincy falsely believes that others are plotting against him and are trying to kill him. He

believes that these agents are putting poison in the hospital's coffee supply and will attack him if he ever tries to leave the ward. This example illustrates a positive symptom of schizophrenia called _____ .

5. Regardless of the situation she is in, Parminder responds in an emotionally flat way, and she consistently shows a greatly reduced or complete lack of emotional responsiveness. She shows little in the way of expressive gestures or facial expressions, and her speech is slow and monotonous, without normal vocal inflections. These schizophrenic symptoms indicate that Parminder suffers from _____ , or _____ .

6. Mrs. Perez usually sits passively in a motionless stupor, but if the nurse moves her arms to a new position, she will stay in that position for a very long time. This symptom of catatonic schizophrenia is called _____ .

7. When Darcy was examined by his psychologist, she noted that he displayed some combination of positive and negative symptoms that did not clearly fit the criteria for _____ , _____ , or _____ types of schizophrenia, so she diagnosed him as having an undifferentiated type of schizophrenia.

Graphic Organizer 3

Write the main positive and negative symptoms of schizophrenia in the spaces provided.

Positive Symptoms	Negative Symptoms
1.	1.
2.	2.
3.	3.

Review of Terms and Concepts 3

Use the terms in this list to complete the Matching Test, then to help you answer the True/False items correctly.

schizophrenia
positive symptoms
negative symptoms
delusion
delusions of reference
delusions of grandeur
delusions of persecution
hallucination
flat affect
alogia (poverty of
  speech)
avolition

paranoid type of
  schizophrenia
catatonic type of
  schizophrenia
waxy flexibility
disorganized type of
  schizophrenia
  (hebephrenic
  schizophrenia)
undifferentiated type of
  schizophrenia
dopamine hypothesis

Matching Exercise

Match the appropriate term with its definition or description.

1. _____ View that schizophrenia is related to, and may be caused by, excess activity of the neurotransmitter dopamine in the brain.

2. _____ Mental disorder in which the ability to function is impaired by severely distorted beliefs, perceptions, and thought processes.

3. _____ Subtype of schizophrenia that is characterized by the presence of delusions, hallucinations, or both; the person shows virtually no cognitive impairment, disorganized behavior, or negative symptoms, but instead, well-organized delusions of persecution or grandeur are operating, and auditory hallucinations are often evident.

4. _____ Unusual symptom of catatonic schizophrenia in which the person can be molded into any position and will hold that position indefinitely.

5. _____ Commonly seen negative symptom of schizophrenia in which an individual consistently shows a dramatic reduction in emotional responsiveness and a lack of normal facial expression; few expressive gestures are made, and the person's speech is slow and monotonous, lacking normal vocal inflections.

6. _____ Falsely held belief that persists in spite of contradictory evidence.

7. _____ Delusion in which the person believes that other people are constantly talking about her or that everything that happens is somehow related to her.

8. _____ False or distorted perception that seems vividly real to the person experiencing it.

9. _____ Label for a subtype of schizophrenia that is used when an individual displays some combination of positive and negative symptoms that does not clearly fit the criteria for the paranoid, catatonic, or disorganized type.

True/False Test

Indicate whether each item is true or false by placing T or F in the space next to each item.

1. ____ In schizophrenia, positive symptoms reflect defects or deficits in normal functioning and include flat affect, alogia, and avolition.

2. ____ Avolition refers to the inability to initiate or persist in even simple forms of goal-directed behaviors, such as dressing, bathing, or engaging in social activities.

3. ____ The catatonic type of schizophrenia is marked by highly disturbed movements or actions and may include bizarre postures or grimaces, waxy flexibility, extremely agitated behavior, complete immobility, echoing words spoken by others, and assuming rigid postures that resist being moved.

4. ____ Alogia, which is also referred to as poverty of speech, is used to describe the symptom in which speech production is greatly reduced.

5. ____ The basic theme of delusions of grandeur is that the person is extremely important, powerful, or wealthy.

6. ____ In schizophrenia, negative symptoms reflect excesses or distortions of normal functioning and include delusions, hallucinations, and disorganized thoughts and behaviors.

7. ____ In delusions of persecution, the person believes that others are plotting against or trying to harm him or someone close to him.

8. ____ The prominent features of the disorganized type of schizophrenia are extremely disorganized behavior, disorganized speech, and flat affect; this subtype is sometimes called hebephrenic schizophrenia.

Check your answers and review any areas of weakness before going on to the next section.

Something to Think About

1. One of the most common misconceptions about mental, or psychological, disorders is that schizophrenia and multiple personality are the same thing. This myth is fostered by inaccurate portrayals and misinformation in the media. What are the important distinctions between these two disorders, and what would you say to someone who thought they were the same thing?

2. Most people are curious about mental, or psychological, disorders. Students frequently recognize aspects of themselves in the descriptions they read and wonder if they could end up suffering from some form of psychological disorder. What is normal, and what is abnormal? What are the chances of developing symptoms of psychopathology, and what causes such disorders? How would you answer these questions?

Check your answers and review any areas of weakness before completing the progress tests.

Progress Test 1

Review the complete chapter (including Concept Reviews and the boxed inserts), review all your study notes, and then test yourself on the following progress test. Check your answers. If you make a mistake, review your notes, review the relevant section of the study guide, and, if necessary, go back and read the appropriate part of your textbook.

1. Phoebe believes that she is the president of the United States and thinks that her indecipherable scribblings are actually top secret memos. Phoebe is most clearly suffering from a(n)
   (a) delusion.   (c) hallucination.
   (b) panic attack.   (d) obsession.

2. Shayna has very erratic, unstable relationships, emotions, and self-image. She is extremely impulsive and goes to great lengths to avoid real or imagined abandonment. It is most probable that Shayna has a disorder called
   (a) agoraphobia.
   (b) borderline personality disorder.
   (c) antisocial personality disorder.
   (d) cyclothymic disorder.

3. Dr. Koopman deals with people who suffer from a variety of problems that cause significant personal distress and impair their ability to function in one or more important areas of their lives. Like most people in his profession, Dr. Koopman uses the term *mental disorder* to describe these symptoms. Dr. Koopman is most likely a
   (a) clinical psychologist.
   (b) psychiatrist.
   (c) social psychologist.
   (d) developmental psychologist.

4. Kaila often appears nervous and agitated. She frequently talks in a loud voice and giggles at almost everything she hears. Her behavior is most likely to be diagnosed as a psychological disorder if it
   (a) is not caused by some biological dysfunction.
   (b) is the result of a genetic predisposition.
   (c) represents a significant departure from the prevailing social and cultural norms.
   (d) is caused by drugs or medication.

5. Sidney, a college student, complains that he feels nervous and fearful most of the time but doesn't know why. He worries constantly about everything in his life, and if he manages to deal with one problem, he starts worrying about a dozen more things. Sidney most likely suffers from _____ disorder.
   (a) generalized anxiety   (c) dissociative
   (b) bipolar   (d) cyclothymic

6. Imogene, a third-grade teacher, sometimes experiences a pounding heart, rapid breathing, breathlessness, and a choking sensation. She breaks out in a sweat, starts to tremble, and experiences light-headedness and chills. These symptoms last for about ten minutes and are characteristic of
   (a) posttraumatic stress disorder (PTSD).
   (b) dysthymic disorder.
   (c) cyclothymic disorder.
   (d) panic attack.

7. Paula has been diagnosed with agoraphobia. Her symptoms include which of the following?
   (a) an extreme and irrational fear of experiencing a panic attack in a public place and being unable to escape or get help
   (b) a sudden, rapidly escalating emotional state characterized by extreme euphoria, excitement, physical energy, and rapid thoughts and speech
   (c) partial or total inability to recall important personal information
   (d) all of the above

8. Dr. Weinberg believes that people acquire irrational fears through learning. Dr. Weinberg's position is most consistent with the idea that _____ may be involved in the development of phobias.
   (a) observational learning
   (b) classical conditioning
   (c) operant conditioning
   (d) all of the above

9. Jaime brushes her teeth 12 times every day. Each time, she uses exactly 35 strokes up and 35 strokes down and three different brands of toothpaste. Jaime suffers from a(n) _____ disorder.
   (a) obsessive-compulsive
   (b) panic
   (c) cyclothymic
   (d) bipolar

10. Kevin was working in a building when an explosion occurred; although he escaped with relatively minor injuries, he can't stop thinking about all the dead and seriously injured people he saw. He has frequent nightmares about the event and feels guilty that he survived when many of his coworkers did not. Kevin's symptoms are indicative of
    (a) dissociative fugue.
    (b) dysthymic disorder.
    (c) cyclothymic disorder.
    (d) posttraumatic stress disorder (PTSD).

11. Mrs. Landon has been diagnosed as suffering from major depression. Which of the following symptoms is she most likely to be experiencing?
    (a) feelings of guilt, worthlessness, inadequacy, emptiness, and hopelessness
    (b) awkward and slower than usual speech, movement, and gestures and frequent crying spells for no apparent reason
    (c) dull and sluggish thought processes and problems concentrating
    (d) loss of physical energy and vague aches and pains
    (e) all of the above

12. Karla suffers from a chronic, low-grade depression characterized by many of the symptoms of major depression but less intense; these problems started many years ago when both her parents were killed in a car accident. Karla is likely to be diagnosed as suffering from
    (a) dysthymic disorder.
    (b) agoraphobia.
    (c) cyclothymic disorder.
    (d) dissociative amnesia.

13. After living in Anchorage for a number of years, Juanitta was diagnosed with seasonal affective disorder (SAD). Episodes of depression are most likely to occur
    (a) when she travels south to visit her family in Florida.
    (b) during the fall and winter months.
    (c) during the day but not at night.
    (d) during the spring and summer months.

14. According to the Application, the best way to help prevent someone from committing suicide is to
    (a) use some well-known platitudes like "every cloud has a silver lining."
    (b) not let the person talk too much about what is bothering him because it will only make him more depressed.
    (c) suggest that seeking professional help would be a total waste of time and money in the present situation.
    (d) ask the person to delay his decision and encourage him to seek professional help.

15. According to Critical Thinking 13.1, which of the following is true?
    (a) People with mental disorders are generally portrayed with great accuracy in the media.
    (b) The statistical risk of violent behavior associated with mental illness is far higher than the risks associated with being young, male, or poorly educated.
    (c) The incidence of violent behavior among current or former mental patients is grossly exaggerated in media portrayals.
    (d) The statistical risk of violent behavior is greater among people with catatonic schizophrenia than among those with any other mental disorder.

Progress Test 2

After you have checked your understanding of the material in Progress Test 1 and have done a complete chapter review with special focus on any areas of weakness, you are ready to assess your knowledge of Progress Test 2. Check your answers. If you make a mistake, review your notes, the relevant section of the study guide, and, if necessary, the appropriate part of your textbook.

1. Dr. Moretti believes that schizophrenia is the result of abnormal brain chemistry. Her views are consistent with the
    (a) viral infection theory.
    (b) dopamine hypothesis.
    (c) genetic predisposition theory.
    (d) cognitive-behavioral theory.

2. When dealing with patients, psychiatrists, psychologists, and other mental health professionals are likely to refer to _____ to determine the criteria for a particular diagnosis.
    (a) pop psychology books
    (b) standard medical textbooks
    (c) DSM-IV
    (d) astrology charts

3. Dr. Crewe believes that people with panic disorder tend to misinterpret the physical signs of arousal as catastrophic and dangerous, and this misinterpretation only adds to the problem by causing even more physiological arousal. Eventually, they become conditioned to respond with fear to the physical symptoms of arousal, and repeated panic attacks lead to panic disorder. Dr. Crewe's explanation is most consistent with the _____ of panic disorder.
    (a) social-cultural explanation
    (b) biological theory
    (c) cognitive-behavioral theory
    (d) genetic predisposition explanation

4. Nima suffers from a type of schizophrenia that is characterized by hallucinations and delusions of grandeur, but she shows virtually no cognitive impairment, disorganized behavior, or negative symptoms. Nima suffers from _____ -type schizophrenia.
    (a) paranoid   (c) disorganized
    (b) catatonic   (d) undifferentiated

5. Tara, a young married women, has wandered from her home to a distant city where she has completely forgotten her family and her identity. This example illustrates
    (a) undifferentiated-type schizophrenia.
    (b) dissociative fugue.
    (c) disorganized-type schizophrenia.
    (d) dissociative amnesia.

6. Maury repeatedly checks to see if the stove is turned off and frequently turns around on his way to work to go back home to double check. This is an example of a(n)
    (a) delusion.   (c) hallucination.
    (b) obsession.   (d) compulsion.

7. Otis turned down a very high-paying job because it meant he would have to fly to the head office in Tokyo two or three times a year. He doesn't know why, but the thought of flying absolutely terrifies him. Otis may have
    (a) undifferentiated-type schizophrenia.
    (b) a phobia.
    (c) bipolar disorder.
    (d) posttraumatic stress disorder (PTSD).

8. Every semester just before midterm exams, Lilly gets very anxious and worries about how she is going to do. To reduce her apprehension, she studies very hard. Lilly suffers from

   (a) anxiety disorder.
   (b) free-floating disorder.
   (c) panic disorder.
   (d) obsessive-compulsive disorder.
   (e) none of the above; her symptoms are quite normal.

9. Jessica rarely leaves her home. She doesn't go shopping because she is frightened of having a panic attack and getting lost or trapped in a crowd. Jessica has symptoms that indicate she may have

   (a) agoraphobia.
   (b) cyclothymic disorder.
   (c) posttraumatic stress disorder (PTSD).
   (d) seasonal affective disorder (SAD).

10. Yvette usually stands motionless and will echo words just spoken to her. She resists directions from others and sometimes assumes a rigid posture to prevent people from moving her. These symptoms suggest that Yvette has a type of _____ called _____ type.

    (a) schizophrenia; catatonic
    (b) mood disorder; cyclothymic
    (c) schizophrenia; disorganized
    (d) mood disorder; dysthymic

11. Brandy's doctor prescribed lithium for her symptoms; as long as she keeps taking the medication, she feels fine. It is very likely that Brandy suffers from

    (a) schizophrenia.
    (b) generalized anxiety disorder.
    (c) bipolar disorder.
    (d) dissociative identity disorder (DID).

12. Regardless of the situation he is in, Philip responds in an emotionally flat manner and consistently shows greatly reduced lack of emotional responsiveness or facial expression. His speech is slow and monotonous, and he is unable to initiate even simple forms of goal-directed behavior, such as dressing, bathing, or engaging in social activities. Philip is suffering from _____ , and his symptoms are _____ .

    (a) schizophrenia; positive
    (b) anxiety disorder; positive
    (c) schizophrenia; negative
    (d) anxiety disorder; negative

13. Perry has dropped out of college because of the extreme distress that being in social situations causes him. He is unemployed because he is unable to bring himself to partake in an interview. Perry has

    (a) disorganized-type schizophrenia.
    (b) a dissociative disorder.
    (c) a generalized anxiety disorder.
    (d) social phobia.

14. Within the last two years, John has been fired from four different jobs for stealing money and goods from his employers. He feels no remorse and thinks his bosses were stupid for making it so easy to steal from them. John has a long history of problems with the law, which started in his early teens when he was diagnosed as having a conduct disorder. It is most likely that John has

    (a) an antisocial personality disorder.
    (b) an obsessive-compulsive disorder.
    (c) paranoid-type schizophrenia.
    (d) dissociative identity disorder.

15. According to Culture and Human Behavior 13.3, which of the following is true?

    (a) The content of schizophrenic hallucinations and delusions is virtually identical across cultures.
    (b) People with a mental disorder who are not actively suffering from the symptoms of the disorder are twice as dangerous and violent as normal people.
    (c) The content of schizophrenic hallucinations and delusions can vary tremendously from one culture to another.
    (d) Schizophrenia is much more prevalent in North America than in any other part of the world.

Progress Test 3

After you have checked your understanding of the material in Progress Tests 1 and 2, and have done a complete chapter review with special focus on any areas of weakness, you are ready to further assess your knowledge on Progress Test 3. Check your answers. If you make a mistake, review your notes, the appropriate parts of the study guide, and, if necessary, the relevant sections of your textbook.

1. Wendell repeatedly steals small items that he doesn't need and could easily pay for if he wanted to. Harman frequently sets fire to property for no obvious reason other than the pleasure he derives from seeing buildings on fire. According to Table 13.1: Some Key Diagnostic Categories in DSM IV, Wendell suffers from _____ and Harman has a disorder called _____ .
   - (a) kleptomania; pyromania
   - (b) Tourette's disorder; hypochondriasis
   - (c) autistic disorder; fetishism
   - (d) agoraphobia; pyrophobia

2. Fear of having a panic attack in a public situation is to _____ as an extreme and irrational of being embarrassed, judged, or scrutinized by others in social situations is to
   _____ .
   - (a) social phobia; agoraphobia
   - (b) bibliophobia; phonophobia
   - (c) agoraphobia; social phobia
   - (d) phobophobia; ergophobia

3. Shayne suffers from posttraumatic stress disorder (PTSD). If he is similar to most people who have this disorder, he is likely to exhibit which of the following symptoms?
   - (a) frequent, intrusive recollections of a traumatic event, numbing of emotional responsiveness, and avoidance of particular situations
   - (b) recurrent episodes of unintended sleep in inappropriate situations, such as during a meeting or while driving a car
   - (c) repetitive behaviors or mental acts that are performed to prevent or reduce anxiety
   - (d) the urge to set fires for pleasure, gratification, or relief of tension

4. Mandy is a forty-five-year-old administrative assistant. Based on the National Comorbidity Survey (NCS), the chance that Mandy may have experienced the symptoms of a psychological disorder at some point in her life is about _____ percent.
   - (a) 10
   - (b) 50
   - (c) 80
   - (d) 100

5. Dr. Burstein explains the development of phobias in terms of basic learning principles. Which of the following are likely to be included in his explanation?
   - (a) classical conditioning
   - (b) operant conditioning
   - (c) observational learning
   - (d) All of the above may be involved in his explanation.

6. After several weeks of feeling very apathetic and dissatisfied with his life, Elmiro has suddenly become extremely euphoric and full of energy. He talks so rapidly that he is hard to understand, sleeps very little, and has gone on a number of very expensive shopping sprees. He gets very irritated when anyone tells him to take it easy and slow down. Elmiro is exhibiting all the signs of
   - (a) obsessive-compulsive disorder.
   - (b) catatonic schizophrenia.
   - (c) dissociative identity disorder (DID).
   - (d) bipolar disorder.

7. Lucille suffers from dissociative identity disorder (DID). If she is like most people diagnosed with this disorder, she is likely to have experienced
   - (a) extreme physical or sexual abuse in childhood.
   - (b) episodes when she believed she was the reincarnation of some famous and powerful person.
   - (c) exposure to a viral infection during prenatal development or early infancy.
   - (d) excess dopamine in her brain during childhood.

8. When Christopher was younger, he became violently ill after eating southern fried chicken Although the cause of his illness was a flu bug, he now feels nauseated at just the sight or smell of southern fried chicken. Christopher's irrational fear of this specific food can best be explained by the _____ explanation of phobia development.
   - (a) operant conditioning
   - (b) classical conditioning
   - (c) observational learning
   - (d) dopamine deficiency

9. Dr. Krane is involved in the scientific study of the origins, symptoms, and development of psychological disorders. Dr. Krane's specialty area is
   - (a) psychopathology.
   - (b) personality.
   - (c) perception.
   - (d) psychosocioimmunology.

10. Vera has been diagnosed with cyclothymic disorder. Her symptoms are likely to include
    - (a) moderate but frequent mood swings for two years or longer.
    - (b) chronic low-grade feelings of depression that produce subjective discomfort but do not seriously impair her ability to function.
    - (c) partial or total inability to recall important personal information.
    - (d) irrational fears of a specific object or situation.
    - (e) all of the above.

11. Nester's sense of self-esteem is wildly inflated, and he exudes supreme self-confidence. He has delusional, grandiose plans for obtaining wealth, power, and fame and is engaged in a frenzy of goal-directed activities that could cost thousands of dollars. This is an example of a(n)
    - (a) manic episode.
    - (b) obsession.
    - (c) social phobia.
    - (d) hallucination.

12. Deidre suffers from frequent and unexpected panic attacks. Despite her apprehension about these episodes, Deidre functions fairly well in her job and has a relatively normal social life. Deidre is likely to be diagnosed with
    - (a) panic disorder.
    - (b) social phobia.
    - (c) bipolar disorder.
    - (d) dissociative fugue.

13. Scott repeatedly thinks that he might get a gun and kill all his colleagues at work. These thoughts are very disturbing, intrusive, and uncontrollable and cause Scott great distress and anxiety. Scott is experiencing a(n)
    - (a) delusion.
    - (b) obsession.
    - (c) hallucination.
    - (d) compulsion.

14. Konrad has experienced numerous psychiatric and physical symptoms and memory loss, and he has a chaotic personal history. During a session with his therapist, Konrad suddenly began speaking in a very childlike voice and claimed that his name was Arnold and that he was only ten years old. A short time later he reverted to his normal adult voice and claimed to have no recollection of the incident. Konrad is likely to be diagnosed as suffering from
    - (a) paranoid-type schizophrenia.
    - (b) dissociative identity disorder (DID).
    - (c) gender identity disorder.
    - (d) posttraumatic stress disorder.

15. According to Critical Thinking 13.2, which of the following statements about DID is (are) true?
    - (a) Much of the skepticism about DID is related to the fact that the number of reported cases has decreased dramatically in the last two decades.
    - (b) Some psychologists suggest that DID patients are consciously or unconsciously faking the symptoms, responding to the therapists' suggestions, or mimicking the symptoms of sensational DID cases portrayed in the media.
    - (c) Cross-cultural research has shown that the incidence of DID outside the United States is almost zero.
    - (d) Most psychologists believe that DID and schizophrenia are identical disorders.
    - (e) All of the above are true.

Answers

Introduction: Understanding Psychological Disorders

1. *Psychopathology is* the scientific study of the origins, symptoms, and development of psychological disorders.

2. *A psychological, or mental, disorder can be defined as* a pattern of behavioral and psycho-

logical symptoms that cause significant personal distress, impair the ability to function in one or more important areas of daily life, or both. These symptoms must represent a serious departure from prevailing social and cultural norms.

3. *DSM-IV stands for* the *Diagnostic and Statistical Manual of Mental Disorders*, fourth edition; it was published by the American Psychiatric Association in 1994 and represents the consensus of a wide range of mental health professionals and organizations. *This manual describes* approximately 250 specific psychological disorders (including the symptoms, the exact criteria that must be met to make a diagnosis, and the typical course for each mental disorder), and provides mental health professionals with a common language to label mental disorders and comprehensive guidelines to diagnose mental disorders.

4. *The National Comorbidity Survey found that psychological disorders were more common than previously thought, which can be interpreted to mean* that many people who could benefit from treatment do not seek it. However, it seems that most of these people seem to weather the symptoms without becoming completely debilitated.

Anxiety Disorders

1. *Anxiety is defined as* an unpleasant emotional state characterized by physical arousal and feelings of tension, apprehension, and worry that often hits during personal crises and everyday conflicts. *It is often adaptive and normal because* it puts you on physical and mental alert and helps you focus attention on the threatening situation.

2. *In the anxiety disorders, the anxiety is* maladaptive, disrupting everyday activities, moods, and thought processes.

3. *The three features that distinguish normal anxiety from pathological anxiety are: (a)* Pathological anxiety is irrational (it is provoked by perceived threats that are exaggerated or nonexistent, and the anxiety response is out of proportion to the actual importance of the situation). *(b)* Pathological anxiety is uncontrollable (the person can't shut off the alarm reaction, even when he or she knows it's unrealistic). *(c)* Pathological anxiety is disruptive (it interferes with relationships, job or academic performance, or everyday activity).

4. *Generalized anxiety disorder is characterized by* excessive, global, and persistent symptoms of anxiety (also called free-floating anxiety).

5. *A panic attack is* a sudden episode of extreme anxiety that rapidly escalates in intensity; the most common symptoms are a pounding heart, rapid breathing, breathlessness, and a choking sensation, often accompanied by sweating, trembling, light-headedness, chills, or hot flashes.

6. *A panic disorder is* an anxiety disorder in which the person experiences frequent and unexpected panic attacks.

7. *A phobia is* an intense fear that is triggered by a specific object or situation (encountering the feared situation or object can provoke a full-fledged panic attack in some people). *A specific phobia is* characterized by an extreme and irrational fear of a specific object or situation that interferes with the ability to function in daily life (e.g., agoraphobia, social phobia, etc.).

8. *Phobias are assumed by some to involve various forms of learning such as* classical conditioning (the feared object is the conditioned stimulus, and the learned fear is the conditioned response, which can generalize to other similar stimuli); operant conditioning, which can also be involved in the avoidance behavior that characterizes phobias (the conditioned response of avoiding the feared object is negatively reinforced by the relief from anxiety and fear that the behavior brings about); observational learning (people can learn to be phobic of certain objects or situations by observing the fearful reactions of someone else who acts as a model in the situation or through seeing media accounts of disasters and catastrophes), and biological preparedness (humans are predisposed through our evolutionary history to acquire fears of certain animals or situations).

Anxiety Disorders: Posttraumatic Stress Disorder and Obsessive-Compulsive Disorder

1. *Posttraumatic stress disorder (PTSD) is* a long-lasting anxiety disorder in which chronic and persistent symptoms of anxiety develop in response to an extreme physical or psychological trauma (extreme traumas are events that produce intense feelings of horror and helplessness, such as a serious physical injury or threat of injury to yourself or to loved ones).

2. *The three core symptoms that characterize PTSD are: (a)* The person frequently recalls the

event, replaying it in his or her mind (it is often unwanted or intrusive and interferes with normal thought processes). *(b)* The person avoids stimuli or situations that tend to trigger memories of the experience and undergoes a general numbing of emotional responsiveness. *(c)* The person experiences the increased physical arousal associated with anxiety (he or she may be easily startled, experience sleep disturbances, have problems concentrating and remembering, and be prone to irritability or angry outbursts).

3. *Factors that influence the likelihood of developing posttraumatic stress disorder are: (a)* People with a personal or family history of psychological disorders are more likely to develop PTSD when exposed to extreme trauma. *(b)* The magnitude of the trauma plays an important role—more extreme stressors are more likely to produce PTSD. *(c)* When people undergo multiple traumas the incidence of PTSD can be quite high.

4. *Obsessive-compulsive disorder is* an anxiety disorder in which the symptoms of anxiety are triggered by intrusive, repetitive thoughts and urges to perform certain actions. *Obsessions are* repeated, intrusive, and uncontrollable irrational thoughts or mental images that cause extreme anxiety and distress (they have little basis in reality and are often extremely far-fetched). *Compulsions are* repetitive behaviors that are performed to prevent or reduce anxiety and are typically ritual behaviors (overtly physical or covertly mental) that must be carried out in a certain pattern or sequence.

5. *People with obsessive-compulsive disorder commonly experience* both obsessions and compulsions, which are often linked in some way, even if the behaviors bear little logical relationship to the feared consequences (in all cases, obsessive-compulsives feel that something terrible will happen if the compulsive action is left undone).

6. *Two biological factors that seem to be involved in obsessive-compulsive disorder are* a deficiency in the neurotransmitter serotonin (drugs that increase the availability of serotonin in the brain decrease symptoms), and dysfunctions in specific brain areas, such as the frontal lobes (which play a key role in our ability to think and plan ahead), or the caudate nucleus (which is involved in regulating movements).

Concept Check 1

1. mental; psychological
2. normal
3. obsessive-compulsive
4. generalized anxiety
5. social phobia
6. posttraumatic stress
7. panic attacks

Graphic Organizer 1

Generalized Anxiety Disorder
Persistent, chronic, unreasonable worry and anxiety, characterized by general symptoms of anxiety, including persistent physical arousal.

Panic Disorder
Frequent and unexpected panic attacks, with no specific or identifiable trigger.

Phobias
Intense anxiety or panic attack triggered by a specific object or situation leads to persistent avoidance of feared object or situation.

Posttraumatic Stress Disorder
Anxiety triggered by memories of an extreme physical or psychological traumatic experience.

Obsessive-Compulsive Disorder
Anxiety caused by uncontrollable, persistent, recurring, and intrusive thoughts (obsessions) and/or urges to perform certain actions (compulsions).

Matching Exercise 1

1. psychopathology
2. DSM-IV
3. obsessive-compulsive disorder
4. anxiety
5. phobia
6. posttraumatic stress disorder (PTSD)
7. agoraphobia
8. specific phobia

True/False Test 1

1. F	4. T	7. T
2. T	5. F	8. T
3. T	6. T	

Mood Disorders: Emotions Gone Awry

1. *Mood disorders are* a category of mental disorders in which significant and chronic disruption in mood is the predominant symptom, causing impaired cognitive, behavioral, and physical functioning.

2. *Major depression is characterized by* extreme and persistent feelings of despondency, worthlessness, and hopelessness, causing impaired emotional, cognitive, behavioral, and physical functioning.

3. *Dysthymic disorder is* a mood disorder involving chronic, low-grade feelings of depression that produce subjective discomfort but do not seriously impair the ability to function.

4. *Seasonal affective disorder is a mood disorder in which* episodes of depression typically recur during the fall and winter and remit during the spring and summer.

5. *Bipolar disorder is defined as* a mood disorder involving periods of incapacitating depression alternating with periods of extreme euphoria and excitement (often called manic-depression).

6. *A manic episode is a* sudden, rapidly escalating emotional state characterized by extreme euphoria, excitement, physical energy, and rapid thoughts and speech.

7. *Cyclothymic disorder is a mood disorder characterized by* moderate but frequent mood swings that are not severe enough to qualify as bipolar disorder.

8. *Multiple factors appear to be involved in the development of mood disorders. These include* genetic predispositions, stress, and brain chemistry (the neurotransmitters serotonin and norepinephrine have been implicated in depression, and glutamate may be involved in bipolar disorder).

Personality Disorders: Maladaptive Traits

1. *Personality disorder is characterized by* inflexible, maladaptive patterns of thought, emotions, behavior, and interpersonal functioning that are stable over time and across situations and that deviate from expectations of the individual's culture.

2. *The antisocial personality is characterized by* a pervasive pattern of disregarding and violating the rights of others (such individuals are often referred to as psychopaths or sociopaths).

3. *Borderline personality disorder is characterized by* instability of interpersonal relationships, self-image, and emotions and marked impulsivity.

The Dissociative Disorders: Fragmentation of the Self

1. *The dissociative experience is* a break or disruption in consciousness during which awareness, memory, and personal identity become separated or divided.

2. *Dissociative disorders are* a category of psychological disorders in which extreme and frequent disruptions of awareness, memory, and personal identity impair the ability to function.

3. *Dissociative amnesia is a disorder involving* the partial or total inability to recall important personal information. *Dissociative fugue is* a disorder involving sudden and unexpected travel away from home, extensive amnesia, and identity confusion.

4. *Dissociative identity disorder (DID) involves* extensive memory disruptions along with the presence of two or more distinct identities, or "personalities" (formerly called multiple personality disorder).

5. *According to one theory, DID is caused by* trauma in childhood and represents an extreme form of coping through dissociation.

Concept Check 2

1. seasonal affective
2. genetic
3. bipolar
4. cyclothymic
5. dissociative fugue
6. dissociative experiences
7. dissociative amnesia
8. antisocial; borderline

Graphic Organizer 2

Major Depression

1. Loss of interest or pleasure in almost all activities
2. Despondent mood, feelings of emptiness or worthlessness, or excessive guilt
3. Preoccupation with death or suicidal thoughts
4. Difficulty sleeping or excessive sleeping
5. Diminished ability to think, concentrate, or make decisions

6. Diminished appetite and significant weight loss or excessive eating and weight gain

Bipolar Disorder
1. One or more manic episodes characterized by euphoria, high energy, grandiose ideas, flight of ideas, inappropriate self-confidence, and decreased need for sleep
2. Usually also has one or more episodes of major depression
3. May alternate rapidly between symptoms of mania and major depression

Dysthymic Disorder
1. Chronic, low-grade depressed feelings that are not severe enough to qualify as major depression

Cyclothymic Disorder
1. Moderate, recurring, up-and-down mood swings that are not severe enough to qualify as major depression or bipolar disorder

Matching Exercise 2
1. antisocial personality disorder
2. bipolar disorder
3. seasonal affective disorder (SAD)
4. major depression
5. manic episode
6. dissociative experience
7. personality disorders
8. dissociative identity disorder (DID)

True/False Test 2

1. T	4. F	7. F
2. F	5. T	
3. F	6. T	

Schizophrenia: A Different Reality

1. *Schizophrenia is a psychological disorder that involves* severely distorted beliefs, perceptions, and thought processes that impair an individual's ability to function.

2. *Positive symptoms include* delusions (false beliefs that persist in spite of contradictory evidence), hallucinations (false perceptions that seem vividly real to the person experiencing them), and severely disorganized thought processes, speech, and behavior. *Negative symptoms reflect* a restriction or disruption of normal functions, including flat affect, alogia, and avolition.

3. *The four subtypes of schizophrenia are (a)* paranoid type (presence of delusions, hallucinations, or both, but no cognitive impairment, disorganized behavior, or negative symptoms); *(b)* catatonic type (highly disturbed movements or actions, such as bizarre postures or grimaces, extremely agitated behavior, complete immobility, echoing words spoken by others or imitating their movements); *(c)* disorganized type (extremely disorganized behavior, disorganized speech, flat affect, and sometimes disorganized delusions and hallucinations; formerly called hebephrenic schizophrenia); and *(d)* undifferentiated type (used to describe individuals who display some combination of positive and negative symptoms but who do not fit the criteria for the other three types).

4. *Evidence that genetic factors are involved in the development of schizophrenia comes from* family, twin, and adoption studies, but studies of identical twins demonstrate that nongenetic factors play at least an equal role.

5. *The idea that schizophrenia is the result of abnormal brain chemistry is supported largely by two pieces of indirect evidence: (a)* Antipsychotic drugs that reduce schizophrenic symptoms in many people reduce or block dopamine activity in the brain. *(b)* Drugs such as amphetamines or cocaine enhance dopamine activity in the brain (use of these drugs can produce schizophrenia-like symptoms in normal adults or increase symptoms in people who already suffer from schizophrenia).

6. *Environmental and psychological factors implicated in the development of schizophrenia include* exposure to a virus during prenatal development and a psychologically unhealthy family environment (adopted children who were genetically at risk were found to be less likely to develop schizophrenia when raised in a psychologically healthy family).

Concept Check 3
1. 50
2. more
3. hallucinations; delusions
4. delusions of persecution
5. flat affect; affective flattening
6. waxy flexibility
7. paranoid, catatonic; disorganized

Graphic Organizer 3

Positive Symptoms
1. delusions
2. hallucinations
3. disorganized thoughts and behavior

Negative Symptoms
1. flat effect
2. alogia (poverty of speech)
3. avolition

Matching Exercise 3

1. dopamine hypothesis
2. schizophrenia
3. paranoid type of schizophrenia
4. waxy flexibility
5. flat affect
6. delusion
7. delusions of reference
8. hallucination
9. undifferentiated type of schizophrenia

True/False Test 3

1. F	4. T	7. T
2. T	5. T	8. T
3. T	6. F	

Something to Think About

1. Multiple personality disorder, now called dissociative identity disorder (DID), involves extensive memory disruptions for personal information along with the presence of two or more distinct identities or personalities. Typically, each personality has its own name and each will be experienced as if it has its own personal history and self-image. These alternate personalities, or alters, may be of widely varying ages and of different genders. Typically, the primary personality is unaware of the existence of the alternate personalities. However, the alters may have knowledge of each other's existence and share memories. Sometimes the experiences of one alter are accessible to another alter but not vice versa. From this description of the disorder, it is clear that symptoms of amnesia and memory problems are a central part of DID. In addition, people with DID have numerous psychiatric and physical symptoms as well as a chaotic personal history.

Contrast DID with a description of schizophrenia and the differences between the two disorders become apparent. Schizophrenia is a psychological disorder that involves severely distorted beliefs, perceptions, and thought processes. During a schizophrenic episode, people lose their grip on reality. The positive symptoms of schizophrenia reflect an excess or distortion of normal functioning and include hallucinations, delusions, and severely disorganized thought processes, speech, and behavior. The negative symptoms reflect a restriction or reduction of normal functions and include flat affect, alogia (poverty of speech), and avolition, or the inability to initiate or persist in even simple forms of goal-directed behavior. There are four different subtypes of schizophrenia: paranoid type, catatonic type, disorganized type, and undifferentiated type. In addition, as noted in the text, the prevalence, course, and cause of schizophrenia are markedly different from those of DID.

2. The first thing to note is that the line that divides normal and abnormal behavior is not clearly defined. In addition, it is affected by the social and cultural context in which the behavior occurs. Psychopathology is the scientific study of the origins, symptoms, and development of psychological disorders, and as you learned in this chapter, DSM-IV is the book that describes about 250 specific disorders, including their symptoms, the exact criteria that must be met to make a diagnosis, and the typical course of each psychological disorder. The main categories of psychological disorders are the anxiety disorders, mood disorders, personality disorders, dissociative disorders, and schizophrenia.

According to your text, the chance that someone will experience symptoms of psychological disorder some time in his or her lifetime is fifty-fifty. About one in three people will have experienced the symptoms of psychological disorder during the last year. However, about 80 percent of those people will not have sought professional help. The good news is that most people seem to weather the symptoms without becoming completely debilitated and without professional intervention. It is estimated that 3 to 5 percent of people have really serious symptoms that demand immediate treatment, and these people usually have developed several mental disorders over time, not just one disorder that suddenly appears. Women tend to have a higher prevalence of anxiety and depression, whereas men tend to have a higher prevalence of substance abuse disorders.

Nobody knows for sure what causes psychological disorders. There is no shortage of theories, however. Biological and genetic factors have been implicated, as have abnormalities in brain structure and chemical imbalances. Various environmental and social explanations have also been suggested. Research continues, and someday we may be closer to finding the cause or causes of these abnormalities.

Progress Test 1

1. a	6. d	11. e
2. b	7. a	12. a
3. b	8. d	13. b
4. c	9. a	14. d
5. a	10. d	15. c

Progress Test 2

1. b	6. d	11. c
2. c	7. b	12. c
3. c	8. e	13. d
4. a	9. a	14. a
5. b	10. a	15. c

Progress Test 3

1. a	6. d	11. a
2. c	7. a	12. a
3. a	8. b	13. b
4. b	9. a	14. b
5. d	10. a	15. b

Therapies

Reading the section below first will give you a general sense of the chapter's contents and an initial introduction to some of the major concepts and terms. This will prime you for what you are about to read and help you to develop a "cognitive map" that will guide your study of the material in this chapter. Likewise, reading the **preview questions** at the beginning of each major section will improve your ability to understand, learn, and retain the information.

CHAPTER 14 . . . AT A GLANCE

Chapter 14 discusses the use of psychotherapies and biomedical therapies to treat psychological disorders. Psychoanalysis, which is based on Freud's theory of personality, is described, including its basic assumptions and the techniques used in the psychoanalytic process. Client-centered therapy is discussed as the prime example of the humanistic approach to psychotherapy, and the basic assumptions of this form of insight therapy are explored. Behavior therapy is based on learning principles and assumes that maladaptive behaviors are learned. The techniques used to facilitate change are examined. The cognitive therapies, which assume that psychological problems are caused by maladaptive patterns of thinking, are explored next.

Group and family therapies are contrasted with individual therapy, and the advantages and benefits of each are examined. The effectiveness of psychotherapy is explored, and it is concluded that, in general, psychotherapy is better than no treatment at all and that no particular form of psychotherapy is superior to any other.

In introducing the biomedical therapies, the text notes that the most common biomedical therapy is psychoactive medication. The discussion includes the nature of these drugs, their effects on the brain, their side effects, and the disorder for which they are prescribed. The main categories of drugs are antipsychotic, antianxiety, and antidepressant medications. Lithium is prescribed for bipolar disorder. Electroconvulsive therapy (ECT), a different type of biomedical therapy, is used for treating severe depression.

Introduction: Psychotherapy and Biomedical Therapy

Preview Questions

Consider the following questions as you study this section of the chapter.

- How is psychotherapy defined, and what types of problems are treated using psychotherapy?
- What is the basic assumption common to all forms of psychotherapy?
- What is biomedical therapy, and what is its basic assumption?

Read the section "Introduction: Psychotherapy and Biomedical Therapy" and **write** *your answers to the following:*

1. Psychotherapy refers to _____

   _____

   _____

2. A basic assumption of all psychotherapies is that _____

   _____

3. Biomedical therapies involve _____

   _____

   _____

4. The biomedical therapies are based on the assumption that _____

   _____

Psychoanalytic Therapy

Preview Questions

Consider the following questions as you study this section of the chapter.

- What is psychoanalysis, and who developed this form of therapy?
- What techniques are used in psychoanalysis, and what is their purpose?
- What role does insight play in psychoanalytic techniques?
- What are short-term dynamic therapies?

Read the section "Psychoanalytic Therapy" and **write** *your answers to the following:*

1. Psychoanalysis is a _____

   _____

   _____

   _____

2. The main psychoanalytic techniques (and their purpose) are

   (a) _____

   _____

   (b) _____

   _____

   (c) _____

   _____

   (d) _____

   _____

   (e) _____

   _____

3. Together, these psychoanalytic techniques are designed to _____

   _____

4. The various forms of short-term dynamic therapies (all based on traditional psychoanalytic notions) have four features in common:

   (a) _____

   _____

   (b) _____

   _____

   (c) _____

   _____

   (d) _____

   _____

After you have carefully studied the preceding sections, complete the following exercises.

Concept Check 1

Read the following and write the correct term in the space provided.

1. During a session with her psychoanalyst, Felicity was asked to elaborate on her negative feelings about her husband. She responded by making a few wisecracks about men and then abruptly changed the subject. Her therapist would say she is engaging in

   _____ .

2. When Felicity's therapist urges her to report all her spontaneous thoughts, mental images, and feelings, he is using the technique called

   _____ .

3. Felicity's therapist offers a carefully timed explanation of her free associations, hoping to facilitate the recognition of her unconscious conflicts or motivations. This technique is called _____ .

4. Although her therapist has remained neutral and nonjudgmental throughout their sessions, Felicity is beginning to express feelings of hostility and anger toward him. This part of the psychoanalytic process is called

   _____ .

5. When Felicity describes a dream she had the previous night, her therapist explores the content and analyzes it for disguised or symbolic wishes and motivations. Her therapist is using

   _____ .

Review of Terms, Concepts, and Names 1

Use the terms in this list to complete the Matching Test, then to help you answer the True/False items correctly.

psychotherapy	resistance
biomedical therapies	dream interpretation
psychoanalysis	interpretation
Sigmund Freud	transference
insight	short-term dynamic
free association	therapies

Matching Exercise

Match the appropriate term/name with its definition or description.

1. _____ Founder of psychoanalysis who theorized that psychological symptoms are the result of unconscious and unresolved conflicts stemming from early childhood.

2. _____ The treatment of emotional, behavioral, and interpersonal problems through the use of psychological techniques designed to encourage understanding of problems and modify troubling feelings, behaviors, or relationships.

3. _____ Psychoanalytic technique in which the psychoanalyst offers a carefully timed explanation of the patient's dreams, free associations, or behavior to facilitate the recognition of unconscious conflicts or motivations.

4. _____ Type of psychotherapy originated by Sigmund Freud in which free association, dream interpretation, and analysis of resistance and transference are used to explore repressed or unconscious impulses, anxieties, and internal conflicts.

5. _____ The use of medications, electroconvulsive therapy, or other medical treatment to treat the symptoms associated with psychological disorders.

6. _____ Psychotherapies that are based on traditional psychoanalytic notions in which therapeutic contact typically lasts for no more than a few months rather than years.

True/False Test

Indicate whether each statement is true or false by placing T or F in the blank space next to each item.

1. ____ Psychoanalysts believe that it is essential to move conflicts from the patient's unconscious to his or her conscious awareness. The process of recognizing and ultimately resolving these longstanding repressed conflicts is called insight.

2. ____ Transference is the process by which emotions and desires originally associated with a significant person in the patient's life, such as a parent, are unconsciously transferred to the psychoanalyst.

3. ___ In psychoanalysis, the patient's unconscious attempts to block the revelation of repressed memories and conflicts is called resistance.

4. ___ Dream interpretation is a technique used in psychoanalysis in which the content of dreams is analyzed for disguised or symbolic wishes, meanings, and motivations.

5. ___ Free association is a technique used in psychoanalysis in which the patient spontaneously reports all thoughts, feelings, and mental images as they come to mind as a way of revealing unconscious thoughts and emotions.

Check your answers and review any areas of weakness before going on to the next section.

Humanistic Therapy

Preview Questions

Consider the following questions as you study this section of the chapter.

- What is the main humanistic therapy, and who developed it?
- What therapeutic conditions and techniques are important in client-centered therapy?
- How do client-centered therapy and psychoanalysis differ as insight therapies?

*Read the section "Humanistic Therapy" and **write** your answers to the following:*

1. In naming his therapy, Rogers deliberately used the word *client* rather than *patient* because

   _____

   _____

   _____

   _____

2. In client-centered therapy, the main conditions are that _____

   _____

   _____

   _____

3. Unlike psychoanalysis, humanistic therapy does not offer _____

   _____

   _____

   _____

Behavior Therapy

Preview Questions

Consider the following questions as you study this section of the chapter.

- What is the basic premise of behavior therapy?
- How are classical and operant conditioning principles used to treat and modify problem behaviors?

*Read the section "Behavior Therapy" and **write** your answers to the following:*

1. Behavior therapists assume that maladaptive behaviors are _____

   _____

   Therefore, the basic strategy in behavior therapy involves _____

   _____

2. Behavior therapists employ techniques that are based on the learning principles of _____

   _____

   _____

3. Mary Cover Jones's procedure, called counterconditioning, involved _____

   _____

   _____

   _____

4. Along with counterconditioning, Jones used ___

   _____

   _____

5. Based on the same premise as counterconditioning, systematic desensitization involves

   _____

   _____

   _____

6. The three basic steps of systematic desensitization are:

(a) _____

_____

(b) _____

_____

(c) _____

_____

7. The bell and pad treatment uses classical conditioning techniques to help bedwetters by _____

_____

_____

_____

8. Aversive conditioning involves _____

_____

_____

9. B. F. Skinner's operant conditioning model of learning is based on the simple principle that behavior is _____

_____

10. The token economy is a form of behavior therapy in which _____

_____

_____

After you have carefully studied the preceding sections, complete the following exercises.

Concept Check 2

Read the following and write the correct term in the space provided.

1. Dr. Soos does not analyze or interpret his clients' motives or problems. Instead, he believes that the client is in the best position to discover his or her own ways of effectively dealing with problems and that the role of the therapist is to provide the right conditions that foster self-awareness, psychological growth, and self-directed change. Dr. Soos is obviously a(n) _____ psychologist who uses _____ therapy.

2. In an attempt to help her husband overcome his deep fear of traveling by sea, Mrs. Bowman brings home travel brochures showing exotic destinations reached by cruise ships. She asks her husband to imagine both of them sitting in their deck chairs enjoying the warm sunshine and cool beverages, and at the same time she reassures him that these big ships are totally safe and comfortable and that he has nothing to worry about. Mrs. Bowman's efforts to reduce her husband's fear most closely resembles techniques used in _____ .

3. To help Trevor overcome his addiction to nicotine, Dr. Clarke asks him to smoke some cigarettes and at the same time administers electric shock to his arm. Dr. Clarke is using a technique called _____ conditioning.

4. Retarded children in a group home are given plastic chips for making their beds, brushing their teeth, washing their hands, and being on time for meals. They are allowed to exchange these chips for candy, cookies, or additional TV time. The group home is using a behavioral technique called the _____ .

5. Eight-year-old Darryl has problems with bedwetting. His mother takes him to a behavior therapist who recommends a procedure that fixes the problem in a matter of weeks. The therapist most likely is using the

_____ .

6. Desiree told her therapist, "I feel so inadequate and useless, and I can't seem to cope with even the smallest things in my life. What should I do?" Her therapist answered, "You are feeling very helpless about things in your life, and sometimes you feel unable to cope. Can you think where these feelings come from?" The therapist is using _____ therapy and appears to be communicating with

_____ .

Review of Terms, Concepts, and Names 2

Use the terms in this list to complete the Matching Test, then to help you answer the True/False items correctly.

humanistic perspective
client-centered therapy
Carl Rogers
genuineness
unconditional positive
  regard
conditional acceptance
empathic understanding
behavior therapy
Mary Cover Jones
counterconditioning

systematic
  desensitization
progressive relaxation
control scene
bell and pad treatment
aversive conditioning
extinction
positive reinforcement
token economy

Matching Exercise

Match the appropriate term/name with its definition or description.

1. _____ American psychologist who conducted the first clinical demonstrations of behavior therapy.

2. _____ Psychological perspective that emphasizes human potential, self-awareness, and freedom of choice.

3. _____ Form of behavior therapy in which the therapeutic environment is structured to reward desired behaviors with tokens or points that may eventually be exchanged for tangible rewards.

4. _____ In client-centered therapy, the critical quality of the therapist that involves honestly and openly sharing his or her thoughts and feelings with the client.

5. _____ Type of psychotherapy that focuses on directly changing maladaptive behavior patterns by using basic learning principles and techniques; also called behavior modification.

6. _____ American psychologist who helped found humanistic psychology and developed client-centered therapy.

7. _____ The first step in systematic desensitization, which involves successively relaxing one muscle group after another until a deep state of relaxation is achieved.

8. _____ Behavior therapy technique used to treat nighttime bedwetting by conditioning arousal from sleep in response to body signals of a full bladder.

9. _____ Type of psychotherapy developed by humanist Carl Rogers in which the therapist is nondirective and reflective, and the client directs the focus of each therapy session.

True/False Test

Indicate whether each statement is true or false by placing T or F in the blank space next to each item.

1. ____ Aversive conditioning is a behavior therapy technique based on classical conditioning that involves modifying behavior by conditioning a new response that is incompatible with a previously learned response.

2. ____ In client-centered therapy, empathic understanding involves active listening and reflecting the content and personal meaning of feelings being experienced by the client.

3. ____ Systematic desensitization is a type of behavior therapy in which phobic responses are reduced by pairing relaxation with a series of mental images or real-life situations that the person finds progressively more fear provoking; it is based on the principle of counterconditioning.

4. ____ In behavior therapy, when a behavior decreases because it no longer leads to a reinforcer, extinction has occurred.

5. ____ In systematic desensitization, the therapist may have the client create a very relaxing scene, unrelated to the hierarchy of anxiety-provoking images, called a control scene.

6. ____ In client-centered therapy, unconditional positive regard is created when the therapist values, accepts, and cares for the client, whatever her problems or behaviors.

7. ____ In behavior therapy, the process by which a behavior is increased as the result of a desirable consequence is called positive reinforcement.

8. ____ When a person has received acceptance by significant others only if she conforms to their expectations, she is said to have experienced conditional acceptance.

9. ____ Counterconditioning, a relatively ineffective type of behavior therapy, involves repeatedly pairing an aversive stimulus with the occurrence of undesirable behaviors or thoughts.

Check your answers and review any areas of weakness before going on to the next section.

Cognitive Therapies

Preview Questions

Consider the following questions as you study this section of the chapter.

- On what assumption are cognitive therapies based?
- What is rational-emotive therapy (RET), and who developed it?
- What is Beck's cognitive therapy (CT), and how does it differ from rational-emotive therapy?

*Read the section "Cognitive Therapies" and **write** your answers to the following:*

1. Cognitive therapies assume that _____
    _____
    _____

2. The goal of cognitive therapy is to _____
    _____
    _____

3. Ellis's rational-emotive therapy (RET) focuses on_____
    _____

4. Beck's cognitive therapy (CT) focuses on _____
    _____

5. Like Ellis, Beck believes that _____
    _____
    _____
    _____

6. In contrast with RET's emphasis on "irrational" thinking, Beck believes that_____
    _____
    _____
    _____

Group and Family Therapy

Preview Questions

Consider the following questions as you study this section of the chapter.

- What is group therapy, and what are some of the advantages of this approach?
- What are family therapy and marital or couple therapy?

*Read the section "Group and Family Therapy" and **write** your answers to the following:*

1. Group therapy involves _____
    _____
    _____

2. Some of the key advantages of group therapy are that _____
    _____
    _____
    _____

3. Family therapy is based on the assumption that
    _____
    _____

4. Marital or couple therapy focuses on
    _____
    _____

Evaluating the Effectiveness of Psychotherapy

Preview Questions

Consider the following questions as you study this section of the chapter.

- What is meta-analysis, and what has it demonstrated about the general effectiveness of psychotherapy?
- Is one form of psychotherapy superior to another?
- What common factors contribute to effective psychotherapy, and what is eclecticism?

*Read the section "Evaluating the Effectiveness of Psychotherapy" and **write** your answers to the following:*

1. When meta-analysis is used to summarize studies, the researchers consistently arrive at the same conclusion: _____
    _____
    _____
    _____

2. Researchers have identified a number of factors that are related to a positive therapy outcome:

   (a) _____

   _____

   (b) _____

   _____

   (c) _____

   _____

   (d) _____

   _____

   (e) _____

   _____

3. Eclecticism refers to the _____

   _____

   _____

After you have carefully studied the preceding sections, complete the following exercises.

Concept Check 3

Read the following and write the correct term in the space provided.

1. Dr. McGilvery wants to determine whether psychotherapy is effective for particular psychological disorders. In attempting to analyze the results of numerous published studies on the issue, he should use a technique called

   _____ .

2. Mike, a mental health professional, tries to tailor his therapeutic approach to the problems and characteristics of the person seeking help. Mike's pragmatic and integrated use of diverse psychotherapeutic techniques would classify him as a(n) _____ therapist.

3. Dr. Samson believes that a key aspect of resolving some psychological problems is getting individuals to realize that others have problems similar to their own. To achieve this goal, _____ therapy would be useful.

4. Jay's therapist attacks and openly criticizes Jay's irrational and self-defeating ways of thinking. Jay's therapist is most likely a(n) _____ therapist.

5. Dr. Beaven tries to help her clients learn to recognize and monitor the automatic thoughts that occur without conscious effort or control; she then encourages them to test the reality of these thoughts empirically. Dr. Beaven's approach is most consistent with _____ therapy.

6. Dr. Sidhu believes that in order to understand psychological problems, it is important to investigate interactions among family members within the context of the dynamic family system in which each member plays a unique role. Dr. Sidhu is most likely a(n) _____ therapist.

Graphic Organizer 1

Fill in each of the following with the correct information.

Type of Therapy	Founder	Source of Problems	Treatment Techniques	Goals of Therapy
Psychoanalysis				
Client-Centered Therapy				
Behavior Therapy				
Rational-Emotive Therapy				
Cognitive Therapy				

Review of Terms, Concepts, and Names 3

Use the terms in this list to complete the Matching Test, then to help you answer the True/False items correctly.

cognitive therapies
Albert Ellis
rational-emotive therapy
Aaron T. Beck
cognitive therapy
group therapy

self-help groups and
 support groups
family therapy
spontaneous remission
eclecticism

Matching Exercise

Match the appropriate term/name with its definition or description.

1. _____ Form of psychotherapy that is based on the assumption that the family is a system and that treats the family as a unit.

2. _____ Group of psychotherapies that are based on the assumption that psychological problems are due to maladaptive patterns of thinking; treatment techniques focus on recognizing and altering these unhealthy thinking patterns.

3. _____ Type of therapy, developed by psychiatrist Aaron Beck, that focuses on changing the client's unrealistic beliefs.

4. _____ Form of psychotherapy that involves one or more therapists working simultaneously with a small group of clients.

5. _____ Type of psychotherapy, developed by psychologist Albert Ellis, that focuses on changing the client's irrational beliefs.

True/False Test

Indicate whether each item is true or false by placing T or F in the space next to each item.

1. ____ Albert Ellis founded cognitive therapy (CT), a psychotherapy based on the assumption that depression and other psychological problems are caused by biased perceptions, distorted thinking, and inaccurate beliefs.

2. ____ Eclecticism is the pragmatic and integrated use of techniques from different psychotherapies.

3. ____ Spontaneous remission is the phenomenon in which people eventually improve or recover from psychological symptoms simply with the passage of time.

4. ____ Self-help groups and support groups deal with a wide array of psychological, medical, and behavioral problems through group processes and interactions that are typically organized and led by nonprofessionals.

5. ____ Aaron T. Beck founded the cognitive psychotherapy called rational-emotive therapy (RET), which emphasizes recognizing and changing irrational beliefs.

Check your answers and review any areas of weakness before going on to the next section.

Biomedical Therapies

Preview Questions

Consider the following questions as you study this section of the chapter.

- What is biomedical therapy?
- What are the most important antipsychotic, antianxiety, and antidepressant medications, how do they achieve their effects, and what are their advantages?
- What are lithium and ECT, and how are they used?

*Read the section "Biomedical Therapies" and **write** your answers to the following:*

1. The biomedical therapies are _____
 _____

2. Antipsychotic medications are _____
 _____

 The most common antipsychotic medications include _____
 _____
 _____

3. The new atypical antipsychotic drugs include
 _____
 _____

4. Antianxiety medications are _____
 _____

 The most common antianxiety medications include _____
 _____
 _____

5. Lithium is _____

_____

_____

_____

6. The antidepressant medications are _____

_____

The most common antidepressant medications

include _____

_____

_____

7. Electroconvulsive therapy (ECT) is a biomedical

therapy used primarily_____

_____

_____

_____

_____

**After you have carefully studied the preceding
section, complete the following exercises.**

Concept Check 4

*Read the following and write the correct term in the
space provided.*

1. For no apparent reason, Mrs. Bell has constant
and persistent feelings of anxiety, nervousness,
and apprehension that interfere with her ability to eat, sleep, and function. Her psychiatrist
is most likely to prescribe a type of psychoactive medication called an _____
medication.

2. Mr. Millis still experiences intense feelings of
despondency, hopelessness, dejection, and suicidal thoughts, despite extensive psychotherapy
and months of psychoactive medication.
Because of this lack of responsiveness, his doctor is likely to consider using

_____ therapy.

3. After being on antipsychotic medications for
many years, Florence has developed a number
of serious symptoms, such as severe, uncontrollable facial tics and grimaces, chewing movements, and other involuntary movements of the

lips, jaw, and tongue. Florence suffers from

_____ .

4. Dwayne has been diagnosed with bipolar disorder. His doctor is most likely to prescribe

_____ .

5. To treat her symptoms, which included hallucinations, delusions, and disordered thought
processes, Debra's psychiatrist prescribed one of
the atypical antipsychotic medications that
affect the levels of the neurotransmitters serotonin and dopamine in the brain. He is likely to
have prescribed either _____ or

_____ .

Review of Terms and Concepts 4

*Use the terms in this list to complete the Matching
Test.*

psychoactive   lithium
  medications   antidepressant
antipsychotic   medications
  medications   electroconvulsive
tardive dyskinesia   therapy (ECT)
antianxiety medications

Matching Exercise

*Match the appropriate term with its definition or
description.*

1. _____ A naturally occurring substance that is used in the treatment of bipolar
disorder.

2. _____ Prescription drugs that alter
mental functions and alleviate psychological
symptoms.

3. _____ Biomedical therapy used primarily in the treatment of depression that
involves electrically inducing a brief brain
seizure; also called *shock therapy* and *electric
shock therapy.*

4. _____ Prescription drugs that are
used to alleviate the symptoms of anxiety.

5. _____ Prescription drugs that are
used to reduce the symptoms associated with
depression.

6. _____ Potentially irreversible motor disorder that results from the long-term use of antipsychotic medications and is characterized by severe, uncontrollable facial tics and grimaces, chewing movements, and other involuntary movements of the lips, jaw, and tongue.

7. _____ Prescription drugs that are used to reduce psychotic symptoms; frequently used in the treatment of schizophrenia.

Check your answers and review any areas of weakness before going on to the next section.

Something to Think About

1. Many people suffer from fear and anxiety about such things as going to the dentist or doctor or to job interviews and taking exams. These kinds of fears are normal, and most people manage to cope with such anxiety-provoking situations. Other fears are more serious and may cause the person intense distress and somehow interfere with his or her normal functioning. Imagine a situation in which a friend or family member comes to you seeking help about how to overcome her fear of flying. Based on what you know about the behavior therapy technique of systematic desensitization, what might you say to this person?

2. Many people with psychological problems do not seek help from mental health professionals. There are many reasons for this. One reason may have to do with a lack of understanding about what to expect in psychotherapy. What are some of the important things a person should know about psychotherapy?

Check your answers and review any areas of weakness before completing the progress tests.

Progress Test 1

Review the complete chapter (including Concept Reviews and the boxed inserts), review all your study notes, and then test yourself on the following progress test. Check your answers. If you make a mistake, review your notes, review the relevant section of the study guide, and, if necessary, go back and read the appropriate part of your textbook.

1. Jacqueline's therapist uses dream interpretation and free association to help her to become more aware of unresolved conflicts in her childhood. The therapist's techniques and goals best reflect the primary aim of
   (a) psychoanalysis.
   (b) client-centered therapy.
   (c) behavior therapy.
   (d) cognitive therapy.

2. Mrs. Alverz gives her third-grade students a silver sticker every time they get a perfect score on their weekly spelling test. At the end of the term, students can exchange their stickers for prizes. Mrs. Alverz is using a strategy based on _____ conditioning called the _____ .
   (a) classical; bell and pad method
   (b) classical; token economy
   (c) operant; bell and pad method
   (d) operant; token economy

3. Laurel's therapist uses rational-emotive therapy (RET). After identifying Laurel's core irrational beliefs, her therapist is likely to
   (a) help her formulate an anxiety hierarchy.
   (b) encourage her to use free association so that she can get insight into her unconscious motivations and feelings.
   (c) provide her with a warm, supportive atmosphere, unconditional positive regard, and empathic understanding.
   (d) vigorously dispute and challenge her irrational beliefs.

4. Dr. Whorley offers a number of explanations for his patient's dreams and free associations in order to help the patient recognize unconscious conflicts and motivations. Dr. Whorley is using a psychoanalytic technique called
   (a) interpretation.   (c) resistance.
   (b) transference.   (d) conditional acceptance.

5. Twenty-five-year-old Melissa told her therapist that she felt worthless and unattractive because she didn't have a boyfriend; she was sure she was going to end up single and unloved. Her therapist said, "Your way of thinking is not only irrational but also totally stupid and absurd! You are worthless only if you *think* you are!" Her therapist is most likely

   (a) a behavior therapist.
   (b) a client-centered therapist.
   (c) a rational-emotive therapist.
   (d) a psychoanalyst.
   (e) none of the above; no therapist would talk like that to a client.

6. Once a week, Gardner attends a local health clinic, where he attempts to deal with some of his psychological problems by discussing them with five or six other people and two psychologists. Gardner is involved in

   (a) individual therapy.
   (b) group therapy.
   (c) a biomedical treatment program.
   (d) a self-help group.

7. Mr. Lansdon's intense feelings of despondency and helplessness are periodically interrupted by episodes in which he experiences excessive feelings of personal power and a grandiose optimism that he can change the world to fit his strange ideological beliefs. A biomedical therapist would most likely prescribe

   (a) electroconvulsive therapy.
   (b) lithium.
   (c) antipsychotic medications.
   (d) antidepressant medications.

8. Gabrielle's feelings of unhappiness, despondency, dejection, and hopelessness have become so extreme that she has attempted suicide. Which of the following treatments is likely to provide her with the quickest relief from her misery?

   (a) systematic desensitization
   (b) the bell and pad treatment
   (c) psychoanalysis
   (d) electroconvulsive therapy (ECT)

9. Because of his persistent psychological problems, Werner has been prescribed a benzodiazepine drug called Valium. It is most likely that Werner suffers from

   (a) bipolar disorder.   (c) anxiety.
   (b) schizophrenia.   (d) depression.

10. When Christos was younger, he experienced a very painful tooth extraction. He now has an extreme fear of going to the dentist and has not been for a dental check up in years. In order to help Christos overcome his irrational fear, a behavioral therapist is likely to use

   (a) rational-emotive therapy.
   (b) systematic desensitization.
   (c) the bell and pad treatment.
   (d) antianxiety medication.

11. Kathleen is on a committee at a community health-care facility that has the task of determining which of the major forms of psychotherapy is most effective. After she reviews studies that used meta-analysis to assess the results of treatment outcomes, she is most likely to conclude that

   (a) behavior therapy is the single most effective therapy available.
   (b) client-centered therapy has been consistently more effective than all the other forms of therapy.
   (c) in general, there is little or no difference in the effectiveness of the different forms of psychotherapy.
   (d) psychoanalysis works best for schizophrenia, and cognitive therapy works best for phobias.

12. Tyler has been diagnosed with schizophrenia. His doctor is most likely to prescribe

   (a) electroconvulsive therapy.
   (b) lithium.
   (c) antipsychotic medication.
   (d) antianxiety medication.

13. According to the Application, which of the following is true?

   (a) Therapy is a collaborative effort.
   (b) Expect therapy to challenge how you think and act.
   (c) Your therapist will not become a substitute friend.
   (d) Your therapist will not make decisions for you.
   (e) All of the above are true.

14. Mr. Keiko, a middle-aged Japanese American, has been referred to a Western-style psychologist because he is displaying the classic symptoms of anxiety and depression. According to Culture and Human Behavior 14.2, Mr. Keiko

    (a) may be reluctant to discuss personal, intimate details of his life with a stranger.
    (b) might try to avoid focusing on upsetting thoughts and resist exploring painful thoughts and feelings that could help resolve his psychological problems.
    (c) may not agree that becoming more assertive, more self-sufficient, less dependent on others, and caring for his own needs first is a good idea.
    (d) might do all of the above.

15. After a session with her therapist, in which she finally expressed all the anger and hostility she felt toward her parents and described the terrible guilt she felt about it, Charlene felt an enormous reduction in and relief from her emotional and physical tension. According to the Application, Charlene has probably experienced

    (a) resistance.
    (b) catharsis.
    (c) extinction
    (d) counterconditioning.

Progress Test 2

After you have checked your understanding of the material in Progress Test 1 and have done a complete chapter review with special focus on any areas of weakness, you are ready to assess your knowledge of Progress Test 2. Check your answers. If you make a mistake, review your notes, the relevant section of the study guide, and, if necessary, the appropriate part of your textbook.

1. Dr. Rassmunsen uses medication and other medical procedures, including electroconvulsive therapy, to treat the symptoms of psychological disorders. Dr. Rassmunsen's approach would most likely be classified as

    (a) cognitive therapy.
    (b) behavioral therapy.
    (c) humanistic therapy.
    (d) biomedical therapy.

2. Mr. Damson suffers from auditory hallucinations and falsely believes that his coworkers are not only trying to steal his "secret inventions" but are also plotting to kill him. A biomedical therapist would most likely prescribe

    (a) electroconvulsive therapy.
    (b) lithium.
    (c) antipsychotic medications.
    (d) antidepressant medications.

3. Mervyn's therapist prescribed a medication that is classified as a selective serotonin reuptake inhibitor (SSRI) for his psychological symptoms. It is most likely that Mervyn suffers from

    (a) schizophrenia.   (c) anxiety disorder.
    (b) bipolar disorder.   (d) depression.

4. When Freda told her therapist that she wanted to get his advice on what she should do about her relationship problems, he replied, "It sounds to me like you are experiencing some difficulties with your relationship. Is that right?" The therapist's response reflects the technique of

    (a) transference.
    (b) free association.
    (c) empathic understanding.
    (d) counterconditioning.

5. It is very probable that Freda's therapist is a _____ therapist.

    (a) cognitive   (c) behavior
    (b) psychoanalytic   (d) humanistic

6. When Greta's psychoanalyst asked her to elaborate on certain aspects of her dream, she couldn't think of anything to say. Her lack of responsiveness is likely to be interpreted as

    (a) resistance.
    (b) extinction.
    (c) transference.
    (d) spontaneous remission.

7. Dr. Whelan believes that people can overcome their problems if they learn to recognize and monitor their automatic thoughts and then try to test the reality of those thoughts empirically. Her approach is most consistent with

    (a) behavior therapy.
    (b) biomedical therapy.
    (c) cognitive therapy.
    (d) psychoanalysis.

8. A behavior therapist trains a child who is a frequent bedwetter to awaken and use the bathroom by arranging for an alarm to sound every time the child wets the bed. This technique is called _____ and illustrates the use of _____ conditioning principles.
   (a) aversive therapy; operant
   (b) the bell and pad treatment; classical
   (c) aversive therapy; classical
   (d) the bell and pad treatment; operant

9. For which of the following is Dr. Kelly most likely to prescribe a benzodiazepine drug called Valium?
   (a) Celia, who smokes three packs of cigarettes a day
   (b) Rachel, who suffers from nervous apprehension, intense anxiety, and an inability to relax
   (c) Garth, who irrationally believes that aliens are trying to steal his thoughts
   (d) Manuel, who fluctuates between extreme moods of euphoria and depression

10. Quentin has an irrational fear of flying. His therapist first teaches him to relax completely, then he asks him to come up with a list of anxiety-provoking images associated with flying. Finally, the therapist asks Quentin to close his eyes and imagine very clearly the least fearful scene on the list. Quentin's therapist is a _____ therapist using _____ .
   (a) behavior; systematic desensitization
   (b) cognitive; rational-emotive techniques
   (c) humanistic; empathic understanding
   (d) psychoanalytic; free association

11. Jeneen is taking a prescription drug that contains a naturally occurring substance called lithium. It is most probable that she is suffering from
   (a) schizophrenia.   (c) chronic depression.
   (b) bipolar disorder.   (d) anxiety disorder.

12. Ursula, who lives in a home for the mentally retarded, is able to earn points for getting dressed, maintaining personal hygiene, and engaging in appropriate social interactions. These points can be exchanged for access to desirable items or special privileges. This example illustrates the use of
   (a) aversive conditioning.
   (b) counterconditioning.
   (c) systematic desensitization.
   (d) a token economy.

13. Seven-year-old Niall chews the ends of all his pens and pencils, so his mother paints them with a foul-tasting, but harmless, substance. After a few days of this treatment, Niall stops chewing his pens and pencils. Niall's mother has used a form of
   (a) transference.
   (b) counterconditioning.
   (c) aversive therapy.
   (d) electroconvulsive therapy.

14. According to In Focus 14.1, the main difference between group therapy and self-help groups is that
   (a) self-help groups are usually organized by nonprofessionals.
   (b) group therapy is typically much less expensive than self-help therapy.
   (c) self-help groups have a very low success rate compared to group therapy.
   (d) group therapies usually follow a twelve-step approach, whereas self-help groups never follow an organized structured format.

15. According to the Application, which of the following is true of catharsis?
   (a) It produces long-term relief from most psychological disorders.
   (b) It is the cornerstone of the relationship between the therapist and the person seeking help.
   (c) It refers to the emotional relief that people experience from the simple act of talking about their problems.
   (d) It refers to the repression of anxiety-provoking emotions into the unconscious mind.

Progress Test 3

After you have checked your understanding of the material in Progress Tests 1 and 2, and have done a complete chapter review with special focus on any areas of weakness, you are ready to further assess your knowledge on Progress Test 3. Check your answers. If you make a mistake, review your notes, the appropriate parts of the study guide, and, if necessary, the relevant sections of your textbook.

1. After reviewing the literature on the use of lithium and the mechanism involved in its effectiveness in treating bipolar disorder, Richelle is likely to conclude that lithium

   (a) stabilizes the availability of glutamate, an excitatory neurotransmitter, preventing both abnormal highs and lows.
   (b) boosts the levels of dopamine in the brain.
   (c) selectively inhibits the reuptake of serotonin.
   (d) stabilizes the levels of both dopamine and serotonin in the brain.

2. Aaron Beck is to _____ as Carl Rogers is to _____ .

   (a) cognitive therapy; rational emotive therapy
   (b) behavior therapy; client-centered therapy
   (c) biomedical therapy; psychoanalysis
   (d) cognitive therapy; client-centered therapy

3. Because of Rhian's persistent feelings of hopelessness, dejection, and guilt, and her suicidal thoughts, her doctor is likely to prescribe an antidepressant drug called

   (a) Prozac.   (c) Valium.
   (b) chlorpromazine.   (d) lithium.

4. When Clifford decided to pursue a career as an artist instead of complying with his father's wish for him to become a lawyer, both parents were angry, critical, and rejecting. Carl Rogers would say that Clifford's parents are demonstrating

   (a) conditional acceptance.
   (b) empathic understanding.
   (c) unconditional positive regard.
   (d) unconscious motivations and feelings.

5. Mrs. Blonska has been diagnosed with generalized anxiety disorder. Because her doctor is concerned with the long-term treatment of her global and persistent feelings of anxiety, he is likely to prescribe

   (a) Buspar.   (c) Depakote.
   (b) Prozac.   (d) Clozapine.

6. Mr. MacKaskill has a serious drinking problem. In order to reduce his intake of alcohol, a behavior therapist might give Mr. MacKaskill a medication called Antabuse, which induces nausea whenever it is taken with alcohol. This behavioral technique is called

   (a) counterconditioning.
   (b) systematic desensitization.
   (c) aversive therapy.
   (d) the token economy.

7. For no obvious reason, Mr. Henderson has recently begun to express feelings of annoyance, irritability, and anger toward his therapist, who has been consistently patient, concerned, and supportive. Freud would most likely consider Mr. Henderson's hostility toward his therapist to be an example of

   (a) insight.   (c) aversion.
   (b) counterconditioning. (d) transference.

8. Dr. Elson uses a therapeutic technique that involves modifying behavior by conditioning a new response that is incompatible with a previously learned undesired response. Dr. Elson is most likely a _____ therapist who is using _____ .

   (a) behavior; counterconditioning
   (b) cognitive; rational-emotive techniques
   (c) psychoanalytic; free association
   (d) biomedical; ECT

9. Nelson's therapist believes that a therapist should be nondirective, providing unconditional positive regard in an open, honest way. Nelson's therapist is most likely a _____ therapist.

   (a) psychoanalytic   (c) cognitive
   (b) behavioral   (d) humanistic

10. During a lecture to students interested in graduate work in clinical psychology, Dr. Barton is asked what factors contribute most to effective psychotherapy. He is most likely to respond that
    (a) mutual respect, trust, and hope in the therapeutic situation are important factors.
    (b) therapists who have warmth, sensitivity, sincerity, and genuineness are usually effective.
    (c) clients who are motivated, expressive, and actively committed to therapy enhance the success of therapy.
    (d) all of the above contribute to effective psychotherapy.

11. Brian's therapist attempts to tailor her approach to his particular problems and characteristics and, in doing so, makes use of techniques from different psychotherapies. Brian's therapist would most likely be classified as a(n) _____ therapist.
    (a) humanistic   (c) behavior
    (b) eclectic   (d) cognitive

12. Which of the following individuals is most likely to benefit from a psychoactive drug that affects the level of the neurotransmitter dopamine in the brain?
    (a) Herman, who hears imaginary voices telling him that he is going to be abducted by aliens
    (b) Marcel, who is very nervous and anxious all the time
    (c) Carla, who feels sad, despondent, dejected, and worthless most of the time
    (d) Faith, who drinks at least a six-pack of beer every day

13. Harriet has asked her psychology professor whether psychotherapy is more effective than no therapy at all. If her professor is familiar with the meta-analytic studies on the topic, he is most likely to answer that
    (a) psychotherapy is no more effective than talking to a friend.
    (b) it is not possible to measure the effectiveness of psychotherapy.
    (c) psychotherapy harms more people than it helps.
    (d) psychotherapy is significantly more effective than no treatment.

14. Self-help groups are discussed in In Focus 14.3. Which of the following points is made?
    (a) Compared with therapy provided by mental health professionals, self-help groups are generally ineffective for the vast majority of psychological problems.
    (b) All self-help groups are organized and led by nonprofessionals.
    (c) Compared with professional mental health services, self-help groups are much more likely to cause harm to the people involved.
    (d) Self-help groups are most useful for people with mood disorders.

15. Masahara goes to a therapist who specializes in a Japanese psychotherapy called Naikan therapy. According to Culture and Human Behavior 14.2, it is very probable that he will be advised
    (a) that being self-absorbed is the surest path to psychological suffering.
    (b) to focus on developing a sense of gratitude and obligation towards significant others.
    (c) to meditate on how much his parents and others have done for him and how he may have failed to meet their needs.
    (d) to reflect on the trouble and problems he may have caused significant others.
    (e) to do all of the above.

Answers

Introduction: Psychotherapy and Biomedical Therapy

1. *Psychotherapy refers to* the treatment of emotional, behavioral, and interpersonal problems through the use of psychological techniques designed to encourage understanding of problems and to modify troubling feelings, behaviors, or relationships.

2. *A basic assumption of all psychotherapies is that* psychological factors play a significant role in a person's troubling feelings, behaviors, or relationships.

3. *Biomedical therapies involve* the use of medications, electroconvulsive therapy, or other medical interventions to treat the symptoms associated with psychological disorders.

4. *The biomedical therapies are based on the assumption that* the symptoms of many psychological disorders involve biological factors, such as abnormal brain chemistry.

Psychoanalytic Therapy

1. *Psychoanalysis is a* type of psychotherapy, originated by Sigmund Freud, in which free association, dream interpretation, and analysis of resistance and transference are used to explore repressed or unconscious impulses, anxieties, and internal conflicts.

2. *The main psychoanalytic techniques (and their purpose) are: (a)* free association, in which the patient spontaneously reports all her thoughts, mental images, and feelings while lying on a couch; *(b)* resistance, the patient's unconscious attempts to block the process of revealing repressed memories and conflicts; *(c)* dream interpretation, the analysis of dream content for disguised or symbolic wishes, meanings, and motivations; *(d)* interpretation, in which the psychoanalyst offers a carefully timed explanation of the patient's dreams, free associations, or behavior to facilitate the recognition of unconscious conflicts or motivations; and *(e)* transference, the process by which emotions and desires originally associated with a significant person in the patient's life, such as a parent, are unconsciously transferred to the psychoanalyst.

3. *Together, these psychoanalytic techniques are designed to* help uncover unconscious conflicts so the patient attains insight as to the real source of her problems.

4. *The various forms of short-term dynamic therapies (all based on traditional psychoanalytic notions) have four features in common:* (a) Contact lasts for no more than a few months. (b) The patient's problems are quickly assessed at the beginning of therapy. (c) The therapist and patient agree on specific, concrete, and attainable goals. (d) In the actual sessions, most psychodynamic therapists are more directive than traditional psychoanalysts, actively engaging the patient in a dialogue.

Concept Check 1

1. resistance
2. free association
3. interpretation
4. transference
5. dream interpretation

Matching Exercise 1

1. Sigmund Freud

2. psychotherapy
3. interpretation
4. psychoanalysis
5. biomedical therapy
6. short-term dynamic therapies

True/False Test 1

1. T	3. T	5. T
2. T	4. T	

Humanistic Therapy

1. *In naming his therapy, Rogers deliberately used the word* client *rather than* patient *because* he wanted to get away from the idea that the person was sick and was seeking treatment from an all-knowing authority figure. He also wanted to emphasize the client's subjective perception of himself and his environment.

2. *In client-centered therapy, the main conditions are that* the therapist should be nondirective; the client should direct the focus of therapy sessions; and the therapist should be genuine, demonstrate unconditional positive regard, and communicate empathic understanding.

3. *Unlike psychoanalysis, humanistic therapy does not offer* solutions or interpretations about the client's unconscious feelings and motivations, but instead is nondirective, providing active, reflective listening, unconditional positive regard, and emphatic understanding, with an emphasis on the client's subjective, conscious perceptions of herself and her environment.

Behavior Therapy

1. *Behavior therapists assume that maladaptive behaviors are* learned just as adaptive behaviors are. *Therefore, the basic strategy in behavior therapy involves* unlearning maladaptive behaviors and learning more adaptive behaviors in their place.

2. *Behavior therapists employ techniques that are based on the learning principles of* classical conditioning, operant conditioning, and observational learning.

3. *Mary Cover Jones's procedure, called counterconditioning, involved* gradually introducing the feared stimulus and at the same time pairing it with a pleasant stimulus, such as food, which elicits a positive response that is incompatible with the original conditioned response (this procedure also eliminated fear of objects

that were similar to the original feared stimulus).

4. *Along with counterconditioning, Jones used* observational learning techniques and demonstrated that seeing others acting in a fearless manner encourages the fearful individual to imitate the fearless behavior.

5. *Based on the same premise as counterconditioning, systematic desensitization involves* learning a new conditioned response (relaxation) that is incompatible with or inhibits the old conditioned response (fear and anxiety).

6. *The three basic steps involved in systematic desensitization are: (a)* The patient learns progressive relaxation. *(b)* The therapist helps the client construct an anxiety hierarchy and develop a control scene. *(c)* The process of desensitization begins by getting the deeply relaxed patient to imagine the least threatening scene in the anxiety hierarchy (over several sessions the client gradually works his way up the anxiety hierarchy).

7. *The bell and pad treatment uses classical conditioning techniques to help bedwetters by* pairing the sensation of a full bladder (conditioned stimulus) with a loud bell (the unconditioned stimulus, which is triggered by a wet bed), which wakens the child (the unconditioned response). Eventually, the sensation of a full bladder by itself (conditioned stimulus) will cause the child to waken (conditioned response) before he wets the bed.

8. *Aversive conditioning involves* repeatedly pairing an aversive stimulus with the occurrence of undesirable behaviors or thoughts (a relatively ineffective type of behavior therapy).

9. *B. F. Skinner's operant conditioning model of learning is based on the simple principle that behavior is* shaped and maintained by its consequences; this model uses positive reinforcement for desired behaviors and extinction (or nonreinforcement) for undesired behaviors.

10. *The token economy is a form of behavior therapy in which* the therapeutic environment is structured to reward desired behaviors with tokens or points that may eventually be exchanged for tangible rewards.

Concept Check 2

1. humanistic; client-centered

2. behavior therapy (systematic desensitization)

3. aversive

4. token economy

5. bell and pad treatment

6. client-centered; empathic understanding

Matching Exercise 2

1. Mary Cover Jones
2. humanistic perspective
3. token economy
4. genuineness
5. behavior therapy
6. Carl Rogers
7. progressive relaxation
8. bell and pad treatment
9. client-centered therapy

True/False 2

1. F	4. T	7. T
2. T	5. T	8. T
3. T	6. T	9. F

Cognitive Therapies

1. *Cognitive therapies assume that* most people blame unhappiness and problems on external events and situations, but the real cause of unhappiness is the way the person thinks about the events, not the events themselves.

2. *The goal of cognitive therapy is to* identify the maladaptive patterns of thinking and then to change them to more adaptive, healthy patterns.

3. *Ellis's rational-emotive therapy (RET) focuses on* identifying, disputing, and changing the client's irrational beliefs (explained by the ABC model [Activating events, Beliefs, and Consequences]).

4. *Beck's cognitive therapy (CT) focuses on* changing the client's unrealistic and distorted beliefs.

5. *Like Ellis, Beck believes that* what people think creates their moods and emotions; like RET, CT involves helping clients to identify faulty thinking and to replace unhealthy patterns of thinking with healthier ones.

6. *In contrast with RET's emphasis on "irrational" thinking, Beck believes that* depression and other psychological problems are caused by distorted thinking and unrealistic beliefs, and the

cognitive therapist encourages the client to empirically test the accuracy of his or her assumptions and beliefs.

Group and Family Therapy

1. *Group therapy involves* one or more therapists working simultaneously with a small group of clients (the group may be as small as three or four people or as large as ten or more people).

2. *Some of the key advantages of group therapy are that* it is cost-effective; therapists can observe clients interacting with other group members; clients can benefit from the support, encouragement, and practical suggestions provided by other group members; and people can try out new behaviors in a safe, supportive environment.

3. *Family therapy is based on the assumption that* the family is an interdependent system; it focuses on treating the family as a unit, rather than on treating the individual.

4. *Marital or couple therapy focuses on* improving communication, problem-solving skills, and intimacy between members of a couple.

Evaluating the Effectiveness of Psychotherapy

1. *When meta-analysis is used to summarize studies, the researchers consistently arrive at the same conclusion:* psychotherapy is significantly more effective than no treatment and no particular form of therapy is superior to any other.

2. *Researchers have identified a number of factors that are related to a positive therapy outcome:* (a) The most important factors are those associated with the therapeutic relationship, such as mutual respect, trust, and hope; (b) certain characteristics of the therapist, such as warmth, sensitivity, responsiveness, being perceived as sincere and genuine, and actively helping people to understand and face their problems; (c) therapists' sensitivity to the cultural differences that may exist between themselves and their clients; (d) client characteristics, such as level of motivation, commitment to therapy, active involvement in the process, along with openness, a willingness to change, expressiveness, and social maturity; (e) external circumstances, such as having the support, understanding, and encouragement of family members or a spouse and having a stable living situation.

3. *Eclecticism refers to the* pragmatic and integrated use of techniques from different psychotherapies (eclectic psychotherapists carefully tailor their approach to the problems and characteristics of the person seeking help).

Concept Check 3

1. meta-analysis
2. eclectic
3. group
4. rational-emotive
5. cognitive
6. family

Graphic Organizer 1

Psychoanalysis:
Founder: Sigmund Freud
Source of Problems: Repressed, unconscious conflicts stemming from early childhood experiences
Treatment Techniques: Free association, analysis of dream content, interpretation, and transference
Goals of Therapy: To recognize, work through, and resolve longstanding conflicts

Client-Centered Therapy:
Founder: Carl Rogers
Source of Problems: Conditional acceptance and dependence that causes a person to develop a distorted self-concept and worldview
Treatment Techniques: Nondirective therapy, with therapist displaying unconditional positive regard, genuineness, and empathic understanding
Goals of Therapy: To develop self-awareness, self-acceptance, and self-determination

Behavior Therapy:
Founder: Various; derived from the fundamental principles of learning
Source of Problems: Learned maladaptive behavior patterns
Treatment Techniques: Counterconditioning, systematic desensitization, bell and pad treatment, aversive conditioning, reinforcement and extinction, token economy, and observational learning
Goals of Therapy: To unlearn maladaptive behaviors and learn adaptive behaviors in their place

Rational-Emotive Therapy
Founder: Albert Ellis
Source of Problems: Irrational beliefs
Treatment Techniques: Very directive therapy: identifying, logically disputing, and challenging irrational beliefs
Goals of Therapy: To surrender irrational beliefs and absolutist demands

Cognitive Therapy:
Founder: Aaron T. Beck
Source of Problems: Unrealistic, distorted perceptions and interpretations of events due to cognitive biases
Treatment Techniques: Directive collaboration: teaching client to monitor automatic thoughts; testing accuracy of conclusions; correcting distorted thinking and perception
Goals of Therapy: To accurately and realistically perceive self, others, and external events

Matching Exercise 3

1. family therapy
2. cognitive therapies
3. cognitive therapy
4. group therapy
5. rational-emotive therapy

True/False Test 3

1. F
2. T
3. T
4. T
5. F

Biomedical Therapies

1. *The biomedical therapies are* medical treatments for the symptoms of psychological disorders.

2. *Antipsychotic medications are* prescription drugs that are used to reduce psychotic symptoms (frequently used in the treatment of schizophrenia). *The most common antipsychotic medications include* reserpine and chlorpromazine, which alter dopamine levels in the brain; while they reduce the positive symptoms of schizophrenia, they have little or no effect on the negative symptoms (they also have potential side effects, including tardive dyskinesia after long-term use).

3. *The new atypical antipsychotic drugs include* clozapine and risperidone, both of which affect serotonin and dopamine levels in the brain (the atypical antipsychotics have fewer side effects and are more effective in treating both positive and negative symptoms of schizophrenia).

4. *Antianxiety medications are* prescription drugs that are used to alleviate the symptoms of anxiety. *The most common antianxiety medications include* the benzodiazepines, which are effective in the treatment of anxiety but are potentially addictive and have many side effects (Buspar is a newer antianxiety drug that is apparently nonaddictive).

5. *Lithium is* a naturally occurring substance that is used in the treatment of bipolar disorder; it appears to work by stabilizing the availability of glutamate, an excitatory neurotransmitter, preventing both abnormal highs and lows. (Depakote has recently been introduced as a new drug treatment for bipolar disorder).

6. *The antidepressant medications are* prescription drugs that are used to reduce the symptoms associated with depression. *The most common antidepressant medications include* the tricyclics; the MAO inhibitors; the second-generation antidepressants trazodone and bupropion; the selective serotonin reuptake inhibitors (SSRIs) Prozac, Zoloft, and Paxil; and the dual action antidepressants Serzone, Remeron, and Celexa.

7. *Electroconvulsive therapy (ECT) is a biomedical therapy used primarily* in the treatment of depression; it involves electrically inducing brief brain seizures (also called shock therapy and electric shock therapy).

Concept Check 4

1. antianxiety
2. electroconvulsive
3. tardive dyskinesia
4. lithium
5. clozapine; risperidone

Matching Exercise 4

1. lithium
2. psychoactive medications
3. electroconvulsive therapy (ECT)
4. antianxiety medications
5. antidepressant medications
6. tardive dyskinesia
7. antipsychotic medications

Something to Think About

1. The first thing to tell someone with a phobia is that there are many different therapeutic approaches in psychology, such as psychoanalysis, client-centered therapy, cognitive therapy, and behavior therapy. It would be appropriate to briefly explain the differences between

each of these approaches and to advise the person to seek professional help if she feels that her problem is severe. Having said that, you can then go on to describe an approach that has been relatively effective in dealing with phobias—systematic desensitization.

The first step in systematic desensitization is for the person to learn how to relax completely. This is because a state of complete relaxation is incompatible with being tense and anxious. The second step is to have the person generate a hierarchy of feared situations associated with flying. For example, the most feared situation the person can imagine might be sitting on the plane during take off and the least fearful might be hearing someone talking about flying. Once the person is totally relaxed, she can start imagining the least fearful situation in the hierarchy. When she can do that for a number of times without tensing up, she can move to the next situation in the hierarchy, and so on. It is also helpful for the person to create an unrelated, relaxing control scene, such as lying on the beach watching the waves roll in, which can be used to help her relax. Over a number of sessions, the person works her way up the hierarchy while relaxing completely, until eventually she can approach the real situation.

In practice, systematic desensitization is often combined with other techniques, such as counterconditioning (pairing pleasant associations, such as being able to travel to exotic islands, with the feared situation) and observational learning (using the real situation or a video), which involves watching other people being calm and relaxed in the anxiety-provoking situation.

2. First, people seek help from mental health professionals not only for psychological problems but also for dealing with troubled relationships, coping with transitions in life, and other troubling situations. Second, there should be no stigma attached to getting help when it is needed. The prevalence of psychological disorders and similar types of problems is much higher than most people realize, so we all probably know someone who is or has been in therapy or perhaps needs to be. So, what should we expect from psychotherapy? The Application gives some important guidelines about the therapist-client relationship and the psychotherapy process.

The cornerstone of psychotherapy is the relationship between the therapist and the person seeking help. This relationship is a collaborative endeavor in which the client is actively involved in the therapeutic process. Therapy requires work not only during the therapy sessions but also outside them. So people should expect to be involved and active. In addition, people should not expect the therapist to make decisions for them. Virtually all forms of therapy are designed to increase a person's sense of responsibility, confidence, and mastery in dealing with life's problems. The therapist is there to help.

A therapist is not a substitute friend. Rather, he or she is more of a consultant, responding objectively and honestly to issues and problems. In addition, ethically and legally, everything that goes on in therapy is totally confidential. And, under no circumstances does therapeutic intimacy include sexual intimacy.

A person should also expect therapy to challenge how he or she thinks and acts, which sometimes can be a painful process. But becoming aware that changes are needed is a necessary step toward developing healthier forms of thinking and behavior. It is important, however, not to confuse insight with change. Just because people gain an understanding of the sources and nature of their psychological problems does not mean that they will automatically resolve these problems. Likewise, the catharsis that often results from therapy is not synonymous with change. With some effort and the help of the therapeutic process, people can move toward changing how they think, behave, and react to other people, but this will not happen overnight.

Progress Test 1

1. a	6. b	11. c
2. d	7. b	12. c
3. d	8. d	13. e
4. a	9. c	14. d
5. c	10. b	15. b

Progress Test 2

1. d	6. a	11. b
2. c	7. c	12. d
3. d	8. b	13. c
4. c	9. b	14. a
5. d	10. a	15. c

Progress Test 3

1. a	6. c	11. b
2. d	7. d	12. a
3. a	8. a	13. d
4. a	9. d	14. b
5. a	10. d	15. e

Statistics:
Understanding Data

PREVIEW   Reading the section below first will give you a general sense of the chapter's contents and an initial introduction to some of the major concepts and terms. This will prime you for what you are about to read and help you to develop a "cognitive map" that will guide your study of the material in this chapter. Likewise, reading the **preview questions** at the beginning of each major section will improve your ability to understand, learn, and retain the information.

APPENDIX . . . AT A GLANCE   Appendix A explains how and when various statistical techniques are used. Descriptive statistics are used to organize and summarize data in a meaningful way. Examples discussed include frequency distributions, which can be presented as a table, histogram, or frequency polygon; measures of central tendency (mode, median, and mean); and measures of variability (range and standard deviation). z scores are explained, and the concept of the normal distribution is presented.

Correlation, which is introduced in Chapter 1, is described, and how the correlation coefficient is calculated is explained. The point is made that correlational research is restricted to prediction and cannot be used to identify cause-and-effect relationships. The scatter diagram can be used to depict graphically the relationship between two variables.

Inferential statistics are used to determine whether outcomes of a study can be generalized to a larger population, and they provide information about the probability of a particular result if only random factors are operating. The text notes that if the probability of the outcome resulting from chance factors is small, the findings are said to be statistically significant.

Descriptive Statistics

Preview Questions

Consider the following questions as you study this section of the chapter.

- What are descriptive statistics, and what are they used for?
- What are frequency distributions, histograms, and frequency polygons?
- What is a skewed distribution, and what is a symmetrical distribution?
- What are the three measures of central tendency?
- What are the two measures of variability, and what are z scores?

*Read the section "Descriptive Statistics" and **write** your answers to the following:*

1. Descriptive statistics are used to _____
   _____

2. A frequency distribution is _____
   _____
   _____

3. A histogram is _____
   _____
   _____

4. A frequency polygon is _____
   _____
   _____

5. A skewed distribution is_____
   _____
   _____

6. A symmetrical distribution is _____
   _____
   _____

7. Measures of central tendency are_____
   _____

   The mode is _____
   _____

   The median is _____
   _____

The mean is _____
_____

8. Measures of variability are _____
   _____

   The range is _____
   _____

   The standard deviation is _____
   _____

9. A z score is _____
   _____

After you have carefully studied the preceding section, complete the following exercises.

Concept Check 1

Read the following and write the correct term in the space provided.

1. Professor Wilson calculated the mode, median, and mean of the scores from the midterm exam. These descriptive statistics are referred to as

   _____ .

2. Professor Wilson noticed that the most frequently occurring score was 73; this score is called the _____ .

3. In order to determine the spread of the scores, Professor Wilson subtracted the lowest score in the distribution from the highest. In this instance, he has calculated a measure of _____ called the

   _____ .

4. Next, he subtracted the mean from each score in the distribution, squared each of these deviations, added them up, divided by the number of scores in the distribution, and finally took the square root of the number just calculated. Professor Wilson has calculated a measure of _____ called the

   _____ .

5. Finally, Professor Wilson graphically represented the frequency distribution by placing a mark above each score at the point representing its frequency and then connecting these points with straight lines. This type of graph is called a(n) _____ .

Review of Terms and Concepts 1

Use the terms in this list to complete the Matching Test, then to help you answer the True/False items correctly.

descriptive statistics
frequency distribution
histogram
frequency polygon
skewed distribution
positively skewed
   distribution
negatively skewed
   distribution
symmetrical distribution
measure of central
   tendency

mode
median
mean
measure of variability
range
standard deviation
z score
standard normal curve
   (standard normal
   distribution)

Matching Exercise

Match the appropriate term with its definition or description.

1. _____ A number, expressed in standard deviation units, that shows a score's deviation from the mean.

2. _____ Statistics used to organize and summarize data in a meaningful way.

3. _____ A symmetrical distribution forming a bell-shaped curve in which the mean, median, and mode are all equal and fall in the exact middle.

4. _____ A summary of how often various scores occur in a sample of scores. Score values are arranged in order of magnitude, and the number of times each score occurs is recorded.

5. _____ Measure of variability; expressed as the square root of the sum of the squared deviations around the mean divided by the number of scores in the distribution.

6. _____ An asymmetrical distribution; more scores pile up on one side of the distribution than on the other.

7. _____ A single number that presents information about the spread of scores in a frequency distribution.

8. _____ Distribution in which the scores fall equally on both sides of the graph. The normal curve is an example.

9. _____ Measure of variability; the highest score in a distribution minus the lowest score.

True/False Test

Indicate whether each statement is true or false by placing T or F in the blank space next to each item.

1. ____ In a positively skewed distribution, most people have high scores.

2. ____ The mode is the most frequently occurring score in a distribution.

3. ____ A measure of central tendency is a single number that presents some information about the "center" of a frequency distribution.

4. ____ In a negatively skewed distribution, most people have low scores.

5. ____ A histogram is a way of graphically representing a frequency distribution where frequency is marked above each score category on the graph's horizontal axis and the marks are connected by straight lines.

6. ____ The mean is the sum of a set of scores in a distribution divided by the number of scores and is usually the most representative measure of central tendency.

7. ____ A frequency polygon is a way of graphically representing a frequency distribution and is a type of bar chart using vertical bars that touch.

8. ____ The median is the score that divides a frequency distribution exactly in half, so that the same number of scores lies on each side of it.

Check your answers and review any areas of weakness before going on to the next section.

Correlation and Inferential Statistics

Preview Questions

Consider the following questions as you study these sections of the chapter.

- How is correlation defined, and what is the correlation coefficient?
- How are correlations depicted graphically?
- What are inferential statistics, and what is meant by statistical significance?
- What is meant by the terms *population* and *sample*?

*Read the sections "Correlation" and "Inferential Statistics" and **write** your answers to the following:*

1. Correlation is the _____

   _____

2. The correlation coefficient is a measure of ____

   _____

   _____

   A positive correlation coefficient indicates that

   _____

   _____

   A negative correlation coefficient indicates that

   _____

   _____

3. Correlations are depicted graphically_____

   _____

   A positive correlation is indicated by _____

   _____

   _____

   A negative correlation is indicated by_____

   _____

   _____

4. Inferential statistics are _____

   _____

   _____

5. Statistical significance refers to the fact that if the results of a study are _____

   _____

   _____

   _____

6. A population is _____

   _____

   Because the entire population of interest usually cannot be studied, researchers use _____

   _____

   _____

After you have carefully studied the preceding section, complete the following exercises.

Concept Check 2

Read the following and write the correct term in the space provided.

1. Dr. Jabul discovers that the more education people have, the more money they tend to earn. Dr. Jabul has discovered a _____ correlation.

2. Based on his research, Dr. Jabul can use one variable to _____ the other, but he cannot say that one variable _____ the other.

3. When Professor Alphonse plotted his data on a scatter plot, he noticed that they clustered in a pattern that extends from the upper lefthand hand corner of the graph to the lower righthand corner. This pattern suggests that the two variables are _____ related.

4. When Kayla analyzed the correlational data for her psychology project, the correlation coefficient was +.07. Kayla can conclude that the two variables _____ (are/are not) correlated.

5. When researchers analyzed the data from their experiment, they found large differences between the control group and the experimental group that were not due to chance. They can conclude that the results are

   _____ .

6. In order to discover how people feel about the level of service provided, the ABC company asks a randomly selected subset of their customers to fill out a brief questionnaire. ABC's customers represent the _____ , and the subset surveyed is a(n)

   _____ .

Review of Terms and Concepts 2

Use the terms in this list to complete the Matching Test, then to help you answer the True/False items correctly.

correlation	scatter diagram (scatter
correlation coefficient	plot)
positive correlation	inferential statistics
coefficient	statistically significant
negative correlation	population
coefficient	sample

Matching Exercise

Match the appropriate term with its definition or description.

1. _____ Graph that represents the relationship between two variables.

2. _____ Measure of the magnitude and direction of the relationship (the correlation) between two variables; the closer the number is to +1 or −1, the stronger the relationship.

3. _____ Statistical techniques that allow researchers to determine whether the outcomes in a study are likely to be more than just chance events and whether they can be legitimately generalized to a larger population.

4. _____ A complete set of something—people, nonhuman animals, objects, or events.

5. _____ The relationship between two variables.

True/False Test

Indicate whether each statement is true or false by placing T or F in the blank space next to each item.

1. ____ Results can be considered statistically significant when the probability of obtaining them, if chance factors alone are operating, is less than .05 (5 chances out of 100).

2. ____ A positive correlation coefficient indicates that as one variable increases, the other tends to decrease.

3. ____ A sample is a subset of a population.

4. ____ A negative correlation coefficient indicates that as one variable increases, the other tends to increase.

Check your answers and review any areas of weakness before completing the progress tests.

Progress Test 1

Review the complete chapter, review all your study notes, and then test yourself on the following progress test. Check your answers. If you make a mistake, review your notes, review the relevant section of the study guide, and, if necessary, go back and read the appropriate part of your textbook.

1. Professor Admunson used a scatter diagram to depict the relationship between her students' high school GPA and their first-year GPA in college. She noticed that the data points clustered in a pattern that extend from the lower left-hand corner of the graph to the upper right-hand corner. This pattern suggests that the two variables

   (a) are negatively correlated.
   (b) have no relationship.
   (c) are positively correlated.
   (d) have a cause-and-effect relationship.

2. A measure of variability is to

   _____ as a measure of central tendency is to _____ .

   (a) mode; median
   (b) correlation; scatter plot
   (c) standard deviation; mean
   (d) histogram; frequency polygon

3. One student in the class got an extremely low score of 10 out of 100 on a test. Which measure of central tendency is most affected by this low score?

   (a) mode   (c) median
   (b) mean   (d) range

4. Following the final exam, Professor Farrar calculated a number of statistics and noticed that the standard deviation was extremely small. This indicates that
   (a) the scores on the exam were clustered around the mean and not spread out.
   (b) the distribution was skewed.
   (c) the scores had a great deal of variability and were not clustered around the mean.
   (d) there were very few students in her class.

5. Mrs. Kodiak has seven children aged 3, 5, 8, 9, 12, 15, and 15. The median age of her children is
   (a) 9.   (c) 12.
   (b) 15.   (d) 67.

6. When the results of an experiment were examined and the appropriate statistics calculated, the researchers concluded that the probability of obtaining these results, if random factors alone were operating, was less than .01. The results are
   (a) probably due to chance.
   (b) statistically insignificant.
   (c) skewed.
   (d) statistically significant.

7. For his class presentation, Liam prepared a graph that depicted a frequency distribution with vertical bars that touched each other. Liam has constructed a
   (a) scatter diagram.
   (b) frequency polygon.
   (c) histogram.
   (d) standard deviation.

8. Liam's graph is a symmetrical distribution with an equal number of scores on each side of the graph. It is very likely that the
   (a) mean is larger than the median.
   (b) mode is larger than the mean.
   (c) mean, mode, and median have the same value.
   (d) median is larger than the mode.

9. When researchers calculated the correlation coefficients for two different sets of data, they discovered that set A had a negative correlation of −.85 and set B had a positive correlation of +.62. They can conclude that
   (a) set A has a stronger correlation than set B.
   (b) set A has a weaker correlation than set B.
   (c) set B has a stronger correlation than set A.
   (d) both (b) and (c) are true.

10. When Gary calculated the mean, median, and mode of the data in his frequency distribution, he was using
   (a) inferential statistics.
   (b) descriptive statistics.
   (c) correlational statistics.
   (d) measures of variability.

Progress Test 2

After you have checked your understanding of the material in Progress Test 1 and have done a complete chapter review with special focus on any areas of weakness, you are ready to assess your knowledge of Progress Test 2. Check your answers. If you make a mistake, review your notes, the relevant section of the study guide, and, if necessary, the appropriate part of your textbook.

1. In addition to calculating the range, Matthew also calculated the standard deviation for his frequency distribution of scores. Matthew is using
   (a) measures of variability.
   (b) inferential statistics.
   (c) measures of central tendency.
   (d) correlational statistics.

2. When Professor Kitahara finished marking the final exams, he plotted the results on a graph by marking the frequency above each score category on the horizontal axis and then connecting the marks using straight lines. Professor Kitahara has constructed a
   (a) frequency distribution.
   (b) histogram.
   (c) frequency polygon.
   (d) scatter diagram.

3. Professor Kitahara observed that the graph was a symmetrical distribution that resembled a bell-shaped curve and that the mean, median, and mode were all equal. A student who scored better than 84 percent of the other students in this distribution would have a z score of
   (a) +1.
   (c) +.84.
   (b) −1.
   (d) −.84.

4. Hanna has a grade point average of 3.5. What measure of central tendency was used to calculate this statistic?
   (a) median
   (b) standard deviation
   (c) mode
   (d) mean

5. In her research, Dr. Simiak found that the more credit cards people have, the less money they have in their savings accounts. Dr. Simiak has found a _____ correlation between the number of credit cards owned and savings.
   (a) positive
   (c) negative
   (b) zero
   (d) skewed

6. Range is to mode as _____ is to _____ .
   (a) correlation; scatter diagram
   (b) median; mode
   (c) correlation coefficient; z score
   (d) variability; central tendency

7. Fydor compared two frequency distributions and noticed that in the first distribution most people had low scores and in the second distribution most people had high scores. The first distribution is _____ , and the second distribution is _____ .
   (a) positively skewed; negatively skewed
   (b) symmetrical; normal
   (c) negatively skewed; positively skewed
   (d) a polygon; a histogram

8. When Tyborg calculated the mean and standard deviation for a set of scores, he found that the mean was 55 out of a 100, and the standard deviation was 15. If the scores are normally distributed, Tyborg can conclude that approximately 68 percent of the scores are between.
   (a) 40 and 70.
   (c) 55 and 70.
   (b) 25 and 85.
   (d) 40 and 55.

9. In the above example, a student with a z score of −1 would have a score of
   (a) 55.
   (c) 70.
   (b) 40.
   (d) 25.

10. During the past month Karianne read 8 books, Kyle read 2 books, Phyllis read 4 books, and Philip read 6 books. The mean number of books read by this group is
    (a) 5.
    (c) 8.
    (b) 20.
    (d) 6.

Progress Test 3

After you have checked your understanding of the material in Progress Tests 1 and 2, and have done a complete chapter review with special focus on any areas of weakness, you are ready to further assess your knowledge on Progress Test 3. Check your answers. If you make a mistake, review your notes, the appropriate parts of the study guide, and, if necessary, the relevant sections of your textbook.

1. A complete set of something (people, objects, events, etc.) is to a _____ as a representative subset is to a _____ .
   (a) descriptive statistics; inferential statistics
   (b) sample; population
   (c) inferential statistics; descriptive statistics
   (d) population; sample

2. Dr. Soryun carried out the appropriate calculations on her data and noticed that results were more extreme than would be expected by chance. She concluded that the probability of obtaining these results if random factors alone were operating was less than 1 chance out of a 100. Dr. Soryun has used _____ statistics, and the results can be called _____ .
   (a) descriptive statistics; statistically significant
   (b) inferential statistics; positively skewed
   (c) descriptive statistics; positively skewed
   (d) inferential statistics; statistically significant

3. Organizing and summarizing data is to _____ as making inferences and drawing conclusions is to _____ .
   (a) descriptive statistics; inferential statistics
   (b) correlational research; experimental research
   (c) inferential statistics; descriptive statistics
   (d) experimental research; correlational research

4. Researchers at State University are interested in determining to what extent personality variables such as impatience, aggressiveness, and hostility could be used to predict the risk of cardiovascular disease. These researchers are most likely to use _____ in their research.
   (a) a measure of variability
   (b) the correlation coefficient
   (c) the standard normal distribution
   (d) the standard deviation

5. After analyzing his data, Jamie decided to depict his results in a graph. He noticed that the data points clustered in a pattern that extended from the upper lefthand corner to the lower righthand corner on his graph. Jamie has constructed a _____ that shows a _____.
   (a) polygon; skewed distribution
   (b) scatter diagram; positive correlation
   (c) histogram; symmetrical distribution
   (d) scatter diagram; negative correlation

6. In his survey research, Dr. Khrod discovered that the more education people have, the less television they watch. Dr. Khrod has discovered a(n) _____ between television watching and level of education.
   (a) negative correlation
   (b) illusory correlation
   (c) positive correlation
   (d) cause-and-effect relationship

7. When Harpinder plotted his data, his graph closely resembled the normal curve and had a mean of 50 and a standard deviation of 5. Harpinder can be confident that approximately 68 percent of the scores are between
   (a) +1 and –1 SDs.
   (b) +2 and –2 SDs.
   (c) +3 and –3 SDs.
   (d) correlation coefficients of +1 and –1.

8. Raphael's z-score on the midterm was +1. If the class scores are normally distributed, Raphael has
   (a) scored better than 34.13 percent of the class.
   (b) scored worse than 34.13 percent of the class.
   (c) scored better than 84 percent of the class.
   (d) scored worse than 84 percent of the class.

9. When Professor Exman compared the statistics from her two introductory biology classes, she noticed that the standard deviation was 8.24 in class A and 3.76 in class B. She can conclude that
   (a) the students in class A studied much harder than those in class B.
   (b) the scores in class A had much more variability than those in class B.
   (c) the range for both classes is likely to be identical.
   (d) one very extreme score probably distorted the standard deviation for class A.

10. As a first step in analyzing her data, Tracianne calculated the mean, the mode, and the median. Tracianne has
    (a) used inferential statistics.
    (b) determined the statistical significance of her results.
    (c) used descriptive statistics.
    (d) calculated measures of variability.

Answers

Descriptive Statistics

1. *Descriptive statistics are used to* organize and summarize data in a meaningful way.

2. *A frequency distribution is* a summary of how often various scores occur in a sample of scores. Score values are arranged in order of magnitude, and the number of times each score occurs is recorded.

3. *A histogram is* a way of graphically representing a frequency distribution. It is like a bar chart with two special features: the bars are always vertical, and they always touch.

4. *A frequency polygon is* another way of graphically representing a frequency distribution. In contrast to a histogram, or a frequency distribution, a mark is made above each category at the point representing its frequency, and these marks are then connected by straight lines.

5. *A skewed distribution is* an asymmetrical distribution with more scores piled up on one side of the distribution than on the other. If most people have low scores, the distribution is positively skewed; if most people have high scores, the distribution is negatively skewed.

6. *A symmetrical distribution is* a distribution in which scores fall equally on both halves of the graph (an example of a symmetrical distribution is the normal curve).

7. *Measures of central tendency are* single numbers that present some information about the center of a frequency distribution. *The mode is* the score or category that occurs most frequently in a set of raw scores or in a frequency distribution. *The median is* the score that divides a frequency distribution exactly in half, so that the same number of scores lie on each side of it. *The mean is* the sum of a set of scores in a distribution divided by the number of scores, and is usually the most representative measure of central tendency.

8. *Measures of variability are* single numbers that present information about the spread of scores in a distribution. *The range is* the highest score in a distribution minus the lowest score. *The standard deviation is* expressed as the square root of the sum of the squared deviations around the mean divided by the number of scores in the distribution.

9. *A z score is* a number, expressed in standard deviation units, that shows a score's deviation from the mean.

Concept Check 1

1. measures of central tendency
2. mode
3. variability; range
4. variability; standard deviation
5. frequency polygon

Matching Exercise 1

1. *z* score
2. descriptive statistics
3. standard normal curve (standard normal distribution)
4. frequency distribution
5. standard deviation
6. skewed distribution
7. measure of variability
8. symmetrical distribution
9. range

True/False Test 1

1. F	4. F	7. F
2. T	5. F	8. T
3. T	6. T	

Correlation and Inferential Statistics

1. *Correlation is the* relationship between two variables; it does not indicate causality between the two variables.

2. *The correlation coefficient is a measure of* the magnitude and direction of the relationship between two variables, and the closer the correlation coefficient is to +1 or −1, the stronger the relationship is. *A positive correlation coefficient indicates that* as one variable increases, the other tends to increase. *A negative correlation coefficient indicates that* as one variable increases, the other tends to decrease.

3. *Correlations are depicted graphically* on a scatter diagram (scatter plot), which is a graph that represents the relationship between two variables. *A positive correlation is indicated by* the upward-sloping pattern of dots, from bottom left to top right (when one variable is high, the other tends to be high too, and vice versa). *A negative correlation is indicated by* the downward-sloping pattern of dots, from upper left to lower right (when one variable is high, the other tends to be low, and vice versa).

4. *Inferential statistics are* statistical techniques that allow researchers to determine whether the outcomes in a study are likely to be more than just chance events and whether they can be legitimately generalized to larger populations.

5. *Statistical significance refers to the fact that if the results of a study are* more extreme than would be expected by chance alone, we reject the idea that no real effect has occurred and conclude that the manipulation of the independent variable is the reason for the obtained results; when this happens, the results are statistically significant, and the probability of getting these results, if random factors alone are operating, is less than .05 (5 chances in 100) or .01 (1 chance in 100).

6. *A population is* a complete set of something—people, nonhuman animals, objects, or events. *Because the entire population of interest usually cannot be studied, researchers use* a sample, which is a subset of a population.

Concept Check 2

1. positive
2. predict; causes
3. negatively

4. are not

5. statistically significant

6. population; sample

Matching Exercise 2

1. scatter diagram (scatter plot)
2. correlation coefficient
3. inferential statistics
4. population
5. correlation

True/False Test 2

1. T	3. T
2. F	4. F

Progress Test 1

1. c	5. a	9. a
2. c	6. d	10. b
3. b	7. c	
4. a	8. c	

Progress Test 2

1. a	5. c	9. b
2. c	6. d	10. a
3. a	7. a	
4. d	8. a	

Progress Test 3

1. d	5. d	9. b
2. d	6. a	10. c
3. a	7. a	
4. b	8. c	